South Asia and United States Policy

NORMAN D. PALMER

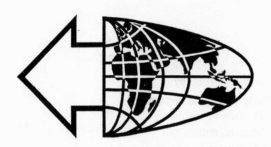

NEW YORK · ATLANTA · GENEVA, ILL. · DALLAS · PALO ALTO

Copyright © 1966 by
Norman D. Palmer
All rights reserved including
the right to reproduce this
book or parts thereof in any form.

Printed in the U.S.A.

Certain quotations on pp. 41, 43, and 272–273 are
copyright © 1946 by The John Day Company. Reprinted
from The Discovery of India by Jawaharlal Nehru by
permission of The John Day Company, Inc., publisher.

Contents

Preface

THE ENCOUNTER BETWEEN ASIA AND THE WEST is increasing in scope and in depth. But it is still far too limited and superficial to provide the basis for a viable relationship between countries and peoples with such a different cultural heritage and historical experience, as well as such different outlook and interests, separated by more than geographical distance but at the same time united by the forces that make for interdependence in the modern world. "The central drama of our age," wrote Walter Lippmann in September 1965, "is how the Western nations and Asian peoples are to find a tolerable basis of coexistence. Today we do not have even the rudiments of an understanding by which Europeans and Americans, Russians and Chinese, Indians and Pakistanis, would be willing to live and let live." This observation underscores the importance of developing what Lippmann has called "a new order of human relationship between the Asian world and the Western world." "In Asia," he pointed out, "the margin of safety is very thin; there is not even the beginning of a meeting of minds, and a catastrophe is possible."

In the growing encounter between Asia and the West, South Asia is obviously an area of special significance. It is today a major center of world attention and concern, but it is still a relatively unknown area, and there is a great deal of confusion and misunderstanding about the internal situation and the external orientation of even the major countries of the area, India and Pakistan.

There is perhaps no major part of the world that presents more complex problems to United States foreign policy than the Indian subcontinent. As a direct ally of the United States, Pakistan is of special importance to American policy, political, strategic, and economic. India's prospects, as the leading nation in non-Communist mainland Asia, are crucial to the future balance of power.

This study, which is the product of five years of field work, research, and reflection, deals with the internal dynamics and the external policies of India and Pakistan, with some attention to Nepal and Ceylon, and the implications of the situation in South Asia for United States policy. It is, in effect, three interrelated studies in one. It deals, in the first place, with the internal dynamics of the area, on the assumption that this approach is essential for an understanding of external relations and orientation. Secondly, it contains a fairly full-length treatment of the foreign policy of both India and Pakistan, with particular attention to Indo-Pakistan relations and to relations between India and Communist China. Finally, it presents an account of United States-South Asian contacts and relations, with special emphasis on the levels of encounter, the course of the relations, and the role and impact of American aid, both economic and military.

For the United States, South Asia is an area of challenge and opportunity, as well as of frustration and occasional despair. The central theme of this study is the need for the United States to give greater depth and meaning to its relations with India and Pakistan, on unofficial as well as official levels, to seek a clearer understanding of the complex and rapidly changing South Asian scene, to reassess its policies toward the countries of that area, and particularly to consider the problems and dilemmas created for the United States by the internal difficulties which India and Pakistan are facing, the unhappy state of their mutual relations, and the impact upon them of external pressures and forces, such as those which arise from the growing power and militancy of Communist China and from what Lippmann has called "the spreading convulsion in Asia."

In view of the present tensions and the continuing changes in South Asia, any analysis of existing conditions must be a tentative one, and any attempt to recommend new directions in United States policy toward the area is certain to provoke disagreement and criticism. Yet the growing importance of South Asia makes such an analysis and such an attempt all the more imperative, whatever the hazards may be. Scholars, as well as those with responsibilities for decision-making in foreign policy, must deal with difficult and changing conditions, in real world situations, and they should even be so bold as to advance policy recommendations and suggestions.

I have tried to be as fair as I can in analyzing conditions and policies in both India and Pakistan, and to strike some sort of balance in evaluating United States policies toward both countries, and toward South Asia as a whole. I am deeply interested in both India and Pakistan, and I feel most strongly that the United States can and should strive constantly to develop more satisfactory relations with both, whatever the difficulties arising from mutual tensions and external conditions may be. This approach will not commend itself to those in India and Pakistan, or elsewhere, who want the United States to "choose" between the two countries, or who desire simple answers or "solutions" for complex questions; but I am confident that in the long run it is in the best interests of the United States, and of India and Pakistan as well. The aim of the United States should be to seek out and to cultivate opportunities for cooperation with both India and Pakistan, and not to attempt to impose "solutions" for complex problems by political, economic, or military pressures.

In the preparation of this study I have received assistance from more individuals and organizations than I can possibly name. For the financial support which made it possible for me to be absent for a year and a half from my regular duties at the University of Pennsylvania in order to work on this project, in South Asia as well as in the United States, I am particularly indebted to the University of Pennsylvania, for a sabbatical leave; to the Council on Foreign Relations, for providing the major support for my firsthand study and observations in South Asia, for setting up a Study Group at the Council to give me the advice and guidance of distinguished specialists from many fields, and for making available supporting facilities and editorial assistance; and to the American Council of Learned Societies (Grants for Research on Asia) and the Guggenheim Foundation for supplementary grants for research in South Asia.

On the personal level I wish to acknowledge especially the assistance and encouragement of Dr. Philip E. Mosely, now Director of the European Institute at Columbia University; Dr. W. Phillips Davison, formerly Senior Research Fellow of the Council on Foreign Relations; Mr. August Maffry, Vice President, Irving Trust Company, who was Chairman of the Council's Study Group on "South Asia and U. S. Policy in the 1960s;" Mr. Robert Valkenier of the Council on Foreign Relations; Dr. A. Appadorai, formerly Director of the Indian School of International Studies in New Delhi; Professor V. K. N. Menon, formerly Director of the Indian Institute of Public Administration in New Delhi; Mr. L. A. Sherwani of the Pakistan Institute of International Affairs in Karachi; Dr. Akhter Hameed Khan, the guiding genius of the Pakistan Academy for Rural Development in Comilla, East Pakistan; and Dr. William Metz and Mr. Ernest Howell, formerly representatives of the Asia Foundation in Lahore and Dacca, respectively. In South Asia I had useful interviews with scores of senior officials, members of the Indian Parliament, scholars, journalists, business and professional men, and many others. Among these were Prime Minister Jawaharlal Nehru, Manzur Qadir, then Foreign Minister of Pakistan, Mr. Tulsi Giri, then Foreign Minister of Nepal, the Governors of both West and East Pakistan and of two Indian States, and the Chief Ministers of three Indian States. In the United States I had the benefit of the guidance not only of the distinguished members of the Study Group set up by the Council on Foreign Relations, but also of many others, in official and unofficial positions, with special expertise and experience in South Asia and/or American foreign policy.

Mr. Maffry and Mrs. Marina Finkelstein read the entire manuscript and made many useful comments and suggestions; and Mr. Valkenier patiently examined and improved several revisions. Portions of the manuscript were also read by Dr. Davison, Colonel Amos A. Jordan, Jr., Mr. Charles B. Marshall, Professor Wilfred Malenbaum, and Colonel Marshall E. Sanders.

I am especially grateful to these individuals, and also to Mr. Richard N. Clark of the Houghton Mifflin Company, who skilfully guided the manuscript through the various stages leading to publication.

Some of the material in this book is based on articles which have appeared in *Current History*, issues of November 1962, March 1963, February 1964, and February and November 1965; *The Journal of International Affairs*, No. 2, 1963; *Orbis*, Summer 1963; *Pacific Affairs*, Summer 1963; *Political Quarterly*, October-December 1962; and in a paper entitled "Experiments in 'Democratic Decentralization' in South Asia," prepared for the Sixth World Congress of the International Political Science Association (Geneva, September 1964).

I want also to acknowledge the patience and support of my wife and daughter, who accompanied me to South Asia when I was engaged in this project, as they have on previous occasions; of my colleagues in the South Asia Regional Studies Program at the University of Pennsylvania; of my students at the University of Pennsylvania; and of the hundreds of friends in India and Pakistan who helped and stimulated me in more ways than they can possibly realize.

NORMAN D. PALMER

Leopard Lake
Berwyn, Pennsylvania
October 2, 1965

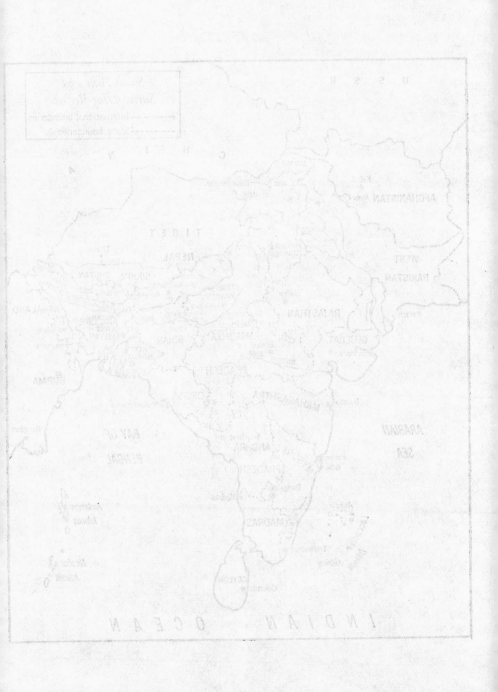

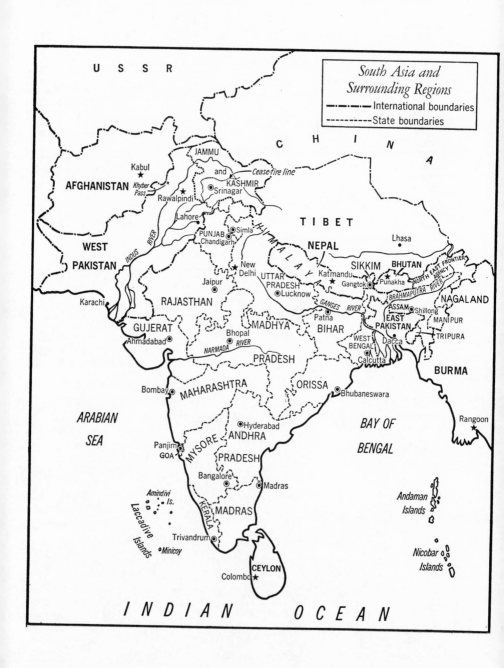

CHAPTER ONE

The United States–
South Asian Encounter

ONE OF THE GREATEST PROBLEMS facing the United States is to evolve a satisfactory relationship with the newly emerging nations of Asia and Africa. Their sudden appearance on the world's stage, and their struggles for identity, unity, and survival, have given new dimensions to contemporary international affairs. In developing this new relationship the United States must give special attention to South Asia, the home of some 40 per cent of all the people of the non-Communist underdeveloped world. In the past the United States-South Asian encounter was limited and relatively unimportant; since the beginning of World War II it has developed rapidly in scope and depth; and it is bound to become increasingly multifarious and meaningful, for South Asia will surely be one of the main areas of concern in the years immediately ahead.

South Asia may be called the heart of the so-called underdeveloped world and a pivotal area in contemporary international relations. It is today one of the world's greatest laboratories of political, economic, and social change. It embodies all the hopes and most of the problems of mankind.

Except for Communist China, South Asia has the largest population concentration in the entire world — nearly 600,000,000 people. It is an area of great geopolitical significance, whether viewed from a regional, continental, or global standpoint. It is also an area full of distressed people, whose living standards are among the lowest in the world. At the moment there is apparent political, economic, and social stability, but underneath the surface great pressures are building up and great changes are under way. It is an area in crisis, even though for the time being the crisis is largely a quiet one — to use a term which Professor John P. Lewis applied to India.[1]

The home of ancient civilizations and new nations, South Asia throughout

[1] *Quiet Crisis in India: Economic Development and American Policy* (Washington, D.C.: The Brookings Institution, 1962).

1

the centuries has had a remarkable degree of geographic and cultural unity, and its peoples have shared a common historical experience; but it has never been united politically or socially. Aside from the great divisions that have separated Aryans from non-Aryans, Hindus from Muslims, caste from caste, region from region, literate from illiterate, villagers from townspeople, Hindi-speaking from non-Hindi-speaking, the peoples of the subcontinent have been torn between the past and the present, and they have found it difficult to reconcile their objectives with realities. History and nature have been unkind to them.[2] They developed one of the most stable and meaningful, but also one of the most rigid and stratified of social systems. This social system is proving to be increasingly inadequate under modern conditions, and the people of the subcontinent are facing the unwelcome prospect of inevitable change in unknown directions.

Inevitably the progress, or lack of progress, of the countries and peoples of South Asia will be compared with the record of Communist China, and the comparison may have fateful consequences in the entire underdeveloped world. South Asia is perhaps the major bulwark against Chinese Communist expansion in non-Communist Asia, and it is presently being subjected to alternating doses of Chinese pressures and blandishments, designed to reveal and exploit weaknesses and divisions and perhaps to provoke a test of wills and to probe for possible targets of opportunity.

The Scope of United States-South Asian Relations

How important is South Asia to the United States? The answer can only be that whereas in the past it has not been an area of major American concern, the United States can no longer enjoy the luxury of continued unconcern. "No thoughtful citizen," declared John F. Kennedy in a speech in the United States Senate on March 25, 1958, "can fail to see our stake in the survival of free government in India," which he called on another occasion "the hinge of fate in Asia."[3] Yet many "thoughtful" citizens have attached little importance to India, and even less to Pakistan. To the extent that the two nations figure in their serious thinking at all, India and Pakistan seem to stand out as countries following rather dubious policies at home and abroad, whose leaders are viewed with many misgivings, and whose people live strange lives in terrible conditions and embrace strange practices and ideas. Fortunately many Americans are now aware of a fact that has long since been accepted by their responsible leaders, namely that South Asia, like all

[2] For a penetrating but controversial analysis of Indian civilization which stresses the lack of a sense of history, see Amaury de Riencourt, *The Soul of India* (New York: Harper, 1960), especially pp. 15–16. For a different interpretation, see *Seminar* (New Delhi), no. 39, November 1962, containing a symposium on "Past and Present"; especially articles by Romila Thapar, R. C. Majumdar, K. M. Panikkar, and S. Gopal.

[3] In an address in the United States Senate, February 19, 1959.

other major areas of the world, is of vital importance to the United States and and that more attention must be given to it. Although past contacts between the United States and South Asia have been quite limited, this is a part of the world which is open to the United States and with which meaningful contacts and cooperative policies are possible.

In the great issues of war and peace, and therefore of human survival, the United States is far less concerned with South Asia than with the Soviet Union or with its NATO allies, where the balance of world power presently rests. In the major foreign policy concerns of the United States, namely survival, the development of effective deterrent power, the prevention of a nuclear war, and the steady pursuit of the national interest during a period of protracted conflict, South Asia does not have a determining place; but even in these areas of vital concern, India, the largest of the nonaligned states, and Pakistan, American's major Asian ally, cannot be ignored.

Since policies toward any country or area have to be considered in the light of global policies, American relations with the South Asian countries are inevitably affected, and sometimes shaped, by larger considerations. During World War II, the major American interest in India was related to the importance of the subcontinent in the CBI theater of operations against the Japanese, and this interest was at times compromised by the impasse between the United Kingdom, America's major ally and the occupying power in India, and the leaders of the Indian independence movement. The extension of arms aid to Pakistan was prompted in part by the overall United States policy, first enunciated by President Truman in 1947, of providing military assistance, upon request, to "freedom-loving nations" for the purpose of resisting external aggression or internal disruption, and also in part by the search for alternatives to the abortive American-sponsored proposal to establish a Middle East Defense Organization. The association of the United States with Pakistan in SEATO and the encouragement to Pakistan to join the Bagdad Pact (later CENTO) may be explained, again in part, by the overall alliance policy of the United States, which had been evolved as a part of the containment policy, and by a desire to build up such collective strength as was possible in "the arc of danger" extending from Turkey to the Far East. American economic aid to the countries of South Asia is occasioned by the recognition of the great stake which the United States has in the survival of the developing nations of the non-Communist world and of the crucial need of these countries for substantial amounts of external assistance for basic development purposes.

Large-scale direct contacts between Americans and South Asians date only from World War II, and official relations between the United States and the independent countries of the area only from the postwar years, when political independence came to the nations of South Asia. These relations have been considerably handicapped and distorted by differences in historical experience, and in ways of life and patterns of thought, by massive ignorance of each other's traditions and values, and by differing priorities and objectives in political, economic, and international policies. They have been enhanced and strengthened by many mutual interests, respect for leaders of the past or present in both areas of the world, and a mutual stake in cooperation rather than conflict.

Until the Second World War contacts between the United States and South Asia, on official or unofficial levels, were limited and rather ephemeral, confined largely to consular officials, traders, missionaries, a few scholars, and in the 1920s and 1930s, a growing number of tourists. These Americans, except the missionaries and a handful of scholars, dealt mostly with certain members of the urban, English-speaking elite, and saw or knew very little about the "real India." South Asian contacts with the United States were even more limited. Until 1947 all official contacts at high levels had to be carried on with the ruling power in South Asia, the United Kingdom. Relatively few Indians visited the United States. None of the outstanding political leaders, except Jayaprakash Narayan, came to the United States for higher education. Some Indians, including a substantial number of Sikhs, settled in the United States, and some of them, assisted by American sympathizers, formed a fairly active but not very influential lobby in the United States for the Indian independence movement. As Harold Isaacs has shown, American images of India took the form of stereotypes, ranging from the extremely favorable to the extremely unfavorable — the "Mother India" image, the Gandhi image, and the like.[4]

After the United States entered World War II, thousands of American GIs were stationed in South Asia. This was the first really extensive contact between Americans and South Asians, and its effects, for good and for ill, have persisted. In general, the American soldiers in South Asia lived under rather unpleasant conditions in Karachi, Calcutta, and the jungles of Assam, and had little opportunity and perhaps even less desire to get to know and to understand the Indian people, whom they saw as masses of humanity living at abysmal levels of poverty and ignorance; whereas most of the Indian people either saw little of the GIs or saw them in their less impressive moments. The net effects of these contacts would be difficult to determine.

In the postwar years the new encounter has been not only far more extensive than the previous contacts; it has been carried on at different levels, and has had a wider impact. It has come at a troubled period in the world's history, when both the United States and the nations of South Asia have been embarking, rather reluctantly and hesitatingly, on new and larger roles in world affairs. The brevity and the still relatively limited nature of that encounter need to be borne in mind, for these help to explain many of the problems that have arisen in United States-South Asian relations, in spite of the obvious desire of the governments and peoples involved to establish new

[4] Harold Isaacs, *Scratches on Our Minds: American Images of China and India* (New York: John Day, 1958), pp. 239–408.

bases of understanding and cooperation. For most Americans South Asia is not a part of their conscious lives in any recognized and direct way, but more and more Americans are becoming involved in South Asian affairs, and on the official level the involvement is deeper than most people realize.

More meaningfully, the heavy American involvement may be traced to the last years of the Truman administration. During the time when Chester Bowles was ambassador, the United States first began to extend substantial assistance to India and to recognize its great stake in India's political evolution and in economic development under the Five Year plan which had just been launched. In the early years of the Eisenhower administration, economic aid to both India and Pakistan reached much larger proportions and the United States entered into its military associations with Pakistan. Since 1951–55 the involvement has grown with each passing year — involvement in the external relations, the inter-regional disputes, and the internal affairs of all the countries of South Asia.

The extension of large-scale economic assistance and technical cooperation has added a new dimension to official American activities in South Asia. India has received far more economic assistance from the United States than any other developing country. Pakistan is the second largest recipient of American economic assistance, and in per capita terms American aid to Pakistan is substantially greater than aid to India. The United States has had direct formal diplomatic relations with Nepal only since 1958, but it has already extended far more economic aid to Nepal than any other country, except India. In February 1963, because of the failure of the government of Ceylon to compensate American oil companies for their expropriated properties, economic assistance to Ceylon was suspended, and was resumed only after the defeat of Mrs. Bandaranaike's government in the elections of March 1965. It was never very large, totaling only $79.4 million between 1945 and mid-1962.

Other aspects of American economic relations with South Asia include efforts to promote trade and private American investment, and the role of the United States and the South Asian countries in the economic organs and agencies of the United Nations, including the specialized agencies, and in other multilateral economic agencies.

Military assistance has been an important ingredient of America's relations with Pakistan since 1954, and, in view of the strong Indian reactions to the extension of such assistance to an unfriendly neighbor, of relations with India as well. The military aid which has been extended to India since late October 1962, first on an emergency basis and then in a more sustained way, has in turn profoundly complicated the whole nature of America's relations with the two countries.

Both economic and military assistance have bulked so large in relations with India and Pakistan, and have involved the United States so deeply in the affairs of South Asia, that they have tended to overshadow other aspects of the encounter. They have created an unnatural and unhealthy relationship between the United States and the South Asian countries. As necessary in fact as they are undesirable in theory, they must be continued until some effective substitute is found or until the countries of South Asia can be relatively "self-sustaining" in both economic development and defense posture.

Another major area of official contacts between the United States and South Asia embraces the more nebulous but equally important realm of educational, cultural, scientific, and information programs of cooperation. Though expanding in scope and in effectiveness, such contacts have not yet made much of an impression on basic attitudes and orientation. Most of the people of South Asia still lie beyond the reach of the American diplomatic and information agencies in the South Asian capitals and other important centers. Nor have the counterpart agencies of the South Asian governments yet reached many Americans, although some South Asian ambassadors have been indefatigable in traveling around the United States and in making contacts with organizations and individual Americans. Officially sponsored and financed American programs of educational and cultural exchange, notably the Fulbright and Smith-Mundt programs, have sent many American scholars and students to South Asia, and have brought many South Asians to the United States. From 5 to 10 per cent of the several thousand South Asians now studying in the United States have come under official auspices, either through grants made to them by their own government or by the American government. Prominent — and not so prominent — Asians have been brought to the United States under the State Department's Leader-Specialist Program and under other official auspices (including several hundred Pakistani officers for special military training under the United States Military Assistance Program), and prominent Americans have been sent to all of the countries of South Asia under official sponsorship. With some exceptions, Indian books, music, films, and artists are not known in America. Indian intellectuals are more familiar with major American writings, but the widespread distribution of American books has been inhibited by price, low levels of literacy, lack of translations into Indian languages, and inadequate support.

American business concerns and universities and other private organizations are providing specialists in various fields in South Asia, under contracts with United States government agencies. On a less specialized and more grass- or rice-roots level, small numbers of Americans, mostly young in years, are now working in all of the South Asian countries as members of the Peace Corps. In time the Peace Corps representatives may have more of an impact on more South Asians than all of the more experienced and more highly paid Americans who have been sent to the subcontinent under official auspices.

Speaking generally, American relations with India are at an all-time high, as a result of the prompt American response to India's request for military assistance when the Chinese attacked in October-November 1962. Relations with Pakistan have been strained in recent years, particularly so since the extension of military aid to India and Pakistan's border and trade agreements with Communist China. Pakistan can be described at present as a disgruntled ally. Relations with Ceylon are rather limited and unsatisfactory; those with Nepal, controlled by King Mahendra, are correct but far from close. In spite of ups and downs in the official relations between the United States and the countries of South Asia, it may be said that these relations are basically good, if not really close or wholly satisfactory.

Areas of Ignorance and Problems of Understanding

Now meeting at many levels and in many ways, officially and unofficially, the results of this encounter between the United States and South Asia are already apparent. Contacts are growing rapidly, and mutual interest is visibly increasing. Paradoxically, almost all educated South Asians have a special interest in and knowledge of the United States, whereas relatively few of the most highly educated Americans have a comparable interest in and knowledge of the subcontinent. In part, no doubt, this paradox may be explained by the fact that the importance of the United States in world affairs is now so great that inevitably any educated person finds himself compelled to make some effort to understand the puzzling phenomenon that is America, whereas South Asia does not occupy a comparable place in the minds of most Americans; but the general ignorance of South Asia in the United States should be a matter of concern, and every effort should be made to correct it.

United States-South Asian contacts are still more extensive than intensive. Americans and South Asians do not really know each other, and in fact most of them have little awareness of the way people in the other part of the world live and what things matter most to them. "The vast multitude of the common masses of India," writes Mrs. Kusum Nair, ". . . have no relationship whatever with the United States of America or its people." This same comment could be made, *mutatis mutandis,* with even greater accuracy of the peoples of other South Asian countries, and with almost equal relevance of the vast majority of the people of the United States. Moreover, Mrs. Nair contends that "there is not, and can never be, a deeper emotional kinship between the two peoples, rooted in a common ethnic, cultural, or historical heritage such as binds the American and the West European communities, or the Arab states, for example. . . . Under the circumstances, it is difficult to envisage any revolutionary change in the basic relationship between America and India. . . . Even so, there is great scope for improvement in the interpretation of the American way of life to India."[5]

[5] Kusum Nair, "Galbraith in India," *Harper's,* December 1961, pp. 50, 53.

The relative superficiality of the United States-South Asian encounter is not a surprising phenomenon, and it need not be a serious barrier in the way of satisfactory relations; but obviously a greater knowledge of each other on a widespread popular scale, and especially among elite opinion-making groups, would create a better background for more meaningful encounters at many levels. The problem of knowledge and understanding is definitely a two-way proposition; but it is perhaps a greater responsibility for Americans than for the peoples of South Asian countries, for in literate circles at least, the American ignorance and misunderstanding are the greater. This lack of really basic contacts and understanding limits severely the scope and profundity of the mutual relations, and gives a kind of unreality or false glow to any claims or evidences that the era of United States-South Asian understanding has really dawned.

Possibly, as Professor Richard L. Park has observed, "The best one can hope for in the relations between two peoples are broad ranges of understanding of each other's viewpoints, plus general tolerance and a resistance against giving ill-tempered criticism. There persists the belief in most nations of the existence of a certain self-righteousness and clear-mindedness sadly lacking in all other nations. A penchant for instructing the rest of the world in these 'self-evident' truths happens to be a weakness shared by America and India."[6]

The dark areas of ignorance and misunderstanding are even more manifest in the American approach to the other countries of South Asia. This is especially true, of course, of Nepal, about which Americans know very little indeed, but it is also true of Ceylon and even of Pakistan. Most Americans are vague even about the geography of Pakistan — all too often they think of it as a part of India, or are surprised to learn that it is divided into two main parts, separated by a thousand miles of Indian territory — and they have only the foggiest notion of the circumstances which led to the creation and which form the *raison d'être* of America's major Asian ally.

Too often ignorance is compounded by indifference, irritation, and sensitivity. Many Americans, for example, think that South Asia doesn't really matter to them; they are exasperated by attitudes, policies, and behavior which seem strange and irrational, and which make South Asians difficult to deal with and hard to understand; and they are sensitive to alleged failures to appreciate American motives or actions, including economic aid, and to the barrage of criticism which comes from the subcontinent. Many South Asians have the same feelings about the United States.

Those who are especially interested in the other part of the world often

[6] "Bases for Political Accord Between India and America," in C. H. Alexandrowicz, ed., *Indian Year Book of International Affairs, 1957* (Madras: Diocesan Press, for the Indian Study Group of International Law and Affairs, University of Madras, 1957), p. 444.

hold ultra-critical or ultra-sympathetic views. Many American views on India, for example, may be subsumed under what might be called either the "Taj Mahal by moonlight" or the "Mother India" approach. Many Indian views on America reflect either excessive faith or excessive disillusionment.

An added complication is the spiraling cycle of criticisms, hostile reactions to criticisms, counter criticisms, and further criticisms which have constantly bedeviled United States-South Asian and especially Indo-American relations. A great deal of the criticism stems from sheer ignorance or prejudice, or from frustrations, or from an inability to appreciate the circumstances that give rise to certain attitudes and policies and the limitations under which policy-makers must operate. As Professor Lewis observed with respect to Indo-American cooperation, it is difficult to sustain "a high quality of . . . collaboration . . . in an atmosphere of aimless ill humor."[7] Fortunately official and most unofficial relations are conducted on a different level, although even on this level influential South Asian spokesmen have shown a considerable frankness and virtuosity in criticizing the United States and sometimes American spokesmen have returned the compliment.

The exchange of unpleasantries has been particularly sharp in the press. Unfortunately, the bitterly critical editorials in the press, and even some of the most caustic columns of prominent journalists, have often mirrored the views of large numbers of people, and therefore have to be given greater consideration than they would otherwise merit in drawing up the United States-South Asian balance sheet. In recent years, particularly in 1962 and the first half of 1963, the press of Pakistan — which, while not directly controlled by the government, is operating under controlled conditions and would hardly venture to express views which are far out of line with government attitudes — has reached new heights of vitriolic criticism of "our incredible ally." The American press has not replied in kind, perhaps in part because American newspapermen have not been fully aware of what the Pakistan press has been printing and because they have had a more obvious target at which they particularly like to shoot. That target is India. For many years India has had a bad press in the United States. Even the more responsible journals have shown a "waspishness" toward India that has often been far from "latent," and what might be called the provincial press — applying the term to outlook and not to location this would include all but a handful of American newspapers — has, with some outstanding exceptions, shown a degree of hostility toward India and toward Nehru, and of course toward Krishna Menon, that has to be read to be believed. After the Indian take-over in Goa, Indians were aroused not so much by American criticisms of this action — although criticisms from many supposed friends of India, notably Adlai Stevenson, hurt them, too — as by the generally anti-Indian

[7] Lewis, *Quiet Crisis in India,* p. 336.

tone of many of the newspaper editorials, feature articles and columns, and cartoons.[8]

Ironically, one might argue that a major stumbling block to good United States-South Asian relations has been the American Congress. Consciously or unconsciously, members of the Congress have often given offense in South Asian countries by their obvious ignorance and apparent callousness, and by their outspoken criticisms of the leaders, policies, and ways of life and patterns of thought in these countries. In a sense they have given too little attention to Pakistan — which is still an "unknown ally" — and even less to Nepal and Ceylon, about which most Congressmen know little, and too much attention to India, even though this country, too, is largely unknown on Capitol Hill.

Many Congressmen have been disturbed because a country which, at least until recently, has been following policies at home and abroad with which they were unsympathetic, has been the major recipient of American economic aid in recent years. The prolonged debates on the wheat loan to India in 1951, and the bitter things that were said in the course of these debates, largely counteracted the goodwill toward America that aid in time of crisis would have otherwise produced. The annual debates in Congress on foreign aid appropriations have occasioned a spate of criticisms of India. In 1962 the criticisms were so strong that the continuance of substantial aid to India — which was vital to the success of India's Third Five Year Plan — was in jeopardy. This feeling was reflected in a sentence in a report of the Senate Foreign Relations Committee on the Foreign Assistance Act of 1962: "Although some members were reluctant to single out one country for reduction in planned programs, others felt that a variety of incidents during the past year . . . had so tended to alienate a large body of American opinion as to justify at least a token reduction of planned U. S. assistance to India." One senator even proposed, with apparent seriousness, that all aid to India should be eliminated.

Distinguished members of the Congress called Nehru a "hypocrite" or worse, and they have spoken contemptuously of many aspects of Indian life and policy. One veteran Senator called the Indian army "no damned good," and stated that he opposed American arms aid to India on the ground that any weapons provided would find their way into the hands of the Chinese Communists. Anti-Indian statements of this sort have had a bipartisan character. Obviously the anti-Indian blasts of Congressmen should be considered in the proper perspective, but it is too much to expect that Indians will be able to fathom the motivations behind ill-tempered words from persons whom they consider to be responsible spokesmen of American policy.

---

[8] Perhaps they were particularly sensitive in this instance because they were thrown on the defensive by the strong criticisms of the move into Goa in the Western world and by their own doubts and misgivings, and because the critical American response to Goa was played up so widely in India.

If anything can be done to persuade members of the Congress to choose their words more carefully or to inform South Asians of the implications of the right of free speech and the peculiarities of the American presidential system, this would be a real contribution to improved United States-South Asian relations.

Since South Asia is of special significance in all of non-Communist Asia, in the "third world" of unaligned and weakly aligned countries, and in the entire underdeveloped world, it is bound to be, as has been noted, an area of increasing concern to the United States. In the years to come ignorance, misunderstanding, and "waspish" impatience regarding South Asia are luxuries which the United States can no longer afford. Hence a major effort of education and mental reorientation, on official and unofficial levels, is clearly needed.

CHAPTER TWO

The Course of United States–South Asian Relations

BROADLY SPEAKING, AMERICAN POLICY toward the countries of South Asia in the postwar years falls into three main periods, corresponding roughly with the terms of the Truman, Eisenhower, and Kennedy-Johnson adminstrations. The Truman administration was primarily absorbed in other and more pressing matters, such as postwar rehabilitation and reconstruction, mainly in Western Europe, and the formulation of a containment policy *vis-à-vis* a threatening Soviet Union. Relations with India were conducted on a rather formal level until 1951; then the question of the wheat loan to India at a time of a grave food crisis attracted much attention, and in the fall of 1951 the appointment of Chester Bowles as ambassador to India marked the beginning of a period of real warmth and interest in Indo-American relations (in the United States Madame Pandit made a similar contribution). Relations with Pakistan and Ceylon had not yet jelled, and Nepal has just emerged from the long period of Rana rule.

During the Eisenhower administration, with its suspicions of "neutrals" and its emphasis on military alliances, attention seemed to shift to Pakistan, although India became the main recipient of American economic aid. Pakistan swung over to a policy of alignment; it received military assistance from the United States, with which it concluded a Mutual Defense Agreement, and it entered into the two American-sponsored multilateral mutual security arrangements in Asia, the Manila Treaty (SEATO), and the Baghdad Pact (later CENTO). India strongly disapproved of the trends in American foreign policy, being particularly disturbed by American arms aid to Pakistan and Pakistan's adherence to military pacts. Toward the end of Eisenhower's term of office, after the death of John Foster Dulles and the crisis in Sino-Indian relations since 1959, United States relations with India seemed to improve considerably, whereas those with Pakistan became rather cool.

With President Kennedy the American approach to South Asia became

12

more than ever an Indian-oriented one. Mr. Kennedy was known as a great friend of India, although he had no firsthand acquaintance with that country. Pakistan was understandably suspicious of the Kennedy administration, and its leaders and its newspapers were quite open in voicing their apprehensions and displeasure. These suspicions were somewhat mitigated as a result of President Ayub Khan's visit to the United States in July 1961, the adverse reactions in the United States to India's move into Goa, and the American support of a resolution in the UN Security Council urging India and Pakistan to enter into direct negotiations on the Kashmir dispute. But all the old suspicions and fears were revived and aggravated when the United States began to give substantial military aid to India after the major Chinese offensive was launched in the North East Frontier Agency and Ladakh in late October 1962. At present Pakistan is a disgruntled ally which seems to be veering away from its alignment policy. India, on the other hand, has been shocked out of what Prime Minister Nehru called "an artificial atmosphere of our own creation" and, while continuing to insist that it still adheres to a policy of nonalignment, it has turned to the Western nations and to the Soviet Union for military aid.

The United States and India

World War II and the Truman Administration

Largely because many Americans had been sympathetic with India's freedom struggle, and because of President Roosevelt's known intervention on India's behalf with Churchill[1] — however unavailing that effort may have been — the United States enjoyed great prestige in India as independence dawned. After independence, however, "the standing of the United States," in the words of Robert Trumbull, "did a nose dive, partly because of resurgent Asianism, resentment over the use of atomic weapons on an Asian target, suspicion of Washington's use of its suddenly emergent position among the world powers and numerous disagreements in the international political sphere."[2]

[1] B. Shiva Rao, "Roosevelt and India," *The Hindu Weekly Review* (Madras), February 4, 1963; William Phillips, *Ventures in Diplomacy* (Boston: Beacon Press, 1952), pp. 343–396; *Foreign Relations of the United States, 1941, v. III, The British Commonwealth, the Near East and Africa* (Washington: Government Printing Office, 1959), pp. 176–177.

[2] Dispatch from New Delhi in *The New York Times*, September 27, 1950. In this dispatch Mr. Trumbull quoted "highly placed Indian officials" and others as expressing the belief that "the United States could regain its lost prestige virtually overnight if American spokesmen in the United Nations came out strongly against the South African 'apartheid' (separation of races) policy and also showed more appreciation of India's point of view in her dispute with Pakistan over Kashmir." Other examples are given in Norman D. Palmer, "Ups and Downs in Indo-American Relations," *The Annals* of the American Academy of Political and Social Science, July 1954, pp. 113–130.

This might be taken as an initial illustration of a fundamental feature of Indo-American relations, namely that they have been characterized by frequent and often sudden ups and downs. These fluctuations, often occasioned by specific developments, have tended to obscure the basic community of interest between the two countries and the gradual maturing of their relations and understanding. Hence the state of Indo-American relations at any particular time should be analyzed in terms of specific developments and issues, whereas the real nature of these relations should be analyzed in terms of basic understanding and misunderstanding.

As a Western nation the United States could never wholly free itself from the taint of inherited and unchangeable suspicions of Western motives; and as the country inevitably became more deeply involved in Asian affairs during and after the war, it was bound to be suspect in such a sensitive new nation as India. These sensitivities were reflected by Prime Minister Nehru in a famous address at Columbia University in October 1949, during his first visit to the United States. "The West," he declared, "has too often despised the Asian and the African and still, in many places, denies them not only equality of rights but even common humanity and kindliness," a theme to which Nehru returned again and again in the first years of India's independence.[3] A new era had dawned, he insisted, in which the countries of Asia and Africa did not intend to be bypassed, or ignored, or to have their decisions made for them by the Western powers.

Even though India reluctantly went along with the first two resolutions of the UN Security Council after the sudden attack from North Korea in late June 1950, its heart was not in military resistance to the aggression; it rather devoted all its efforts to bring about a cease-fire in Korea and to avert a widening of the war. The Korean crisis, apparently, was viewed as a regrettable involvement of Asians in a struggle which primarily concerned the United States and the Soviet Union. Widespread anti-United States feeling in India became even more pronounced after the United Nations forces, under American command, crossed the 38th parallel in Korea, in spite of warnings relayed by India that such a move would bring the Chinese Communists into the war.

This growing anti-Americanism was, however, compounded of many ingredients. In January 1951 A. T. Steele reported that during a two-month stay in India he encountered "more criticism of the United States than applause." The main criticism, he found, centered round America's policy toward China and Indo-China, its stand on the Kashmir question, its niggardly economic assistance, always extended with "strings," the war talk

[3] A representative sample of Mr. Nehru's statements on this theme is contained in Jawaharlal Nehru, *India's Foreign Policy: Selected Speeches, September 1946–April 1961* (New Delhi: The Publications Division, Ministry of Information and Broadcasting, Government of India, 1961), pp. 248–268.

in the United States, the American "failure to appreciate the Asian viewpoint" and to take "full cognizance of Asian sensibilities," and inept American propaganda.[4]

Early in 1951 the United States was confronted with what Robert Trumbull called "a peculiarly favorable moment . . . for a fruitful United States venture to cement the friendship of the elusive Indian public opinion at this critical time in Asia."[5] Faced with the prospect of a desperately critical food shortage, Prime Minister Nehru abandoned his standoffish attitude toward American economic aid and requested substantial shipments of food from the United States.

In a special message on February 12, 1951, President Truman recommended emergency assistance to India. Three days later a bill to provide this assistance, calling for an immediate shipment of a million tons of American surplus wheat on a grant basis to India, and authorizing the eventual shipment of another million tons, was introduced into the Congress by a bipartisan group of forty senators and representatives. Early in March the House Committee on Foreign Affairs reported the bill favorably; but, as *The New York Times* stated, "a small group of men concentrated in that legislative graveyard called the Rules Committee blocked the measure for several weeks until it was rewritten in the form of a loan."[6] In late April the Senate Foreign Relations Committee, which had been quite desultory in its consideration of the presumably emergency legislation, recommended a version of the original bill that had been revised to be partly loan, and partly grant. At about the same time the House of Representatives postponed floor action on the bill, apparently out of pique over a statement by Prime Minister Nehru to the effect that he would "not barter away India's self-respect or freedom of action even for something we need so badly." As *The New York Times* declared on May 4, "What could and should have been a magnanimous, humanitarian gesture from one people to another has had all the heart taken out of it."

About a week later Nehru announced both the acceptance of the American terms for emergency aid, which he said involved no political strings, and also the beginning of a Russian shipment of a promised 50,000 tons of wheat to India. The latter announcement, of shipments of Russian wheat which were insignificant in comparison with the promised two million tons from the United States and the approximately 100,000 tons of wheat a month that were arriving from the United States through regular trade channels, was given greater publicity and attracted more favorable attention in India than the news of the major assistance that would be forthcoming from the United States. Paradoxically, therefore, although the

[4] "How India Feels about the U.S.," *New York Herald Tribune,* January 29, 1951.
[5] "Aloofness of India to U.S. Aid is Easing," *The New York Times,* January 14, 1957.
[6] "Aid to India" (editorial), *The New York Times,* May 4, 1951.

United States responded to India's need, making available some two million tons of wheat valued at about $190 million, under a long-term loan, much of the goodwill that might have accrued was lost.

In the summer of 1951 India experienced a new wave of anti-American and pro-Soviet feeling, accentuated by differences over the proposed Japanese Peace Treaty. India refused to go along with the American plan, evolved by John Foster Dulles, for a conference of all nations involved in the war against Japan to agree on the terms of a peace treaty, and it resented what it regarded as American indifference and callousness toward Indian and Asian views on this matter. On September 1, 1951, Robert Trumbull reported: "The intermittently poor relations between India and the United States have reached the lowest ebb of all time this week through India's rejection of the proposed draft treaty with Japan and her boycott of the San Francisco conference."[7]

Six months later, again illustrating the ups and downs of the cycle, Trumbull noted that "The past few months have seen a remarkable improvement in relations between India and the United States."[8] He attributed this improvement to a variety of factors, including increasing contacts between Indians and Americans, the favorable impression created by Chester Bowles, the new ambassador, the actual arrival of the first shipments of wheat under the wheat loan agreement of 1951, and the announcement in January 1952 of a $54 million program of direct assistance to India.

The "remarkable improvement" in Indo-American relations did not last long. The results of the American presidential election in November 1952 were something of a surprise, and even a shock, in India. Almost all the leading Indian newspapers indulged in a "somewhat bewildered analysis" of the factors behind General Eisenhower's victory, and publicly expressed their regret at the decision of the American voters, which they felt boded no good for India. Once again there was a sudden sharp deterioration in relations, symbolized, for example, by rumors that a political appointee unknown in India would replace Chester Bowles. No single American has been as widely known or as genuinely popular as Mr. Bowles, who with Mrs. Bowles and their children had made a great personal impact on India. But the Bowles era was short-lived. When Mr. Bowles and his family left India in March 1953, shortly after the Republican administration assumed control in Washington, many Indians, unaccustomed to the ways of American politics, could not understand why the new administration would replace a man whom they particularly liked, unless it was less friendly to them than the Truman administration had been.

---

[7] "U.S.-India Relations Grow Steadily Worse," *The New York Times*, September 2, 1951.

[8] "India's Views Changing in Regard to the U.S.," *The New York Times*, March 9, 1952.

The Early Eisenhower Years: Arms Aid to Pakistan and Its Repercussions

In addition to the Republican victory at the polls, several other developments in late 1952 and early 1953 raised Indian apprehensions about a change for the worse in Washington's policies in Asia. Among these were United States co-sponsorship of a resolution on Kashmir, strongly opposed by India, in the UN Security Council; reports that the United States and the United Kingdom were negotiating with Pakistan concerning the proposed Middle East Defense Organization and a mutual security arrangement; and rumors that the new Secretary of State, John Foster Dulles, would come to South Asia to sound out India and Pakistan about their willingness or unwillingness to align themselves with the Western nations in the cold war.

On the whole, the first year and a half or more of the Eisenhower administration were bad years for Indo-American relations. The gulf between the personalities and orientation of John Foster Dulles and Jawaharlal Nehru was conspicuously wide, and policy divergencies were particularly marked.[9]

The nadir of Indo-American relations was plumbed in the spring of 1954, when the United States announced its decision to extend military assistance to Pakistan and entered into a mutual security arrangement with that country. Rumors of these impending moves were rife for several months before they were actually made. Apparently Vice-President Nixon came back from a trip to South Asia late in 1953 with the conviction that these moves would be desirable, in spite of the certainty of incurring Indian hostility as a result. By December 1953 public sentiment in India was already aroused by the reports of United States military aid to Pakistan, and Mr. Nehru and other Indian spokesmen, as well as Indian newspapers, were warning of the unhappy consequences of the contemplated moves. "Nothing in the realm of foreign affairs," wrote Robert Trumbull from New Delhi on January 9, 1954, "has so exercised India since she became free . . . . there is no doubt that if the Karachi arms deal goes through, the United States will have forfeited its position in India, whatever that may be and whatever it may be worth."[10]

---

[9] In May 1954 a correspondent of *The New York Times,* reflecting on the course of Indo-American relations, wrote: "Since early in 1953 . . . friction between the United States and India . . . has been frequent. India criticized the ending of the United States blockade of Formosa and was irritated by United States opposition to Indian participation in a conference on Korea. India has advocated admission of Communist China to the United Nations, reacted angrily to United States plans to arm Pakistan, condemned United States hydrogen bomb experiments, opposed Secretary of State Dulles' 'united action' scheme in Southeast Asia, and barred the United States Air Force from flying French paratroopers over India to Indo-China," Dana Adams Schmidt, "India Aid Status under Challenge," *The New York Times,* May 3, 1954.

[10] "India Fights the Pact," *The New York Times,* January 10, 1954.

There can be no doubt that President Eisenhower and his policy-planners carefully considered the effects of the contemplated arrangements with Pakistan upon United States relations with India; indeed, this was clearly the most important consideration militating against these arrangements. Rightly or wrongly, the decision was that the advantages of going ahead outweighed the disadvantages. When President Eisenhower announced his momentous decision on February 25, 1954, he wrote a personal letter to Prime Minister Nehru, assuring him that the new associations with Pakistan were in no way aimed at India, pledging that if Pakistan used American military aid against India the United States would come to India's aid, and promising that any request from India for military assistance "would receive my most sympathetic consideration." Anyone familiar with India's relations with Pakistan or with its views on military aid or alliances could have predicted that these assurances would by no means allay India's apprehensions, and would indeed be regarded as an insulting act of condescension. This was the way Nehru regarded them, as was evidenced by his coldly formal reply to Mr. Eisenhower's letter and by his bitter attack on the decision in the Indian Parliament a few days later. In this speech, Nehru charged that American military aid to Pakistan would upset "normality" and "create conditions which facilitate and encourage aggression." He scornfully rejected President Eisenhower's offer of similar military aid to India: "in making this suggestion," he declared, "the President has done less than justice to us or to himself. If we object to military aid being given to Pakistan, we would be hypocrites and unprincipled opportunists to accept such aid ourselves."[11] Nehru undoubtedly voiced his deepest convictions as well as those of the great majority of Indians who had any views at all on such matters; but his statement takes on a different complexion when viewed against his request for and acceptance of American arms aid when the Chinese launched their major offensive in October 1962.

The predicted Indian reactions to American military aid to Pakistan were not so vehement or so persistent as some Americans had feared. Nevertheless, this momentous step has been the greatest single irritant in Indo-American relations in the postwar years, though it has not jeopardized these relations beyond repair.

Three events in the April following the announcement of the American decision widened the gulf between India and America. The United States formalized its new relationship with Pakistan in a mutual security arrangement. In the same month, apparently in attempted retaliation against India's alleged softness on communism, growing criticisms of the United States, and specific actions such as the refusal to allow United States planes to pass through India en route to Indo-China, some Republican senators

[11] Robert Trumbull, "Nehru Decries U.S. Policy in Asia and the 'Cold War,'" *The New York Times,* March 2, 1954.

led a fight to reduce economic and technical assistance to India, thus creating the impression that America's economic assistance program was tied to political conditions. And India signed a treaty with China regarding Tibet, which included the "Five Principles of Peace" — the *Panchsheel* — and which presumably presaged a closer and more friendly relationship with the Communist regime in Peking. This pro-China orientation was pointed up in June, when the Chinese Premier, Chou En-lai, was given a most enthusiastic reception on a visit to New Delhi and joined with Nehru in a declaration endorsing the *Panchsheel*.

When the Manila Treaty was signed in 1954, joining Pakistan with the United States and six other nations in the multilateral security arrangement which soon became known as SEATO, India's low esteem of the United States was reconfirmed. After a temporary improvement, the strains in Indo-American relations continued through 1955 and were again accentuated in late 1955 and early 1956. The continuing tensions coincided with a marked improvement in Indian-Soviet relations, and with the beginnings of a major Soviet economic, cultural and political "offensive," aimed particularly at India, as the largest of the "neutralist" states. In July 1955 Nehru was given the "red carpet" treatment during an official visit to the Soviet Union. In November and December Nikolai Bulganin and Nikita Khrushchev returned his visit, and were given a tumultuous reception wherever they went in India. Making the most of their opportunities to score propaganda gains with the Indian people, the two Soviet leaders were in fact so outspoken in their attacks on the Western powers that Nehru and other government spokesmen were rather embarrassed, but the Indian people applauded these attacks. In Srinagar Khrushchev publicly endorsed the Indian stand on Kashmir. Both Soviet representatives vehemently denounced the Portuguese for hanging on to Goa, and gave complete support to India's claims. Never was Soviet prestige higher than when Bulganin and Khrushchev left India after their successful "barnstorming" tour.

By an unfortunate coincidence, at about the same time Secretary Dulles joined the Foreign Minister of Portugal in a statement which criticized the Soviet leaders for their intemperate language on Goa and which referred to it, Damão and Diu, the other possessions in India, as Portuguese "provinces."[12] This statement brought down on Dulles' head a storm of denunciation and protest in India and in other former colonial dependencies as well. Dulles was startled at the outcry, for he thought he was simply en-

[12] The exact wording of this much-criticized statement was as follows: "Various statements attributed to Soviet rulers visiting in Asia, which included references to the policies of Western powers in the Far East and allegations concerning the Portuguese provinces in the Far East, were discussed by the two Foreign Ministers." Communiqué by the Secretary of State and the Portuguese Minister of Foreign Affairs, December 2, 1953; *American Foreign Policy: Basic Documents*, v. I, Department of State Publication 6446, General Foreign Policy Series 117 (Washington: Government Printing Office, July 1957), p. 1689.

dorsing a statement of fact. His statement on Goa, however, "did the United States as much word-for-word harm as any declaration ever made."[13] The press in India and some neighboring countries called it "one of the great diplomatic blunders of modern history." The editor of *The Times of India*, often regarded in India as too pro-American, declared that the Dulles-Cunha statement would have a worse effect on Indo-American relations than American military aid to Pakistan. "Such a gesture," he wrote, "can only imply that Washington is writing off India from the democratic slate."[14] This charge was so palpably untrue to most Americans that they could not take it seriously, but the fact was that it expressed the views of millions of Indians. Dulles' seemingly innocuous statement on Goa haunted him for the rest of his life, and it continues to rank high on the list of complaints which Indians frequently advance against the United States. It increased already existing Indian doubts about American views and policies on colonial issues, just as the famous article in *Life* on Dulles' acts of "brinkmanship"[15] tended to confirm the Indian impression of Dulles as a dangerous "warmonger."

Another statement at the time by a prominent American was also resented in India. In a widely-publicized speech in New York on December 13, 1955, George Meany, president of the AFL-CIO, asserted flatly: "Nehru and Tito are not neutral. They are aides and allies of Communist imperialism in fact and in effect, if not in diplomatic verbiage."[16] Indians were accustomed to reports of such statements in American newspaper editorials and in columns by right-wing American journalists, but they were particularly hurt and indignant when a prominent American labor leader made this kind of charge. The harm done to Indo-American relations by Meany's blunt criticisms was partially offset by the public disagreement frequently expressed by Walter Reuther, vice-president of AFL-CIO, who repeated his views many times during a highly successful visit to India in April 1956.[17]

Improving Relations: 1956–61

Whereas the years 1953–55 were on balance rather bad years for Indo-American relations, the next five years were rather good ones, though with the usual ups and downs. Toward the end of 1956 relations improved markedly. In August the United States entered into an agreement with India to supply large quantities of wheat, rice, cotton, and other farm products out

---

[13] A. M. Rosenthal, "India: A Case History in the 'Cold War'," *The New York Times Magazine*, February 5, 1956.

[14] See editorial, "Midwinter Madness," *The Times of India*, December 7, 1955.

[15] James Shepley, "How Dulles Averted War," *Life*, January 16, 1956, pp. 70–72, 77–78, 80.

[16] A. H. Raskin, "Meany Says Nehru and Tito Aid Reds," *The New York Times*, December 14, 1955.

[17] "Indians Acclaim Reuther's Visit," *The New York Times*, April 15, 1956; Arthur Bonner, "Through India with Walter Reuther," *The Reporter*, May 17, 1956, pp. 31–34.

of its surplus supply, largely on a loan basis. The surplus products to be provided were valued at reduced prices at $305 million. The American opposition to the Anglo-French-Israeli invasion of Egypt in October 1956, and the efforts of the United States to work through the United Nations in bringing pressure upon the invading powers to withdraw their forces, won much goodwill in India. Americans were highly critical of the official Indian reactions to the Hungarian crisis, which were symbolized by abstentions on resolutions in the UN General Assembly condemning the Russian brutalities in Hungary (Krishna Menon even voted against one of these resolutions), and by Nehru's long delay in speaking out strongly against the Russian actions; but in this instance public opinion in India was ahead of the official views, and in due time internal as well as external criticism, plus fuller and more reliable reports on the actual happenings in Hungary, persuaded Nehru to take a stronger position on the issue.

In December 1956 Nehru made his second official visit to the United States, a visit generally regarded as quite successful. Nehru seemed to be in a better frame of mind than in 1949. On his extensive travels around the United States, his observations and speeches were reported at length. At an informal press conference, Mr. Nehru said that his long talks with President Eisenhower had persuaded him that United States policy was "not as rigid as I thought," but was instead "a flexible policy adapting itself to circumstances."

In the winter of 1957–58 it became apparent that India was in "grave, potentially even catastrophic financial difficulties," as a result of many adverse developments at home and abroad. Although the Second Five Year Plan, inaugurated in 1956, was cut substantially, large amounts of foreign aid were needed to save even "the core." To meet this new crisis the United States came to India's aid in a major way. In March 1958 it agreed to loan India $225 million for the support of the Second Plan, 70 per cent to be made available through the Export-Import Bank, and 30 per cent from the Development Loan Fund. Also, since India was again faced with a food crisis, the United States entered into two agreements with India in 1958, under Public Law 480, for the provision of large quantities of wheat and other foodgrains, valued at more than $350 million. The United States also played a major role in persuading other Western nations to come to India's aid. The experience in cooperative planning and assistance at this time laid the foundations for a major new approach to developing countries, through the medium of what later came to be known as the International Consortium of Nations.

The Chinese moves in Tibet and along the Sino-Indian borders in 1959 led India to undertake a fairly searching reappraisal of the bases of its foreign policy, with particular reference to its views on Communist motivations and probable behavior, the value of *Panchsheel* in dealing with China or other expansionist states, defense policies, and nonalignment. As relations with China went from bad to worse, Indian attitudes toward the United States changed for the better. Another high point in Indo-American relations came with President Eisenhower's visit in December 1959, while Indians were still in a state of indignation and disillusionment over the actions of the Chinese Communists. Visiting India at a psychologically auspicious time, the American President was given one of the most enthusiastic receptions ever accorded a foreign dignitary. He made a deep personal impression on those who saw and heard him. India obviously also had a profound impact on him, and he said on his departure that he had enjoyed his Indian trip more than his visit to any other country.

The Dulles era in Indo-American relations was over. Eisenhower, the Indians learned, was really a man of peace and goodwill, even though he was an ex-general and a Republican. Actually, under the pressures of economic necessity and foreign danger from the north, Indian policies and attitudes had probably changed far more than had those prevailing in Washington. Without doubt, too, the "Dulles image" in Indian eyes was always a distorted one. But certainly, for whatever reasons, relations between India and the United States in the last months of the Eisenhower administration were more relaxed and cordial.

The Kennedy-Johnson Era: Goa and the Chinese Attack

This did not mean, however, that Indians could view the results of the presidential elections of 1960 with any objectivity. Most Indians had no difficulty in choosing in their own minds between Senator Kennedy, a known friend of India and a young liberal of refreshing personality, and Vice-President Nixon, whose views and personality appealed to them less. Hence Kennedy's victory was applauded in India, and the good impression which Indians had of the new President was confirmed by his top-level appointments — especially that of Chester Bowles as Under Secretary of State, and of Professor J. K. Galbraith as Ambassador to India — by his words and behavior in the weeks just before and after his inauguration, and by his magnificent inaugural address. The Cuban fiasco of 1961 appreciably tarnished the Kennedy image in India, but on the whole the President's words and actions in the first months of his administration were well received in India.

The International Consortium announced a proposed loan to India which would amount to more than $2 billion for the first two years of the Third Five Year Plan, and there was close cooperation between the two countries in the Congo, in Laos, and in the United Nations. In addition, as M. C. Chagla stated upon retiring as ambassador, "Today neutrality has become respectable, and the United States wants newly emerging countries of Africa and the countries in South Asia to be neutral ... today I am proud to say that our Foreign Policy has been accepted by the United States as the correct policy which India has pursued."[18] Ironically, this more charitable view of India's foreign policy came at a time when the bases of that policy were being challenged seriously, for the first time, in India itself.

When Nehru made his third official visit to the United States in November 1961, Indo-American relations were still at a high point. He and President Kennedy had several lengthy and friendly meetings, and there seemed to be every reason to believe that his visit would consolidate cordial ties between the two countries. Instead, an event occurred which illustrated once again how susceptible the surface relations of the two countries were to the trends and tides of particular happenings.

The event was the sudden Indian move into Goa in December 1961. The move was hailed in India, in most of the other newly independent countries, and in the Communist states as a long-overdue elimination of a particularly obnoxious relic of colonialism. In the United States and other Western states, however, it was criticized as a basic violation of India's oft-repeated professions in foreign affairs, and of the Charter of the United Nations.

Indians were quite taken aback by the vehemence and universality of the American reactions to the take-over in Goa, and particularly by the criticisms in American liberal circles. Perhaps the greatest blow was the position taken by Adlai Stevenson in the United Nations. In criticizing the Indian action before the Security Council, in tones more of sorrow than of anger, Stevenson argued that unless actions of this kind could be interdicted they might lead to "the beginning of the end of the United Nations." To Indians this attitude reflected a failure to understand the circumstances which had prompted the move into Goa, and the remark about the possible effects upon the United Nations stung them to the quick, especially since they regarded Stevenson as one of their most sympathetic friends.

In creating new tensions and misunderstandings, the Goa incident seemed to wash away the cordiality that had prevailed in the preceding months. When the Consortium met in January 1962 and postponed further commitments to India, this was interpreted in India as being dictated by official displeasure with the Goa action. India was in turn highly displeased by United States and British support of a resolution in the Security Council, defeated in June 1962 only because of a Soviet veto, requesting India and Pakistan to try anew to solve the Kashmir dispute. In 1962 the annual battle in the American Congress over the President's request for foreign aid was unusually prolonged and bitter, with many criticisms of India.

From this trough Indo-American relations rose to what was probably an all-time crest as a result of the extraordinary developments of the latter weeks of the year. India was ill prepared, mentally and militarily, to meet the unexpected offensive which the Chinese launched in late October, and

[18] Quoted in *Indiagram* (issued by the Information Service of India, Washington), July 14, 1961.

which within a short time had sliced well into Ladakh and NEFA, threatening the plains of Assam. In this grave national emergency Nehru and his fellow-countrymen did not hesitate to drop many of their past illusions and attitudes. They did not allow their adherence to nonalignment or their aversion to military aid to stand in the way of seeking outside military assistance, whatever the source. In late October Nehru dismissed Krishna Menon from the Defense Ministry, thereby removing a major psychological obstacle to Indo-American cooperation, and formally requested military weapons and equipment from the United States. The request was immediately granted, without conditions or preachments, and soon huge transport planes were ferrying emergency weapons and supplies to India. Very shortly steps were taken to meet India's long-term military needs. British and American missions, headed respectively by Duncan Sandys and Averell Harriman, made an on-the-spot survey of India's defense situation and military needs. Sandys and Harriman were able to persuade Ayub Khan and Nehru to agree to direct talks, first at the ministerial level, on the Kashmir question.

India found the sympathy and concrete assistance it sought from many nations, especially from the United States and the United Kingdom. While the Soviet Union was hedging on the promised deliveries of MIG-21s and on other commitments, advising Nehru not to appeal to the West for arms and to enter into direct negotiations with China, and while most of the other nonaligned nations were being singularly unresponsive, the much-abused Western powers came, without quibbling or hesitation, to India's aid. This made a deep impression on Indians, who kept repeating, as if in a state of wonder and bewilderment, "Now we know who our real friends are." Government spokesmen, the press, and the people referred to the United States in unaccustomed terms of appreciation and warmth. For the moment, at least, the Chinese Communists had unwittingly performed a great service to Indo-American cooperation and friendship, costly lesson that it was.

To predict continuing good Indo-American relations is foolhardy. Past experience indicates that fluctuations in these relations will occur, and should therefore be expected. But if the changes in Indian policies and attitudes since the Chinese struck in 1962 do indeed create a "new India," the probability is that in the protracted conflict the United States and India will be thrown together by considerations of immediate interest as well as of shared beliefs and aspirations.

Indo-American Differences: General and Specific

India and the United States have often been at odds on fundamental questions of international policy, as well as on specific issues. The differences reflect radical divergencies in outlook, historical circumstances, present conditions, and attitudes. Although the two countries are seeking common ends, they often do not agree on the proper means to secure these ends.

Since they do not share a common assessment of present dangers, they are inclined to have different priorities and emphases.

The United States is inclined to stress the seriousness of the Communist threat, and to advocate a policy of containment and of collective security in dealing with it. India is inclined to minimize the Communist danger. As Chester Bowles once observed: "Americans . . . have been depressed by what seems to them to be India's failure to see the world struggle in fair perspective; by her application of what seems to be a double standard for judging the action of the Communist and Democratic blocs; . . . and for an outspoken admiration of many of her non-Communist citizens for alleged Communist achievements which have been brought about by methods which Gandhi spent and gave his life in opposing."[19]

India regarded colonialism as a far greater danger to world peace and to the aspirations of mankind than communism and the policies of the Communist states. In an oft-quoted statement in the Rajya Sabha in August 1954, Prime Minister Nehru declared: "We talk about the crisis of our time and many people do it in different ways. Probably in the United States of America the crisis of the time is supposed to be communism versus anti-communism. Maybe so to some extent. Well, the crisis of the time in Asia is colonialism versus anti-colonialism."[20] On this issue Indians, like all formerly colonial peoples, are very sensitive, seeing colonialism in most of the actions of the former colonial powers. Until recently, at least, the actions of Communist states have by definition not been classified as colonialist in nature. In contrast, the American position on colonialism is regarded as at best an ambivalent one, and at worst one reflecting a willingness to sacrifice anti-colonial professions in order to avoid disagreements with NATO and other Western allies.

With such assessments of present dangers and policy priorities, it is hardly surprising that the United States and India have differed rather fundamentally on the proper approaches to peace. Writing in the *Hindustan Times* of March 3, 1955, the veteran Indian statesman, C. Rajagopalachari, asserted that "the great difference between America and India is that the means America is adopting for establishing peace on earth do not appeal to India." "Many thoughtful Indians," Chester Bowles said at the same time, "now have come to think of America as belligerent, militaristic, imperialistic and even worse." Indians seem to feel that American policies have tended to exacerbate instead of alleviate international tensions, that they place too much emphasis on military measures and alliances and too little on peaceful coexistence and international cooperation. SEATO has been a favorite object of Indian attack, a prime illustration of what India regards as the wrong

[19] "Bowles Urges India to See 'What's Right' with U.S. Policy and Not to Stress Faults," *The New York Times*, March 5, 1955; report of an address to the Indian Council of World Affairs in New Delhi.
[20] Quoted in *The Times of India*, August 27, 1954.

road to peace. They have been particularly critical of America's atomic policies, from the decision to drop the first atomic bombs to the latest evidences that the United States is still developing its atomic arsenal. They have consistently called for a cessation of nuclear testing, and for nuclear disarmament, as a preliminary to complete disarmament. In these areas they seem to be far more critical of the United States than of the Soviet Union.

India's negative attitude toward basic American policies, such as the development of mutual security arrangements, is matched by a running American criticism of the basic Indian policy of nonalignment, which Americans are more likely to describe as neutrality or neutralism. Pakistan has often been praised for being willing to "stand up and be counted," in happy contrast to India's professed policy of "belonging to no camp" and of considering each issue as it arose "on its own merits." In recent years, however, the United States government has shown a more sympathetic understanding of the nature and reasons for nonalignment, at the very time that the Indian interpretation and application of this concept has become less moralistic, less rigid, and more flexible.

Policies toward Pakistan have been poles apart, and since relations with Pakistan have been the major concern of India's foreign — and even to a large degree of domestic — policy, these disagreements have been particularly vexing. They have centered mainly around arms aid to Pakistan and the Kashmir question. India's recent acceptance of similar aid from the United States will undoubtedly modify its attitude toward military assistance to Pakistan, but as long as Pakistan is a hostile neighbor India will naturally be disturbed by any moves which increase Pakistan's military capability. The same comment may be made with even greater relevance to Pakistan's views of American arms aid to India.

Both India and Pakistan have been dissatisfied with the American position in the Kashmir dispute. India expected a greater understanding of its views, whereas Pakistan expected less qualified endorsement of its case. On the whole, however, the official and unofficial American views on Kashmir have been more sympathetic with the Pakistani than with the Indian case, an attitude reflected in votes by American representatives whenever the Kashmir question has been brought before the Security Council. But aside from supporting the United Nations resolutions of August 1948 and January 1959, which call for extensive demilitarization in Kashmir and the determination of Kashmir's future by reference to the people of that state, the United States has not supported any specific solution of the Kashmir question.

The China policies of India and the United States have also been poles apart. India was the second non-Communist state to recognize the Central People's Government, and until the Chinese forfeited India's trust and friendship it was a leading champion of the Communist regime. It does not recognize the Nationalist regime on Formosa. Until 1959 the China impasse was a serious barrier to improved Indo-American relations. Since then, thanks to the callous behavior of the Chinese Communists themselves, India has ceased to champion the claims of Peking (although it still favors UN acceptance of the Communist regime as the rightful representative of China), and has reversed its previous contention that Communist China is not a threat to India or to world peace.

On innumerable other specific issues during the past fifteen years and more India and the United States have differed rather sharply. These issues include foreign aid, specific policy issues in the United Nations, issues which are immediate for one country but seem remote to the other, such as Goa and Cuba, criticisms of specific actions by the other country, such as the dispatch of American troops to Lebanon in 1958, differences over Korea, Indo-China, Algeria, Hungary, or almost any other trouble spot in the post-war period.

All these differences seem to suggest that an unbridgeable chasm yawns between India and America. Actually the opposite conclusion would be closer to the truth. Their foreign policies and international posture have been quite divergent. But they also have a great deal in common, including faith in the open society, in democratic processes, and in basic human freedoms, and they have the will and the incentive to cooperate on many levels for their mutual benefit. On April 1, 1953, in an address to the India League of America on the eve of his departure for New Delhi to assume the post of ambassador, George V. Allen said: "America's interest, in one sentence, is that India, which has achieved full sovereign status, shall retain that status completely, and that the faith which the vast majority of the Indian people have in democracy's ability to give them a better and fuller life be sustained and fortified." This view may still be taken as an accurate reflection of the official position of the American government. Despite the ups and downs in Indo-American relations, the basic relations have in fact been consistently good.[21]

The United States and Pakistan

If economic assistance has been the major factor in Indo-American relations, military as well as economic aid has dominated the relations between

---

[21] This conclusion is in line with the concluding paragraph of a study of Indo-American relations by an American and an Indian scholar: "Despite the differences of approach and of policy that have so far troubled Indian-American relations and that may for some time continue to do so, this study has shown that the mutual interests of India and the United States far outweigh the differences, that it is strongly in the interests of both India and the United States for the two countries to cooperate effectively on important world problems, and that the mutual advantage of cooperation is being increasingly recognized in both countries as their policy interests touch at a growing number of points. There is clear evidence that both peoples wish profoundly to live in a world of peace and progress. Despite difficulties they should be able to work toward this goal in closer cooperation in the future than they have in the past." Phillips Talbot and S. L. Poplai, *India and America* (New York: Harper, for the Council on Foreign Relations, 1958), p. 193.

the United States and Pakistan. Relations between the two have been complicated by the cold war preoccupations and global responsibilities of the United States, the changing political scene in Pakistan, the unhappy state of Indo-Pakistan relations, American interests in and aid to India, and the general American ignorance of Pakistan.

For most Americans Pakistan is perhaps the least known of America's major allies. They are puzzled about the circumstances leading to the creation of Pakistan, the nature of the country, the attitudes and ways of life of its people, and the character and motivations of its leaders. Relatively few Americans have had first-hand experience in Pakistan; the obvious exceptions are missionaries and, since Pakistan's independence, aid officials, military advisers, diplomatic personnel, and increasing numbers of businessmen and scholars.

The unofficial meeting of Pakistan and the United States is therefore still in the future, while on official levels the contacts have centered around cooperation in economic development, military preparedness, and alliance politics. In these respects relations have been close and usually cordial, although they have been adversely affected by differences in priorities and interests. In recent months cooperation has been less close, and there have been many strains on the alliance. Pakistan has been having second thoughts about its alliances, and it has been increasingly dissatisfied with the returns on its international commitments and seems to have abandoned its pro-American orientation.

Early Relations

For the first six years after Pakistan became independent its relations with the United States were formally correct but not close, and its impact upon the American consciousness was virtually nil. The story is told that when an American congressman, who visited Karachi soon after independence, was asked by a Pakistani reporter what Americans thought of Pakistan, he replied: "My boy, they've never even heard of it!" This story is doubtless apocryphal, and certainly exaggerated, but it does have a point. The Father of Pakistan, Mohammed Ali Jinnah, was not well known to Americans, as were the two great leaders of the new Indian state, and he died hardly more than a year after independence. The visit of his chief lieutenant, Prime Minister Liaquat Ali Khan, in May 1950 gave officials in Washington an opportunity to learn something of Pakistan's interests and policies, but, unlike Nehru's first visit a few months previously, it was given relatively little publicity and attracted little popular interest. Understandably absorbed in its efforts to lay the bases of nationhood and to deal with urgent internal problems, Pakistan had little opportunity to take an active part in world affairs. Its foreign policy until 1953 may be described as "neutralist." Liaquat Ali Khan stated in 1951 that "sometimes we agreed with the Western bloc, and sometimes with the Communist bloc, as the situation and the matter under consideration demanded.[22]

After Liaquat's assassination in October 1951, "effective control of Pakistan passed from the League and the politicians to Governor General Ghulam Mohammed and a group of men whom Philip Deane of the *Observer* has aptly called 'the hierarchs' — the senior Army officers and the civil servants."[23] To secure outside economic and military aid, strengthen themselves *vis-à-vis* India, and compensate for rebuffs in their overtures to fellow-Muslims of the Middle East, the new leaders of Pakistan began to put out feelers to the United States. For a time Dean Acheson, then Secretary of State, was rather cool, and Ambassador Chester Bowles was strongly opposed to any military aid to Pakistan from the moment he got wind of the feelers, but the Pakistanis received solid support from the Pentagon and from Assistant Secretary of State Henry Byroade. Apparently they were sufficiently encouraged sometime in 1952 to assume that a formal agreement was simply a matter of time. The change of administration and Bowles' departure from New Delhi shortly thereafter created a more receptive mood in Washington, and the collapse of the American-sponsored idea of a Middle East Defense Organization led Secretary Dulles to turn to the alternative proposal of a "northern tier" alignment, with Turkey as the anchor in the west and Pakistan in the east. Apparently his visit to South Asia and the Middle East in the spring of 1953 convinced him that the idea was both sound and feasible.

Arms Aid, Military Alliance, and Economic Aid

By the latter part of 1953 rumors of an impending arms aid program to Pakistan were in common currency. Some of these, it seems, were prompted by Pakistan, although they were denied by the United States. In November 1953, both Governor General Ghulam Mohammed and General Ayub Khan, then Commander-in-Chief of the Pakistan Army, were in the United States, the former ostensibly for medical treatment, the latter in response to an invitation to tour American military installations. Both leaders talked with highly placed American officials.

By early December the reports of the forthcoming United States-Pakistan military pact seemed by this time to be so well substantiated, in spite of official American denials or reticence, that Prime Minister Nehru made official remonstrances and the Congress Party staged protest rallies. Whether because of the vehemence of the Indian reactions, which were surely anticipated from the beginning, or because of other complications, for several

---

[22] Quoted in Selig S. Harrison, "India, Pakistan and the United States: II — Cost of a Mistake," *The New Republic*, August 24, 1959, p. 22. See also K. Sarwar Hasan, *Pakistan and the United States* (New York: Manhattan Publishing Co., 1960), p. 51.

[23] Selig S. Harrison, "India, Pakistan and the United States: I — Case History of a Mistake," *The New Republic*, August 10, 1959, p. 14.

weeks the United States seemed to be hesitating, and in its turn Pakistan became alarmed. The details were worked out, however, and in February 1954 the decision was finally made and officially announced.[24]

On May 19, 1954, the United States and Pakistan formalized their new relationship in a Mutual Defense Assistance Agreement. Pakistan promised that it would not undertake any act of aggression and would use the American military aid "exclusively to maintain her internal security and legitimate defense, or to permit her to participate in the defense of the region or in United Nations collective security arrangements." In the following September Pakistan joined with the United States, the United Kingdom, France, Australia, New Zealand, the Philippines, and Thailand in the Manila Treaty, which was concerned with the defense of Southeast Asia and which resulted in the establishment of the Southeast Asia Treaty Organization (SEATO). Fourteen months later, Pakistan became associated with Turkey, Iran, Iraq, and the United Kingdom in what was then known as the Baghdad Pact and later, after Iraq's withdrawal, renamed the Central Treaty Organization (CENTO).

Thus, by entering into a series of bilateral and multilateral military agreements in 1953–55 Pakistan changed its foreign policy from one of neutrality to one of alignment. The main motive of the United States in agreeing to provide military aid and in encouraging Pakistan to enter into military alliances was to develop a more organized counterpoise to possible Communist aggression. Occupying a key position, Pakistan became the eastern anchor of the Baghdad Pact (now CENTO) and the western anchor of SEATO.[25]

There can be little doubt, however, that in accepting military assistance from the United States, and even in entering into multilateral military alliances, Pakistan was seeking to strengthen itself not so much against the U.S.S.R. as against India. From the beginning Pakistanis were inclined to measure the value of their new allies from this point of view, and since this was a viewpoint which none of their allies shared, they were often disappointed and frustrated.

Pakistani doubts about the real value of its alliances were seldom expressed in the early years of its alignment. Even then, however, a few Pakistanis called attention to the different purposes motivating the United

[24] For the story of the events and circumstances leading to the U.S. decision to extend arms aid to Pakistan, and the repercussion of this decision, see *ibid.*, and James W. Spain, "Military Assistance for Pakistan," *American Political Science Review*, September 1954, pp. 738–751.

[25] Former Vice-President Nixon's biographer insists that Mr. Nixon urged that the United States extend arms aid to Pakistan not so much to enable that country to be in a stronger position to defend itself against any possible Communist attack but "as a counter-force to the confirmed neutralism of Jawaharlal Nehru's India." If this was his real objective, it was shared by relatively few Americans at the time, although it would have commended itself to Senator Knowland and other strongly anti-Nehru members of the American Congress. Ralph Toledano, *Nixon* (New York: Henry Holt, 1956), p. 164. See also Harrison, "Case History of a Mistake," cited, p. 17.

States and Pakistan. The *Christian Science Monitor* of March 25, 1954, for example, carried this comment from a Pakistani correspondent: "Pakistan's great hope — American military aid — may become, in the final analysis, its greatest disillusionment and provide communism with a foothold it otherwise might never have gained. This paradox stems from the fact that military aid has meant one thing to the United States negotiators and the Pakistan Government and something entirely different to a majority of the Pakistani people." Actually, the Pakistan government was primarily motivated by considerations which were closer to the desires of its own people than to those of the American government.

Few Americans publicly opposed the idea of giving military aid to Pakistan. Such a move, after all, seemed wholly consistent with the overall objectives of American policy since March 1947, when President Truman enunciated what came to be known as the Truman Doctrine. Chester Bowles continued to warn against the consequences of arms aid to Pakistan. One powerful voice was raised in opposition in the United States Senate. On March 2, 1954, Senator J. William Fulbright declared: "I think the decision to supply arms to Pakistan is an unfortunate mistake.... I have the greatest respect for the people of Pakistan, as I do for the people of India. ... Their mutual difficulties have threatened war, so we are not unaware of the tension between them and therefore should have been extremely careful in our relations with both." By then, however, the decision had been made, and announced by President Eisenhower.

The exact amounts and types of military aid to Pakistan have not been officially divulged, although their general nature is fairly well known. The appropriations for Pakistan have been included every year in the foreign aid appropriations bill in a general item for military assistance for countries in the Near East and South Asia. But since Turkey and Pakistan are the only countries in the area receiving any substantial amounts of military aid, some educated guesses of the amount allocated to Pakistan can be made from the published figures. Selig Harrison has estimated that the total amount up to the time of the U-2 incident in May 1960 was approximately $1.5 billion;[26] H. R. Vohra has estimated that the total up to the end of 1961 was about $2 billion.[27]

The United States has provided Pakistan with a variety of equipment, including tanks and such sophisticated weapons as F-104A jet fighters and Sidewinder missiles. In return the United States has apparently been permitted to install detection and communications centers and to use Pakistan air fields for certain military purposes, although Pakistan has consistently denied that it has agreed to the establishment of American military bases on its soil. The United States has maintained a large Military Advisory

[26] Selig S. Harrison, "South Asia and U.S. Policy," *The New Republic*, December 11, 1961, p. 12.
[27] *The Times of India*, December 10, 1961.

Group in Pakistan, whose members keep in close touch with the political as well as the military leaders and assist the Pakistani armed forces in a number of advisory ways. Hundreds of Pakistani officers have been sent to the United States for special training. Pakistan and the United States have been active in both SEATO and CENTO (with which the United States is associated, even though it is not a fully participating member). As a reaffirmation and strengthening of the ties the Pakistan-United States Bilateral Agreement of Cooperation, in which the United States pledged to "take appropriate action, including the use of armed force" in the event of aggression against Pakistan, was signed in March 1959.

Another major factor in United States-Pakistan relations during the past decade has been American economic aid. The total value of this aid is now more than $3 billion. It has been extended chiefly in the form of grants, hard and soft loans, and surplus food under PL 480. The sizeable United States Aid Mission has worked closely with Pakistan's planners in the development efforts. Some United States-assisted projects, such as the Karnaphuli hydro-electric project in East Pakistan, have been large and spectacular, but most of the American aid has been used for smaller projects in the overall development programs. One of the most appreciated kinds of American aid was the prompt shipment in 1953–54 during a grave food crisis of some 610,000 tons of wheat, valued at approximately $68 million, which helped to save many lives and probably did more than any other single action to create goodwill.[28] The speedy response to Pakistan's needs contrasted favorably with the long delay and the congressional criticisms that accompanied American assistance to India during the crisis of 1951. Since 1953–54 much larger amounts of surplus foodgrains have been shipped to Pakistan.

The impact of American military and economic assistance was undoubtedly affected by the deterioration in Pakistan's economic and political situation while the First Five Year Plan (1955–60) was being haltingly implemented. The United States viewed with genuine sympathy and general approval the efforts of the military regime which assumed control in October 1958 to "clean up the mess" it had inherited and to press needed reforms. Economic and military assistance was continued on a substantial scale.

The United States was very much involved in the long negotiations over several years which finally led to an agreement between India and Pakistan, signed in September 1960, for the use of the waters of the Indus Basin. David Lilienthal first proposed the procedures which were instrumental in securing the agreement, and Eugene Black, the American President of the International Bank for Reconstruction and Development, took an active part in working out the formula whereby several nations will contribute nearly a billion dollars in grants and long-term loans to the Indus Basin

[28] See *Summary Report: The Pakistan Wheat Program of 1953–54* (*P.L. 77, 83rd Cong.*), submitted by Marion H. Hardesty (Washington: Foreign Operations Administration, July 7, 1954).

Development Fund, with the United States itself contributing about half of the total amount.

On the whole, relations between the United States and Pakistan during the last years of the Eisenhower administration and the first two years of the Ayub Khan regime were good. The U-2 incident in May 1960 caused some embarrassment for both countries. The American reconnaissance plane that was shot down over Soviet territory had taken off from the Peshawar airfield on its ill-fated mission. Apparently the Pakistan government was not fully informed of this mission. Khrushchev warned Pakistan that it was playing with fire by granting the United States the use of its territory for U-2 flights, and that Pakistan might suffer the full fury of a Soviet atomic attack if it continued to collaborate with the American "aggressor." Ayub Khan spurned this threat, but the U-2 affair must have given him some anxious moments and sober second thoughts. Many Pakistanis questioned the wisdom of such direct involvement in the "cold war."

Tensions in United States-Pakistan Relations

Since the fall of 1960, criticisms of American policies and actions have been bluntly and frequently expressed by the leaders of Pakistan and especially by the press. The outcome of the presidential elections in November 1960 was as unwelcome in Pakistan as it was welcome in India. Under President Kennedy the South Asia policy of the United States became even more India-oriented than it had before, as the nation adopted a more sympathetic attitude toward "neutralist" states generally and seemingly placed less value on SEATO or on its Asian allies. There were reports that the Kennedy administration would try to extricate itself from the inherited commitments to provide military aid to Pakistan. Certain of Kennedy's early actions and policies, notably his failure to act decisively at the time of the "Bay of Pigs" invasion of Cuba, were interpreted as indicating a lack of resolution. The President's firm action in the face of the Soviet build-up of nuclear missiles in Cuba in the fall of 1962 helped to counteract this impression, although some Pakistani newspapers, perhaps reflecting official views, complained that the American President had taken grave risks without even informing Pakistan.

Pakistanis were also highly critical of American "weakness" in the Goa affair. American criticisms were not followed by the kind of measures which Pakistanis wanted to invoke against India. Many Pakistani editorials criticizing the American position alleged that if India attempted to do in the Pakistan-held portion of Kashmir what it had done in Goa, the United States would probably find various reasons for inaction.

The United States was deeply disturbed in turn because Pakistan took certain major policy decisions and actions without in any way consulting, or even informing, its American ally. Two major examples were the actions leading to the severance of diplomatic relations between Pakistan and

Afghanistan in August 1961 (they were not resumed until May 1963), and
the new Pakistani orientation toward the Communist countries, particularly
Communist China, which resulted in several important agreements and a
great deal of anti-American, as well as anti-Indian, feeling in Pakistan.
Pakistan, in turn, was alienated and alarmed by the United States decision to
extend military assistance to India following the Chinese attack in 1962, and
it was further offended because it claimed that it had not been consulted
or informed before this important American decision was made.

In August 1961 Ayub Khan ordered the closing of Pakistan's consulates in
Kandahar and Jalalabad and of Afghanistan's consulates and trade agencies
in Pakistan. These measures, taken without even informing the American
ambassador, were embarrassing to the United States in many ways. Because
the Afghan government retaliated not only by severing diplomatic relations
but also by closing its borders to all goods from Pakistan, it cut itself off
from its normal supply routes, thereby becoming more dependent than ever
on the Soviet Union. American economic aid could no longer be sent to
Afghanistan through Karachi and the Khyber Pass.

To help resolve the impasse and try to restore trade, President Kennedy
offered to send Livingston T. Merchant, then ambassador to Canada, to
confer with the leaders of both countries. The offer was accepted by both
parties, though Pakistan had many misgivings. The Pakistanis gave the
United States credit for good intentions, but they felt that in its zeal to
resume aid shipments it might try to pressure Pakistan into making undesirable concessions, and that it was letting itself be used by Afghanistan, which
in Pakistan's view was virtually a Soviet satellite, against its own ally.
Mr. Merchant, who was unfamiliar with the issues in dispute, conferred
with Pakistani and Afghan officials but was unable to make any progress
in bringing the two countries together. Unofficially the Pakistanis were
quite frank in expressing their doubts about the wisdom of the Livingston
Merchant mission.

Even more disturbing to the United States were the various indications
that Pakistan was showing more and more interest in establishing closer
relations with the Soviet Union and especially with Communist China. In
1961 Pakistan entered into an agreement for Soviet assistance in the exploration and development of its oil resources. In an important speech in the
new National Assembly on June 27, 1962, Foreign Minister Mohammed Ali
said that "we have been anxious to improve our relations" with the Soviet
Union, and "we hope that the Soviet leaders appreciate our desire to establish concrete relations with them in scientific, economic and cultural fields."
Still smarting from the recent Soviet veto of the resolution on Kashmir in
the Security Council, he pointed out, however, that their relations could
never be really cordial until the Soviet Union reconsidered its position
on Kashmir.

In the same address Mohammed Ali went out of his way to praise China and to express Pakistan's desire for closer relations with that country. In another major statement in the National Assembly, on November 22, 1962, a month after the Chinese attack on India, Pakistan's Foreign Minister said: "I am glad to say that our relations with China are cordial and that our border negotiations are proceeding apace and satisfactorily." On December 26, on the eve of talks on Kashmir between ministerial representatives of India and Pakistan, Pakistan and Communist China announced that they had "reached complete agreement in principle in regard to the alignment of the common border of the China-Sinkiang contiguous area, the defense of which is the responsibility of Pakistan." On March 3, 1963, the border agreement was signed in Peking, the most widely publicized of a series of agreements which Pakistan concluded in 1963 with Communist China, and with other Communist states as well.

Quite naturally, the United States takes a rather dim view of Pakistan's overtures to Communist China at a time of increasing tension between India and China and of a further hardening of China's international and ideological line. Pakistan's leaders argue that by reaching agreement on the demarcation of boundaries — which they believe was the main source of the trouble between India and China — they are removing any possibility of a border conflict with China and are in fact furthering the interests of SEATO and of the United States. Pakistan's recent overtures to China are looked upon by the United States as a dangerous and ill-advised attempt to enhance its bargaining position *vis-à-vis* India and its allies. India is particularly irritated because the agreement with China affects a border between Sinkiang and northern Kashmir, of which Pakistan, in India's view, is in illegal possession.

The provision of American military assistance to India, following the Chinese attack in 1962, led to unprecedented tensions in United States-Pakistan relations. Unconvinced that the Chinese attack was a real threat to the security of the subcontinent, or even of India, Pakistan protested vigorously over the military strengthening of a hostile neighbor. President Kennedy did his best to reassure Pakistan. In a news conference on November 20 he said: "In providing military assistance to India, we are mindful of our alliance with Pakistan. . . . Our help to India in no way diminishes or qualifies our commitment to Pakistan." The sole purpose of American aid to India, he insisted, was to defeat "Chinese Communist subversion."

India has pledged that the arms and military equipment it receives from the United States will not be used against Pakistan. On its part, the United States has promised, as it did in 1954, that if the arms it supplies are used aggressively, it will promptly take "appropriate action both within and without the United Nations to thwart such aggression."[29] What more assurance, Americans may ask, does Pakistan want? The answer is that Pakistan

---

[29] This pledge was made by President Eisenhower in a letter to Prime Minister Nehru on the same day (February 24, 1954) on which he announced the U.S. decision to give

wants much more assurance than the United States will or can provide.

In a speech on November 22, 1962, Foreign Minister Mohammed Ali alleged that, contrary to its promises, the United States had given arms aid to India without consulting its ally, and its "action in arming India to the teeth is bound to have the effect of encouraging India to engage in a major conflict." In Mohammed Ali's judgment the American action was an act hostile to Pakistan, and raised the gravest problems for his country.

Agreeing with the Indian and not the Pakistani assessment of the gravity of the Chinese threat, the United States not only extended military assistance to India but it also put pressure on both countries to "freeze" their differences, or even to attempt to reach some kind of agreement on Kashmir, in order that Indian troops could be moved to the north without fear of a hostile move by Pakistan and that both countries could concentrate on the common defense. For some weeks Pakistan seemed to resent the efforts to persuade it to make a fresh effort to reach a new basis of understanding with India. In his November speech Mohammed Ali referred with considerable bitterness to this kind of pressure and expressed a complete lack of confidence in India's word.

Many of the standard complaints against the United States were voiced in a bitter editorial in the Dacca *Morning News* of January 15, 1962. The editorial, entitled "End of a Delusion," minced no words. After referring to "American duplicity in the game of power politics," the editorial declared:

> Whether the Government of Pakistan did or did not subscribe to our view of American policy, we have always been convinced that pact or no pacts, if America were to choose between Pakistan and India, the choice would be against us. The basic motivation of American policy throughout these years has been its opposition to Communism and at no stage was it inspired by a genuine desire to preserve peace and stability . . . American policy-makers are not so senile as to imagine that the spectre of Communism, of which the American is so terribly scared, can be exorcised by economic invocations. Behind the economic facade can clearly be seen the military hand and the objective of arming India to the teeth as a counter-poise to China regardless of the peril such a policy will spell to the small countries in the region inside and outside the SEATO. The SEATO and CENTO are America's own babies, one of whom she is now prepared to disown (the other was never fully owned by her) and we have, therefore, no business to nurse them. The sooner we abandon them to their fate the better it will be for us.

Pakistan's Alliance Policy: Expectations and Realities

Common currency in Pakistan since the fall of 1962, statements of this kind reflect a widespread sense of disillusionment and frustration, directed as much against the military commitments which Pakistan has undertaken

---

arms aid to Pakistan. The text of the letter is printed in *The New York Times*, February 26, 1954.

as against the United States. These commitments have never been popular among the mass of the Pakistani people, to the extent that there has been any general popular opinion on the subject.[30] Although Pakistan's alliance policy has brought tangible results, political leaders have constantly been faced with the problem of justifying this policy in terms that Pakistanis could understand and accept.

Because of its alignment policy Pakistan has undoubtedly received more attention and more economic and military assistance than it would have obtained as a "neutral" state. Many Pakistani leaders appreciate this fact, but relatively few of the people do. They are inclined to feel that the disadvantages have outweighed the advantages; they tend to be more impressed with the arguments that the alliance policy has restricted their freedom of action in world affairs, has involved them in the "cold war," and has therefore meant, as Feroz Khan Noon once remarked when he was Prime Minister, that "we have made new enemies for the sake of others."

There can be no question that Pakistan's main purpose in entering into its mutual security arrangements was to improve its position *vis-à-vis* India, even though this was obviously not the intention of its allies. "When we entered into these pacts and arrangements," declared Foreign Minister Mohammed Ali in the National Assembly on November 22, 1962, "we did so purely for defensive purposes. . . . Our main and only purpose was to safeguard the safety and security of Pakistan and we needed support from like minded and peace loving nations. We have never made any secret of the fact that we apprehended the threat to our security from India." Pakistanis apparently expected their great ally to support it on all important issues, definitely including Kashmir. Apparently they expect from their diplomatic friends the same kind of unquestioned support that they expect from their personal friends. As Mohammed Ali phrased it: "If friends let us down we shall not consider them as friends. Friends that stand by us, we will stand by them."

This is an attitude which Americans should understand more clearly. It helps to explain some of the criticisms of the United States since the two countries became allies, i.e., in Pakistani terms, "friends." A true friend, it seems, would give Pakistan wholehearted support on the Kashmir issue, not so much on the merits of the issue as because it is a friend. One can argue that Pakistan's views of what it may reasonably expect of its diplomatic

---

[30] According to former Prime Minister H. S. Suhrawardy, an off-again on-again defender of the alignment policy, the decision to enter into military alliances was "the business of a few ministers sheltered by secrecy. The result has been a set of commitments in the legal sense, yet not sufficiently felt as commitments in the consciousness of the people themselves. . . . The very secrecy with which our engagements have been entered into, the lack of thorough public airing in debate, has left them vulnerable to suspicion that they have somehow rendered us subservient and have drained away our autonomy." "Political Stability and Democracy in Pakistan," *Foreign Affairs*, April 1957, p. 431.

friends are naive and unrealistic, but he must take the existence of such attitudes into consideration as a fact to be reckoned with.

Since 1961 President Ayub Khan has reflected the widespread disillusionment in Pakistan toward the United States and military alliances, and he has often publicly criticized the United States, although usually in relatively moderate terms. Shortly before his state visit to the United States in July 1961, he complained to a correspondent of *The New York Times* that "our American friends . . . seem to put right and wrong on an equal level," and he confessed that he was "not entirely satisfied with military alliances of which Pakistan is a member." Six months later he spoke more critically of Pakistan's "half or quarter friends," and said that while Pakistan's allies were "an evil," they were a "necessary evil."[31] In an important article in *Foreign Affairs* of January 1964, he expressed again his doubts about the recent course of American foreign policy, which he believed would have grave consequences for the United States as well as for Pakistan. "As soon as India arrives at some sort of settlement with China," he warned, it would revert not only to its "traditional policy of intimidation of Pakistan," but also to its "traditional policy of eliminating United States influence in Asia."[32]

In February 1964, between conversations with Chou En-lai, Ayub stated that Communist China had only peaceful intentions whereas United States military aid to India was creating new tensions in Asia and "more problems" for Pakistan. "Serving global interests is all very well, but if it is done at the cost of your friends' security it's not at all a good thing."

Pakistan, therefore, is going through a process of reassessment of the value of its military alliances, and it is trying to develop what Mohammed Ali called a "positive, independent line." In adding to fears and suspicions, American military aid to India has accentuated the "new realism" characteristic of Pakistan's recent foreign and domestic policy.

Bases of Understanding

The evidences of estrangement between Pakistan and the United States are fortunately counteracted by many continuing ties and common interests, and by the continuing economic and military assistance. Doubtless much of the criticism of the United States in Pakistan springs from frustrations arising from wholly different sources, such as extreme sensitivity regarding India and internal problems and pressures. In the years ahead the United States should not neglect its South Asian ally while it develops new relations with India.

Ayub Khan's visits to the United States have helped to lay a better basis for American identification and understanding of Pakistan and for

[31] At a question-and-answer meeting at Mardan, January 21, 1962; quoted in *Dawn* (Karachi), January 22, 1962.

[32] Mohammed Ayub Khan, "The Pakistan-American Alliance: Stresses and Strains," *Foreign Affairs,* January 1964, pp. 199, 204, 209.

cordial personal relationships. On his state visit in July 1961 he made a strong impression on most of those who met or heard him, whether in person or by television. Before a joint session of the American Congress on July 12, he delivered one of the bluntest speeches that the members of Congress had ever heard from a visiting Head of State. It included the following observations: "We are pressing against you today as friends. . . . If we do not make good and if, heaven forbid, we go under communism, then we shall still press against you — but not as friends. So, to my mind, there is very little choice as far as the affluent countries like yours are concerned. As far as the problem of aid is concerned — you have to give to us — because it involves the fate of the world and also your own destiny . . . if there is real trouble there is no other country in Asia on whom you will be able to count. The only people who will stand by you are the people of Pakistan, provided you are also prepared to stand by them." His ending was on a more modest note: "I would like you to please remember that whatever may be the dictates of your worldwide commitments, you will, I hope, take care that you will not take any steps that might aggravate our problems or in any fashion jeopardize our security. As long as you remember that, I have no doubt in my mind that our friendship will grow in strength." There was every prospect after his visit of improved United States-Pakistan relations and of a toning down of public criticism of the United States. Unfortunately, shortly after his return the Chinese attack and the prompt extension of American military aid to India led to new strains and misunderstandings. If the negotiations on the Kashmir question had led to results which were gratifying to Pakistan, this would undoubtedly have helped to improve its attitude toward its "incredible ally." Since nothing came of them, and since Pakistan felt that it was being pressured by the United States to make concessions to India on Kashmir which it is not prepared to make, United States-Pakistan relations again took a turn for the worse.

In August 1963, however, obviously on the recommendation, or orders, of the Government of Pakistan, the vehemently hostile tone of the Pakistani press noticeably changed. Possibly the immediate reason for the change was to create a better atmosphere for official talks in Pakistan and the United States which seemed to lead to a marked improvement in relations.

The improvement did not last long. In 1965 the relations between the United States and its major Asian ally plummeted to a new low. The United States became increasingly critical of Pakistan's continued associations with the Communist states, especially Red China. The Government of Pakistan seemed to be determined to lessen the American presence and American influence in every possible way, and the Pakistani press, obviously under official inspiration, again became bitterly critical of the United States. In April President Johnson suddenly requested Ayub Khan to postpone a state visit to the United States, scheduled to begin a few days later. In July he informed Ayub that the United States Government was asking the World Bank to postpone for about two months a consortium meeting scheduled for July 27, which was to be held to consider the amounts of economic assistance which the participating nations in the consortium (the Aid Pakistan Club) would pledge during the first year of Pakistan's Third Five Year Plan, and he added insult to injury by suggesting that the period of postponement could be utilized for discussing "other matters," presumably relating to the many areas of disagreement between the two countries. Smarting under this latest affront, President Ayub Khan, in his first-of-the-month broadcast to the Pakistani people on August 1, 1965, said:

> While countries strive for freedom in order to develop they will not seek development at the cost of freedom. The country's economic progress and prosperity of its people are of the utmost importance, but its security and independence come first. It is our right as an independent nation to normalize our relations with our neighbors however different our ideologies might be and that right we shall not allow to be compromised. It was in this context that I said we are looking for friends not masters.

The situation became more sensitive in 1965 because of the armed clashes between Indian and Pakistani troops in the Rann of Kutch and in Kashmir. Each country protested to the United States against the alleged use of American weapons and military equipment against it, and each was obviously unhappy over the failure of the United States to support it in the controversy.

In recent months, it seems, both Pakistan and the United States have been nourishing various grievances against each other, and have been increasingly dubious about the general course of each other's foreign policy. Ayub Khan expressed Pakistan's view in his 1964 *Foreign Affairs* article when he charged that "over the last decade, the policies of the United States have undergone a change which has operated progressively to the disadvantage of her ally, Pakistan, vis-a-vis neutral India.[33] Undoubtedly President Johnson's actions in 1965 reflected American reservations about Pakistan's recent external orientation.

Thus America's relations with Pakistan, like those with India, are subject to many ups and downs in response to general trends in the world situation and to particular developments. Although not based on either extensive contacts or on real understanding, they have been generally good, in spite of many differences. But the recent estrangement between the two allied countries has reached disturbing proportions, and a major effort should be made by both countries, on both official and unofficial levels, to reverse this unhappy trend.

[33] *Ibid.*, p. 198.

CHAPTER THREE

The Politics of Creation and Survival

To AN INCREASING DEGREE the study of international relations is encompassing the internal dynamics of the nation-states, an approach which is particularly pertinent to the many new states of Asia and Africa. Both Jawaharlal Nehru and Mohammed Ayub Khan, who were not often in agreement, repeatedly stressed the point that the foreign policies of their countries are closely related to domestic policies, whose ends are unity, survival, and development.[1] The internal dynamics and political development of the major countries of South Asia, therefore, provide a logical starting point for an analysis of their international behavior and orientation. This will be the main theme of the present chapter; but before the contemporary situation in these two countries can be intelligently assessed, a brief glance at their political heritage is necessary.

The Political Heritage of India and Pakistan

Though they are new nations, India and Pakistan have behind them a long history and a complex cultural tradition. "For we are very old," wrote Nehru in The Discovery of India, "and trackless centuries whisper in our ears."[2] With the possible exception of China, the Indian subcontinent has been the home of the oldest continuous civilizations of high level that history records. Although few of the peoples have been historically minded and there are few historical records of any reliability before the twelfth century

---

[1] "Foreign policies depend ultimately on internal conditions and developments." Jawaharlal Nehru, India Today and Tomorrow (New Delhi: Indian Council for Cultural Relations, 1960), p. 29. "The foreign policy of a country is in a sense a projection of its internal policies, social, political and economic." Mohammed Ayub Khan, "Essentials of Pakistan's Foreign Policy," Pakistan Horizon, Fourth Quarter 1961, p. 263.

[2] Jawaharlal Nehru, The Discovery of India (New York: The John Day Company, 1946), p. 144.

41

A.D., Indians and Pakistanis today are mindful of their traditions and experience, and their daily thoughts and efforts are greatly affected by the whispers — some loud and clear, others faint and of uncertain meaning — that impinge upon their inner consciousness from the depth of their cultural inheritance.

Virtually hemmed in and isolated by the world's highest mountain ranges and by the Indian Ocean and its great arms, the Arabian Sea and the Bay of Bengal, the Indian subcontinent has nevertheless been a meeting place of peoples and cultures through the centuries. Long before the vast folk-movement of Indo-European peoples, the Aryans, into the subcontinent in the second millenium B.C., the Indus Valley had been the home of an urban civilization — the so-called Harappa culture. Even today the division between the descendants of the Aryans and of the longer-established peoples they found in the area — most of whom were so-called Dravidians, whose descendants now inhabit the south of India — is important ethnologically, linguistically, and socially.

Until the coming of the Muslims, peoples of different origins and race met and mingled in the subcontinent, although the relationships, tempered by intermarriage, were often of a superior-inferior nature. In general, the invaders did not preserve their separate identity and tended to adopt the customs of the indigenous peoples. The Muslims, who began to come in small bands of raiders shortly after the death of the Prophet in the seventh century, gradually expanded their numbers and power, until, under the Moguls, they ruled most of the subcontinent for nearly two centuries. But they did not become absorbed in the predominantly Hindu population, remaining separate with a different religion and customs. Many of the troubles besetting modern India and Pakistan in their internal life and their mutual relations may be traced to this fundamental fact. There was likewise little intermixture between Indian peoples and the European invaders, especially during the two centuries of British rule, but the number of Westerners in the subcontinent was never large, in relative terms, and their impact was mainly on ideas and institutions.

The point has often been made that never in its long history has the subcontinent been united from the Himalayas to Cape Comorin, and from the Khyber Pass to the Naga Hills. For brief periods, under the strong rule of Asoka, Chandragupta II, Akbar, and the British, most of the subcontinent was controlled, however loosely, from a single center. But the fact remains that political unity has been generally absent from the Indian experience. When the people of the subcontinent finally won their independence, they could not even then achieve national unity, but emerged as two nations, under circumstances which embittered their relations from the outset.[3]

[3] Jawaharlal Nehru and many other Indian commentators have rung the changes on the theme of India's "unity in diversity." They see diversity as an obvious and persistent feature of Indian life through the centuries, but they also find an underlying unity which

Historians in India and Pakistan are reinterpreting their past, often in the light of the preconceptions or national imperatives of the present. The tendency is to glorify the ancient past and to emphasize the less happy aspects of foreign rule. Hindus find their golden age in the ancient Hindu period, and Muslims find theirs in the days of Akbar and Jehangir and Shah Jehan. The traditions of both Hindus and Muslims are largely authoritarian, although contemporary Indian politicians and historians like to point to the ancient panchayats and "village republics" and certain traditions of justified revolt against rulers who abused their power, while Muslims like to emphasize the essential democracy and equality of Islam. The strong, but not necessarily predominant, traditions of democracy in India and Pakistan today owe more to the impact of modern democratic ideas and to the modern experience in operating representative institutions, however limited and imperfect in their nature, than to any natural inclination toward representative democracy springing from religious traditions or historical experience.

Modern India, to be sure, as Sardar K. M. Panikkar pointed out, "does not live under the laws of Manu."[4] Yet one cannot even begin to understand modern India unless he has some acquaintance with those aspects of the political and cultural heritage which even today help to shape the religion, the outlook on life, the thought patterns, and the ways of living of the vast majority of the people.

Three-fourths of the inhabitants of modern India are Hindus, and more than any other factors Hinduism and its view of life have shaped the character of Indian society. The caste system, one of the most rigid and pervasive of social systems, is embedded in Hinduism. For centuries, in the absence of stable government, it helped to give order and stability and meaning to an otherwise fragmented society. Although it is under severe criticism and attack, it still dominates the life of the majority of Hindus, especially in the rural areas, and it is an increasingly important factor in Indian politics.

Still very much a part of the living tradition, the great classics and epics have formulated most of the basic beliefs and doctrines of India. For example, *dharma* (an untranslatable term which is related to duty, justice, morality, or virtue), is perhaps the central concept in Indian political thought and philosophy. *Ahimsa* (nonviolence), which Gandhi made one

should not be overlooked. In *The Discovery of India* (pp. 49, 50) Nehru wrote: "The diversity of India is tremendous; it is obvious; it lies on the surface and anybody can see it." Yet, he added, the peoples of India "have been throughout these ages distinctively Indian, with the same national heritage and the same set of moral and mental qualities. There was something living and dynamic about this heritage which showed itself in ways of living and a philosophical attitude to life and its problems. . . . Some kind of a dream of unity has occupied the mind of India since the dawn of civilization."

[4] K. M. Panikkar, *The State and the Citizen* (Bombay: Asia Publishing House, 1956), p. 18.

of his motivating doctrines, is another pervasive concept of thought and action.[5]

It is difficult to determine precisely to what extent the goals and values of ancient Hindu India have influenced contemporary thought and action. Their persistence in one form or another through the centuries argues that they are unquestionably a part of the modern cultural heritage. Among strictly orthodox Hindus they are still the touchstones of behavior and indeed of life itself. In ways that can hardly be defined, but which are nonetheless real, they have influenced the most Westernized of Indian leaders as well. Even Jawaharlal Nehru himself, for all his professed agnosticism, his Western training, and his intellectual admixture of liberal democracy, Fabian socialism, Marxism and scientific humanism, was conscious of the pull of the past upon him, and "the discovery of India," to use his own expression, was a never-ending quest for him.

In analyzing nonalignment as a basis of India's foreign policy, some Indian commentators often insist that it is in keeping with India's traditions and values, and represents, at least in some measure, a twentieth-century application of basic Hindu views.[6] Nehru himself, in a statement in the Indian Parliament on December 9, 1958, called nonalignment "a policy inherent in the circumstances of India, inherent in the present thinking of India, inherent in the whole mental outlook of India, inherent in the conditioning of the Indian mind." Whatever the connection between nonalignment and Hindu and Buddhist traditions of mediation and tolerance and the middle way, Westerners are more inclined to find the explanation for Indian foreign policy in tangible and recent sources, such as the legacy of the freedom struggle and contemporary facts of geopolitics and power.

Western influences on modern India are more readily discernible, although they are less deeply entrenched than many influences out of India's past. Western contacts with Asia were of longest duration and most intense in India. Whatever their faults and failings, the British had a profound impact. They developed a system of government and administration which has formed the pattern for the political structure of India and Pakistan; they instilled a concept of law and order, of justice under law, which is still the backbone of their judicial system; they trained several generations of Indians of all religious faiths, and associated them in the gigantic task of governing a vast subcontinent. In an area of linguistic diversity and rivalry, they gave the educated elite a common language, which enabled them to

[5] See Norman D. Palmer, *The Indian Political System* (Boston: Houghton Mifflin Company, 1961), p. 21; S. Radhakrishnan, *Indian Philosophy*, v. I (New York: Macmillan, 1922), p. 52; and K. P. Mukerji, *The State* (Madras: The Theosophical Publishing House, 1952), Appendix I "The Hindu Conception of Dharma," pp. 321–346.

[6] See, for example, A. Appadorai, "Traditional Indian Values in the Direction of Peace," *Comprendre*, No. 20 (1959), pp. 1–10; and Lakshmi N. Menon, "Our Policy," *Seminar*, No. 19 (March 1961), pp. 17–22.

communicate more effectively with each other and to keep in touch with the outside world.

The Legacy of Gandhi and Jinnah

One towering figure bestrides modern India, which is a very different place because of his teachings and example. Almost every contemporary Indian leader, in politics or society, was in one way or another influenced by Mahatma Gandhi. He gave a new twist to the nationalist movement; he brought the masses of the people into the movement in an effective way; he developed the techniques of *satyagraha* (nonviolent noncooperation) and *ahimsa* into effective principles of action; he fought foreign rulers and native bigotry and superstition with the same detached passive resistance; he taught the importance of means as well as ends, and of selfless devotion to the common good; and withal he remained a saint in politics, a strange mixture of an intensely practical man and an impractical visionary.

It is difficult to determine the extent of his influence on independent India.[7] Some observers find little evidence of Gandhi's influence in India today; but they tend to overlook the all-pervasive nature of the Mahatma's impact, and the hold which he still has on the minds of millions of his countrymen. Even in the political realm, where his teachings seems to have been disregarded, he receives more than lip service in public addresses. In domestic politics programs such as Panchayati Raj and cottage industries, and the constant talk about decentralization and "partyless democracy," seem to reflect some of his ideas; in foreign affairs, Indian moralizing about ends and means — less commonly heard in recent years — and the whole policy of nonalignment seem to have some Gandhian touches. In politics and foreign policy, however, one should conclude that Gandhi's impact has been more environmental than specific; the memory of his teachings and example seems to give many Indian spokesmen at least a guilty conscience, and to call their attention repeatedly to first principles. The greater impact

[7] An all-India survey of "the Gandhian Impact on the Indian People" by the Indian Institute of Public Opinion, conducted in 1959, suggested the following conclusions: "The extent of awareness of Gandhi is surprisingly high — over 90 per cent in urban areas and as much as 80 per cent in rural areas. But there is no clear image in the public mind of the Mahatma's many-sided personality, or that the image has today a concrete application to practical affairs. He is best known as an outstanding leader of the nationalist movement and as a social reformer. In neither of these is the unique character of his contribution fully realized. The range of application of Gandhi's doctrines in practice is disappointingly small. Thus there is a wide, though receding, Gandhian impact, without any corresponding hard core generating continuing impulses under which Gandhian doctrines can renew themselves in every generation." "An Analysis of the Gandhian Impact on the Indian People," an All-India Urban and Rural Survey, March-April, 1959, *Monthly Public Opinion Surveys* of the Indian Institute of Public Opinion, v. V, Nos. 2 and 3 (November-December 1959), p. 1.

of the Mahatma, however, is on Indian life and society and on the masses of the Indian people even today, more than a decade and a half after his assassination.

To Muslims generally the great days of the past were in the heyday of Mogul rule, in the late sixteenth and seventeenth centuries. After the decline of the Moguls, Muslims found that their status had changed from membership in the ruling minority to a distinctly subordinate role in most aspects of Indian life. Under the British they fared less well than did the Hindus, and they did not take full advantage of the opportunities afforded by the British in administration and education and business. In the last decades of British rule, however, they found more effective leaders and began to assert themselves more positively in many ways.

Much of the credit for this more positive role is due to Sir Syed Ahmad Khan, who in the late nineteenth century advised his fellow Muslims to co-operate with the British rather than to sulk in their tents and complain of their lot, but not to cooperate with the Hindus in the National Congress or other early nationalist organizations. Though Sir Syed did not recommend the formation of a separate Muslim state, many of his ideas contributed to the movement which culminated in partition.[8]

The movement itself took organizational form with the founding of the Muslim League in 1906, and found its great leader in an ascetic Bombay lawyer, Mohammad Ali Jinnah, the *Quaid-i-Azam*.[9] At times, especially during and immediately following World War I, the League cooperated after a fashion with the Indian National Congress, and Jinnah was for some years a champion of Hindu-Muslim unity. But, for various reasons, some of which are still being debated, the League and the Congress came to a parting of the ways, especially after the provincial elections in 1937 when the Congress refused to include Muslims in the governments formed, unless they joined the Congress. After the demand for a separate Muslim state was put forward in the famous Lahore resolution of the Muslim League in 1940, Jinnah would settle for nothing less than an independent Pakistan — although his ideas regarding the territorial boundaries of the Pakistan-to-be changed considerably over the years, and he actually described the Pakistan that emerged in 1947 as a "truncated" country.

In staunchly upholding and proclaiming the "two-nation" theory, Jinnah insisted that Muslims should be treated on terms of absolute equality with the Hindus. The leaders of the Indian National Congress flatly rejected this

[8] See Percival Spear, *India, Pakistan, and the West* (Second Edition, London: Oxford University Press, 1952), pp. 189–190; J. M. S. Baljon, *The Reforms and Religious Ideas of Sir Saiyyad Ahmad Khan* (Lahore: Orientalia Publishers, 1958); and Hafeez Malik, *Moslem Nationalism in India and Pakistan* (Washington: Public Affairs Press, 1963), pp. 208–222.

[9] See Malik, cited, pp. 249–256; Hector Bolitho, *Jinnah: Creator of Pakistan* (London: John Murray, 1954); and M. H. Saiyid, *Mohammad Ali Jinnah: A Political Study* (Lahore: Shaikh Muhammad Ashraf, 1953).

theory and its implications, but they did agree, reluctantly and with heavy hearts, to the partition of the subcontinent in 1947, simply because they saw no acceptable alternative.

Though the events leading to partition can be traced in detail,[10] no one can say definitely when or why partition became "inevitable." Its roots lie in many places, and stem from many events — above all, perhaps, from the unwillingness of most Muslims to trust the Hindu majority after the British left.

The immediate aftermath of partition left a bitter taste, and deepened the forebodings of those who wonderd whether independence itself was worth this price. In India today partition is still widely regarded as a tragedy, and the creation of Pakistan as a mistake, although perhaps an unavoidable mistake.[11] Pakistanis may feel dissatisfied with the division of land and resources, but they naturally believe that they are better off in a separate national status.

The Dangers Within

"The world asks two questions about India: Will it hold together? And will it succeed in pulling itself up to the level of a modern nation?[12] Thus did the official journal of the Indian Planning Commission sum up the most important questions about India today, questions equally relevant about Pakistan. The answer to the first question may be largely dependent on the answer to the second; so too may the answers to such questions as these: Will the effort at national integration and development be made by democratic or nondemocratic means? What will be the foreign policy orientation of these South Asian countries, and their role in world affairs?

Some Indians and Pakistanis, and a few outside observers, appalled by the many divisive forces in the two countries, believe that political fragmentation is a real danger. Others feel that because of these divisive forces, and the necessity of forcing the pace of development, India and Pakistan

[10] See V. P. Menon, *The Transfer of Power in India* (Princeton University Press, 1957).

[11] Lord Wavell, the next to the last British Viceroy of India, felt strongly that the partition of the Indian subcontinent would be a great mistake, and that it would be preferable for British rule to continue until and unless the leaders of the Indian National Congress and the Muslim League could agree on some basis of political federation. In retrospect, at least, the most distinguished Muslim who cast his destinies with the Indian National Congress, Maulana Abul Kamal Azad, agreed with him. In his autobiography, published posthumously, Maulana Azad wrote: "If Lord Wavell's advice had been followed and the solution of the Indian problem deferred for a year or two, . . . it is even possible that the tragedy of Indian partition might have been avoided. . . . Perhaps history will decide that the wiser policy would have been to follow Lord Wavell's advice." *India Wins Freedom: An Autobiographical Narrative* (Bombay: Orient Longmans, 1959), p. 178.

[12] *Yojana* (New Delhi), February 18, 1962, p. 12.

will become increasingly authoritarian in their political organization and policies.[13]

The most obvious divisive forces in India today are caste, the many languages, and communalism. To these should be added regionalism, especially the North-South problem (the feelings of non-Hindi-speaking Indians against their Hindi-speaking countrymen in the north), and the tensions attendant upon change. Perhaps the greatest gulf intervenes between those who want India to be a really modern state, with all of the risks and effort involved, and those who would sacrifice modernity to a quest for a simpler pattern of society and organization, more in keeping with ancient forms and values. In a sense Gandhi sought a formula for India along the latter lines, and many of his followers, including Vinoba Bhave and Jayaprakash Narayan, advocate an extremely decentralized unacquisitive society, based on simple village communities, with a minimum of government, industrialization or planning. Others take a very un-Gandhian approach, and demand some kind of a Hindu Raj, with non-Hindus tolerated to the extent that they will accept a subordinate role in a Hindu state.

The drive for economic progress has given further momentum to the already strong tendencies toward centralization, which are only partially offset by the growing role of some of the stronger Chief Ministers in the states, by the introduction of a more coordinated and effective system of democratic decentralization in Panchayati Raj, by the formation of linguistic states and the urge for linguistic autonomy, and by the Bhoodan, Gramdan, and *sarvodaya* movements. Conflicting trends toward centralization and decentralization are very strong, and the relative balance seems to fluctuate from year to year.

In Pakistan the most obvious divisions are between East and West Pakistan, between the present ruling groups and those who are out of power, and between those who want to create a modern state, with due deference to the principles of Islam, and those who would pattern all their institutions along more orthodox Muslim lines. On the whole, the dangers of political fragmentation or of a reversion to extreme authoritarianism seem more imminent in Pakistan than in India. But Pakistan has in Islam a unifying influence which India lacks.

The odds in favor of the survival of India and Pakistan as national entities are nevertheless relatively high in this uncertain world. The danger of in-

---

[13] The danger that one or the other of these unfortunate developments might occur in India is forcefully brought out in a number of penetrating studies by Indian and Western observers. See, for example, C. Rajagopalachari, *Our Democracy* (Madras: B. G. Paul, 1951); Amaury de Riencourt, *The Soul of India* (New York: Harper, 1960); and Selig S. Harrison, *India: The Most Dangerous Decades* (Princeton University Press, 1960). These rather gloomy analyses, however, should be considered in perspective. There are many unifying as well as disruptive forces in the present Indian scene. As Jawaharlal Nehru has said: "'India is a large country, in which many forces are at work. Some tend to disrupt; others to consolidate."

creasing authoritarianism is also real, and perhaps more likely to come to pass. Pakistan is controlled by a relatively popular and benevolent authoritarianism, which could become far tougher if for any reason those who hold the reins of power are dissatisfied with the way things are going. India has a wider spectrum of democratic groupings, any combination of which, even in the event of a split in the Congress, would probably continue the democratic experiment. In spite of the obstacles in the way, whether inherited or current, the Indian commitment to democracy is a genuine one, and is in fact one of the most significant aspects of the contemporary Indian scene. This commitment is less obvious in Pakistan, but it exists among many Pakistanis, and it is a force which may gain strength in future years.

The present balance of forces in South Asia would be profoundly affected by a major outside threat to one or both countries, a significant change in the relative power position of the two, or a significant change in the internal situation in either. Fortunately, for the time being at least, none of these eventualities seems likly to occur, though each must be considered in any estimates of South Asia's future.

The Political Experience of India and Pakistan

Despite a rather different political experience since independence, India and Pakistan are faced with similar problems and they are pursuing many similar policies. Having survived more than a decade and a half of independence, which is in itself a major achievement, they are finding that the consolidation of independence is even more difficult than the winning of it. With many solid achievements to their credit, they have not found answers to such basic problems as national unity and living with each other.

At the outset certain great decisions were made determining the basic nature of the two states. India was to be a secular state, Pakistan an Islamic one. Both were to be federal states: India with some twenty-eight political units constituted by integrating the former princely states into the Union of India and redrawing political boundaries, Pakistan with four political units in West Pakistan and one in East Pakistan (containing a population larger than all of the units in West Pakistan combined).

In 1955 a single political unit was created in West Pakistan. Two years earlier in India, after much agitation among the Telegu-speaking peoples, a separate state of Andhra was created, largely out of what had been northeastern Madras state, and thereafter the demand for the reorganization of states, primarily along linguistic lines, grew more vehement, until it was largely met by the reorganization of November 1956, which redivided the map of India into fourteen states, of equal status although of unequal size and population. In Bombay, where the linguistic nationalism was not largely appeased, the agitation for two states continued, until in May 1960 the states of Gujarat and Maharashtra were created. In December 1963 a sixteenth state, Nagaland, was officially inaugurated.

Almost as a matter of course, both India and Pakistan adopted a system of parliamentary democracy, patterned largely along British lines. The Government of India Act of 1935, with certain necessary amendments, continued to be the basic law of both countries until their new constitutions went into effect, India's in January 1950, Pakistan's in March 1956 (but this was suspended in October 1958, and Pakistan did not get another constitution until June 1962). Familiar though the leaders of India and Pakistan were with the theory and practice of parliamentary democracy, their actual experience with it had been under the unfavorable circumstances of limited representation during colonial rule and a lack of popular participation.

Parliamentary democracy in Pakistan was given a peculiar twist from the start, as Jinnah, for various reasons, chose to be governor-general, with his chief lieutenant and faithful follower, Liaquat Ali Khan, as prime minister. Wherever Jinnah sat, there was the center of power. Thus a tradition was established of a strong governor-general and a relatively weak prime minister.[14] Of Pakistan's four governors-general, Jinnah, Ghulam Mohammad, and Iskandar Mirza were strong men, more important than their prime ministers. The only exception to this statement came after Jinnah's death in September 1948, when Liaquat Ali Khan remained as prime minister and Nazimuddin was governor-general, and possibly also in 1956–57 when H. S. Suhrawardy, probably the ablest politician Pakistan has produced, was prime minister.

For reasons that are still being debated, parliamentary democracy did not work in Pakistan. Some critics would argue that it was never really given a fair trial, and that therefore the question of its failure is beside the point. The Constitution Commission, appointed in 1960 by Ayub Khan as leader of the martial law regime, concluded that the parliamentary form of government did fail, and that "the real causes of the failure . . . were mainly the lack of leadership resulting in lack of well-organised political parties, the general lack of character in the politicians and their undue interference in the administration."[15] The situation became so serious that in early October 1958, when Iskandar Mirza suspended the constitution of 1956 and assumed complete power by "right of revolution," and when Ayub Khan ousted Mirza about three weeks later, most Pakistanis, whatever their devotion to the principles of democracy, heaved sighs of relief.

For three years and eight months the country was ruled by Ayub Khan

[14] See Khalid Bin Sayeed, *Pakistan: The Formative Phase* (Karachi: Pakistan Publishing House, 1960), Chapters VII and VIII.

[15] *Report of the Constitution Commission, Pakistan, 1961* (Karachi: Manager of Publications, Government of Pakistan, 1962), p. 13. See also G. W. Choudhury, *Democracy in Pakistan* (Dacca: Green Book House, 1963), pp. 132–142. As Professor Choudhury points out, the view of the Constitution Commission that the parliamentary system had been a failure in Pakistan was "challenged by the politicians." *Ibid.*, p. 138.

and his associates in the military, with the cooperation of the civil service, under martial law, and with an almost complete absence of normal political activity. The dictatorship was a benevolent one, and was generally popular. Against the advice of some of his closest associates, Ayub Khan insisted on terminating the martial law administration as soon as possible, and in restoring "democracy," but a democracy which people could work and understand. In February 1960, he appointed a Constitution Commission, headed by a former chief justice, "to examine the progressive failure of parliamentary government in Pakistan" and "to submit constitutional proposals" which would secure "a democracy adapted to changing circumstances and based on . . . Islamic principles," "the consolidation of national unity," and "a firm and stable system of government."[16] In the end result, whatever Ayub Khan's real hopes and intentions, the last two objectives took precedence over the first. The Constitution Commission, reporting in May 1961, recommended a presidential system of government, a bicameral national parliament, with the lower house elected on the basis of restricted direct suffrage, a revival of political parties, and an independent judiciary. Since Ayub Khan found some of these recommendations unacceptable, a cabinet subcommittee worked for months to produce a constitution which would reflect Ayub's views.

The new constitution, promulgated by Ayub on March 1, 1962, attempted to combine authoritarianism and democracy, to make genuine concessions to the people while at the same time keeping the reins of power in essentially the same hands. It gave so much power to the president and contained so many restrictions on the national and provincial assemblies, the judiciary, political parties, and the electorate, that it seemed more like a legal façade for the continuation of military rule than a framework for the restoration of democracy in Pakistan.

Whether this experiment in making further steps in the direction of truly representative government dependent on the success of the limited concessions that have been granted will prove to be a workable compromise remains to be seen. The first elections under the new constitution (with only some 80,000 "Basic Democrats" constituting the electorate) to the National Assembly and to the provincial assemblies, held in late April and early May 1962, returned a large number of former party members, especially members of the Muslim League, some of whom publicly expressed a preference for the restoration of parliamentary democracy and for the revival of the banned political parties. Since they first convened in June 1962, the members of the new National Assembly and the provincial assemblies have been quite vociferous in insisting on fundamental modification of the new constitution. Because of the pressures, President Ayub

---

[16] *Report of the Constitution Commission, Pakistan, 1961*, p. 1. See also, Choudhury, cited, Chapter VI, "The Constitution Commission," pp. 143–175. Professor Choudhury served as Honorary Adviser to the Constitution Commission.

has gradually relaxed many of the restrictions which he felt were necessary for orderly political development. Political parties and other political groupings have been permitted, under rather unhealthy circumstances, and some of the curbs on the role of the judiciary and the rights of the citizens have been removed.

After considering the recommendation of the Franchise Commission that henceforth the members of the national and provincial assemblies, and the president himself, should be chosen by direct and universal suffrage, Ayub decided that the electorate in the promised national elections in the spring of 1965 would continue to be the "Basic Democrats" only. The presidential election was held on January 2, 1965, and resulted in a decisive majority for Ayub Khan, even though Miss Fatima Jinnah, sister of Mohammed Ali Jinnah, was persuaded by the major opposition parties to run against him. About three-fourths of the members of the new National Assembly, elected by the same procedure in March, were avowed followers of President Ayub. Thus, through the process of direct if limited franchise, Ayub Khan received a clear mandate to govern for another five years.

In all probability Ayub Khan will continue for some time to dominate the political life of Pakistan; but it is not at all certain whether he will be willing to endure the trials of operating under the new constitution and will permit the gradual relaxation of controls and the revival of political activities, or whether he will put an end to the new experiment in representative government, as he and General Mirza previously did in 1958. Should martial law again come to Pakistan, it will probably last longer and will be more difficult to "phase out" in favor of a third effort to give Pakistan a democratic system.

On the whole, parliamentary democracy has worked in India, despite all the conditions militating against it. In view of its failure or unsatisfactory operation in India's near neighbors, and indeed in most underdeveloped countries, this is an impressive fact, calling for some reassessment of the prerequisites and prospects for democracy generally.

In India there seems to be little likelihood that a more violent shift, placing power in the hands of the extreme right or the extreme left, will occur by political means. If violent means are used, the result would probably be either a Communist take-over or a military coup. Fissiparous tendencies are so strong that the danger of political fragmentation on regional, linguistic, communal, or other lines cannot be wholly discounted, although it seems even less likely than a swing from the experiment in parliamentary democracy to some kind of extreme left-wing or right-wing authoritarianism.

The People — Yes?

One of the greatest problems which India and Pakistan face is that of bringing the people into the mainstream of political life and the tasks of national development. Thus far neither country has had much success in breaking through the isolation, geographic and mental, the apathy, and distrust of the masses, to give them a feeling that they have a real stake in the existing system. Until the people are more directly involved in public affairs, the use of the term "democracy" to apply to the politics of India and Pakistan is subject to serious qualifications. Possibly a genuine democracy can be initiated from above, but sooner or later it must rest on a counter-response from below.[17]

Well aware of this absence of adequate popular participation in the national effort, the leaders of both India and Pakistan have been trying in various ways to overcome it. In India the grant of universal adult suffrage and the experience of three national elections, several state elections, by-elections, municipal elections, and elections to village *panchayats* have presumably given India's millions a feeling of political action and participation in determining their own affairs; but, as Jayaprakash Narayan has observed, such experiences give only "transient contact with the workings of democracy." In Pakistan the contact has been even more fleeting, for there has never been a nationwide election on the basis of universal suffrage, except to the basic units of the Basic Democracies; and experience with provincial and other elections prior to the institution of martial law in October 1958 was generally not a happy one.

In their five year plans India and Pakistan have stressed the importance of popular participation and support, and many phases of planning, notably the Community Development Program and the National Extension Service in India and the Village AID program in Pakistan, have called for extensive participation in rural areas. The greatest failures of these programs lay in this very area of popular understanding and cooperation. Now they have been fused into more ambitious and comprehensive programs, the Basic Democracies program in Pakistan and Panchayati Raj in India, which are bold and exciting experiments in local government, administration, and development. Both rest on directly elected bodies at the village or town

[17] "The most striking fact that has emerged from the working of ten years of our Constitution," wrote Jayaprakash Narayan in 1962, "is that the people of the country . . . have felt *left out of it all*. They have no doubt had the opportunity of participating in two General Elections, but beyond that transient contact with the workings of democracy, they have had nothing further to do with it. . . . The truth must be faced that the people have not been able to experience the sensation of *Swaraj*. It is only the very thin layer of the educated middle class, and even of them only those directly engaged in political activity, who are involved in the working of our democracy. The result of this state of affairs is that our democracy is found to be resting on a very narrow base. It is like an inverted pyramid that stands on its head." *Swaraj for the People* (Kashi: Akhil Bharat Sarva Seva Sangh Prakashan, 1961), pp. 1–2. Italics in original. This observation by the well-known *sarvodaya* leader, which is perhaps even more applicable to Pakistan than to India, poses a real dilemma for those who really believe, as does Jayaprakash Narayan, in "human freedom and the democratic way of life." Its accuracy will be vouched for by almost anyone who has had any contacts with the masses of the people in South Asia.

level — union councils in the villages and town and union committees in the towns and cities in the case of Pakistan, village *panchayats* in the case of rural India. Both have at least two more tiers, composed partly of indirectly elected and partly of appointed members.[18]

There is a fundamental difference between the two systems. Basic Democracies were conceived of from the beginning as serving as the basis of the new political structure of Pakistan. The elected members of the union councils and the town and union committees — the "Basic Democrats" — constitute the electorate for choosing the president of Pakistan, and also members of the provincial assemblies and the National Assembly. Thus these bodies represent an extension of the Basic Democracies pattern up to the national level. In India the institutions of Panchayati Raj stop at the district level. There was no intention to make it the political pattern of the country, except to some extent at the district and sub-district levels.[19]

Both Panchayati Raj and Basic Democracies were inaugurated in 1959 — the former on a limited scale in Rajasthan and Andhra Pradesh, the latter throughout Pakistan. As integrated programs for rural development and administration, they have achieved some success, and above all, they have won some popular interest and support, but it is still too early to assess their real impact.

Just as official and unofficial American agencies gave significant assistance to the predecessor programs, so should interest and support be extended to these even more comprehensive programs. In the long run their success or failure may do much to determine the pattern of rural South Asia.

Political Parties and Their Critics

Neither in India nor in Pakistan has a healthy party system developed, and in both many people are quite disillusioned with political parties.

---

[18] For information on Panchayati Raj see B. Maheshwari, *Studies in Panchayati Paj* (Delhi: Metropolitan Book Company, 1963); S. K. Dey, *Panchayati Raj* (New Delhi: Ministry of Community Development and Co-operation, 1962); *Agenda Papers: Seminar on Public Administration in Panchayati Raj* (Mussoorie, India: Central Institute of Community Development, Ministry of Community Development and Cooperation, Government of India, 1962); *The Indian Journal of Public Administration*, October-December 1962, a special issue on Panchayati Raj; and numerous articles in various Indian journals, notably the *Economic Weekly, Kurukshetra,* and *Panchayati Raj.*

For information on Basic Democracies see *The Basic Democracies Order, 1959* (Karachi: Ministry of Law, Government of Pakistan, 1959); R. L. Mellema, "The Basic Democracy System in Pakistan," *Asian Survey*, August 1961; K. J. Newman, "Basic Democracy as an Experiment," *Political Studies*, February 1962; and Maheshwari, cited, Chapter 16, "Basic Democracy in Pakistan."

[19] Some Indians, notably Jayaprakash Narayan, have advocated a larger political role for Panchayati Raj. Even S. K. Dey, the energetic and enthusiastic Minister of Panchayati Raj, seems to share this view. In 1961 he wrote: "Panchayati Raj will grow thus to be a way of life and a new approach to government as against a unit of government. It will bring about a complete link up of our people from the Gram Sabha to the Lok Sabha." *Panchayati Raj — a Synthesis*, p. 91.

In India Jayaprakash Narayan favors some kind of "partyless democracy." His views on this subject, presented in many articles and speeches, have attracted much attention and some support.[20] He apparently envisages an "organic democracy" consisting of a series of related "communities," based on the most important of all social units after the family, namely the village. Decisions in Jayaprakash's participating democracy would presumably be made by some method of obtaining consensus. He would abolish parliamentary democracy as well as parties and elections, and he would instead extend the institutions of Panchayati Raj up to the Center, as suggested in his slogan, "from Gram Sabha to Lok Sabha." While Jayaprakash and Vinoba Bhave, India's "walking saint," are the most vocal and best known advocates of a "partyless democracy" and of an extremely decentralized society, many other Indians have expressed doubts about the desirability of a party system in the circumstances of their country.

In spite of the frequent pleas for a "partyless democracy" — pleas which are usually based on disillusionment with the actual operations of parties, or on a feeling that the national emergency calls for "a broad national front," or on a vision of a different type of decentralized society — it is probable that in India, as elsewhere, the abolition of political parties will also end the efforts to move in the direction of democracy. This would be a classic example of throwing out the baby with the bath water. Theoretically, no doubt, it is possible to conceive of a functioning democracy without political parties, but the fact is that no modern democracy has been able to operate without them.[21]

In Pakistan Ayub Khan is highly critical of political parties, and the new constitution, reflecting his views, continued the ban on parties promulgated by the "revolution" of October 1958. The Constitution Commission, however, took a very different view. Holding that "we fail to see how parties can be avoided," the Commission recommended: "If we want to have a democratic form of government, our endeavor should be to create conditions in which parties based on principles can emerge."[22] In response to strong demands by many members of the new National Assembly and the provincial assemblies Ayub himself sponsored a constitutional amendment which gave limited scope to the revival and functioning of political parties; in May 1963 he made the startling announcement that he had decided to join the pro-Government Convention Muslim League; and in the following December he became President of this party. Nevertheless, his aversion to parties is obviously deep-seated, and it has not been lessened by the erratic behavior of the political groupings that have emerged since June 1962.

[20] See especially *Swaraj for the People* and *A Plea for the Reconstruction of Indian Policy* (April 1961).
[21] See John A. Vieg, "The Mirage of 'Party-less' Democracy," *The Indian Journal of Political Science*, January-March 1962, p. 40. See also Hugh Gaitskell, "Opposition in the Older Democracies," in *Democracy in the New States: Rhodes Seminar Papers* (New Delhi: Congress for Cultural Freedom, 1959), pp. 73–74.
[22] *Report of the Constitution Commission, Pakistan, 1961*, p. 80.

Pakistan's experience with political parties has not been a happy one. The Muslim League, which had led the independence movement, began to disintegrate soon after the assassination of Liaquat Ali Khan in 1951, and it suffered a humiliating and unexpected rout, from which it never recovered, in elections in East Pakistan in 1954. The main groups which had formed the United Front to oppose the League in East Pakistan, headed by A. K. Fazlul Huq and H. S. Suhrawardy, soon came to a parting of the ways. The Muslim League encountered increasing difficulties in West Pakistan and at the Center, although prior to the suppression of all political parties in October 1958 it seemed to be experiencing a revival. For a time the Awami League was influential in East Pakistan, and the Republican party in West Pakistan, but no party or coalition of parties was able to supplant the Muslim League for long. The relative strength of the various parties was never tested in nationwide elections. Parties revolved around personalities rather than principles, and unfortunately for Pakistan some of the leading personalities seemed to have few principles.[23]

Contrary to the experience of the Muslim League, the Indian National Congress has continued to be the dominant political force in independent India, as it was in the nationalist movement. Almost all of the older generation of Indian politicians were associated with it, and most of the leaders of other parties were at one time or another members of the Congress Party. Many post-independence parties emerged from its ranks; even the Communist Party of India was at one time associated with it. The founder of the Jan Sangh, now the most important of the right-wing communal parties, was once a prominent member of the Congress.

No other political party has been able to provide an effective opposition to the Congress on the national scene or (with very few exceptions) in the states. Nearly three-fourths of the members of the Lok Sabha have been, and are, Congressmen. The next largest representation in the Lok Sabha has been around thirty members, a distinction which has usually gone to the Communist Party in recent years. The only other parties of any real national significance are the Swatantra and the Praja Socialist parties, and these have substantial strength in only a few states.

The Communist Party, whose candidates received some 10 per cent of the total popular vote in the general election of 1962, continues to retain its identification with various domestic groups and interests, especially in Kerala, Andhra, and West Bengal, in spite of the Chinese incursions, the split among its top leaders on the Chinese and other issues, and the efforts of the Congress and other "nationalists" parties to identify it with the Chinese. In 1964 the pro-Chinese faction of the CPI held a convention, and formed what is virtually a second Communist party in India. The main faction of the CPI, which is pro-Soviet, espouses "the parliamentary road

[23] Keith Callard, *Pakistan: A Political Study* (London: George Allen & Unwin, 1957), especially Chapter II, "The Decline of the Muslim League."

to power," but the pro-Chinese wing seems to favor more forceful methods. For all its recent difficulties, however, the CPI is a vital, and perhaps even a growing force in Indian politics.

The Swatantra Party, a non-communal conservative party whose "super-leader" is the veteran C. R. Rajagopalachari, once a leading member of the Congress hierarchy, and India's first — and last — Indian governor-general, is a new phenomenon in Indian politics, but it has not as yet won any mass following. The Jan Sangh is experiencing a recrudescence of strength, but its support is confined almost solely to the Hindi-speaking states of north India. The Praja Socialist Party, until 1964 the leading non-Communist socialist party, aside from the Congress itself, failed to establish a recognizable identity, and lost support both to the Congress and to the Communists. Its plight seems typical of the difficulties which democratic socialism has experienced, at least in Asia. In the third general elections in 1962 it suffered such severe reverses in every state except Mysore that it was virtually eliminated as a national party. In 1964, it joined with the even weaker Socialist Party to form the new Samyukta Samajvadi (United Socialist) Party; but this merger did not survive its first national convention.

The extreme dominance of the Congress Party has naturally given a lopsided character to the Indian party system. Many observers regard this as a threat, for they argue that a parliamentary democracy cannot function effectively in the absence of an effective opposition. On the other hand, India has probably benefited greatly from the remarkable continuity of leadership and the high degree of political stability which the continued dominance of the Congress, the spearhead of the independence struggle, has afforded.[24] Because of this dominance much of the politics of India has been carried on *within* the Congress. In the Lok Sabha the weakness and disunity of the opposition are partially compensated for by the watchdog activities of some of the important committees, notably the Estimates Committee and the Public Accounts Committee.

In all probability, the Congress Party will remain in power at the Center and in most if not all of the states for some time to come. Certainly there is no discernible effective alternative in sight. But the picture of an allpowerful Congress has to be modified in many ways. In fact, all is not well with the Congress. As the third general elections revealed sharply, it is by no means as strong as its position at the Center would indicate. It is confronted with at least three serious threats: weak leadership, poor organiza-

---

[24] "A well-organized party system might have hindered the relative stability. . . . Much of the success of the legislative and planning programs in these countries can be traced to the large, disciplined majorities held by the party in power in the respective parliaments. The hard test of parliamentary government, of course, will come when this situation no longer prevails." Richard L. Park, "Problems of Political Development," in Philip W. Thayer, ed., *Nationalism and Progress in Free Asia* (Baltimore: The Johns Hopkins Press, 1956), p. 104. See also W. H. Morris-Jones, "Parliament and Dominant Party: Indian Experience," *Parliamentary Affairs,* Summer 1964, pp. 296–307.

tion, internal divisions, and "groupism;" growing opposition to it on the part of many of the Indian people, especially the urban intellectuals; and increasingly effective opposition in many of the states.[25]

"Groupism" within the Congress leadership was a conspicuous feature of the election campaign of 1962, and was undoubtedly a major cause of severe election reverses which the Congress suffered in many of the states. A number of disgruntled prominent Congress leaders secretly — and some even openly — supported opposition candidates, because of their dissatisfaction with the party nominations; some even left the party, and ran against Congress candidates as Independents or joined other parties.

The Congress survived the immediate crisis of leadership occasioned by the death of Nehru in late May 1964. In fact, the problem of the succession was handled with remarkable smoothness and dispatch, although the consequences of the temporary struggle that went on in top Congress circles between the supporters of Lal Bahadur Shastri and Morarji Desai cannot yet be fully assessed. As was generally predicted, a pattern of collective leadership has succeeded Nehru's charismatic leadership. In this collective leadership Kamaraj Nadar, the president of the Congress Party, supported by a few party bosses, seems to be playing the central role.

Dissatisfaction with Congress policies or representatives, or simply satiation with a party that has been so long in power, has created a growing opposition among people generally, which is not yet reflected in the results of elections to the Lok Sabha. For various reasons fewer than half of the voters in each of the three national elections have supported Congress candidates, even for the Lok Sabha, although the absence of a united opposition in most constituencies has given the Congress a larger representation than its popular vote would suggest. The party has reason to be concerned about its growing failure to attract the support of Indian intellectuals, and about its hold in its main centers of strength in rural areas now that Nehru is gone.

In almost every state the Congress is faced with real opposition, which in many instances centers around one opposition group. As a result of the 1962 general elections the Swatantra Party became the major opposition in Bihar, Gujarat, Orissa, and Rajasthan, the Communist party in Andhra, Kerala, and West Bengal, the Jan Sangh in Madhya Pradesh and Uttar Pradesh, and the Praja Socialist Party in Mysore (it has appreciable strength also in Madhya Pradesh and Uttar Pradesh). The Akali Dal, a militant Sikh party, provides the main opposition in the Punjab. In Madras the Dravida Munnetra Kazagham, which advocates a separate South Indian state of Dravidinad, made surprising gains in the third general elections. Weaker opposition is provided by the remnants of the Samyukta Maharashtra Samiti

[25] See Norman D. Palmer, "Growing Pains of Indian Democracy," *Current History,* March 1963, pp. 147–154; Myron Weiner, "India's Third General Elections," *Asian Survey,* May 1962, pp. 3–18.

in Maharashtra, and by the Hill Leaders Conference in Assam. Almost all of the members of the Assembly in Jammu and Kashmir belong to the National Conference or to affiliated parties, but this local version of a united front cooperates with the Congress, at least on national matters, and most of its members have joined the Congress Party. About 60 per cent of all members of state assemblies, however, are members of the Congress. After the 1962 elections Congress ministries remained in power in every state, although they were in a tenuous position in Madhya Pradesh and Rajasthan, and in an even more shaky position in Kerala, where the Congress was able to elect only six of the eighteen members of the Lok Sabha from Kerala, while the Communists won the same number of seats. In September 1964 the Congress government in Kerala was forced to resign when several dissident congressmen joined with the opposition parties in a vote of no confidence. President's rule was proclaimed, and this continued after elections in March 1965 left the Congress with fewer seats in the State Assembly than the pro-Chinese Communist faction of the CPI.

Just as there has been a more discernible split between a left and a right wing within the Congress Party, so does a growing polarization of politics to the right and left of the Congress seem more apparent. The second general elections in 1957 witnessed the emergence of significant groups to the left of the Congress, and the third elections in 1962 led to a greater polarization of that strength in favor of the Communists, who generally maintained their representation and actually increased their percentage of the popular vote from less than 9 to over 10 per cent. The PSP, which fared quite well in 1957, lost heavily in 1962 both in popular vote (from 10.41 to 6.88 per cent) and in the number of successful candidates for state assemblies or the Lok Sabha, to which it elected only five members.

The third elections, beside polarizing that challenge, produced the phenomenon of an emergent right. The Jan Sangh, the only important Hindu communalist party, registered impressive gains in Madhya Pradesh and Uttar Pradesh, and more than doubled its representation in the Lok Sabha (from six to fourteen members). The new Swatantra Party, which criticized the whole approach to planning of the Congress government, made a surprising showing in Bihar and Rajasthan, fared well also in three other states, and elected eighteen members of the Lok Sabha. The emergent right has not polarized around a single party, and can hardly be expected to do so because of the communal divide. Rajaji and other Swatantra leaders tried to rescue conservatism from communalism. The Swatantra Party tries to appeal to voters in all parts of the country, and to all classes and castes, but it is still identified as a party of rich businessmen and "feudal" interests, and it has no significant following outside of five or six states. The Jan Sangh, which denies that it is a communal party, is supported almost wholly by Hindu communalists and Hindi-speaking people of north India. Hence the polarization on the right is not so impressive as the upsurge of the Jan Sangh and the Swatantra Party would seem to suggest.[26]

If a major change occurs in Indian politics, it will probably come as a result of a split-up of the Congress rather than a merger of opposition parties or a swing to the extreme left or the extreme right. If such a split occurs, some members of the Swatantra Party and other conservatively inclined Indians might join the right wing of the Congress to form the nucleus of a right-of-center party, and many members of the non-Communist leftist opposition parties might join with the left wing of the Congress to form a party espousing the principles of democratic socialism. In such an event the new socialist grouping would probably prevail over the more conservatively inclined party, which might nevertheless command enough support to provide the kind of opposition on the national scene which India has not experienced thus far.

Although a split in the Congress — which is a possibility, but not the most likely political development in the near future — would introduce some new elements of instability, it would probably mark no major change in India's external or internal policies or orientation. A swing in favor of a more conservative grouping might lead to more fundamental changes, but doubtless the United States could adjust to them without great difficulty. Since such changes would be within the broad democratic framework which India has built and strengthened during the formative years of its nationhood, the United States should not express a strong preference for any particular change. It would obviously have reason to be deeply concerned if the Communists began to prevail, or if a shift toward Hindi communalism set in on the political level. A decided trend toward either form of authoritarianism, or toward military rule, would raise justifiable apprehensions in the United States and in other democratic countries.

Leaders and Leadership

Political development cannot occur without effective political leadership, a quality in scarce supply in most developing countries. In the countries of South Asia political leadership has in the past been confined largely to certain privileged groups, and to Western-educated intellectuals, but new patterns of leadership are emerging.

Thus far India has been more fortunate in the character and continuity of its leadership than has Pakistan, although it lost Mahatma Gandhi less than six months after independence, and in 1951 one of its strongest administrators and party bosses, Sardar Vallabhbhai Patel, who successfully engineered the delicate task of bringing the princely states into the Indian

[26] See Palmer, "Growing Pains of Indian Democracy," pp. 151–152.

Union. But Jawaharlal Nehru, who was the prime minister from 1947 until his death in 1964, gave India a continuity of leadership that is almost unparalleled in the modern world.

Nehru was much more than the prime minister and the leading figure in the Congress Party; he was the leader of the Indian revolution, known and loved by the masses. As the years passed Nehru often was withdrawn, moody, impatient, and irritable, and he increasingly showed a reluctance to make difficult decisions, but he was still the colossus of post-Gandhian India. In an oft-quoted statement S. K. Patil, a strong man in the Congress Party and a former member of the Indian cabinet, compared Nehru to a banyan tree: "Nehru is the greatest asset we have because he is just like a banyan tree under whose shade millions take shelter," but he is also a liability "because in the shade of that banyan tree, biologically, nothing grows.[27]

In the closing years of his life the questions "After Nehru, who?" and "After Nehru, what?" insistently intruded themselves into almost every discussion of India's future.[28] The Nehru era in Indian politics has ended, but the country is being run by his lieutenants along the lines he charted. The first question has already been answered and the procedures for selecting successors seem to have been established. But the answer to the second question lies hidden in the mists of the future. Though Nehru's towering stature pushed almost all other leaders into the background, they exist at all levels of Indian political life. Nevertheless India is faced with a severe crisis of leadership in the post-Nehru era, as lesser men try to carry on in the tradition of the great leader.

Although the Congress is by all odds the most extensive political organization in the country, its leadership is weak and divided at most levels. The relationship between the party and the government has always been one of tension and uncertainty. From 1955, when Nehru last gave up the Congress presidency, until 1963, his successors in that office were relatively inconspicuous politicians. The selection of Kamaraj Nadar, former chief minister of

[27] Quoted in *Time*, December 14, 1959, p. 22.

[28] An interesting exercise in speculation, based on extensive observations and interviews in India, was made by Welles Hangen, representative of the National Broadcasting Company in India, in 1963. In a book entitled *After Nehru, Who?* (New York: Harcourt, Brace & World, 1963) Hangen devoted separate chapters to the following Indian leaders whom he considered as possible successors to Mr. Nehru: Morarji Desai, V. K. Krishna Menon, Lal Bahadur Shastri, Y. B. Chavan, Indira Gandhi, Jayaprakash Narayan, and General Brij Mohan Kaul.

A poll taken by the Indian Institute of Public Opinion in 1960 indicated that the Indian people, if the small sample reflected the popular view, had no clear preference for Nehru's successor. More voted for Jayaprakash Narayan than for any other person, but only about 12 per cent of those polled favored Jayaprakash. Fewer than 10 per cent favored the next two in order of preference, Moraji Desai and Krishna Menon, who ended in a dead heat. The poll simply confirmed that not only was Nehru's successor in doubt but that the balance of political forces in the post-Nehru era was unpredictable.

Madras, as president of the Congress in 1963 brought to the office a more independent and vigorous political leader.

The Congress has always been a kind of umbrella party, embracing in its ranks at all levels persons with the most diverse views. Within its top leadership there seems to be a conservative wing, of which Moraji Desai, the former finance minister, is the chief spokesman, and a left wing, embracing a large number of top Congress leaders. This leftist group is still a rather amorphous one. Possibly a third, or centrist, group should also be distinguished, consisting of those leaders not clearly identified with either of the wings. At present this group seems to be dominant; in the long run, however, it may lose influence, either by a shift in direction within the ranks of the party leaders during the struggle for power which set in after Nehru's death, or by a break-up of the party into two or more political groupings.

After the Chinese attack of 1962 a real shift in the balance of power among the potential successors to Mr. Nehru seemed to be occurring. This shift seemed to enhance the prospects that Nehru's successor would come from the moderate or conservative groups in the Congress top command, rather than the leftist group, as seemed more probable after the general election of February 1962. On the other hand, the mass resignations from the cabinet, and from the ranks of chief ministers, in August 1963 — the most dramatic and extensive political shake-up in the Indian government since independence — removed from office more conservative or middle-of-the-road leaders than leftists, including Morarji Desai and S. K. Patil, and some of the strongest of the chief ministers. But one of the chief ministers whose resignation was accepted, B. Patnaik of Orissa, was prominently identified with the extreme leftist group within the Congress. Thus no clear evidence of the relative strength of the various groups within the Congress could be discerned.

During the struggle for power in the Congress in the post-Nehru era effective control of the party was seemingly seized firmly, not by representatives of any of the three so-called groups in the party, but by party bosses, most of whom, including the man who seems now to dominate the party, Kamaraj Nadar, were not clearly identified with any particular group. The same comment could be made of Lal Bahadur Shastri, Nehru's successor as prime minister. Lal Bahadur's chief strength lay in the fact that he was a gifted compromiser who was not prominently identified with any group and who was generally acceptable to all.[29]

A few years ago some of the strongest political leaders were chief ministers of the states, but many were brought to New Delhi to assume important cabinet posts. For example, Y. B. Chavan of Maharashtra became union minister of defense in November 1962. Their successors in the states, while men of lesser reputation, have been discharging their new responsi-

[29] Lloyd L. Rudolph and Susanne Hoeber Rudolph, "India Turns to a Conciliator," *The New York Times Magazine,* June 14, 1964.

bilities with considerable success and have become quite active in party affairs. It is probably that chief ministers will have an increasing role in national politics.

In politics and in other phases of Indian life new groups are becoming more influential and new leaders are emerging. In business middle-level and even small businessmen are becoming more important. In politics, thanks largely to the power of the ballot, the lower castes and classes are having more to say and are learning how to say it effectively.[30] In Kerala, for example, where both the Communists and the Congress-PSP coalition ministries made rather sorry records, the low-caste Ezhevas, the largest single community in the state, are finding new leaders. In the districts and even at the subdistrict levels, thanks largely to the importance of the block and district organizations connected with Panchayati Raj, new leaders are emerging.

In general Pakistan's problem of leadership has been more serious than has India's. Its great leader, Mohammed Ali Jinnah, died hardly more than a year after Pakistan came into existence. His chief lieutenant, Liaquat Ali Khan, carried on as prime minister until he was assassinated in October 1951. Between 1951 and 1958 Pakistan had some strong leaders, including Ghulam Mohammad (Governor-General, 1951–55), Iskandar Mirza (Governor-General, 1955–56, and President, 1956–58), and H. S. Suhrawardy (Prime Minister, 1956–57), but they are not strong enough to avert the deteriorating political situation in the country, and in some ways they contributed to it. Some men of great integrity held high office, such as Kwaja Nazimuddin (Governor-General, 1948–51, and Prime Minister, 1951–53) and Chaudhri Mohamad Ali (Prime Minister, 1955–56), but they were ineffective as political leaders. In these years, indeed, as the Constitution Commission pointed out, Pakistan suffered heavily from "the general lack of character in the politicians."[31]

General — now Field Marshal — Mohammed Ayub Khan has been the strong man of Pakistan ever since he first assumed power "by right of revolution" in October 1958. In January 1960 he was elected President by 80,000-odd elected members of the "Basic Democracies." He remained in power when martial law was officially ended in June 1962 and when the new constitution, establishing a presidential system of government, went into effect. In January 1965, again through the process of election by the "Basic Democrats," he was re-elected for a five-year term. He has continued to exercise virtually dictatorial powers, and while the original glamour and appeal of his rule have given way to more resigned acceptance, he has managed to retain a considerable amount of popularity and public support.

No obvious successor to Ayub is in sight. None of his chief lieutenants in

[30] Rajni Kothari, "Developing Political Pattern," *Seminar* (New Delhi), no. 34, June 1962, pp. 47–50.
[31] *Report of the Constitution Commission, Pakistan, 1961*, p. 13.

the military seems fitted for the role, and some of his closest associates, including Generals K. M. Sheikh and Azam Khan, apparently differed sufficiently from Ayub to be relegated to lesser roles. Almost every formerly prominent politician, except former Prime Minister Mohammed Ali (Bogra), was EBDOed (that is, disqualified from holding political office), and some have been in and out of custody. Many of them are now dead, or are in retirement. In time the institutions of Basic Democracy may produce effective national leaders, but this possibility is most remote. Pakistan, like India, has no lack of able and qualified leaders, but most of these people are either debarred from political activity, or are suspect because of their associations with the discredited prerevolutionary past, or are engaged in other pursuits, or have not yet gained recognition and general confidence.

Ayub Khan has proved to be a strong and effective leader. He has introduced many significant reforms; he has lived up to his promise to end martial law and give the people another chance to live under a constitutional government, albeit under controlled conditions; above all, he has given Pakistanis a badly needed upsurge of pride and confidence. There are signs of increasing dissatisfaction in the country, especially in East Pakistan and on the part of students and intellectuals, who have had little opportunity to assert themselves or to exert any influence under the rule of the military and the civil service. The immediate question is whether Ayub can and will be content to be the President of the new Republic of Pakistan, if, as is likely, he is subject to pressures for changes in the Constitution and for greater speed than he desires in the institution of more representative government. In such an event, will he then retire in disgust, or will he revert to more authoritarian controls in another effort to "save the country"?

The Political Role of the Military

Both India and Pakistan inherited from the British the tradition of the subordination of the military to the civil authorities. Broken in Pakistan in October 1958, this tradition still prevails in India, although some signs indicate an erosion of the principle.

In Pakistan in 1951 the Army Chief of Staff and several other high-ranking officers were involved in a plot to overthrow the government, which culminated in the famous Rawalpindi Conspiracy Case. While the story has never been fully revealed, the nature of the plot was thus explained in March 1951 by the prime minister, Liaquat Ali Khan:

> They planned . . . to resort to force with the support of Communist and revolutionary elements, making use of such members of the armed forces as they could tamper with. . . . The country was to be brought under a military dictatorship, when the existing authorities, both civil and military, had been eliminated. The Government was thereafter to be patterned on the Com-

munist model, but under military domination. For this purpose economic and constitution-making missions were to be invited from a certain foreign country.[32]

On several occasions after he assumed power, General Ayub Khan revealed that Governor-General Ghulam Mohammad had once or twice suggested that Ayub, as chief of staff, should step into the frustrating political picture and assume control, with the support of the military. Ayub resisted all such temptations, and frequently boasted publicly that he was not interested in politics and disapproved of political activity on the part of the military. Obviously he changed his mind by October 1958, when he ousted General Mirza, a man with a military background who had been both Governor-General and President of Pakistan, and who had taken over absolute control by "right of revolution" in early October 1958.

From October 1958 until June 1962, when the new Constitution went into effect, Pakistan was governed under martial law, and was in fact a military dictatorship, although a relatively mild one. Ayub Khan governed with a firm hand, and military officers held cabinet posts and other top positions in the national and provincial governments which were normally held by civilians. Even under the new constitution, which has professedly restored "democracy," Ayub Khan enjoys extraordinary powers, and the military are the most important influence in the politics of the country. It is an open question whether under military supervision Pakistan can and will be restored to civilian rule. In view of the recent experience it seems likely that the military will continue to play a dangerously conspicuous role for some time to come.[33]

If the military in India have generally eschewed politics, they have not been wholly immune to political influences, especially when V. K. Krishna Menon, whose whole life has been devoted to politics and political propaganda, was defense minister. Some of the controversy which surrounded him had an impact on the military establishment of which he was the civilian head from 1957 to 1962. Many critics charged that he deliberately played politics with the armed forces, making appointments and transfers and promotions to place his supporters in key positions, courting the favor of the junior officers and enlisted men, and indoctrinating the members of the armed forces with left-wing socialist views. These criticisms were made most strongly in India by General Thimayya, who resigned as chief of staff in 1961 because of basic disagreements with Krishna Menon, by leaders and supporters of the Swatantra Party, and by Acharya Kripalani, an outspoken critic of India's foreign and defense policy. Kripalani made a typical attack on the defense minister in a speech in the Lok Sabha on April 11, 1960, long before he decided to stand against Menon in North

---

[32] Constituent Assembly (Legislature), *Debates*, 1951, vol. 1, p. 34, March 21, 1951.
[33] See Norman D. Palmer, "Pakistan's Mood: The New Realism," *Current History,* November 1962; and Norman D. Palmer, "Pakistan: New Directions," *Current History,* February 1964.

Bombay. Charging that Krishna Menon had introduced "groupism and politics into the Army," the Acharya added: "He has made it a hotbed of intrigue and maneuverings, setting officer against officer."

It is difficult to ascertain the basis of these rumors and charges, or to pinpoint individual examples of Krishna Menon's alleged machinations. They are a part of the larger problem of determining the extent to which Menon built up a personal following and independent strength in the country, and the nature of his relations with the Communists, who were alleged by persons as diverse in their views as Jayaprakash Narayan and Benegal Rama Rau to be infiltrating the Congress party to an alarming degree.

If the danger that Krishna Menon and his henchmen in the army and elsewhere might use the army as an instrument for gaining political power ever existed in fact, it was removed with the abrupt dismissal of the controversial defense minister in late October 1962, a few days after the Chinese attacked. The collateral danger that the army will continue to be politicized, and that it may henceforth be a major factor in Indian politics, has, however, probably increased rather than diminished since Krishna Menon's departure. The danger of a military coup is still remote, but it can no longer be wholly ruled out. If the "angry young officers" become increasingly frustrated and "fed up" with indecision, weakness, and lack of support on the part of the political leaders, they might decide to take matters into their own hands, as the military in so many other developing countries have already done.

Since the Chinese attack the enlarged army has assumed a new and more influential role, and the political climate in India has been more receptive than previously to stronger military policies and actions. This change has many beneficial aspects, but it does tend to strengthen the political role of the military and of militant political groups. "Domestically," as Selig Harrison pointed out, "Nehru has always feared the rise of militarism in alliance with business-dominated rightist forces and Hindu xenophobes more than the Communist left-wing. The 'emergency' has aggravated these fears. . . . Talk of a million-man army persists and a climate of jingoistic nationalism inevitably invigorates the right wing."[34]

"Open Societies"

By almost any standards India and Pakistan could not be classified as "free" societies, without many qualifications. They are still essentially tradition-bound, relatively static societies, beset now by "the wind of change," and torn between the past and the present, the old and the new,

[34] Selig S. Harrison, "India Is Studying a Harlequin Map," *The Washington Post*, January 27, 1963.

the simultaneous quest for the best in their heritage and the best in the modern world. They are governed by a relatively small group, constituting a thin upper crust, and the masses of the people are not yet sufficiently involved as participants in the tasks of modernization and development. Personalities still seem to be more important than principles, and the standards of public life are regrettably low. On the whole, the people have little confidence in officials at any level, except perhaps at the very top.

For a year or two after the "revolution" of October 1958, Pakistan experienced a needed "shot-in-the-arm." The marked upsurge of confidence has largely been dissipated, and the prospects for anything but a "controlled" democracy seem quite dim. India has experienced a series of shocks and disappointments, culminating in the loss of its greatest leader in May 1964, and is not a happy country at the present time. In part this chastened mood may be attributed to a more realistic facing of its basic problems, and to the apprehensions and pressures presented by a suddenly hostile China; in part it may be due to a feeling that things are not going as well as is necessary for growth, or even survival. But both India and Pakistan are making visible progress, and both are trying to deal with their problems in a democratic way — Pakistan much more hesitantly than India. In any event, in both countries the beliefs and the *intentions* of the top leaders are of surpassing importance.

However the present political systems of India and Pakistan may be described, they are certainly not totalitarian systems. As far as the outside world is concerned, they are open and not closed societies.

Many of the present-day leaders of India and Pakistan, in nearly all walks of life, were educated in the West; many more were educated in institutions patterned along Western lines. In no other part of the world has "the meeting of East and West" been more extensive or had a greater impact. India and Pakistan have not rejected the West since they became independent. Thousands of Indians and Pakistanis are today studying in Western institutions, especially in the United Kingdom and the United States. Contacts between South Asians and Westerners were never more extensive.

The fact that India and Pakistan are open and not closed societies and that continuing dialogues and continuing contacts with them are possible is a matter of great importance for the United States, which should certainly bend every effort to assist the South Asian countries to keep the channels of communication open in every possible way. This will be particularly important in the critical transition period — "the most dangerous decades" — that lie ahead.

The United States and South Asian Political Development

At the moment, the political situation in almost every country in South Asia seems to be relatively stable. But beneath the surface many signs of impending changes may be detected, which the United States should follow with particular care and interest. Even though it may be accused of intervention in internal affairs, it must take as much interest in political as in economic development, for economic and social progress in freedom is not possible without adequate political and administrative institutions and leadership. The object should not be political stability *per se*, but political change by orderly rather than disruptive means to lay the basis for genuine political stability.

The United States has given substantial economic and military assistance to India and Pakistan. Obviously this assistance has had a considerable political impact; its effective use has depended in large measure on the capacity and intentions of the political leaders and the administrative personnel. For obvious reasons, the United States has been wary in giving advice and direct assistance in the political field; but it cannot be unconcerned with political trends in these countries, and with the aims and policies of those who hold political power. Under public or private auspices, many Americans have given assistance to India and Pakistan, in the field of governmental administration and finance. Their contributions in the higher levels of policy-making are less obvious, partly because such contributions should properly be made behind the scenes, with no expectation of publicity or general recognition, and even more because this is a sensitive area in which Americans should generally not presume to tread. Even here some examples could be cited, although they cannot be documented in full. Such efforts, even in sensitive areas, should be encouraged, but they should not be pressed beyond the point of receptivity and tolerance on the part of the officials concerned. Publicly voiced official criticisms of the policies or political practices of India and Pakistan should generally be avoided. It is no secret that the United States is not enamored with many aspects of the internal and external policies of India and Pakistan; but sweeping condemnation of these aspects would only alienate both countries without persuading them to reverse their policies.

Parliamentary democracy may not be the most suitable form of democracy in underdeveloped countries. Some kind of presidential form, for example, may be preferable, at least during the difficult transition period. Yet when those in power in the new nations have turned from the parliamentary form to a presidential system, they have usually in fact been turning to a nondemocratic approach. Their claims that they are simply introducing a form of democracy which is more suited to their needs and traditions have usually been thin disguises for increasingly authoritarian trends.[35] It remains to be seen whether Pakistan will be a major proof of, or an exception to, this generalization.

Obviously the United States should be alert to signs of impending changes

[35] See Saul Rose, "Political Institutions," in Saul Rose, ed., *Politics in Southern Asia* (New York: St. Martin's Press, 1963), pp. 330–331.

of a violent nature, tending either toward an authoritarianism of the right or the left or toward political fragmentation, no less than to changes of an orderly nature within the democratic framework. It should do what it can to strengthen the forces of unity and of democracy against the pressures in other directions. Clearly this involves a deep concern for the political development of the countries of South Asia, as well as for their economic and social progress.

CHAPTER FOUR

The Economics of Planning and Development

WHATEVER THEIR DIFFERENCES in political structure, orientation, and objectives, India and Pakistan are faced with similar economic problems and, in general, are trying to deal with these problems in essentially similar ways. Each country is engaged in a major effort in economic development, the success of which is by no means assured, even assuming a continuation of national integration and political stability.

South Asia is perhaps the greatest laboratory of economic development in the modern world. Few, if any, other developing nations have had as much experience or as much success in preparing and implementing development programs as have India and Pakistan.

There seems to be general agreement on the part of the leaders of both countries and of foreign observers that the next few years will be an unusually critical period. Impressive as the present development efforts are, they must be stepped up considerably if the targets of the national plans are to be reached. There is also rather general agreement that the plan targets, however ambitious they may be in terms of available resources and absorptive capacity, are quite modest in terms of minimal needs. If the targets are not substantially achieved, the consequences will be serious in more than the economic sphere. "Each successive year," said the finance minister of India, Morarji Desai, in presenting the interim budget for 1962–63 to the Lok Sabha, "will call for greater effort on the part of everyone if we are to move forward as fast as we must." Yet, as *The Times of India* observed in commenting on this warning, "the basic question whether the conditions in which the necessary effort can be fruitfully made remains unanswered. Also it is by no means certain that economic and meaningful utilization of resources can be achieved. To fulfil targets is rather more difficult than fixing them."[1]

[1] "Central Budget" (Editorial), March 16, 1962.

These observations could be applied with equal validity to Pakistan. They call attention to the conditions, or preconditions, for economic development, which are not primarily economic at all, but political and administrative, social and cultural, philosophical and psychological.

The political and administrative prerequisites for effective economic development are often lacking in the new nations, or exist only to such a limited degree that the efforts are retarded. Fostering growth is a complex process, and is far more than a matter of effective economic planning. Possibly, as John P. Lewis has remarked about India, development should be considered as "an essentially political phenomenon requiring major economic implementation."[2]

Background Factors and Considerations

The Indian and Pakistani planners are well aware that it is in these broader aspects of the problem that progress has been least satisfactory, and the obstacles to development most pervasive and persistent. They have found it easier to make plans than to implement them, to mobilize material resources than to mobilize human resources. For all their efforts the masses are not yet really enlisted in the task of national development, with all of the consequences this implies for their traditional patterns of thinking and ways of life. The political and administrative machinery is not yet really geared to the needs of development — it is most difficult to reorient the thinking and attitudes of civil servants and politicians to such tasks — and the political climate, especially in Pakistan up to October 1958, has often been unfavorable for constructive work.

The growing interaction between traditionalist and modern cultures is a major cause of the "torment in our minds" to which Nehru often referred. Increasing numbers of South Asians are torn between the past and the present, the old and the new, indigenous and foreign ways and ideas. It is obvious even in the minds of the Westernized elite, as one of Nehru's most frequently quoted remarks — "I am a strange mixture of the East and West . . ." — reminds us. Gandhi, a Western-educated and widely cosmopolitan man, exemplified it in his teachings and example. Seeking his inspiration in ideas and traditions of the past, he deliberately turned against many of the ways of the modern world. His influence on social attitudes, if not so clearly on economic policies, is patent. But even in the economic sphere, in a country following the very un-Gandhian approach of centralized planning and industrialization, the Gandhian influence can be found, for example, in the views of such national leaders as Vinoba Bhave and

[2] *Quiet Crisis in India* (Washington: The Brookings Institution, 1962), p. 11.

Jayaprakash Narayan, in the emphasis on decentralization, cottage industries, and rural uplift.[3]

Many other basic conflicts characterize the setting in which the Indian
and Pakistani experiments in economic development must be conducted.
Some of these are suggested in an arresting sentence by an eminent Indian
economist, V.K.R.V. Rao:

> Tradition *versus* modernity, rural *versus* urban, materialism *versus* spirituality,
> superstition *versus* rationality, employment *versus* efficiency, machine *versus*
> hand, income through work *versus* income through agitation, self-reliance *versus*
> state patronage, cost-consciousness *versus* quick profit, casteism, linguism, and
> communalism *versus* nationality, parliamentary processes and the voluntary
> principle *versus* total resource mobilisation and the totalitarian threat, public
> sector *versus* the private sector, socialism *versus* capitalism, inequality *versus*
> equality, rights *versus* obligations, individual profit *versus* social welfare —
> these are some of the dilemmas that befog the Indian goal of economic growth
> and tend to make India's attempt at planned economic development such a
> fascinating chapter in the world's social and economic history.[4]

Indian and Pakistani Approaches to Economic Development

In view of the many obstacles to development, it is hardly surprising
that the economic climate should be a rather unfavorable one. It is particularly difficult for American policy-makers and investors to appraise this
climate, for it is foreign to their own conditions and experience, and it
seems to be extraordinarily unpredictable or even unfathomable. There
are also serious semantic misunderstandings in the American-South Asian
economic dialogue. Words such as "socialism" and "capitalism" are dif-
ferently understood, and evoke different reactions. Americans are disturbed
over the strong and apparently growing role of the government in almost
all phases of economic life. They realize that in India and Pakistan economic
development has to follow, since it did not precede, political independence,
but they wonder whether the imperatives of economic development, and

[3] Morarji Desai, for example, formerly chief minister of Bombay State and union
minister of finance, a strong prohibitionist, a man of abstemious habits, and a devoted
Gandhian in many respects, referred to this dilemma when he told a prominent American businessman: "I believe in the wearing of homespun cloth but I promote the
building of textile plants; I believe in healing people by the regenerative forces of
nature, but I endorse the building of antibiotic plants." Quoted by Dr. Antonie Knoppers, President, Merck Sharp & Dohme International Division, in an address on "India,
an Appraisal of Its Investment Climate," at the Pharmaceutical Manufacturers Association, New York, December 8, 1958. It is rather ironical, but not untypical, that one of
the heaviest investors in the Indian Industrial Finance Corporation, established to provide financial assistance to large industries, is the Mahatma Gandhi National Memorial
Fund!

[4] "Some Problems Confronting Traditional Societies in the Process of Development,"
a paper read at a UNESCO Symposium on Social Development (mimeograph), p. 19.
Italics in original.

of the controlled economy that results, may not lead to increasing political as well as economic regimentation.

Although the Indian and Pakistani approaches to economic development are quite similar, in their economic policies, as in their political orientation, the two countries *seem* to be following divergent paths. Briefly stated, Pakistan has more stringent political controls than India but less stringent economic controls. India is consciously and strongly dedicated to "the socialist pattern of society," whereas Pakistan proclaims its belief in "policies of economic liberalism." India is placing an increasing emphasis on the public sector, whereas Pakistan insists that it wishes to give the widest possible scope for the private sector.

A few quotations from official documents will reveal this apparent difference in economic approach. The Indian Industrial Policy Resolution of 1956 asserted that "it is essential . . . to expand the public sector" and that "accordingly, the State will progressively assume a predominant and direct responsibility for setting up new industrial undertakings and for developing transport facilities. It will also undertake State trading on an increasing scale." The Draft Outline of India's Second Five Year Plan, released in February 1956, contained the following statement of policy:

> The achievement of a socialist pattern of society has been accepted as the objective of economic policy. This means that the basic criterion for determining the lines of advance is not private profit but social gain. Major decisions regarding production, distribution, consumption and investment — and in fact the entire pattern of socio-economic relationships — must be made by agencies informed by social purpose. The benefits of economic development must accrue more and more to the relatively less privileged classes of society, and there should be a progressive reduction of the concentration of incomes, wealth, and economic power . . . the State has to take on heavy responsibilities as the principal agency speaking for and acting in behalf of the community as a whole. The public sector has to expand rapidly and the private sector has to play its part within the framework of the comprehensive plan accepted by the community.[5]

A similar statement of policy was included in the Third Five Year Plan.[6]

Pakistan's Second Five Plan, made public in June 1960, strikes a very different note:

> The creative energies of the people can be best harnessed to the needs of development if policies of economic liberalism are pursued . . . the aim is to push ahead with industrial development by encouraging private enterprise in all practicable ways and by freeing the economy from superfluous restraints . . . . Controls which have a strangulating effect on private initiative will need to be relaxed, and replaced progressively by fiscal and monetary measures and

[5] Planning Commission, Government of India, *Second Five Year Plan: A Draft Outline* (New Delhi: Author, February 1956), p. 9.

[6] Planning Commission, Government of India, *Third Five Year Plan* (New Delhi: Author, 1961), pp. 8–10.

operation of the market mechanism. . . . Where it is necessary to retain controls, their rationalization and simplification will be necessary . . . . in regard to the respective roles of the public and private sectors, a pragmatic approach has been followed . . . . No industries are reserved for the public sector; public investment is provided only in those activities which are not ordinarily developed with private capital or where, on present indications, private investment will not be forthcoming. Disabilities of the private investor are now being steadily removed.[7]

In actual practice, the differences in economic policies of India and Pakistan are not so great as these statements would indicate. For many reasons, including the desperate shortage of foreign exchange and the necessity of giving priority to national development, private enterprise is subjected to innumerable controls and restrictions in both countries; yet it accounts for by far the greater part of the productive capacity of each country — a greater proportion than in most of the Western countries, including the United States. Those who are engaged in industry enjoy a protected and near-monopoly market, in which the demand for most goods far exceeds the supply, and they were probably never better off. Industry in India and Pakistan is now attracting many young people who would normally try to obtain posts in the civil service, and even some senior civil servants are being lured into industry, after and sometimes before they reach the early retirement age. New business and managerial classes, with enhanced prestige, are emerging in both countries, and will undoubtedly be increasingly influential in the national life.[8]

The present trend in Pakistan toward "freeing the economy from superfluous restraints" does not mean that free enterprise will really play the dominant role in the economic life of the country, as far as basic decisions and directions are concerned. Its role rather is to provide the sinews of economic strength and development, along the lines charted and directed by the government planners and the political leaders. In India the trend is clearly toward an increasing role for the public sector, and toward increasing controls on private enterprise. Justified more on grounds of national needs than on economic doctrine, this is described as a policy of cooperation and not of encroachment.

If any one word were to be chosen to characterize the present Indian and Pakistani approach to economic policy and planning, it should probably be the word "pragmatic." Indians and Pakistanis would like to add another word, "flexible." Even "the socialist pattern of society," which conjures up so many spectres in the minds of Western capitalists, is by no means a rigid doctrine or dogma. In fact, it has never really been defined, except in terms of objectives, which almost anyone interested in India's welfare would

---

[7] Planning Commission, Government of Pakistan, *The Second Five Year Plan* (1960–65) (Karachi: Author, June 1960), pp. xiv, 8.

[8] H. Venkatasubbiah, "Mixed Economy Succeeds," *The Times Survey of India*, January 26, 1962, p. xi.

endorse. It seems to have more of Gandhism and Fabianism in it than of Marxism in any rigid form.

In Pakistan the pragmatic approach is even more evident. The Preface to Pakistan's Second Plan contains a statement which could be applied with equal validity to India: "No doctrinaire assumptions underlie the Plan, and neither an exclusively capitalist nor an exclusively socialist economy is postulated. The approach throughout is pragmatic. The fundamental problem is how, under severely limiting conditions, to find some way towards the liberation of the people from the crushing burden of poverty. Viewed in this context, economic growth becomes a necessity for sheer survival."[9]

Faced with the necessity of achieving economic growth "under severely limiting conditions," India and Pakistan have to attempt to harness the public and private sectors in the interests of development. The nature of the Indian economic system is vividly described by Professor V.K.R.V. Rao in words which would apply to Pakistan as well: "A mixed economy, with a public and a private sector on the one hand and a modern and a traditional sector on the other, this is the uneasy compromise that is being forced on India by the size of her population, the limitations of her resources, and the laudable but difficult determination to achieve economic growth within the framework of a free society."[10]

By reason of experience and conditioning, civil servants and officials generally in societies like India and Pakistan have a built-in suspicion of private enterprise.[11] G. D. Birla, a prominent Indian industrialist who supports the Congress Party, has complained that "not a blade of grass" can be grown in India unless it is approved in New Delhi, and that "nothing seems to be moving in Delhi."[12] This kind of statement reflects the concern of many Indian businessmen over the degree of government control, and the apparent lack of a sense of urgency, in governmental circles. Birla himself, however, has also said that his real concern is with the efficiency of the administration and not with its dedication to "the socialist pattern."[13] So long as India, like Pakistan, continues to pursue a pragmatic approach, the danger of doctrinaire socialism seems rather remote; but, as Dr. Antonie

[9] *The Second Five Year Plan* (1960–65), p. xiii.

[10] "Some Problems Confronting Traditional Societies . . . ," cited, p. 17.

[11] As *The Economist* (London) observed with reference to Pakistan, "The official's beliefs incline him toward an absolute priority for all projects in the public sector and a tendency, in allotting foreign exchange, to treat the private sector as residual." Special supplement on "Pakistan: A Survey," December 2, 1961, p. 932.

[12] Address in Bombay, March 4, 1962; quoted in *The Times of India*, March 5, 1962.

[13] Statement in interview with the author, Birla House, New Delhi, in late 1961. In *An Analysis of the Third Plan* (New Delhi, n.d., p. 18) Mr. Birla wrote: "At present the administration is not at all geared to the needs of the Plan. . . . The administration is getting more and more complicated and inefficient. Parkinson's Law is extending its tentacles to all Government departments without creating any extra efficiency. . . . Nothing has happened so far to make us take an optimistic view of the future of administration."

Knoppers, an American businessman familiar with the economic climate in India and sympathetic with that country's endeavors, has warned, "history has demonstrated over and over again that a 'public sector' tends to usurp more and more power. After a time the 'pragmatism' gets its rationalization and justification as 'dogma.' "[14]

It is in the interest of the United States, and in keeping with its own experience and convictions, to encourage India and Pakistan to pursue the path of pragmatism in their economic policies, and to eschew economic doctrinairism or excessive public encroachment on the private sector. It can hardly be enthusiastic about many of the experiments which both countries are carrying on. On the other hand, the conditions leading to the present orientation should be appreciated and understood, and the United States should not be deterred from increasing cooperation with both countries because of any qualms about "basic democracies" or "the socialist pattern of society." In general, in its economic policies it should do what it can to assist and strengthen the private sector, and to influence the political authorities and the planners to maintain a true mixed economy and not to move rapidly toward an extremely centralized economic system. In certain instances, official and unofficial American cooperation and assistance may well be extended to public sector undertakings and more frequently such cooperation should be undertaken in the kinds of enterprises, involving both public and private, foreign and domestic cooperation, which in Pakistan's Second Five Year Plan are classified in the "semi-public sector." Private American companies and investors should continue on an increasing scale to look for mutually advantageous opportunities for collaboration and investment in the wide areas where private enterprise is finding increasing scope for its activities and initiative.

General Problems

Before proceeding to a brief examination of the approaches, the nature, and the scope of the development plans, some general and special problems must be mentioned, if only cursorily, for these have a direct and profound bearing on the environment in which the planning efforts must be carried on. Four may be singled out for special mention: population growth and its effect on economic development; education; administrative efficiency and integrity; and the mobilization and use of human and material resources.

Population and Economic Development

No problem facing the underdeveloped countries of the word is more widely discussed than population growth. There seems to be rather general

[14] Address on "India, an Appraisal of Its Investment Climate," cited.

and almost desperate agreement that "something must be done," but there is far less agreement on precisely what must be done and very little evidence either that countries are undertaking effective programs to curb population growth or that they are having any appreciable effect.

The rate of population growth in India and Pakistan is less than in many other countries, but it is higher than it was thought to be prior to the census of 1961. Apparently it has counteracted most of the progress that has been made during the period of the Five Year Plans. Instead of a rate of population growth of about 1.4 per cent a year, as was estimated by both Indian and Pakistani planners in drafting the development programs, the census of 1961 in both countries revealed that the actual rate was perhaps 2.1 per cent in India, and something like 2.2 per cent in Pakistan. This forced some rather fundamental revisions in the plans and figures.

Both countries are well aware of the seriousness of the problem and are trying to do something to check population growth. There are relatively few religious inhibitions, but there are many obstacles arising from the social customs and attitudes, the ignorance and superstitions, of the masses of the people. Almost nowhere in the world do "family planners" find a more cordial reception or a more eager audience. In both countries various experiments have been undertaken — the "rhythm method," various kinds of contraceptives, birth control centers, monetary inducements for sterilization, intrauterine devices, even some new pills — but these experiments have either been inconclusive, or have had little if any visible effect. India's Third and Pakistan's Second Five Year Plan contain appropriations for "family planning" of $100 million and $6 million, respectively.

This whole question is a peculiarly sensitive one, about which the United States can do little, not only because in the last analysis this depends on the people in the developing countries but also because on this issue the United States is divided against itself. In testifying before the House Committee on Foreign Affairs in 1962, Ambassador Galbraith commented on this problem:

> I am personally in favor of a population policy, or birth control. This, however, is an issue which deeply divides the American people. Therefore, as the servant of the American Government, I have taken the position that it is something which should lie within the discretion of the Indian Government, something which should lie within the discretion of governments which are not similarly divided by this issue; that we should and can in good conscience leave this problem to others, even though, as I say, speaking as an individual, I regard it as a problem of great importance.[15]

In view of the growing importance of this problem many Americans may be inclined to share the view of Professor Alvin Hansen: "I do not believe

[15] *Foreign Assistance Act of 1962,* Hearings before the House Committee on Foreign Affairs, 87th Cong., 2d Sess., March 29, 1962 (Washington: Government Printing Office, 1962), p. 604.

that it will be possible even for our politicians to close their eyes for long to the urgent necessity of population control.[16] Indeed, he argues that "what India needs is a much larger *aggregate* program, with the bulk of the increase going into education, agriculture, and population control."[17] Most of the additional funds to finance such a program, as Professor Hansen admits, would have to come from foreign aid, and presumably the United States would make a major contribution to this end. But the fact is that the United States Government feels, probably rightly for the reasons indicated by Ambassador Galbraith, that it cannot officially encourage, much less finance, any programs of population control.[18] Fortunately, private American foundations have fewer inhibitions.[19]

At the very least, however, the United States should encourage unofficial and official efforts in India and Pakistan to develop effective techniques for curbing population growth. It should assist these countries, perhaps indirectly through the World Health Organization and other international agencies especially concerned with this problem, and through private channels, in obtaining and applying the best techniques of modern scientific research.

[16] *Economic Issues of the 1960s* (New York: McGraw-Hill, 1960), p. 164.

[17] *Ibid.*, p. 165. Italics in original.

[18] In Section V of its Third Interim Report, entitled "Economic Assistance Programs and Administration," transmitted to the President on July 13, 1959, the President's Committee to Study the United States Military Assistance Program (the Draper Committee) recommended: "That, in order to meet more effectively the problems of economic development, the United States (1) assist those countries with which it is cooperating in economic aid programs, on request, in the formulation of their plans designed to deal with the problem of rapid population growth, . . . and (3) strongly support studies and appropriate research as a part of its own Mutual Security Program, within the United Nations and elsewhere, leading to the availability of relevant information in a form most useful to individual countries in the formulation of practical programs to meet the serious challenge posed by rapidly expanding populations." This was almost the first positive recommendation on the subject in any officially-sponsored American report. No action, however, was taken on this recommendation. President Eisenhower felt that this was a task for private organizations, not for United States government agencies. (In 1965 he announced that he had changed his mind on this issue.) A Gallup Poll indicated that the American public was overwhelmingly in favor of making birth control information available to other nations. See Statement of Purpose presented to the Founding Conference of the World Population Emergency Campaign, held at Princeton, New Jersey, on March 20, 1960; quoted in a full-page advertisement on the "Population Explosion" by the World Population Emergency Campaign, in *New York Times, International Edition,* May 8, 1960.

[19] A report on the work of the Ford Foundation in India, issued in 1961, contained the following statement: ". . . the Foundation has granted $933,000 to the Indian government for an intensive research program to be carried out primarily by six centers around the country. The centers will explore popular attitudes and beliefs regarding family planning and optimum family size, and will devise educational techniques suited to these conditions. Foundation funds will also be used for research grants, fellowships for training Indians in communications both at home and abroad, and outside consultants." *Roots of Change: The Ford Foundation in India* (New York: The Ford Foundation, November 1961), p. 26.

Education

Historical experience suggests that effective population control can come only with an improvement in living standards and economic status; but in South Asia such improvement may be largely vitiated by population growth. The long-range answer lies not so much in improved methods and techniques of birth control, but in education, which will help to remove the barriers of ignorance and superstition and make people better qualified to contribute to the development efforts.

Some people in India and Pakistan, fearful that it will simply upset old ways and attitudes, develop a false sense of values, and add to the already large numbers of the educated unemployed, seem to believe that too much emphasis on education is undesirable at the present stage of development; but most who express any views on the subject seem agreed that education is fundamental to everything they are trying to do. In a broadcast on December 30, 1959, introducing and explaining the forthcoming Second Five Year Plan, President Ayub Khan declared: "Education is an investment in human resources, and on it more than on any other single factor, depends the social and economic development of the country." It is of course far easier to express this point of view, with glib assurance, than to translate it into meaningful programs.

The importance of education is fully recognized, and educational institutions and programs of all kinds are mushrooming in both countries. Even in quantitative terms, however, the archievements, while truly impressive, still fall far short of minimal needs. It will be some years before the stated objectives of universal education for all children of school age can possibly be attained, and problems of adult education can only be resolved with the passage of time. There is rather general agreement that standards of higher education have declined markedly since independence, partly as a result of the rapid increase of the number of students, and this decline can hardly be arrested until some solutions are found for poorly prepared students, inadequately qualified teachers and school administrators, inadequate physical facilities and resources, and language and other problems.

In the field of education in India and Pakistan the United States government and private American foundations have been particularly active and have given many kinds of assistance. They should give even more attention to this vital area, and especially to the improvement of educational standards and facilities as well as to the establishment of more educational institutions and programs.

Administrative Efficiency and Integrity

Political development is essential for the effective implementation of economic plans. One gets the impression that both India and Pakistan still have far to go in this vital area, and that the general political and administrative climate is in many ways less healthy than it has been in the recent past. A marked upsurge in political and administrative efficiency and integrity occurred after the "revolution" in Pakistan in October 1958, in stark contrast to the sorry state of affairs in the preceding months. Since the lifting of martial law in 1962, Pakistan may be moving from relative efficiency and integrity in a near political vacuum to a slump in standards and in national morale as efforts are made, under rather stifling and unhealthy conditions, to revive some of the institutions of representative government. In India one hears on all sides complaints of widespread corruption and declining moral standards in politics and administration. Increasingly these complaints reach close to the top levels of leadership in New Delhi itself.

In both India and Pakistan there is growing concern over the rigidities and inadequacies of the administrative system, which seems, in the words of Professor D. R. Gadgil, "extremely unsuitable for a democratic structure."[20] Almost every specialist in public administration, native or foreign, including such sympathetic American observers as Paul Appleby and Rowland Egger, has called attention to the need for radical changes and expansion of the administrative structure and for fundamental reorientation of the administrative personnel.

The United States can do little to change the administrative structure in India and Pakistan, or to reorient the thinking and attitudes of civil servants. These are matters which Indians and Pakistanis must resolve for themselves, in keeping with their traditions and their consciences. But the United States can and should continue to support and encourage the growing efforts in India and Pakistan to improve the standards and broaden the base of their administrative structure, and to provide more adequate training, whether in foreign or indigenous institutions or by inservice training and field experience. Here the work of the Public Administration Division of the Agency for International Development and its predecessor organizations, through direct assistance and through contracts with American universities and other organizations, and of the Ford Foundation deserve special commendation.

Mobilization and Use of Human and Material Resources

One of the many frustrating paradoxes in underdeveloped countries is that whereas capital resources are never adequate to meet even minimal national needs, the available human and natural resources are never effectively mobilized and used. Millions of people in India and Pakistan are either idle or underemployed, or are barred from really productive contributions by ignorance and lack of skills and training. The human resources of South Asia, the area's richest resources, are not being effectively used.

Strenuous efforts are being made to discover and develop the rich natural

[20] "Prospects for the Second Five-Year Plan Period," *India Quarterly*, January-March 1957, p. 16; Birla, cited, p. 18.

resources of the subcontinent, but the fruits of these efforts are not yet widely apparent. In time the impact of such major undertakings as the vast multipurpose river valley projects and the steel mills will doubtless be felt, but thus far they have constituted drains on scarce resources without commensurate returns. Many economists believe that India and Pakistan can make a greater contribution to their own development, that even in these desperately poor countries it is possible to increase both monetary and non-monetized investment, and to divert a larger share of such investment to purposes of national development. Above all, there is a feeling that neither country has really geared itself, either mentally or physically, for dealing with a situation so serious and so urgent that it involves the very question of national survival. "I do not see any sense of urgency anywhere in New Delhi," complained G. D. Birla, "except in public speeches."[21] Certainly all the public speeches and all the efforts of India's leaders have not really aroused "the sleeping Leviathan" that is rural India.

Special Problems

A number of somewhat more specialized problems should also be mentioned before India's and Pakistan's planning efforts are discussed. Four of the most urgent of these are waste and disinvestment, unemployment and underemployment, urban and rural planning and development, and regionalism and regional development.

Waste and Disinvestment

Waste and disinvestment — "the attrition of existing resources" — are conspicuous phenomena in almost every society, but in underdeveloped countries, where austerity has to be the rule for the people and should be for the favored elite as well, these constitute serious drains on available resources. In India and Pakistan evidences of waste — and allied with it, conspicuous consumption — are everywhere to be seen, from the dusty and cheerless villages to the spectacular new government buildings and the homes of the wealthy in the urban centers. Some of the waste which is particularly commented upon by foreign observers — such as that occasioned by the destructiveness of the millions of "sacred" monkeys, the care of sacred cows, mostly unproductive animals, the excessive sums spent even by poor people on marriages and festivals and at least until recently upon dowries, the gifts to sadhus and other "holy men," are due largely to tradi-

---

[21] Birla, cited, p. 18. This is an underlying theme of Mrs. Kusum Nair's much-discussed book, *Blossoms in the Dust* (London: George Duckworth, 1961). See also the text of her lecture on "The Problem of Limited Aspirations" at the Central Institute of Study and Research in Community Development, Mussoorie, in *Yojana* (New Delhi), February 4, 1962.

tional religious practices and could not be eliminated without profound changes in basic beliefs and habits. The traditional custom of hoarding wealth in the form of gold or jewels, and thereby making it largely unavailable as savings which can be mobilized for national development, could also be described as a form of waste.

Disinvestment in either tangible or intangible form obviously tends to offset the effects of development programs. Examples of tangible disinvestment are the loss of thousands of acres of once arable land each year as a result of water-logging and salinity of the soil, and insufficient or inefficient maintenance of wells, irrigation works, houses, plants, and other properties. In some of the large cities, notably in Bombay where rent controls are in effect, the effects of inadequate maintenance of apartments and rented buildings are shocking to observe. The sad state of the Port of Calcutta, partly resulting from inadequate maintenance, is another clear example of disinvestment, approaching the dimensions of a scandal. Intangible disinvestment would include those features of the national scene which are formidable barriers to creating an environment favorable for integration and development. Sir Theodore Gregory, for example, calls particular attention to the "the threat of 'linguistic nationalism,'" which to him means that the unity of India is threatened by the growing inability of the younger generation to get into contact with each other and with the outside world."[22]

Underemployment and Unemployment

The extent of underemployment in India and Pakistan can be no more than guessed at; it defies statistics, and is in any event partly a matter of definition. Even casual observation suggests that its dimensions are vast, especially in the countryside. Millions of people, because of their desires, customs, professions, health, or lack of opportunity, work only part of each year, and millions more do not put in what would be generally regarded as a full day's work.

More reliable figures are available for the extent of unemployment in the two countries. It is apparently much greater than the planners envisaged. The Second Five Year Plan in India, for example, contained an estimate that a backlog of 5,300,000 unemployed would remain at the end of the Plan; the actual backlog was about 9,000,000. Apparently unemployment in both countries is still increasing. India's planners estimated that during the Third Plan jobs will be provided for an additional 14,000,000 people, but they also estimated that during the same period the increase in the labor force will be in the neighborhood of 17,000,000. Even if the estimates are not so far from the facts, India will have a backlog of some 12,000,000 unemployed by 1966.

[22] *India on the Eve of the Third Five Year Plan* (Calcutta: The Associated Chambers of Commerce of India, 1961), p. 18.

In spite of an almost total failure to implement the manpower and employment programs outlined in its First Five Year Plan, Pakistan, unlike India, hopes to reduce the backlog of unemployment by 1965; but there is considerable doubt whether this "important goal of the Second Plan" can be achieved.

There is the further problem of the so-called educated unemployed, a growing group which will be an increasingly restless and dangerous element in these countries unless some means are found to provide them opportunities for constructive work. At least a partial answer is perhaps suggested in a summary of India's Third Plan: "With rapid industrialization there will be larger employment opportunities for the educated, and the educational system will have to be geared to meet the rapidly changing pattern of personnel requirements."[23] In any event, a substantial amount of manpower training — and retraining — will be necessary. The United States Government and various American agencies, notably the Ford Foundation, are providing substantial assistance to India and Pakistan in improving facilities for manpower planning and training. This is an area in which Americans have had extensive experience and success, and the fruits of their experience and the services of some of their specialists should be made available to the fullest possible extent to the developing nations of South Asia.

Urban and Rural Planning and Development

Two very different patterns of life exist in India and Pakistan — one in the urban areas, with fewer than 20 per cent of the population; the other in the thousands of villages, large and small, scattered throughout the subcontinent. Inevitably special attention is being given to problems of urban and rural development.

In 1961, 115 Indian cities had a population of over 100,000. In spite of a vast amount of new construction, these cities are increasingly unable to cope with the deterioration of existing housing and sanitary and transport facilities and with the vast influx of people. Urban India is fast becoming a seething megalopolis. The estimates of the expenditures required to provide adequately for the growing population are fantastic. Some of the urban centers will have to be developed as urban complexes, extending far beyond the present municipal boundaries, and in some instances accommodating as many as 25 to 30 million people, perhaps even more.[24]

Current plans of both India and Pakistan contain provisions for urban development, with emphasis on housing, slum clearance, and urban planning. Pakistan's Second Plan allocates Rs. 18 million[25] for plans for selected towns

[23] Planning Commission, Government of India, *Third Five Year Plan: Summary* (New Delhi: Author, n.d.), p. 52.

[24] See Roy Turner, ed., *India's Urban Future* (Berkeley, Calif.: University of California Press, 1962).

[25] Rs. is the symbol for rupees. A rupee is worth about 21 cents in American currency; there are 4.76 rupees to the dollar.

and cities in East and West Pakistan. Pakistan, of course, has a special task of urban planning in the building of an entirely new capital of Islamabad, outside of Rawalpindi, for which Rs. 200 million were provided during the period of the Second Plan, and another Rs. 20 million "to meet the auxiliary needs of the new Capital at Dacca."

Urban planning scheduled in India during the period of the Third Plan is even more ambitious. Master plans are tentatively scheduled for twenty metropolitan cities, state capitals, and port towns, twenty-eight industrial centers, and five so-called resource regions. A twenty-year master plan for Delhi, "probably the most ambitious ever undertaken in Asia," has been in preparation since 1957. "It postulates a composite rural-urban development of the Union Territory of Delhi within an integrated 'Delhi metropolitan area' of 800 square miles . . . , a larger 'national Capital region' extending over an area of about 4,500 square miles and . . . an even larger 'Delhi resource region.' "[26] In 1961 a similar planning project was launched in Calcutta, India's largest city, "whose problems are among the most severe in the world."[27] The Ford Foundation has given substantial assistance in the formulation of the Delhi Master Plan, and it has already made even more generous grants for the Calcutta Project.

Many of the problems of rural development will be considered in the discussion of agricultural production and elsewhere in this and other chapters; but it should be borne in mind that the task of mobilizing the South Asian countryside has been one of the most frustrating that has faced the Indian and Pakistani planners.

There is much talk about "the revolution of rising expectations," which presumably is ushering in a "new India" and a "new Pakistan." But if the masses of South Asia are awakening, few of them seem aware of this fact. "My experience," Mrs. Kusum Nair wrote after a year in rural India, "would seem to indicate that a majority of the rural communities do not share in this concept of an ever-rising standard of living. This does not mean that the desired standard is always fixed at the subsistence level. . . . But whatever the level, it tends to be static, with a ceiling rather than a floor, and it is socially determined." This is a challenging conclusion, for, as Mrs. Nair has pointed out, "If my observation is correct, it largely invalidates one of the principal assumptions on which present planning for economic development in the rural sector is based."[28]

Regionalism

Regionalism is so strong in South Asia that some observers hold that India and Pakistan should be considered not so much as two integrated nations as

---

[26] B. G. Verghese, "Town and Country Planning," *The Times of India*, November 1, 1961.

[27] *Roots of Change: The Ford Foundation in India*, p. 51.

[28] "The Problem of Limited Aspirations," cited, p. 12. Mrs. Nair's book, *Blossoms in the Dust*, has the significant subtitle: "The Human Element in Indian Development."

a series of sub-national regions, each with its own history, culture, language, and special interests, and very sensitive at the same time about real or imagined neglect by the central government and encroachments on its local autonomy. Regionalism can obviously be a source of strength to a nation, and in time this may be the case in South Asia; but under present conditions regionalism in India and Pakistan has tended to be a disruptive and disturbing force.

The main problems of regionalism in India arise between the Hindi-speaking North and the non-Hindi states of the South and East. On the whole the non-Hindi states, which are becoming more important economically and politically, feel that they are being discriminated against and they fear this discrimination will become more serious as Hindi becomes increasingly the language of administration and education. The most serious aspects of this problem are on the political and psychological levels. The economic aspects are reflected in problems of plant location and the general allocation of resources and projects under the national plans.

For Pakistan the main regional problem is that between the two wings, although there is a great deal of rivalry among the various regions within West Pakistan in relation to the Punjab. The problem of the two wings is so serious that Pakistan's survival as a single state is constantly in jeopardy. In this rivalry, East Pakistan is the aggrieved party. East Pakistanis feel that they are being discriminated against in innumerable ways by West Pakistanis, who, though numerically a minority, dominate the army, the civil service, the business community, the legal profession, and almost all other preferred callings. They particularly resent what they regard as something akin to carpetbagger rule by West Pakistanis in East Pakistan itself, and as an unfair relative allocation of resources between the two wings. Because East Pakistan earns something like 70 per cent of all of Pakistan's foreign exchange, includes well over half of the total population, and is considerably less developed economically than West Pakistan generally, they argue that they should receive more than half — and not less, as they are receiving at present — of the revenues of the nation and the amounts made available under the development programs.

Planning in India

India is well along in its program of economic planning. The only vigorous objection to the approach comes from the Swatantra Party, and from those who, invoking the teachings and example of Mahatma Gandhi, profess abhorrence of the whole effort to turn India into a modern industrialized economy. Some economists, Indian and foreign, question the extent or the soundness of India's planning.[29] Professor D. R. Gadgil, for example,

[29] See P. T. Bauer, *Indian Economic Policy and Development* (London: George Allen and Unwin, 1961), and *United States Aid and Indian Economic Development* (New

believes that in spite of more than a decade of experience, "the Indian economy is not yet being operated in any planned manner."[30]

The Five Year Plans

The First Five Year Plan was launched in the year following the creation of the Planning Commission in 1950, although it was not "finalized" until December 1952. In many respects it was not a plan at all. Even Mr. Nehru admitted in 1957 that it had not involved "any particular effort. We just took what was there and called it a Plan."[31] This observation does less than justice to those who helped to prepare and implement the Plan, but it contains at least a kernel of truth.

The broad objective of the First Plan was "to lay the foundations on which a more progressive and diversified economy could be built up." The bulk of the total expenditure of nearly five billion dollars in the public sector went for social services, chiefly education, health, and rehabilitation, transport and communications, irrigation and flood control, agriculture and community development, and power. Only about 7 per cent was spent on industrial development. All of the important targets of the First Plan were realized, in both the public and private sectors, and some were in fact exceeded. National income was estimated to have increased by 18 per cent, instead of the original expectation of about 12 per cent.

This successful experience in preliminary and rather modest planning emboldened the planners to more than double their targets for the Second Plan, launched in 1956. The principal objective of this Plan was "to secure a more rapid growth of the national economy and to increase the country's productive potential in a way that will make possible accelerated development in the succeeding plan periods." Four somewhat more specific objectives were also highlighted: (1) "a sizable increase in national income"; (2) "rapid industrialization with particular emphasis on the development of basic and heavy industries"; (3) "a large expansion of employment opportunities"; and (4) "reduction of inequalities in income and wealth and a more even distribution of economic power."[32]

Midway in the period 1956–1961 the Second Plan ran into difficulties, occasioned by such unanticipated factors as serious droughts, a rise in prices of imported goods, and overly ambitious estimates in certain key areas. In general, in contrast to the success of the First Plan, the Second fell short of

---

York: American Enterprise Association, 1959); B. R. Shenoy, *Indian Planning and Economic Development* (Bombay: Asia Publishing House, 1963). For more balanced, but basically critical, analyses, see D. R. Gadgil, *Planning and Economic Policy in India* (Poona: Gokhale Institute of Politics and Economics, 1961); and Wilfred Malenbaum, *Prospects for Indian Development* (London: George Allen and Unwin, 1962).

[30] *Planning and Economic Policy in India,* p. 109.
[31] Statement to National Development Council, September 1957.
[32] *Second Five Year Plan: A Draft Outline,* pp. 6–7.

■ TABLE 1: India's First Three Five Year Plans, 1951–1966

Sectoral Distribution of Expenditures in the Public Sector
(at 1960–61 prices, in millions of dollars)

	First Plan		Second Plan		Third Plan	
	Expenditure	Percentage	Expenditure	Percentage	Expenditure	Percentage
Agriculture and community development	611.1	15	1113	11	2242.8	14
Major and medium irrigation	651	16	882	9	1365	9
Power	546	13	934.5	10	2125.2	13
Village and small industries	90.3	2	367.5	4	554.4	4
Industries and minerals	155.4	4	1890	20	3192	20
Transport and communications	1098.3	27	2730	28	3120.6	20
Social services and miscellaneous	963.9	23	1743	18	2730	17
Inventories					420	3
TOTAL	4116	100	9660	100	15,750	100

Source: Planning Commission, Government of India, **Third Five Year Plan** (New Delhi: Government of India Press, 1961); adapted from tables on pp. 33 and 58.

its targets by nearly 30 per cent. The increase in national income during the Plan period was about 20 per cent, instead of the planned target of 25 per cent. Real progress in industrialization, especially heavy industry, was made in both the public and private sectors. The expansion of employment opportunities was not even sufficient to keep up with the additions to the labor force. Little, if any, progress was made in reducing "inequalities in income and wealth." Total expenditures under the Second Plan were about double those of the First, amounting to approximately $10 billion in the public sector.

Profiting from the experimentation of the First Plan, and from the hard lessons of the Second, India's planners devoted particular care to drafting the Third Plan, which called for a substantial increase in expenditures in both the public and private sectors — approximately $15.225 and $8.4 billion respectively. Parenthetically, the relative expenditures in the public and private sectors in each of the three Plans has been progressively weighted in favor of the public sector; for the three Plans the ratios are approximately 50:50, 60:40, and 65:35, respectively. It should also be noted that the private sector has generally exceeded the targets assigned to it, whereas shortfalls in the public sector, including critical areas such as transport and power, and especially in the targets allocated to the states, have sometimes been substantial.

The principal objectives of the Third Plan, substantially the same as those for the Second Plan, were stated to be: (1) an increase in national income of more than 25 per cent; (2) "self-sufficiency in foodgrains," and increased agricultural production generally; (3) the expansion of "basic industries like steel, chemical industries, fuel and power," and of machine-building capacity; (4) "a substantial increase in employment opportunities"; and (5) "reduction in disparities in income and wealth and a more even distribution of economic power."[33]   The singling out of "self-sufficiency in foodgrains" was a recognition of the special importance of a substantial increase in food production to meet India's food crisis and to reduce the drain on foreign exchange.

Even before the Chinese attack of October-November 1962, serious short-falls were already in sight in crucial areas, such as coal production, power and transport. Agricultural production was lagging badly. Apparently steel production by 1966 will fall far short of the target of nearly 10 million tons, and food production will be well below the target of 100 million tons. The enlarged crisis with China has forced India to more than double its defense budget and to review the whole Plan in the light of new priorities and needs.

The amount of foreign assistance required for each year of the Third, and apparently also for the Fourth, Plan periods will amount to over a billion dollars, counting assistance needed for the Plan and for maintenance and interest payments on foreign loans. The percentage of foreign assistance in-creased from approximately 4 per cent of the total expenditures in the First Plan, to 10 per cent in the Second, to more than 25 per cent in the Third, but it will decline relatively, if not absolutely, during the Fourth and sub-sequent Plans. To obtain the necessary foreign exchange resources, India must depend on continued assistance of a substantial nature from the members of the International Consortium — the "Aid-to-India Club" — and especially from the United States, and from international agencies like the World Bank, and to a lesser extent on the success or failure of India's efforts to increase the level of its exports.

The draft outline of the Fourth Plan, which will officially enter into effect on April 1, 1966, was ready in the spring of 1965. According to a note pre-sented to the National Development Council by the Planning Commission in March 1964, the Fourth Plan will "ensure among other things, a minimum level of income, expanding employment opportunities, and balanced regional development. The strategy for attaining these objectives, in broad terms, was faster development of agriculture, combined with a rapid extension of the industrial sector and suitable provision for transport, fuel, power and education."[34]   The draft Plan called for total expenditures of between $40 and $45 billions and for a heavy emphasis on agricultural development and related programs. In response to criticism that the Plan was too ambitious, Prime Minister Shastri said in the Lok Sabha in August 1965 that "in fact what we have planned for falls far short of fulfilling our needs and require-ments."

The conflict with Pakistan in August-September 1965 led to a considerable

[33] *Third Five Year Plan*, p. 48.
[34] Quoted in *India News*, issued by the Information Service of India, Washington, November 22, 1963.

reorientation in the approach to the Fourth Plan. In October Finance Minister T. T. Krishnamachari said that the first year of the Fourth Plan would have to be treated as "a one-year emergency Plan with a defense bias" and that "we will have to depend largely on our own resources." Asoka Mehta, Deputy Chairman of the Planning Commission, stated that every effort would be made to implement the Plan as originally contemplated, and especially to step up agricultural production, but he warned that this would mean the mobilization of more resources internally, the observance of strictest economy in administration, and the postponement of all non-essential schemes.

Planning in Pakistan

Pakistan is one plan behind India in number, and considerably farther behind in terms of the magnitude and consistency of the planning efforts. Launched in 1956, the First Five Year Plan did not receive the formal approval of the Government until 1957, and it never received full support until the present Government came into power. It was a very modest plan, and even its target expenditures had to be scaled down by some 20 per cent because of exaggerated estimates of available financial resources, foreign and domestic. The total expenditures under the Plan were hardly more than $2 billion — about $1.3 billion in the public sector, and $705 million in the private sector, a ratio of nearly 65:35. Major emphasis was placed on industrialization, water and power development, transport and communications, and housing and settlements. Industrial development was quite impressive, especially in cotton textiles and sugar production. Substantial

■ TABLE 2: Pakistan's First and Second Five Year Plans, 1955–1965

Sectoral Distribution of Expenditures
(at 1960–61 prices, in millions of dollars)

	First Plan (Actual expen- diture)	Revised Second Plan (Proposed ex- penditure)	Percentage Increase
Agriculture	302.5	718	138
Water and power	483	922	91
Industry, fuels and minerals	861	1285	49
Transport and communications	479	850.5	78
Housing and settlements	542	716	32
Education and training	86	220.5	156
Health	29.5	88	200
Manpower and social welfare	10.5	29.5	180
TOTAL	2793.5	4829.5	73

Source: Planning Commission, Government of Pakistan, **Second Five Year Plan and Revised Estimates** (Pakistan: Author, November, 1961); adapted from table on p. 12.

progress was made in transport and communications, except for inland water transport and roads in East Pakistan. Housing and settlements received a real impetus only after the October 1958 "revolution," when some amazing results were achieved in record time. The water power and power development program fell considerably behind schedule. Because of a serious lag in agricultural production, Rs. 700 million of precious foreign exchange had to be spent for imported foodgrains, as compared with Rs. 410 million provided in the Plan. Instead of estimated increases in national income of 15 per cent and of per capita income of 7 per cent, the actual figures at the end of the Plan were 11 and 3 per cent, respectively. As explained in the Second Plan:

> Shortfalls in implementation of the Plan were due to several causes. Nondevelopment expenditures exceeded expectations; earnings of foreign exchange fell considerably short of the Plan projection; and arrivals of foreign aid were slower than expected. A considerable rise took place in both external and internal prices, upsetting the cost calculations included in the Plan. Adverse factors beyond the control of public policy and human effort, particularly unfavourable weather and the deterioration in the terms of trade, were exceptionally serious. Many projects took longer to complete than was expected, due chiefly to deficient advance planning, shortages of key personnel, equipment and materials, and ineffective coordination between government agencies. Above all, there was failure to observe the discipline of the Plan.[35]

The measure of achievement in the public sector can be attributed largely to the improved political situation after October 1958, and to the initiative of Ayub Khan and his associates. It is a striking fact that the targets of the First Plan in the private sector were slightly exceeded.

In preparing the Second Five Year Plan, the Planning Commission took a more realistic view of the needs and the resources of the country and the prospects of foreign aid, and produced a plan which, as it soon turned out, was overly modest. The main objectives of the Plan, summarized by President Ayub, were:

> First, we must increase the wealth of the country by a determined effort to raise our agricultural and industrial production. In agriculture, our primary aim must be to grow enough food on our own soil to feed the nation. . . . In industry, we must aim at substantial but selective development. . . . Second, we must earn our own living in the world by exporting more . . . and by making for ourselves more of the goods we have previously imported. . . . Third, we must provide work for our people. . . . Fourth, we must improve the social services — education, health, and housing especially. . . . Finally, we must do all we can to help the less prosperous areas of our country.[36]

As originally announced, the Second Plan called for an expenditure of slightly less than $4 billion — $2.4 billion in the government-financed sector, and $1.575 billion in the private-financed sector. A part of both the govern-

[35] *The Second Five Year Plan* (1960–65), pp. 2–3.
[36] Broadcast over Radio Pakistan, December 30, 1960.

ment and private contribution was allocated to a new sector, called the "semi-public sector." A year after the Second Plan was launched, it was revised and substantially enlarged, due to "under-estimation of the cost of several projects in the original Plan, increase in prices since 1959, and enlargement of the physical size of the Plan."[37] A number of changes were made in accordance with suggestions by a World Bank Mission, which visited Pakistan in January and February 1961. The revised version of the Plan raised the estimated expenditures to $4.8 billion — $2.6 billion in the public sector, about $800 million in the semi-public sector, and $1.428 billion in the private sector. In the public sector the emphasis was to be heavily on water and power, and then on transport and communications and agriculture. In both the semi-public and the private sectors, the main emphasis was to be on industrial development. The foreign exchange requirements were estimated at $2.3 billion.

During the period of the Second Plan it was estimated that an additional $693 million would be expended on the Indus Basin replacement works (the financing of which is specially provided for under the Indus Basin Development Fund Agreement of 1960) and $336 million on a "Works Programme." All of the amounts budgeted for the Works Program, and nearly one-third of the sums to be spent on the Indus Basin replacement works, would, it was anticipated, come from P.L. 480 counterpart funds.

The Third Plan, covering the years 1965–70, will be somewhat more than twice the size of the Second, involving an estimated expenditure of $9.9 billion, $6.7 billion for the public and $3.2 billion for the private sector. "The main aims of the Plan are to increase national income by 30 per cent and per capita income by 15 per cent, reducing per capita income disparity between East Pakistan and West Pakistan by 5 per cent, creating 5,000,000 new jobs for unskilled workers and moving toward a social welfare state."[38] Through additional taxation, increased exports, and other measures, it is hoped that the heavy dependence on foreign aid will be considerably reduced.

Agricultural Development

On the whole, the greatest disappointments in the implementation of the development programs of India and Pakistan have been in the crucial agricultural sector, comprising the major part of what Professor P. C. Mahalanobis has aptly termed "the diffuse sector." With very few exceptions, neither India nor Pakistan achieved the targets of agricultural production set for the Second and First Plans, respectively. In India the shortfall of production of foodgrains was nearly 3,000,000 tons. Both countries were forced to import

[37] Planning Commission, Government of Pakistan, *The Second Five Year Plan* (*Revised Estimates*) (Karachi: Author, November 1961), p. 9.
[38] Dispatch from Karachi in *The Asian Student* (San Francisco), February 8, 1964.

far more foodgrains than they had anticipated, with a consequent heavy drain on foreign exchange, which was badly needed to pay for imports for development purposes.

Self-sufficiency in food production must therefore be one of the major targets of the entire development efforts; and this is related to other aspects of agricultural development, with all their broader social and political implications.

Food Production and Other Targets

A major target of India and Pakistan is to achieve self-sufficiency in food-grains. For a time India's prospects in this vital sector looked quite bright. An important report in 1962, based on long-term projections, concluded that India would achieve self-sufficiency in foodgrains by the end of the Third Plan, and would have a surplus of about 6,000,000 tons by 1975–76, at the end of the Fifth Plan, with a daily consumption per capita of 18 instead of 16 ounces.[39] Other estimates, however, were much gloomier. A much-discussed report of an American agricultural team sponsored by the Ford Foundation, submitted in 1959,[40] presented an alarming picture of "India's Food Crisis," and estimated that India's foodgrain needs by 1965–66 would be around 105,000,000 tons annually. Other estimates were even higher, and the predictions of the possibility of reaching such targets even gloomier.

The gloomy forecasts proved to be the more accurate. At the end of the Third Five Year Plan India was far from self-sufficiency in foodgrains. The production of foodgrains did not increase at all in 1962, 1963, and 1964, due mainly to a series of bad harvests, but instead remained around the 80,000,000 tons a year mark, far below the requirements for self-sufficiency. The harvest of 1964–65 was fortunately a good one; but in all probability India cannot hope to achieve self-sufficiency in foodgrains for several years, perhaps not until the Sixth Plan period or even later, and another long period of bad harvests would make even this gloomy forecast impossible of achievement.

For some years Pakistan's food crisis seemed to be even more severe. When the First Five Year Plan was drawn up, it was estimated that 6,000,000 tons of foodgrains would have to be imported in the Plan period. The actual food imports during this period were about 20,000,000 tons. The First Plan called for an increase of 9 per cent in food production, a modest target indeed, but the actual increase, if any, was negligible. During the period of the Second Plan, however, the food picture brightened considerably, and by the end of the Plan in mid-1965 the Government of Pakistan claimed that it was close to self-sufficiency in food production.

[39] For a summary of this report, prepared by the National Council of Applied Economic Research and sponsored and financed by the U.S. Department of Agriculture, see *India News*, June 4, 1962.

[40] *Report on India's Food Crisis and Steps to Meet It*, by the Agricultural Production Team sponsored by the Ford Foundation (New Delhi: Ministry of Food and Agriculture, Government of India, April 1959).

Another major objective of the two countries is to increase substantially the production of commercial crops for export, chiefly cotton and jute. Since the production of these products, except sugarcane, has not increased significantly during the past ten years or more, increases in acreage and in production per acre, and improvements in organization and administration, will obviously be necessary.[41]

Agricultural development obviously involves far more than food production, important as this single factor is. In Pakistan's Second Plan, "Agriculture is viewed ... as a comprehensive operation which, in its broad sense, includes crop production, animal husbandry, fisheries, forestry, and the associated mechanisms such as land reforms, rural credit, cooperation, marketing, and Village AID" (for India substitute Community Development for Village AID).[42] It also includes important aspects of irrigation and power, village and small industries, housing and rural planning, and education and social services. Responsibility for the actual implementation of agricultural programs devolves more on the states of India and the provinces of Pakistan than on the central government and, in the last analysis, upon the agencies of Panchayati Raj and Basic Democracies.

Land Reform

Major efforts in land reform have been made in both India and Pakistan; yet, as India's Third Plan frankly confessed, "the total impact of land reform has been less than had been hoped for."[43] Every state of India has enacted legislation regarding land reform, and the Bhoodan and Gramdan movements of Vinoba Bhave have stressed land-giving and redistribution as a means toward higher goals. Intermediary tenures, like *zamindaris, jagirs,* and *inams,* which formerly controlled some 40 per cent of the country, have been abolished. Most states have passed legislation for the resumption of tenancies on ground of personal cultivation, for security of tenure, and for ceilings on land ownership. Except in five states, little progress has been made in the consolidation of holdings.

Substantial land reform was implemented in East Pakistan in the 1950s, especially in 1956, when the Government acquired all intermediary holdings. Since the Ayub Khan regime came into power further progress has been made, including compensation for the former owners or rent-receivers and consolidation of holdings. In West Pakistan, however, where much of the land was held by big landlords, many of them absentees, and where holdings were small and subject to frequent subdivision, almost nothing was done prior to October 1958. One of the first acts of Ayub Khan was to appoint a Land Reforms Commission; and in January 1959, almost immediately after the Commission made its report, "the Government announced its land re-

---

[41] *The Second Five Year Plan* (1960–65), p. 135.
[42] *Ibid.,* p. 127.
[43] *Third Five Year Plan,* p. 221.

forms policy . . ., imposing a ceiling on holdings, forbidding partition of economic and subsistence holdings, abolishing *jagirs* and other intermediate interests, making consolidation of holdings compulsory, assuring security of tenure to tenants, and conferring ownership rights on certain types of existing tenants."[44] This announcement seemed to herald a major political and social, as well as economic, revolution in West Pakistan.

If these reforms were fully implemented, they would deprive the big land-lords of West Pakistan of their political power by undermining their economic base, laying the basis for a new kind of existence for the millions of tenants and small proprietors of the Province. Trends in these directions can be seen, but to date the reforms have not been implemented on anything like the planned scale. Many of the large landowners have been able to retain a large part of their holdings by a kind of paper division among members of their families and by other devices, relatively few of the smaller farmers have been able to get full ownership rights to their lands, and the amount of land actually taken over by the Government, presumably for redistribution, has apparently been less than 3,000,000 acres, mostly uncultivated waste land.

Cooperatives

"In a planned economy pledged to the values of socialism and democracy," reads India's Third Five Year Plan, "cooperation should become progressively the principal basis of organisation in many branches of economic life, notably in agriculture and minor irrigation, small industry and processing, marketing, distribution, supplies, rural electrification, housing and construction, and the provision of essential amenities for local communities."[45] India now has some 75,000 service cooperatives, and by the end of the Third Plan it expects to have between 7,000 and 8,000 cooperative farming societies.

Pakistan places far less emphasis on cooperatives, but its Second Plan does refer to "the development of the cooperative movement," and it contains specific provisions for rural credit and marketing cooperatives, cooperative societies of fishermen, and cooperative farming societies. In East Pakistan, at least, cooperative societies seem to be spreading rapidly, under government encouragement, and some of the real leaders of the villages are officers in such societies.

Waterlogging and Salinity in Pakistan

Buried in a section of Pakistan's Second Plan, under the heading of "Drainage, reclamation, and tubewells," is the following significant passage:

> Salinity and waterlogging pose a serious threat to the national economy. It is estimated that over 50 per cent of the irrigated land is affected, an area

[44] *The Second Five Year Plan* (1960–65), p. 184.
[45] *Third Five Year Plan,* p. 200.

of some 12 million acres. . . the cost of drainage, creation of additional water supplies through storage, and revamping of the canal systems needed to deal with the problem effectively has been calculated to be as high as Rs. 25,000 million. Expenditures on this scale are clearly beyond the resources of the country. In the circumstances, measures to control and depress the water table, and to reclaim the land, will have to be spread over several Plan periods. This is an unfortunate position, since the great urgency of counteracting the menace of salinity and waterlogging is incontestable.[46]

In West Pakistan (in East Pakistan the problem is not a serious one), every year some 100,000 acres of formerly arable land become unfit for cultivation. The Second Plan allocates a small sum for measures to attempt to arrest this continuing loss, chiefly for the drilling of "strategically located tubewells," but it is doubtful if such small actions can even check the spread of the blight.

The United States is already deeply involved in the effort to devise ways and means to cope with waterlogging and salinity. For some years its experts have been working with Pakistan authorities on projects, such as drainage and tubewells, which are designed at least to arrest the loss of arable land. President Kennedy himself took an active interest in this problem. In July 1961 an American team headed by Dr. Jerome Wiesner, Special Assistant to the President for Science and Technology, visited Pakistan to make a special study of the problem of waterlogging and salinity. Nearly a year later it submitted a bulky report, which recommended a phased program over a period of twenty-five years, in which the affected land would be divided into twenty-five areas, with one area to be treated every year.

In view of the gravity of this problem, which is getting progressively more serious, immediate steps should be taken to implement a long-range program. These steps must of course be taken mainly by the Government of Pakistan and by Pakistani experts; but they obviously cannot be effective unless substantial outside technical and financial assistance is forthcoming. Apparently an effective program will take between ten and twenty-five years, and will cost between one and five billion dollars. This will dwarf even the Indus Basin development project, which calls for an expenditure of something like one billion dollars over a ten-year period. Perhaps the same countries which have pledged their support to the Indus Basin Development Fund, plus other countries and international agencies, should agree to set up a fund along similar lines and of even greater dimensions. It would be appropriate for the World Bank to assume the initiative, as it did in the canal waters dispute; in any event, steps should be taken immediately. The success of the project will depend largely on the United States, which will undoubtedly have to provide a major portion of the substantial sums required.

[46] *The Second Five Year Plan* (*1960–65*), p. 209.

Community Development and Panchayati Raj in India

On October 2, 1952 — Mahatma Gandhi's birthday — the Community Development Program was launched with great fanfare in certain parts of India. In the following year, with much less fanfare, the National Extension Service program was also inaugurated, as a means of extending the scope of the development efforts on a less intensive basis than the Community Development blocks. Eventually, the NES projects were to be absorbed in the Community Development Program. As a result of recommendations of the so-called Balvantray Mehta Report, the distinction between NES and CD blocks was dropped, and was replaced by a single scheme of community development spread over two stages.

The Third Plan, in 1961, reported that "The community development programme now serves over 3,100 development blocks comprising about 370,000 villages. Of these, about 880 blocks have been completed more than five years and entered the second stage of the community development programme. By October 1963, the programme will extend over the entire rural area of the country."[47] This date has repeatedly been postponed.

Impressive as were the undertakings in community development, one of the most widely publicized aspects of India's planning efforts, the program was in fact lagging badly in many parts of the country and in many important ways. Problems arose because of the unresolved question of the relations between the village-level workers, the block development officers, and officials of state administration and local bodies in rural India. Production targets were not being met. Above all, in spite of concentrated efforts, the program was failing at its most vital level, namely that of popular understanding and cooperation. Something had to be done to revive and rescue the lagging CD Program. This was one of the reasons for the appointment of the Balvantray Mehta Study Team, which was instructed to review the progress of the NES and CD Programs and to make recommendations for their improvement.

Taking a very liberal view of its mandate, the Study Team recommended what was in effect a radically different pattern of government and administration, as well as of development, in rural India — the Panchayati Raj system.[48] This system has now been introduced, in varying degrees and in varying forms, within the broad framework of a three-tier program in nearly all of the Indian states. As has been noted, this is much more than a development program, but all development efforts at the district and sub-district

---

[47] *Third Five Year Plan*, p. 332.

[48] *Report of the Team for the Study of Community Projects and National Extension Service* (Balvantray G. Mehta, Leader) (New Delhi: Committee on Plan Projects, Government of India, 1957), Vols. I and II (November 1957); vol. III (Parts I and II) (December 1957).

levels are now embraced within it. Thus, as the Third Plan stated, "the concept of rural extension has broadened into that of Panchayati Raj, that is to say, the development of a set of interconnected democratic and popular institutions at the village, block and district levels in which the representatives of the people in the Village Panchayats, Panchayat Samitis and Zila Parishads and cooperative organisations function with the support and assistance of the various development agencies of Government working as a team."[49]

The limited experience to date with Panchayati Raj suggests that it is indeed a major new factor in rural India, which has unlimited possibilities but which also may, like the Community Development Program, fail to live up to the hopes placed in it. No more comprehensive or ambitious program has been inaugurated in rural India, or in any other countryside; but no program has to face more formidable obstacles — created alike by human and physical limitations.

Village AID and Basic Democracies in Pakistan

In almost every respect, save in size and cost, Pakistan's program of Basic Democracies is as comprehensive and as ambitious as Panchayati Raj; and in certain respects it is even more so, for it extends beyond the district, and is conceived by some as providing also a framework for the political structure of the country. As a comprehensive program for the rural areas, however, it is strikingly similar to the Panchayati Raj system.

Like its counterpart, the Basic Democracies program has now absorbed what in Pakistan was known as Village AID (Agricultural and Industrial Development) Program. This step was taken largely for the same reasons, namely the lags in the Village AID program and its uncertain status with respect to "the nation-building departments," to use the language of Pakistan's Second Plan.

When the Second Plan was drawn up, it was assumed that Village AID would become a permanent organization associated with the Basic Democracies. However, when the revised estimates for the Plan were made public in November 1961, it was announced that Village AID was being disbanded, and that "its agricultural development functions are being taken over by the Agricultural Departments and (in the selected areas) by the Corporations [the Agricultural Development Corporations which have been established in the two wings] and its other functions by the Basic Democracies."[50]

The impact and implications of these changes and developments cannot yet be properly appraised, but again we are reminded that food production leads to many other aspects of agricultural development, that community development is an important agency for agricultural development, and that

[49] *Third Five Year Plan,* p. 332.
[50] *The Second Five Year Plan (Revised Estimates),* p. 11.

through community development, and, above all, through Panchayati Raj and Basic Democracies, agricultural development becomes a part of the even more important work of rural uplift and nation-building.

Industrialization

In happy contrast to the limited progress in agricultural production and development, India and Pakistan have forged ahead rapidly in the industrial field. In India industrial production nearly doubled during the period of the First and Second Five Year Plans. During substantially the same period Pakistan achieved a fivefold increase in production in large-scale manufacturing industries, in spite of shortages of foreign exchange and other difficulties. In India the rate of industrial growth averaged between 9 and 10 per cent a year in the decade of the 1950s. In Pakistan the announced rate of industrial growth was 6.6 per cent in 1957 and 1958, 11.6 per cent in 1959, and 12.4 per cent in 1960, and it has maintained these high levels since 1960. In fact, Pakistan's achievements in the industrial field have been characterized as an "economic miracle."

Indian and Pakistani Approaches to Industrial Development

India and Pakistan give the appearance of seeking to deal with roughly similar problems of industrial development in different ways. As has been indicated, India is giving increasing emphasis to the public sector, whereas Pakistan is relying more heavily on the private sector; but both countries are in fact developing a mixed economy. In setting forth the basic policies of the Government of India, the Industrial Policy Resolution of 1956 stated that it was necessary "to expand the public sector, and to build up a large and growing co-operative sector." The resolution announced the Government's decision to classify industries into three categories. Industries in the first category would be "the exclusive responsibility of the State." These included iron and steel, heavy plant and machinery, heavy electrical plant, coal and lignite, as well as most types of mining and minerals, atomic energy, defense production, air, rail, and ship transport, communications, and electricity. Industries in the second category would be "progressively State-owned," with private enterprise expected to "supplement the effort of the State." These included almost all other minerals, aluminum, machine tools, antibiotics and "other essential drugs," fertilizers, chemical pulp, road and sea transport. The Resolution insisted, however, that "the private sector will have the opportunity to develop and expand."

The Third Plan took what appeared to be a more conciliatory and less rigid view:

With the rapid expansion of the economy, wider opportunities of growth arise for both the public and private sectors and in many ways their activities are complementary. The private sector includes not only organised industry but agriculture, small industry, trade and a great deal of activity in housing construction and other fields. . . . It is mainly within a limited area in the field of large-scale industrial enterprise that the question arises whether, in the special circumstances of the country, in accordance with the Industrial Policy Resolution of April, 1956, and in view of the social goals aimed at, particular tasks should be assigned to the public sector or to the private sector. In the context of the country's planned development the private sector has a large area in which to develop and expand.[51]

By contrast, Pakistan's Second Plan states, "it is a basic assumption of the Plan that for the implementation of the industrial development programme, reliance will be placed primarily on private enterprise." "The cardinal principle," states the Plan, in what seems to be an oblique criticism of the Indian approach, "is that there should be no public industrial sector in the sense of reservation of complete industries for public enterprise, but that the Government should remain generally responsible for promoting all industries by providing the required facilities, and should directly participate only in those enterprises which are essential for overall development and where private capital is not forthcoming or high considerations of national security intervene."[52]

In spite of the announced aversion of the Government of Pakistan to an excessive expansion of the public sector and to "strangulating" controls, businessmen in Pakistan complain almost as bitterly as do those in India about such controls, especially about the rigidities of the licensing system and the difficulties and delays in obtaining permits. Pakistan, like India, is in danger of becoming a "license-permit-control Raj," to use a term which Rajagopalachari and other spokesmen of the Swantantra Party in India have popularized.

Industrial Priorities, Targets, and Production

The relative results of the Indian and Pakistani approaches to industrial development will be watched with absorbing interest in South Asia and elsewhere. Both countries have drawn up basic priorities for industrial development. During the Third Plan period the largest sums were expended in India on steel mills, heavy machinery and heavy electrical plants, oil refineries, plants for making antibiotics and other drugs, carbonization plants, fertilizer factories, ship-building, aluminum plants, automobile and ancillary industries, heavy chemicals, newsprint factories, cement plants, oil exploration, textile industries, and sugar production. In Pakistan, during the Second Plan period, the largest appropriations in the public and private sectors were for sugar mills, woolen and cotton mills, jute mills, fertilizer factories, oil refineries, cement plants, and steel mills.

Almost certainly the remarkable industrial growth of India and Pakistan

[51] *Third Five Year Plan,* pp. 7–8.
[52] *The Second Five Year Plan* (*1960–65*), pp. 225–226.

in recent years will continue. There are, however, grounds for doubt that the targets of the current Plans in many of the vital industrial sectors can be achieved.

At the end of the Third Plan India had significant shortfalls in the production of iron and steel, fertilizers, textile machinery, aluminum, dyestuffs, and other crucial products. Continuing problems and shortages of foreign exchange plague all efforts at industrial development. Construction of plants and other facilities almost always takes longer than anticipated, and the costs are invariably much higher than the original estimates.

The shortages in coal, power, and transport are particularly serious. Production of coal was increased from 38.3 million tons in 1955 to 54.6 million tons in 1960–61, but by the latter date the target was 60 million tons. The target for 1965–66, the last year of the Third Plan, was 97 million tons, but it was not attained. The steel mills and other large industries are already feeling the pinch of the coal shortage, which will almost certainly get worse in the next few years. Industries consume more than three-fifths of all the electricity generated in India. Total generating capacity more than doubled during the course of the Third Five Year Plan — from about 5.7 million kilowatts to about 12.7 million — but even this ambitious increase was inadequate for India's total power needs by 1965–66. The rapid development of the economy has placed new strains on the already overburdened transport system, especially upon the railways, which are faced with the problem of "the rehabilitation of overaged assets," to use the gentle language of the Third Plan, as well as with the addition of new lines and equipment.

Pakistan, like India, is faced with serious shortages of fuel, transport, and power, as well as of foreign exchange. The long search for oil, which thus far has led to disappointing results in its main objective, did uncover large fields of natural gas. The fields at Sui and Mari "are capable of providing West Pakistan with ample quantities of gaseous fuel and petro-chemical raw materials for many decades."[53] Coal production is low and inadequate. The railways of Pakistan, which were in an appalling condition at the beginning of the First Plan, are still handicapped by overage rolling stock, inefficient operation, and inadequate facilities generally. Rapid improvements are being made in roads and road transport, especially important in West Pakistan, and in inland water transport in East Pakistan, most of which is a vast delta. Electric power generating capacity is being rapidly expanded. Most of the increased capacity in East Pakistan comes from the Karnaphuli hydroelectric station, built by American engineers, largely from American funds. Additional capacity in West Pakistan comes mainly from hydroelectric and thermal plants in the Indus Basin, and from thermal stations in and near Karachi.

The increasing diversification of industry in India is reflected in the rapid

[53] *The Second Five Year Plan* (*1960–65*), p. 269.

growth of small-scale as well as medium-sized and large industries. The National Small Industries Corporation and the Khadi and Village Industries Commission are actively promoting and assisting the development of village and small industries. The Third Plan allocates Rs. 264 crores for this purpose, more than half of which will be spent by the states.[54] The largest expenditures, in order of size, will be for khadi (hand-woven cloth) and village industries, small-scale industries, the handloom industry, and industrial estates. The popularity of the industrial estates is attested by the fact that 60 of these estates were set up during the Second Plan period, about 300 during the Third Plan years. In contrast to the older industrial estates, which were usually located near large cities, the new ones are being located as far as possible near small- and medium-sized towns, and even in selected rural areas where essential facilities are available.[55]

Pakistan's Second Plan frankly admitted that in the First Plan period "the major problems of small industries remained unsolved because of lack of a concerted effort to tackle them." The problems were stated to be "weakness in organization for production and marketing; shortage of raw materials, spares and equipment; credit difficulties; inadequate marketing facilities; lack of standardization; and deficiencies in production facilities."[56] A Provincial Small Industries Corporation has been set up in each Province. One of the responsibilities of these Corporations is to promote the establishment of industrial estates, for which the Second Plan allocated Rs. 75 million. Most of the estates have been located in West Pakistan, by far the more heavily industrialized part of the country. To right this imbalance the Plan allocated Rs. 60 million for industrial estates to East Pakistan. The main responsibility for the development of these estates, however, rests with the private sector.

Public Enterprises

More than 100 public corporations and other state enterprises are now operating in India. In addition to those which have long existed in power, transport, communication, and other public utilities, these include such gigantic state corporations as the controversial Damodar Valley Corporation, a kind of Indian T.V.A.; Hindustan Steel, which supervises the huge steel plants in the public sector at Rourkela, Durgapur and Bhilai; the State Trading Corporation, which is becoming increasingly active in foreign trade, especially with the Communist countries; the National Industrial Development Corporation, which is concerned with the establishment of new industries, and in many cases with their transference to private hands; the Small Industries Corporation; the National Coal Development Corporation; the

---

[54] A crore is 10,000,000 (a lakh is 100,000). "Rs. 10 crore" would be ten crores of rupees, or approximately $21 million.

[55] See P. C. Alexander, *Industrial Estates in India* (Bombay: Asia Publishing House, 1963).

[56] *The Second Five Year Plan* (*1960–65*), pp. 255–256.

Life Insurance Corporation; Hindustan Machine Tools; the Heavy Engineering Corporation; the Heavy Electricals Corporation; Hindustan Antibiotics; Bharat Electronics; the Chittaranjan Locomotive Works; and the Sindri Fertilizer Factory. Many public corporations also exist in the states.[57]

State enterprises in India normally fall into one of three categories: (1) those under Departmental management, such as the Chittaranjan Locomotive Works; (2) statutory corporations, such as the Damodar Valley Corporation, or the Life Insurance Corporation; and (3) joint-stock companies, organized under the Indian Companies Act. The third category is the most common form, and includes such enterprises as Hindustan Steel and the State Trading Corporation. A fourth form, probably transitory, is for state enterprises to be supervised by control boards, a pattern which has been followed in the actual planning and implementation of two of the largest of all the multipurpose river valley development projects, the Bhakra-Nangal and the Hirakud projects.[58]

A great many questions have been raised about the desirability of state enterprises, the form which they should take, their proper scope and functions, and their management and administration. Moreover, there is considerable confusion regarding "the proper relationship between the public body and the chief executive" of a public enterprise. "If the chief executive is subjected to a force outside the organization, he will no longer think automatically of the goals of the organization. Exposed to constant public scrutiny, the management will be afraid of making the day-to-day decisions necessary in commercial operations and the organisation will be virtually stifled by red tape and bureaucracy."[59]

Dissatisfaction with the public enterprises, especially with such controversial enterprises as the Damodar Valley Corporation or the State Trading Corporation or Hindustan Steel, has often been voiced in India. The Estimates Committee of the Lok Sabha has made scathing criticisms, especially of the Damodar Valley Corporation and the State Trading Corporation, and the parliament has established an important new Committee on Public Undertakings.

Until recently, at least, there was a curious ambivalence of attitude on the question of profits in public enterprises. A prevalent feeling seemed to be that "profits were somehow shameful, and it were better that the public

[57] See 122nd Report of the Estimates Committee, on the National Industrial Development Corporation (New Delhi: Lok Sabha Secretariat, March 1961).

[58] M. V. Pylee, "Government Enterprises in the Indian Economy," *Asian Survey*, September 1961, pp. 16–26. "The Bhakra Nangal was executed by the Punjab State through its public works department and Hirakud (in Orissa State) was executed directly by the Central Government, in accordance with the departmental code. Both were under the supervision of non-statutory Control Boards." Venkatasubbiah, *Indian Economy Since Independence*, p. 128.

[59] R. C. Joshi, "Problems of Administration," *The Times of India*, February 20, 1962.

sector did not sully itself with them."[60] In any event, the primary purpose of public enterprises, it was felt, was to serve some social or noncommercial purpose, and the test of the efficiency should be service and not profits. There is a growing feeling in India, however, that the provision of needed social services does not exempt a public enterprise from being operated on a sound commercial basis as far as possible, and that profits, far from being shameful or undesirable, are definitely desirable. "It is held that it is the duty of public enterprises not only to make profits, but also to strive for even bigger ones, so as to contribute as much as possible to the development funds available for the Five-Year Plans."[61] Profits — i.e., surplus earnings — of these enterprises range from nearly 10 per cent, which the State Trading Corporation was reported to have earned in 1961–62, to nothing, and of course many operate at a monetary loss.[62]

Pakistan too has a number of important public enterprises. Some of these, like the Water and Power Development Authorities, and the Karachi Gas Company, are classed in the public sector, while others, which have a greater degree of autonomy and which derive a part of their resources from other than government sources, are classed in the semi-public sector. Among the central agencies in the semi-public sector are the Pakistan Industrial Development Corporation, the Small Industries Corporation, Pakistan International Airlines Corporation, the Port Trusts in Karachi and Chittagong, the Karachi Electric Supply Corporation, the Karachi Development Authority, and similar provincial agencies.

Some of the public enterprises in India may be more accurately described as semi-public sector undertakings, for they involve nonofficial participation in various significant ways. Several of the institutions which provide financial assistance to Indian industry and for other development purposes may properly be described as semi-public agencies, though not the three major public financial institutions — the Reserve Bank, the State Bank, and the Life Insurance Corporation.

The most hybrid arrangement of all is the Industrial Credit and Investment Corporation of India. "The I.C.I.C.I. is an international, 'mixed' and private venture. There is both Indian and foreign investment in the equity part of its capital structure and internal and external public finance in the loan part of it."[63] It has been very active in promoting and partially financing large- and medium-sized industries in India, and has been helpful in obtaining foreign exchange.

[60] R. Leslie Mitchell, "Profits and the Public Sector: I — Social Purposes," *The Times of India,* March 17, 1962.

[61] *Ibid.*

[62] According to *The Times of India* of March 16, 1962, the return on an investment of approximately Rs. 870 crores in State enterprises was expected to be no more than 0.4 per cent in the coming year.

[63] Venkatasubbiah, *Indian Economy Since Independence,* p. 176.

The Pakistan equivalent is P.I.C.I.C., the Pakistan Industrial Credit and Investment Corporation. The Government has also set up a Pakistan Industrial Development Bank and an Investment Promotion Bureau. The P.I.D.C. has taken the initiative in the development of many needed industries and has turned these over as speedily as possible to the private sector. It has made direct investments of equity capital in industries, ranging from 100 per cent to 10 per cent or even less and has associated in joint ventures, in which foreign companies also have an equity interest.

Planning in South Asia: Plans and Performance

Few if any answers to the basic questions relating to the development plans of India and Pakistan can be found by a detailed examination of the voluminous plans or of the statistical and other data accumulated by the Planning Commissions. Among the basic questions are these: Is the overall pattern of and approach to planning in these countries the right one, under the existing circumstances? Are the plans sound and realistic? What are the prospects for their success, in non-economic as well as in economic terms, in terms of long-run objectives as well as in the achievement of specific targets? What will be the consequences if they fall far short of success? What, indeed, will be the consequences if they succeed?

Obviously no really valid answers can be given to these basic questions. The answers which any observer will give will depend upon his own attitudes and interests, and upon his own assessment of the relative importance of the factors which he believes are most vital. Even a skilled economist will be influenced largely by such considerations, and he will doubtless be forced to conclude that the answers will depend more upon non-economic than upon economic factors. Although the Plans were prepared on the basis of the most competent economic advice available, and on the basis of a painstaking accumulation of relevant data, one gets the impression that they rest even more on hope and faith than on economic forecasting.

India's First Plan was hardly a plan, and was very modest in its dimensions. The Second reflected a rather doctrinaire approach, and seemed to give excessive emphasis to industrialization; it was only a partial success, for it ran into serious difficulties, some of which could not have been anticipated, and its targets had to be scaled down considerably. The Third Plan was far more ambitious, and seemingly more realistic; but its implementation was slowed down by serious shortages in such fundamental things as foodgrains, coal, transport, power — and foreign exchange — and by the new demands and stresses occasioned by the Chinese attack of October-November 1962. Many of its targets were not realized.

Pakistan's First Plan contained some shockingly bad cost estimates and other unrealistic features, and its implementation was adversely affected by the deteriorating political situation in the country in the first half of the Plan period. The Second Plan was more carefully prepared, with far greater support from more effective political leaders under more favorable political conditions; but sustantial revisions had to be made in it within the first year after it was officially launched.

Both countries are woefully short of trained administrators and technicians, and the political and educational and administrative systems are still inadequate and far too rigid for the needs of a developing economy. The growing shortage of foreign exchange, an inescapable concomitant of economic development, and the difficulties of raising the level of exports, have led to a growing dependence on foreign assistance, which raises all kinds of problems and complications. Large sections of the Plans are relatively unplanned. It is particularly difficult to make detailed estimates for the private sector, which accounts for most of the actual productivity of each country. There is a wide gap between stated objectives and planned programs, and an even wider gap between plans and performance. And there is always the haunting fear that India and Pakistan are not doing enough, perhaps because they cannot do enough, and are not getting enough outside assistance, to ensure their national survival or to meet even the minimal needs of a growing population.

For the actual implementation and support of the Plans, the leaders and planners of the central governments of India and Pakistan have had to rely heavily on the states and the provinces, as well as on the private sector, and on the people generally. The private sector, to be sure, has more than fulfilled its allocated share of the Plans, but the proper balance and relationship between private and public sectors are delicate problems at best, and the private sector encompasses the larger part of economic activity in rural India. The states and the provinces have constantly lagged in their development responsibilities; and yet the Central Government must depend on them for the implementation of most of the planned programs, and for the mobilization of a substantial part of the needed internal resources. The greatest failure of all has probably been the failure to enlist the widespread cooperation of the people in the work of planning. If these are "people's plans," this fact is more apparent and more generally accepted in New Delhi and Karachi than it is in the countryside.

No underdeveloped country has made more progress in democratic planning and its implementation than has India; and Pakistan has not lagged far behind. In spite of the deficiencies in their planning, and the obstacles to development in their own societies, the results of their planning efforts have been truly impressive. From the beginning the Plans have been in the public domain. They have been prepared and implemented in consultation with a fantastically large number of presumably qualified specialists and interested agencies and organizations, in the private as well as the public sector, and from many foreign countries, and in draft outline the Plans have been submitted to public scrutiny and criticism.

"The primary question in assessing the realism of any national plan," stated a report on planning in Pakistan issued by Political and Economic Planning in London, "is whether it is too ambitious in relation to the available resources." Measured by this standard, both India's and Pakistan's Plans are quite ambitious, but, as the PEP report concluded regarding Pakistan's Second Plan, "not wildly out of scale with the resources, foreign and indigenous, which are likely to be available."[64] India's Third Plan was nearly five times as large as Pakistan's Second Plan, but this is roughly in proportion to the relative size, population, and resources of the two countries.

If the yardstick to be applied is need rather than available resources, then neither India nor Pakistan is planning on a sufficiently ambitious scale. Possibly the two countries, by more rigorous measures, still within the framework of democratic planning, could mobilize greater human and financial resources for development purposes within their borders and they might be able to raise even larger sums from foreign sources. Although the needs are so great, however, there are limits to the absorptive capacity of the economies of India and Pakistan, under existing conditions; both countries, in fact, have had difficulty in using all the funds that have been available to them. Moreover, there are limits to the amounts of foreign assistance that can be obtained.

With the growing demands for development and for internal consumption for a large and expanding population, living at or close to the subsistence level, the problem of the mobilization and allocation of scarce resources, human as well as natural, will inevitably become, to use a phrase in common currency in South Asia, "almost intractable." Under these circumstances, much of the current discussion of the prospects for "take-off to self-sustaining growth" in India and Pakistan seems to represent hope rather than reality. In his much-discussed book, *The Stages of Economic Growth*, W. W. Rostow expressed the belief that India had entered the "take-off" stage in the early 1950s, at the beginning of its Five Year Plans, and that Pakistan was "likely to be less than a decade behind — or at least not much more."[65] If so, both countries are still in the process of taking off.

[64] "Planning in Pakistan," *Planning* (London), April 20, 1959, pp. 330, 331.
[65] W. W. Rostow, *The Stages of Economic Growth* (Cambridge: Cambridge University Press, 1960), pp. 38, 126.

CHAPTER FIVE

Foreign Economic Relations

As the pace of economic development quickens, India and Pakistan will become increasingly part of the world economy. The success or failure of their development efforts will of course depend primarily on themselves, but they will be greatly affected, for better or for worse, by the economic policies of the more developed nations, and by trends in the world economy. They must look abroad for essential materials and supplies insufficiently available at home, for markets for their exports, for capital, and especially for foreign exchange to supplement their own capital resources, and for technical assistance and cooperation.

The Foreign Exchange Dilemma

Their foreign exchange dilemma is particularly acute. An inescapable feature of the "crisis of development," it must be largely resolved before they can hope to reach a self-sustaining stage, in which they will not have to depend unduly on foreign assistance, except through the normal channels of international finance. For some years the terms of trade — the ratio of import and export prices — have been running against them, and will continue to do so as long as their imports increase rapidly while their exports are relatively stagnant. The unfavorable balance of trade of course adds to their foreign exchange problems. They must have foreign exchange not only for "development imports," but also for "maintenance imports," and even for what might be called "survival imports," for they have been forced to use some of their scarce foreign exchange to pay for substantial imports of foodgrains. They can obtain some credits from the World Bank and the Export-Import Bank; but these agencies will make loans only for certain specified purposes, their interest rates are high, and the principal must be repaid, often in a relatively short time. Some foreign capital is made available by private foreign enterprise, but thus far this has been too small to have any appreciable effect. This means that for the bulk of the needed

107

foreign exchange India and Pakistan must rely on foreign assistance — soft loans and grants — on a large scale.

In each of the preceding Plan periods the foreign exchange needs have been greater than the original estimates. During India's Second Plan, for example, the balance of payments deficit was about $4.62 billion, as compared with Plan estimates of $2.3 billion. This was financed by external assistance amounting to somewhat over $2.9 billion, by drawing on the foreign exchange reserves to the amount of nearly $1.25 billion, and by a draft on the International Monetary Fund for $115.5 million. The balance of payments gap for the Third Plan period was estimated in the Draft Outline of the Plan, made public in May 1960, at $6.7 billion. It will probably be considerably higher. The gap during the Third Plan period will, it is assumed, be covered almost wholly by foreign assistance. The foreign exchange reserves are at a dangerously low level, and presumably none will be drawn upon to help to provide the foreign exchange requirements of the Third Plan.

India and Pakistan look to the United States, their main source of foreign assistance and their second best market, for understanding and help in dealing with their foreign exchange problems. They would appreciate American support in obtaining more foreign private investment in their economies, and "hard loans" from the Export-Import Bank and the World Bank. The amount of foreign private investment that can be attracted to South Asia in the near future is, however, clearly quite limited, and India and Pakistan are in no position to meet the terms and conditions of "hard loans" on an extensive scale. Their main reliance, which they regret as much as the United States and other donor countries, must for the present be upon soft loans and grants, which they hope will be made available in generous amounts and without political or other "strings," aside from those which they can accept as reasonable and not affronting their sovereignty or dignity. Above all, they would like the United States and other developed countries to provide greater help in expanding their exports and in obtaining easier access to foreign markets, and thereby to give more reality to the oft-expressed aim of "trade, not aid."

Foreign Trade

A developing economy usually has an unbalanced foreign trade, but this statement of natural economic fact does not ease the foreign trade dilemma faced by India and Pakistan. They must earn substantial amounts of foreign exchange through trade surpluses, if they are ever to free themselves of the heavy dependence on foreign aid; yet their present trade patterns impose a further drain on their available foreign exchange.

Trade Patterns

The annual average value of India's imports was $1.5 billion during the period of the First Five Year Plan and $2.25 billion during the Second Plan. The estimated average annual value during the Third Plan was $2.67 billion. Thus, as the size of India's Plans expand, so too do the import requirements. Indian exports, however, present a very different picture. For more than a decade their average annual value hovered around $1.25 billion. Since 1962 they have showed a steady upward trend. This trend is encouraging, but it is due in part to rises in price, and it is far below the export level of $2.94 billion which the Indian planners hope to reach within the next five years.

Pakistan's trade pattern is in some ways even more dismal, although export earnings seem to be increasing slightly. The First Plan provided for foreign exchange earnings of $2.2 billion and for imports, developmental and nondevelopmental, including food, of $3.5 billion. Because foreign earnings were actually about 10 percent below estimates, foreign exchange expenditures on imports had to be reduced drastically, and this reduction was "a principal factor accounting for shortfalls in implementation of the Plan." The situation was made even worse by a sharp deterioration in the terms of trade and by a serious food shortage. The outlook for the Second Plan period was not very hopeful:

> Export earnings are expected to increase by 15 per cent during the Plan period. . . . But despite maximum efforts to increase exports and to save on imports through import substitution, there will still be a large gap between foreign exchange earnings and the import requirements of the economy under the Plan. The gap is estimated at Rs. 8,000 million: Rs. 1,500 million for general balance of payments support and Rs. 6,500 for the import requirements of the development programmes of the Plan. It will also be necessary to import Rs. 1,000 million worth of foodgrains before self-sufficiency is reached by the end of the Plan period. In addition, Rs. 700 million worth of other agricultural commodities will be required under U.S. Public Law 480 to generate rupee funds to finance a part of the rupee cost of the Indus Basin replacement works.[1]

India's two major exports, by far, are tea and jute manufactures, which have each averaged somewhat more than $250 million for many years. In 1960 these two items alone accounted for more than one-third of India's total exports. Next came cotton textiles, which in 1963 showed an increase for the first time in several years. Pakistan's main exports are the same as India's, with the addition of raw jute and raw cotton, but the proportions are somewhat different. Raw jute is by far the major export item; in 1960 it brought in nearly 45 per cent of Pakistan's export earnings, and jute manufactures

[1] Planning Commission, Government of Pakistan, *The Second Five Year Plan* (1960–65) (Karachi: Author, June 1960) pp. 81–82.

accounted for another 13 per cent. East Pakistan is credited with some 70 per cent of the total export earnings. West Pakistan's main export items are raw cotton, cotton textile, and raw wool.

In the international trade of the two countries, the United Kingdom and the United States play an almost dominating role. Imports from and exports to these nations have varied considerably in recent years. For example, 18.5 per cent of India's imports came from the United Kingdom in 1952, 25 per cent in 1956, and 20 per cent in 1960. For imports from the United States the percentages for the same years were 33.6, 11.3 and 23.7, respectively. These marked variations can be explained mainly by food imports to meet India's changing needs. Indian exports to the United Kingdom were 20.5 per cent of the total in 1952, 29.8 in 1956, and 27.5 in 1960. For exports to the United States the comparable percentages were 19, 14.7, and 16.

For India, "the structure of imports now follows a fairly uniform pattern — plant and machinery accounting for 17½ per cent, industrial raw materials for 67 per cent and consumer goods including foodgrains just over 15 per cent."[2] Consumer goods have been a far greater percentage of Pakistan's imports; during the past decade they have almost invariably been at least double the combined total value of imports of capital goods and industrial raw materials.

Trade Restrictions

The foreign trade of both India and Pakistan is subject to strict government supervision and control, through licensing, quotas, and other requirements, in the interest of the objectives of the development programs. Not only is this a result of the serious foreign exchange problem and the necessity of utilizing all available resources for national development and survival, but also to some extent of economic and social ideology. A report by the Economic Research Service of the United States Department of Agriculture, issued in June 1960, thus described the foreign trade policies of the two countries:

> India's foreign trade policy may be described as one of permitting carefully selected imports and of encouraging but controlling exports along with organized export promotion of specific commodities. It includes supplementary imports of essential raw and semimanufactured materials not produced in sufficient quantities indigenously, and allows large imports of equipment and machinery needed for its development projects; but it provides for tight controls over nonessential items and consumer goods. Tariffs and duties are used only as a subsidiary means of trade control and to earn revenue for the Indian treasure . . . .
> Pakistan's foreign trade is controlled by means of quotas and licensing. Import tariffs are used to protect domestic industry and to earn revenue for the

[2] "Import & Export Position During 1961," *India News* (issued by the Information Service of India, Washington), May 18, 1962. These figures are suspiciously exact, but the general trend seems clear.

treasury. Export duties are maintained on jute and cotton and are an important source of revenue.[3]

India's trade policies were reviewed and to some extent revised in the light of the recommendations of the Report of the Import and Export Policy Committee (A. Ramaswami Mudaliar, Chairman) in the spring of 1962. The Committee made more than one hundred recommendations, some of them of a rather sweeping nature. Pakistan has been moving toward a policy of increasing liberalization of its import and export policies.

India is trying to achieve a proper balance between development and maintenance imports. Its already heavy emphasis on the imports of capital goods and industrial raw materials needed for development projects will in all probability become further accentuated, if the imports of foodgrains can be reduced substantially. In response to pressures from Indian businessmen and from other sources, the Government of India announced in the spring of 1962 that a system of annual, instead of semi-annual, licensing will be followed as far as possible, subject to the availability of foreign exchange. At the same time it reduced the import quotas on a large number of items, presumably because these were being manufactured in India to a greater extent.

When the present regime assumed power in Pakistan in October 1958, it immediately imposed severe import restrictions; but these have been steadily relaxed and liberalized since then, with encouraging results. This has been particularly the case since the introduction of the Export Bonus Scheme in January 1959, and of a new licensing system in January 1960. At least one-third of all import items now have been placed under an automatic licensing system, and many items have been placed under "Open General License."[4]

Export Promotion

If a developing country is ever to reach the stage of relative self-sustaining growth, it must earn substantial amounts of foreign exchange through exports. Yet, because of external as well as internal factors, this is a particularly difficult objective to achieve. Professor J. K. Galbraith has referred to the "inherent economic disadvantage of exports in the developing economy," and he has declared that if he had "to single out the major problem of a development economy it would be that of maintaining a satisfactory rate of increase in exports and export earnings."[5] In the export field India and Pakistan are faced with very special and very serious problems. The record of the past decade and more is mainly one of stagnation, and there

[3] Economic Research Service, U.S. Department of Agriculture, *Notes on the Agricultural Economies of the Far East: II — South Asia* (Washington: Author, June 1960), pp. 18, 25.

[4] Agra M. Ghouse, *The Economy of Pakistan: A Review* (Lahore: Assembly Chambers, 1961), pp. 49–50.

[5] Address in Shillong, Assam, April 28, 1962. See also *Economic Survey of Asia and the Far East, 1961*, United Nations Publication 62.II.F.1, p. 89.

are few hopeful signs on the horizon. They are at a serious disadvantage in world markets, where the competition is getting keener every year. And internal needs and demands often compete or conflict with export priorities.

India's Third Five Year Plan calls for export earnings of $7.77 billion, an annual average of about $1.55 billion. Since actual export earnings were well below $1.55 billion until 1963, India is clearly behind its targets in this vital area. India may in fact have difficulty in maintaining present levels of exports of its major export items, tea, jute manufacture, and cotton piece-goods. Prices of these items fluctuate considerably in the world markets, and they are in other ways particularly vulnerable. Many other countries compete for the world markets in tea. Pakistan is a major competitor in jute production, and a number of other countries are establishing jute mills. Cotton textiles must face the formidable competition of long-time producers, such as the English mills, and the Japanese are having increasing success in competing for foreign markets for their textile products. The internal demands for all of these items are growing rapidly, requiring important governmental decisions regarding the relative allocation for internal consumption versus exports.

As the government is well aware, if India is to increase substantially its earnings from exports, it will have to give special attention to export promotion. The Third Plan itself mentions a variety of proposals. "The primary object of the general policies envisaged in support of the export programme is to create the necessary climate in the country for the export effort, to restrain domestic demands and enlarge surpluses available for exports, and to reduce production costs."[6] The Plan calls attention to a number of measures that had already been taken to promote exports:

> The measures in question were fairly widely conceived and included organisational changes, increased facilities and incentives and diversification of trade. To the first group belong Export Promotion Councils, which have been set up for cotton textiles, silk and rayon, engineering goods, chemicals, tobacco, spices, cashew, leather, plastics, sports goods and mica; establishment of the Export Risks Insurance Corporation; assignment to Commodity Boards for tea, coffee and coir of duties of Export Promotion Councils; and increased facilities for publicity, fairs, exhibitions, etc. In the second group may be mentioned measures such as the removal of export controls and quota restrictions, abolition of most export duties, refund of excise duties, special import licenses for raw materials for exports, and priorities for transport facilities. Thirdly, through the activities of the State Trading Corporation and development of trading relations with U.S.S.R. and countries in Eastern Europe, there has been progress in the diversification of India's foreign trade.[7]

The Mudaliar Committee suggested a large number of measures to promote exports, including tax relief incentives, a rebate by the railways on

[6] Planning Commission, Government of India, *Third Five Year Plan* (New Delhi: Author, 1961), p. 139.
[7] *Ibid*, p. 136.

goods destined for export, a revolving fund to enable export-oriented industries to obtain adequate supplies of essential raw materials, the setting up of an Export Stabilization Board, and measures designed to reduce administrative formalities and delays. A few of the recommendations of the Committee have been rejected, but many have already been adopted and others are still under study. The Export Promotion Councils and the Commodity Boards have been particularly active, and their activities have been encouraged by the Ministry for International Trade, which was created after the third general election in 1962, with Manubhai Shah as the Minister. The Government of India has also announced that it intends to set up a Board of Trade somewhat along the lines of the British Board of Trade, export promotion cells in all of the central Ministeries concerned with exports, and four regional directorates of export promotion in the United States, Europe, Africa, and East and Southeast Asia. In January 1964 Mr. Shah announced the formation of the Export Credit and Guarantee Corporation, which he said would be a "vital and integral part of the export promotion machinery of the country."

The State Trading Corporation, established in 1956, is a major agency for the promotion of trade, especially with the Soviet Union and Eastern Europe. It has been able to increase the volume of trade in certain commodities, such as iron ore and manganese, through bilateral negotiations with a number of countries, including the United States and Japan, and it has been instrumental in obtaining such needed materials as chemicals, fertilizers, and cement. It has even given some encouragement to small Indian industries which are interested in marketing some of their products abroad. In many respects it seems to be functioning effectively and to be meeting a real need. The Mudaliar Committee commented favorably on its work. Its surplus of 9 per cent of investment in 1961–62 was perhaps the highest in any public enterprise. The S.T.C. has, however, been much criticized, notably by the Estimates Committee of the Lok Sabha, in its 86th Report. Many Indians wonder whether such an organization is compatible with the objectives of democratic planning and practice. Indian businessmen seem to feel that the S.T.C. is a competing rather than a complementary organization, and they question its management and its operations.[8]

The most interesting program of export promotion in Pakistan is the Export Bonus Scheme, "the sheet anchor of the commercial policy of the present regime."[9] In effect since 1959, the E.B.S. covers all exportable commodities and manufactured goods, except raw jute, raw cotton, raw wool, raw hides and skins, tea, and most varieties of rice (cotton yarn was added

---

[8] See *State Trading Corporation: A Report on India's Export Performance* (Bombay: Council for Economic Education, 1962), and H. Venkatasubbiah, *Indian Economy Since Independence* (Bombay: Asia Publishing House, 1958), p. 244.

[9] "Economist," "Export Bonus Scheme," *Enterprise* (Karachi), August 14, 1961.

to the list of exceptions as of January 30, 1961). Exporters of all manufactured goods except cotton and jute manufactures are entitled to receive bonus vouchers, which may be used to obtain foreign exchange for the import of any authorized commodities to the extent of 40 per cent of the foreign exchange earned by their exports; for the exports of all other items, including cotton (except cotton yarn) and jute manufactures, the bonus is 20 per cent. Bonus vouchers may be bought and sold freely within Pakistan, and they may be used to obtain import licenses for consumer goods as well as industrial requirements.

Although most of the major exports of the country were excluded from the scheme, the E.B.S. has given a real boost to exports. Unfortunately, this increase has been largely offset by the decline in export earnings of items not on the E.B.S. list and by the removal of cotton yarn from the list, because of domestic shortages and a developing black market for this commodity. The scheme offers "an indirect subsidy to exporters and manufacturers at the cost of general consumers,"[10] and it has had an inflationary impact in Pakistan. Although some of the bonus vouchers have been used to import foreign automobiles and other luxury items, in the first eighteen months of the scheme nearly 78 per cent of the amount made available under the vouchers was used to import industrial goods.

India and Pakistan, in common with all other developing countries, believe that the industrialized nations of the world should show a greater awareness of their specific problems of export promotion and a greater willingness to make special concessions and provide other special opportunities for them in the difficult arena of international trade. For this reason they welcomed the recognition by the GATT countries in 1963, and again in 1964, that no reciprocity in terms of tariff reductions could reasonably be expected or demanded of the less developed countries, and they attached great importance to the United Nations Conference on Trade and Development which met in Geneva in the late spring of 1964.

"Trade, Not Aid?"

Since the United States and the United Kingdom are by far their best customers, as well as their main source of essential imports, India and Pakistan are particularly affected by the trade policies of these two powerful states. The western giants might make a greater and more lasting contribution to South Asian development by a relaxation of their own trade policies, by using their influence in international agencies such as GATT for a general liberalization of trade policies, and by bearing in mind the needs of developing countries as they develop new associations with the European Economic Community, than by all the assistance which they make available through foreign aid. For some time to come — probably for a much longer time than many people realize — the developing countries

[10] Ghouse, cited, p. 57. For an excellent analysis of the Export Bonus Scheme, see *ibid.*, pp. 53–63.

must have substantial amounts of foreign assistance as well as expanding markets abroad; but the amount of aid might be decreased markedly if more trade opportunities were provided.

In a sense, therefore, the United States and the United Kingdom, as the major industrialized states of the non-Communist world and the states to which India and Pakistan must look for a large share of their outside assistance and economic contacts, may be following rather short-sighted policies by failing to give sufficient consideration to the developing nations as they frame their own trade policies. "It is indeed paradoxical," remarked Morarji Desai in addressing a UN meeting devoted to "the decade of development" in 1962, "that rich and technologically advanced countries, which because of their resources and know-how have an advantage in producing the most complex products of the modern industrial society, should insist on protecting and subsidizing simpler forms of manufacture in the production of which the less industrialized countries have a comparative disadvantage. They do this at a considerable cost to themselves and an immeasurable harm to the developing countries." The Indian Finance Minister was calling attention to the important point that developing countries must find markets for "processed goods, semi-manufactures and simple manufactures" as well as for primary products.

Illiberal and restrictive trade policies may in fact largely counteract the beneficial results of foreign aid programs. Apparently this point is recognized in the United Kingdom and the United States, although it does not seem to be reflected in trade policies as much as would seem to be desirable. The Trade Expansion Act of 1962 is a step in the right direction. Unfortunately, it is not as long a step as was contemplated. The "Kennedy round" of tariff negotiations in GATT has become bogged down in endless frustrations and complications, giving point to a warning of Pakistan's Minister of Commerce at the ministerial meeting of GATT in May 1963, with reference to an eight-point "Programme of Action"[11] which India and Pakistan and nineteen other developing nations proposed: "If acceptance of the action programme is delayed now, we will be lost in the complexities

---

[11] GATT Doc. MIN (63), 7, 22 May 1963, para. 1. The eight point "Programme of Action" called for:

(1) a standstill on increases in tariff and non-tariff barriers against the trade of the developing countries;

(2) elimination of quantitative restrictions inconsistent with GATT on imports from less developed countries;

(3) duty-free entry into industrialized countries of tropical products by 31 December 1963;

(4) elimination by the industrialized countries of customs tariffs on primary products important in the trade of less developed countries;

(5) a reduction by 50 per cent over the next five years and eventual elimination of tariff barriers to exports of semi-processed and processed products from less developed countries;

(6) progressive reduction and elimination by 31 December 1965 of internal charges and revenue duties on products wholly or mainly produced in the less developed countries;

of the Kennedy round."[12] His warning was all too prophetic. The "Programme of Action" was not accepted, and the "Kennedy round" has proved to be a seemingly interminable merry-go-round.

Through its policies in GATT, in OECD, in the economic agencies of the United Nations, in its negotiations with the European Economic Community, in the negotiation of international commodity agreements, and in other ways the United States can do much to create wider markets for the products of India and Pakistan. These efforts, however, will be at least partially counteracted by pressures from domestic producers and their supporters in the Congress, by American tariff and other restrictive policies, by balance of payments difficulties, by "Buy American" and "Ship American" requirements, and by other measures which, however necessary they may appear to be, nevertheless add to the burdens of underdeveloped countries as they try to accelerate their painfully slow economic progress.

Here, again, the wisdom of the old slogan, "trade, not aid," seems to be clearly demonstrated. Unfortunately, the slogan commands more lip service than concrete support. If countries like India and Pakistan are ever to get off the treadmill of continuing dependence on large amounts of foreign assistance from reluctant donors, chiefly the United States, they must step up markedly their production and their exports. Even a relatively small degree of liberalization of trade opportunities could be of far greater assistance to countries like India and Pakistan than large amounts of aid, a point forcefully brought out by a prominent American industrialist, Mr. Harvey Williams. "If simple manufactured imports from the less developed areas to the Atlantic Community were to equal only one per cent" of the combined Gross National Product, he estimated, the total in a very few years "would approximate $10 billion annually — over twice the largest annual economic aid appropriation which has been proposed to the United States Congress." "How much sounder, and how much more secure," he argued, "would be the position of the United States if the equivalent of several billions a year was flowing to the less developed areas for new products of their own production rather than being provided through grants and loans as economic aid. This alternative would be a bona fide two-way trade."[13]

---

(7) annual reporting by the industrialized countries on steps taken to provide greater access for the products of the less developed countries; and

(8) consideration of other appropriate measures to facilitate the efforts of the developing nations to diversify their economies, strengthen their export capacity, and increase their export earnings.

This summary of the "Programme of Action" is taken from "Issues Before the Eighteenth General Assembly," *International Conciliation*, No. 544, September 1963, p. 142.

[12] Quoted in an editorial entitled "GATT Again," *Far Eastern Economic Review*, May 30, 1963, p. 451.

[13] Harvey Williams, "Our International Position: The Challenge and the Opportunity," an address to the 14th annual New Jersey Business Conference at Rutgers University, New Brunswick, New Jersey, May 8, 1962.

In the realm of commercial policy we enter what Professor John P. Lewis has called

> the most difficult of the essential policy adjustments that must be made by the United States and other Western powers. . . . If the West cannot overcome its own political inhibitions enough to extend India some solid assistance on the trade front, the rest of the help it is supplying will lose much of its importance . . . . For probably it is in the field of international trade policy, more than in its foreign aid programs or in its policies toward American private overseas investment, that the United States is most apt to fall short of supporting and facilitating Indian economic development in the manner that this country's own best interests dictate.

Professor Lewis suggests "action on three trade fronts": (1) "selective United States tariff reduction," and "a friendly reception," and perhaps also some technical assistance, "to the intensified marketing efforts that the Indians should be making on their own behalf"; (2) American help to India and other developing countries "on the European trade front," which means that "responsible United States policymakers at every opportunity — in their own trade and negotiations with the Common Market, in OECD, and in their dealings with their European allies — should use this country's bargaining leverage to champion easier access to European markets for the developing economies' industrial as well as agricultural products"; and (3) assistance to India in the expansion of exports, including industrial exports, and in "the development of industrial capacity, not just for supplying the recipient countries' domestic markets, but for producing exports, even when these exports may compete with American exports in third markets."[14] These suggestions are important ones, and indicate areas of action by the United States which might prove to be far more important and in the long run far more beneficial than large amounts of foreign aid. The fact is that for political and other reasons the United States is doing very little to assist India and other developing nations along these lines. One persistent question intrudes itself at this point: To what extent is the American Government using foreign aid as a substitute for the politically more difficult measures which would in fact contribute far more than foreign aid to the political survival and economic development of the newer countries?

Private Foreign Investment

Neither India nor Pakistan is relying heavily on private foreign investment for financing the development programs, but both countries are making special efforts to step up the level. "Private foreign investments . . . ," said Finance Minister Morarji Desai at the inauguration of the New York office

[14] John P. Lewis, *Quiet Crisis in India: Economic Development and American Policy* (Washington: The Brookings Institution, 1962), pp. 233, 245–247, 334.

of the Indian Investment Centre in 1961, "are essential not only for the foreign exchange they bring in but also for bringing in knowhow, new managerial techniques and also for giving new ideas of efficiency which they have evolved as a result of the advancement that they have made in industries and science." This is of course an approach which the United States government wishes to encourage in every possible way.

Levels of Foreign Investment

The total amount of private foreign investment in India and Pakistan is quite substantial, and it is growing steadily. In India it rose from about $540 million in 1948 to $882 million in 1953 to $1.2 billion in 1960 to $1.5 billion in 1964. As would be expected, by far the largest share of this investment — about 65 per cent in 1960 — is British. Perhaps half of the total amount was invested in manufacturing, tea and other plantations, and mining. The same situation exists in Pakistan, where the total foreign private investment in 1962 was approximately $550 million.

Private foreign investment may take many different forms. It may be in the form of direct equity investment, ranging all the way from complete ownership and control to only token participation, direct private lending to indigenous enterprises, various kinds of managerial, professional, or organizational services under contract, technical cooperation, and licensing arrangements. In past years the emphasis was heavily on direct investment and control, but more recently the trend has been toward other forms of investment, such as joint ventures, usually with minority participation, and professional services and technical cooperation under licensing or other arrangements.

In spite of the rather substantial total amounts of this kind of investment, much of which was made even before independence, India and Pakistan are disappointed at the low level of investment from foreign private sources. India's Third Five Year Plan does not indicate separately the amount which India expects to obtain from private foreign investment during the Plan period. A publication of the Planning Commission lists a sum of $630 million which, it is anticipated, will be realized during this period from "Direct Foreign Investment and Loans including Suppliers' Credits."[15] Apparently private foreign investment in India is somewhere between $100 and $200 million annually. Pakistan's Second Plan estimates that only $126 million will be available from this source during the Plan period. This estimate is certainly too conservative, for the actual amounts seem to be somewhere between $50 and $100 million each year. These sums are small in comparison both with the needs of the two countries and with the total amount of foreign private investment.

[15] Planning Commission, Government of India, *Towards a Self-Reliant Economy: India's Third Plan 1961–66* (New Delhi: Publications Division, Ministry of Information and Broadcasting, Government of India, December 1961), p. 127.

American private investment in South Asia has been disappointingly small, although it is growing rapidly, increasing from $38 million in 1950 to around $200 million in 1962.[16] At the end of 1959 it was $173 million, about 13.4 per cent of the total investment in India. According to a study of the United States Department of Commerce American private investment in the countries of the Far East and South and Southeast Asia amounted to $1.289 billion in 1962, but only 15 per cent of this was in India, which had 60 per cent of the population of the area. Not more than $50 million in private American capital is being invested in India each year.

In Pakistan private American investment is of course much less, totaling only $38 million in 1962, with a current annual rate of investment of only a few million dollars. Former Ambassador Aziz Ahmed has said that of a total of $50 million of private foreign investment in Pakistan during the first eighteen months of the Second Plan, only $10 million came from U.S. investors.[17]

Incentives for Foreign Investment

Both India and Pakistan insist that they offer an unusually favorable investment climate for foreign investors. Among many investment incentives they offer equality of treatment with indigenously owned enterprises, the right to remit profits, the right to the repatriation of capital investment at any time, flexible requirements regarding joint ventures involving equity arrangements, royalty payments, guarantees against nationalization, generous depreciation allowances, liberal tax holidays or tax exemption for new industries, income tax exemptions for foreign technicians, relief from double taxation, and other tax concessions.

Special assistance to foreign enterprises or investors is now provided by the Indian Investment Centre, a nonprofit, semi-official service organization established in 1960, with its headquarters in New Delhi and an office in New York.[18] During the first three years of its operations, the Indian Investment Centre assisted in the conclusion of 72 joint venture agreements. Of the 57 which had been approved by the Government of India by February 1964, 31 involved participation by American companies.

No similar Centre has been established by Pakistan, although that country has a number of agencies, including the Investment Promotion Bureau, the P.I.C.I.C., and the P.I.D.C., which provide extensive information about

[16] *India Investment Analysis,* a memorandum prepared for the use of officials of Merck Sharp & Dohme International Division, December 2, 1963. I am indebted to Dr. Antonie T. Knoppers, President of Merck Sharp & Dohme International, for making this memorandum available to me.

[17] Address to the Harvard Business School Club, Washington, May 24, 1962, on "The Chemistry of Economic Growth and Investment Opportunity in Pakistan." See also Shams Siddiqui, "Foreign Investment in Pakistan," *Forward* (Karachi), October 1961, pp. 22–23.

[18] *Investing in India: Indian Investment Centre . . . Objects and Functions* (New Delhi: Indian Investment Centre, August 1961), p. 31.

investment opportunities and regulations in Pakistan and which are interested in promoting collaboration between Pakistani and foreign concerns.

The United States Government also provides a great deal of information, assistance, and encouragement to private American interests which are involved in or which are looking into the potentialities of investment in foreign operations. The agencies most concerned with this kind of assistance are the Bureau of Foreign Commerce and the Agency for International Development, especially its Office of Development Finance and Public Enterprise and its Office of Small Business. The Bureau of Foreign Commerce keeps closely in touch with business conditions and opportunities all over the world. The Office of Development Finance and Private Enterprise seeks "to encourage private enterprise to play a larger development role, . . . and to assist in locating specific business opportunities arising out of the AID program." The Office of Small Business "is reponsible for assisting American business, particularly small independent enterprises, to participate equitably in the furnishing of commodities and services financed by the Agency for International Development." It also is interested in assisting small business concerns to organize their own export trade groups.[19]

American private enterprise obviously benefits greatly from the aid given to foreign nations, for the greater part of the credits made available to these nations is spent in the United States. This is especially true of credits made available as development loans by AID, the main channel of developmental assistance today, for since 1959 recipients of such loans are required to use the credits for purchases in the United States, with limited exceptions.

The government also provides American foreign investors with specific guarantees, incentives, and services. Some of these are dollar loans to United States or foreign business enterprises involving a two-step lending procedure whereby loans are extended to a private enterprise on relatively short terms but ultimate payment is made to the United States in dollars through the host government over a longer period of time, and Cooley loans from the foreign currency proceeds of sales of surplus agricultural commodities, which "may be made to domestic or foreign firms for the establishment of facilities abroad to assist in the use, distribution or increased consumption of United States agricultural products." There is also encouragement to private concerns to undertake surveys of investment opportunities in developing countries by agreements to share up to 50 per cent of the cost of such surveys and feasibility surveys. Specific risk investment guarantees assure protection "in whole or in part" against inconvertible currencies or losses due to expropriation or to "war, revolution, or insurrection," and

---

[19] Foreign Assistance Act of 1962, Hearings before House Committee on Foreign Affairs, 87th Cong., 2d Sess., March 26, 1962 (Washington: Government Printing Office, 1962), pp. 354, 357; statement by Frank M. Coffin, Deputy Administrator for Programs, Agency for International Development.

there are also extended risk guarantees, first incorporated into the Foreign Assistance Act of 1961.[20]

For some time the United States has been negotiating with both India and Pakistan for the conclusion of tax treaties, which, if ratified, would provide special incentives for American private investors. Even if these treaties are concluded, however, they may never receive the approval of the United States Senate, which has many reservations regarding this kind of treaty.

American banking institutions, and especially a number of large New York banks, have played an important role in calling the attention of their clients to investment opportunities in South Asia, in providing essential information about investment regulations, and in financing joint ventures and other business arrangements between American and South Asian private enterprises.

In view of all of the efforts that are being made to attract private foreign investment and of all of the incentives and guarantees that are afforded, the question naturally arises: Why has so little American private investment been made in India and Pakistan? These countries are relatively stable politically, they are engaged in planned programs of economic progress, their record of meeting obligations is impeccable, they offer potentially large markets under almost monopoly conditions, they have a generally favorable investment climate. Nevertheless, the amount of American private investment in South Asia is increasing but slowly and the prospects are not bright.

The reasons for this state of affairs are fairly obvious. There are at present many claimants for foreign private capital. Opportunities for American investment are great at home as well as abroad; and much of the American foreign private investment still goes to more developed countries, or to Latin America where American business interests have had extensive experience, or for the development of American-owned and operated oil facilities.

For most American businessmen investment in India or Pakistan represents a venture into the unknown. They are not so convinced as are the spokesmen of these two countries that the investment climate is unusually favorable. G. L. Mehta realized this when he observed: "We feel that people abroad seem to hear more about the controversy between the public and the private sectors, government controls and burden of taxation, than they do about the remarkable growth that has taken place both in the private and public sectors."[21] American businessmen who have dealings in South Asia, especially those who are new to the area, have all kinds of doubts and reservations about the political situation, the prevailing economic policies and orientation, the social attitudes, the red tape and regulations, the

---

[20] *Ibid.*, pp. 355–357.

[21] Address at the inauguration of the branch office of the Indian Investment Centre in New York, October 2, 1961.

reliability and efficiency of the South Asian companies and individuals with whom they try to deal, the real market opportunities in countries with such low standards of living. On the whole, American private enterprise is not oriented toward investment in such underdeveloped countries as India and Pakistan.

In the opinion of many middle-sized and small South Asian businessmen American private enterprises are missing a real opportunity to establish themselves solidly in a vast potential market, at an early stage of its development; they are being much too conservative and hesitant in their approach; they are too easily discouraged by their unfamiliarity with this area and by the difficulties which they encounter at an early stage of their explorations; they are too easily frightened by the bogeys of "socialism" or of economic planning; they insist on having everything spelled out "in black and white" from the beginning; they try to get too large a share of control in their joint venture arrangements, whereas a minority interest will in fact often give them a major say in the affairs of such ventures and will in most cases open up other profitable opportunities; they tend to gravitate too much toward the Indian business interests with which they are at least somewhat familiar. In short, they are not sufficiently venturesome or imaginative and thereby are being almost "un-American."

There is much substance to these criticisms. Fortunately, they do not apply to a growing number of American private interests, which seem to be finding real opportunities for profitable investment in South Asia in spite of all the uncertainties and difficulties.

While the investment climate in South Asia seems to be increasingly favorable in most respects, it is always subject to policies of the governments and the dictates of the Five Year Plans. During a six-day conference in New Delhi in October 1961, between leading Indian industrialists and a large number of prominent American businessmen, several major American doubts and reservations were frankly discussed. The two points which the Americans raised again and again were the reservation of key industries to the public sector (Schedule A of the Government's Industrial Policy Resolution of April 30, 1956) and the general insistence, subject to some exceptions as approved by the Government of India, on minority participation by foreigners in joint industrial ventures.

Experience of Foreign Oil Companies in India

The experience of foreign oil companies in India, notably Burmah-Shell and Standard Vacuum (now Esso Standard Eastern), illustrates some of the difficulties as well as some of the potentialities of doing business in India. The oil companies have obviously not been happy with some of the new restrictions imposed upon them by the Government of India, and with some of the prevailing economic policies. Unfortunately for them, some of the officials with whom they have had to deal, notably K. D. Malaviya, former

Minister for Mines and Fuel, have been markedly unsympathetic and rigid. Accustomed to a near-monopoly market and to complete ownership and control of their branches in India, they have found it hard to adjust themselves to a "new deal," when they face competition from the Government-owned and -operated Indian Oil Company and from other foreign competition, including that of the Soviet Union, and when the prevailing emphasis is on minority participation for foreign interests, and certainly not on 100 per cent ownership, such as the Western oil companies insisted upon in the past.

Differences between the Government and the oil companies have been acute since 1958. Malaviya charged that the privately owned refineries in India were processing crude oil far beyond the capacities for which they were licensed, and that their refusal to reduce the price of refined products was motivated by "the purpose of extracting concessions from the Government of India under threat of breakdown of supplies." In July 1961 a committee appointed by the Government of India to look into the whole matter (the Damle Committee) "recommended greater discounts to be obtained by the companies from their Associates and imposition of additional non-recoverable duties by Government and reductions in distribution and marketing charges and the profit margin of the companies."[22] Although the Government, according to Malaviya, "was not satisfied with the quantum of discounts suggested by the Damle Committee," it accepted the Committee's recommendations and declared them to be in effect as of October 1, 1961. The oil companies refused to accept the recommendation of reduced prices of refined products on the ground that discounts were not available to them on such products. They indicated, however, that crude oil could be imported at reduced prices and that oil products refined in India could be sold at the price levels suggested by the Damle Committee. The Government of India did not accept this approach. As a result a stalemate on the basic issues has existed between the Government and the oil companies, and an uneasy compromise, satisfactory to neither party, has been evolved, under which the Government sanctions foreign exchange for the import of refined oil products at discounted prices but the oil companies use the exchange to import such products at fully posted prices. The oil companies insist that the Government policy has already reduced their earning to less than 12 per cent, a figure which the Damle Committee suggested should be guaranteed by way of minimum profits.

One consequence of the protracted dispute has been to expand the scope and activities of the public operated Indian Oil Company, which acts not only as a distributing agency but which operates oil wells, refineries, and pipe lines, especially in Assam and Gujerat. Another consequence has been to bring other countries and oil interests onto the Indian scene. In the early

[22] Burmah-Shell — A Survey of Its Colossal Activities During 1960," *Forum* (Bombay), November-December 1961, p. 52.

stages of the dispute Malaviya said that the attitude of the oil companies would compel the Government of India to look for "alternative sources" of supply. The E.N.I., a public sector Italian company, has entered into an agreement to assist the Indian Oil Company, and the Italian Government has granted a special loan to India to defray the costs of this assistance. The Soviet Union, of course, has often expressed a willingness to meet all of India's requirements for petroleum products under most attractive terms, and it has entered into some agreements with the Indian Government for oil exploration and technical cooperation with the Indian Oil Company, and for the shipment of limited amounts of oil to India.

In the meantime, the oil dispute drags on, with both the oil companies and the Government as the losers. Generally public opinion in India has been with the Government in this dispute. "The oil companies," declared *The Times of India* on November 21, 1961, "like their counterparts elsewhere, have made such an excessive secret of their trade for so long and have acquired such a reputation for hard bargaining that they have only themselves to blame if their case is not received with the degree of sympathy that they believe it deserves." The Damle Committee held that "petroleum and petroleum products come within the definition of 'essential commodity' under the Essential Commodities Act, 1955," which empowers the Government of India to impose statutory price control on essential commodities.[23] The Government has not yet invoked this power, but it may do so. As *The Times of India* stated, however, "There is even now room for a reasonable and mutually satisfactory settlement between the Government and the oil companies."

Possibly the main lesson of the oil controversy is that both foreign private concerns and the Government of India lose if they take too rigid positions, and do not make sufficient concessions to the need for compromise. From the point of view of the American private investor, however, it is clear that the experience of Stanvac and Caltex and other private oil companies in India raises doubts and questions in his mind. He cannot be impervious, moreover, to the growing role of public-sector operations in such an important field of activity, and to the possible implications of the increasing involvement of the Soviet Union in this field.

The expropriation of foreign oil companies in Ceylon in 1962, with no agreements regarding compensation, and Ceylon's arrangements with the Soviet Union for the importation of oil products at prices well below the prevailing world prices and for the establishment with Russian help of oil refineries in Ceylon, did not make the investment climate in South Asia generally more attractive to potential American investors. The oil companies felt that if Ceylon could expropriate their properties and, while promising to make adequate compensation, could drag out negotiations in-

[23] See "Oil Crisis," *Link* (New Delhi), November 26, 1961, p. 18.

definitely and make offers that were little better than expropriation without compensation, a dangerous precedent would be set which might be followed in other countries, such as India, where the companies have a far larger investment. Foreign private companies, however large and powerful, will be reluctant, and perhaps even unable, to compete with state trading companies, which fix prices and other terms on political more than on economic grounds, unless they too are subsidized heavily by their own governments. They will be reluctant too to engage in operations in countries which follow such quixotic and mercurial economic and political policies as Ceylon followed between 1956 and 1965.

Joint Ventures

One of the most common and currently popular forms of private investment in India and Pakistan is through joint ventures. Although they do not account for the bulk of private foreign investment in these two countries, their numbers are increasing rapidly. In India they rose from 17 in 1956 to nearly 500 in 1963. By the end of 1963 some 125 American companies were engaged in operations in India under joint venture arrangements.

Joint ventures may be equity or non-equity arrangements, the latter being the general rule in cooperative arrangements with any public sector enterprise. Foreign companies may also have special arrangements with Indian or Pakistani companies through contracts for managerial, professional, or organizational services or through licensing agreements. Normally the Governments of India and Pakistan insist that a foreign firm shall have no more than a 49 per cent equity in a joint venture, although many different arrangements are actually in existence.

In the past, many American companies wanted 100 per cent ownership and control, and they have gradually modified their position with great reluctance. American companies are still not happy with minority equity, although they are becoming more used to it. Their attitude is rather different from that of some foreign firms, notably the Japanese. South Asian businessmen, as well as Government spokesmen, often point out that there are definite advantages to minority participation, and that if American firms would show more willingness to enter into joint ventures with less than majority equity they would then be in "on the ground floor" in expanding enterprises and would soon find many opportunities for increasing their role in the ventures as well as for increasingly profitable investment.

From the point of view of the South Asian governments, and business concerns, as well as of national interests generally, there are obvious reasons why Indian or Pakistani interests should retain majority participation in joint ventures, wherever possible. In India the insistence on Indian majority participation has increased, in fact if not in announced policy. As early as April 6, 1949, Prime Minister Nehru declared: "The major interest in ownership and effective control of an industrial undertaking should, as a rule, be in Indian hands."[24] In actual practice the Government of India allowed many deviations from this rule, but recently it is becoming more and more difficult for foreign companies to get majority ownership in India. As a revealing summary of the present attitude of the Government of India regarding joint ventures indicates:

> Foreign participation is not indiscriminately welcome in India. It is sought as a scarce resource to be alloted to strategic areas, and the terms of any collaboration are carefully scrutinized to insure that the price India pays is commensurate with the value received. Decisions regarding foreign investment are not left exclusively to private negotiation; the government has ultimate sanction. A new foreign investment must give definite assurances on the terms of capital participation, on the terms of payment for imported materials, on a program of eventual manufacture within India of components for the product involved, and on the training of Indians for responsible managerial positions.[25]

Pakistan has tended to liberalize its policy regarding foreign participation in joint ventures. A declaration on industrial policy issued by the Government of Pakistan in April 1948 stated that "Pakistan would welcome foreign capital seeking investment from a purely industrial and economic objective and not claiming any special privilege," with the condition that "opportunities for participation of indigenous capital are provided and monopolies avoided." This condition was interpreted to mean that Pakistani nationals should hold at least 51 per cent of the equity in some thirteen specified industrial fields, and at least 30 per cent in others. A policy statement of November 1958 made this interpretation even more liberal. "Normally," it declares, "the Government will expect that the regional local expenditure (in a new enterprise) will be met from local equity capital" and that "in the case of oil refining the Government will expect substantial participation of Pakistani capital in equity."[26]

An examination of specific joint ventures in India and Pakistan would reveal a bewildering variety of arrangements and connections. Some of the ventures are most complicated, involving public and private domestic and foreign capital and participation.

Non-equity joint ventures also may take many different forms. The most common would be those involving foreign technical collaboration, foreign loans or grants, and licensing arrangements. They exist in both the private and public sectors, and many examples can be found in the fields reserved for state enterprises. They are the prevailing pattern in the steel industry of India, in both the three public mills in the public sector and in the Tata Iron and Steel Company plant at Jamshedpur and other private sector steel enterprises as well. As is well known, a substantial part of the costs of the

---

[24] Quoted in Wolfgang G. Friedmann and George Kalmanoff, eds., *Joint International Business Ventures* (New York: Columbia University Press, 1961), p. 194.
[25] *Ibid.*
[26] *Ibid.*, pp. 194–195.

three steel mills in the public sector in India was provided by loans from the Soviet Union, Great Britain, and Western Germany, and the plants were built and are now being expanded by agreements between the Government of India and the Government of the Soviet Union, and private British and German interests, backed by their governments. The Kaiser Engineering Corporation provides technical collaboration under a joint venture arrangement with Tata Iron and Steel.

In December 1961 the Government of Pakistan announced that it had decided to award the contract for the construction of a steel mill of 350,000 ton capacity at Karachi to the Swindell Bressler Corporation of the United States, and Rheinstahl-Sybetra of West Germany, which had agreed to subscribe 30 per cent of the capital required to build the mill and to supervise the actual construction. The remaining shares will be owned by Pakistanis. The Government also announced that plans for a smaller steel mill (about 100,000 ton capacity) to be built in Chittagong would be drawn up by John Miles & Partners of London. The Japanese Government has indicated a willingness to provide credits sufficient to meet most of the costs of the Chittagong mill, and in all probability the contract for its construction will be awarded to a Japanese firm or firms.

The United States Government has been noticeably cool toward participation either by official or private American interests in state enterprises abroad, or even in enterprises where a foreign government exercises substantial but not majority control. American private concerns are generally rather cautious in considering any proposed arrangements with state enterprises, or with foreign private concerns in collaboration with state enterprises. In a few cases in Pakistan, however, American companies have favored a small participation by the P.I.D.C. in joint venture arrangements which they were considering with private Pakistani interests. Private American concerns have entered into nonequity joint ventures with state enterprises in India and Pakistan, or with both governments and private companies.

Economic Relations with Britain and the EEC

For both India and Pakistan, economic relations with the United Kingdom, the center of the Commonwealth and the sterling area and their major market, are of special interest and concern. They watched with mixed feelings and considerable apprehension the negotiations following Britain's decision in 1961 to apply for admission to the European Economic Community. Some Indian and Pakistani spokesmen professed to welcome this historic shift in British policy toward Europe. Ayub Khan himself said: "Although financially our interests will be affected because we have a protected market in Britain for certain goods, we feel that it would be in the interests of the world that Britain should join the Common Market.[27] Britain kept the members of the Commonwealth fully informed of the circumstances which led it to apply for membership in the EEC; it assured the other Commonwealth countries that it would make every effort to obtain adequate economic safeguards for these countries as a condition for its entry into EEC; and it argued that they would in the long run benefit from its association with EEC, which would bring into being a major trading area and would lead to a fundamental reshaping of the patterns of world trade.

But while there was a widespread appreciation in India and Pakistan of the factors which impelled the British to seek membership in EEC, there was an even more widespread apprehension of the consequences of this momentous step. Politically, India and Pakistan feared that British association in the EEC would weaken the Commonwealth, involve Britain in commitments which would jeopardize its relations with other Commonwealth countries, increase international tensions, and create an "inward-looking community" in Western Europe which would function as a unit in its relations with the weaker underdeveloped countries.

All of these points were raised by Nehru and Ayub Khan during the Commonwealth Prime Ministers' Conference in London, in September 1962. According to newspaper reports of the closed session, Nehru said, with reference to the trade of India, Pakistan, and Ceylon: "I do not see how the Commonwealth will survive unless a radical change is made in the present proposals." He was reported to have described the Common Market "as a political grouping with a military basis" and to have said that "for Britain to join such a body could strike at the political cohesion of the Commonwealth." He also charged that the EEC "has already created alarm on the other side of the Iron Curtain" and thus added "to the tension between East and West." Ayub Khan joined in the criticism by warning the Common Market countries against "turning their organization into a sort of rich man's club and thereby re-establishing imperialism of the worst sort."[28]

From an economic point of view India and Pakistan feel that their interests are bound to suffer if Britain joins the Common Market. Both nations would naturally like to maintain the present preferential arrangements for their exports to the United Kingdom. Since this would not be possible with Britain's adhesion to EEC, they wanted to obtain as many safeguards for their exports as possible. They were not at all satisfied with the proposals that were made at meetings between representatives of Britain and the EEC members. These proposals, in their view, reflected the "inward looking

---

[27] Quoted in A. T. Chaudhri, "Possible Effects on Pakistan If Britain Enters E.C.M.," *Forward*, October 1961, p. 14. *Forward* is an official publication of the Pakistan Industrial Development Corporation.

[28] AP dispatch from London, dated September 11, 1962; in the *Philadelphia Inquirer*, September 12, 1962.

attitude" on the part of Common Market countries which they have frequently deplored. K. C. Reddy, Indian Minister of Commerce and Industry, stated in the Parliament in March 1962: "The really crucial question is whether in the highly prosperous economies of Western Europe, which have formed the Common Market, there is sufficient recognition, not only in economic terms, but also in political and human terms, of the importance of enabling countries to increase their exports and thus reduce their dependence on aid." Most Indians and Pakistanis would be inclined to answer this question in the negative. In fact, they seemed to feel that they are bound to be the losers in the negotiations between Britain and the Common Market countries, whether Britain finally enters or not.

When Britain's bid to enter the Common Market was at least temporarily stalled by General de Gaulle's brusque obstinacy in January 1963, the reactions in India and Pakistan were mixed, but regret seemed to predominate over relief. Both countries realize that they have a practical as well as a sentimental stake in the economic health of the United Kingdom, and they tended to share British bewilderment and resentment over the abrupt "veto" of General de Gaulle. They were relieved that the *status quo* would be preserved with respect to their exports to Britain, but they also hoped that some of the tariff concessions which Britain had persuaded the Common Market countries to accept with reference to important exports of the South Asian countries, and the agreement to permit duty-free entry of tea, handloom goods, and cashew nuts, might be granted, even with the postponement of the negotiations for British adherence to the EEC. They were increasingly concerned over the heavy deficit in their balance of trade with the Common Market countries, and especially with West Germany, and they hoped that the contemplated tariff and duty-free concessions and other more liberal measures on the part of the EEC countries, coupled with enhanced effort on their own part, would help them reduce the heavy imbalance of trade. Looking to the more distant future, they hoped to be able to conclude a general trade agreement with the Common Market or a series of bilateral trade agreements with West Germany and perhaps other Common Market Countries.[29]

International Economic Associations and Agreements

Both countries have been actively interested in all kinds of international economic and financial associations and agencies, such as the Colombo Plan, GATT, international commodity agreements, the Commonwealth Economic Consultative Council, ECAFE, the World Bank, the International Monetary Fund, the International Development Association, the UN Special

[29] See, for example, the editorial entitled "India and E.C.M.," in *The Hindu*, February 10, 1963.

Fund, and other UN agencies. They have been the beneficiaries of most of these agencies, but they have also made definite contributions to them, chiefly by making available technical experts and by providing limited funds for technical assistance.

The Colombo Plan, which started in 1950 as a Commonwealth program of assistance to the member countries and British possessions in South and Southeast Asia, has been expanded to include all of the countries of the area (except North Vietnam), and also Japan and the United States. Donor countries affiliated with the Plan have contributed more than $12 billion in capital and technical assistance, but most of this has not been under Colombo Plan arrangements. Among major projects undertaken in South Asia with assistance provided under the Colombo Plan are the Warsak hydroelectric project in West Pakistan (Canada), the Durgapur steel plant in India (United Kingdom), the Tribhuvan Rajpath in Nepal (India), and the Mutwal fisheries project in Ceylon (Canada).

At their nineteenth session, in 1961, the countries associated in the General Agreement on Tariffs and Trade adopted a declaration on the promotion of trade of the less developed countries, which India and Pakistan welcomed. They were particularly pleased that it showed an awareness of the special problems facing developing countries in their efforts to expand their exports, and recognized their inability to reduce tariffs on a reciprocal basis. In 1962 President Kennedy asked Congress for permission to reduce tariffs jointly with the Common Market countries, up to 50 per cent of the existing duties. Shortly thereafter the United States and the EEC signed an agreement for the mutual reduction of tariffs on selected commodities to the extent of 20 per cent. Although the commodities covered by this agreement were mostly industrial goods, all such reductions in tariffs will apply also to India and Pakistan, under the provisions of GATT for most-favored-nation treatment.

India and Pakistan are parties to a number of international commodity agreements, and they have been interested in revising some of these in the direction of more liberal quotas or other concessions to producing countries. They regarded the nineteen-nation cotton textile agreement, concluded in Geneva in 1961, as a step in the right direction, but they would like a further reduction of restrictions on textile exports. The agreement to admit tea into the Common Market area without tariff was welcomed by India, Pakistan, and Ceylon; but the former two countries would be more interested in obtaining lower duties on their textile exports. India, the world's largest producer of sugar, would like to have a larger sugar quota from the United States. Only after the embargo was imposed on sugar imports from Cuba did the United States include India in the list of countries from which its sugar would be imported. The cut in that quota in 1961 roused a storm of criticism and protest in India.

As the United Nations regional economic commission especially concerned with the Far East and South and Southeast Asia, ECAFE sponsors a number of studies and reports and carries out other activities which are useful to the South Asian countries. The first Secretary-General of ECAFE was an Indian, Dr. P. S. Lokanathan, and Indians and Pakistanis have played prominent roles in the Commission. ECAFE has attempted, with indifferent success, to foster closer economic cooperation among the countries of South and Southeast Asia. The activities of various agencies of the United Nations in South Asia, and the role of South Asian countries and nationals in these agencies, are too extensive to summarize in a few brief comments. India and Pakistan have been especially active in the work of the Economic and Social Council and its affiliated commissions and specialized agencies. The United Nations maintains field offices and/or special missions in all of the South Asian countries, and several of the specialized agencies also have offices in India and Pakistan. In the economic commissions and agencies Indian and Pakistani nationals have occupied many of the highest positions, or have served as technical specialists.

The International Bank for Reconstruction and Development, by far the most important international lending agency, has made substantial loans for South Asian development. Its role in the eventual resolution of the canal waters dispute, and in organizing the group of developed nations which have joined in pledging assistance to the Indus Basin Development Fund, was a new departure for the Bank, and one of its greatest international services. The Bank took the initiative in organizing major capital-exporting countries into the International Consortium of Nations to consider the foreign exchange needs of India and Pakistan in furtherance of their development program and to propose ways by which these needs can be met.

India and Pakistan still have substantial drawing rights on the International Monetary Fund. For various reasons India has been hesitant to approach the Fund for all or part of the more than $410 million which it is entitled to draw from the Fund, subject to certain conditions. India shares the views of many developing countries that the Articles of the Fund should be modified and its financial resources strengthened in order that it may give, as the *Economic Weekly* urged, "the kind of assistance which may be called balance of payments support until the developing countries have finally emerged."[30]

The International Development Association makes available — thus far in too limited amounts — the kind of soft loans which countries like India and Pakistan prefer to get for long-term development purposes. The Special Fund has made a number of small grants for technical assistance to South Asian countries, as has the UN Technical Assistance Program and the Expanded Program for Technical Assistance. Among the specialized agencies,

[30] "India and the IMF," *Economic Weekly*, July 7, 1962.

in addition to the Bank and the Fund, India and Pakistan are perhaps most interested in the work of FAO, WHO, and UNESCO.

India and Pakistan, in common with other underdeveloped countries, are particularly interested in securing international cooperation and support in widening their markets and in obtaining higher prices for their exports. They argue that a major breakthrough, calling for fundamental changes in international trade patterns, is necessary to enable them to resolve their trade problems. They vigorously advanced these views at the United Nations Conference on Trade and Development in 1964, which the Indian Minister for International Trade called "the first World Conference in the real sense of the word." The Conference adopted a number of principles, proposals, and resolutions embodying these points of view. For the developing countries this represented some progress in their uphill struggle to obtain wider and more favorable trade opportunities. They are now awaiting, with mingled feelings of doubt and expectation, the effective implementation of the recommendations of the Conference of 1964.

CHAPTER SIX

Foreign Aid in United States–
South Asian Relations

THE HEAVY AND INCREASING DEPENDENCE of India and Pakistan on foreign aid is an unfortunate but inescapable feature of their development efforts. Aid, defined in this context, "should be limited to financing made available on terms more liberal than those available in the commercial market."[1] It would include "soft" loans, grants, technical assistance, and, for American aid, commodities made available under Public Law 480. For a developing country, as W. B. Reddaway points out, aid plays two main roles: "it adds to the amount of savings available for capital formation, and it helps with the balance of payments problems."[2] Both roles are of major importance, the second perhaps even more than the first.

Foreign Aid and Economic Development in South Asia

The assumption at the present stage of Indian and Pakistani development is that if the amounts of foreign exchange specified in the current Plans are made available, chiefly through foreign aid, the need for large amounts of foreign assistance will decline within a relatively short period of time — perhaps ten to fifteen years — and the two countries will be able to get along more or less on their own momentum. The planners are careful to avoid the use of such terms as "take-off" and "self-sustaining growth," but they obviously aim at attaining this in the foreseeable future.

India's Third Plan states that it "has been formulated on the basis that it would be advantageous from the point of view of the recipient country

---

[1] *An Act for International Development: Summary Presentation*, June 1961, Report of the President's Task Force on Foreign Economic Assistance (Henry R. Labouisse, Director) (Washington: Government Printing Office, 1961), p. 144. Hereafter referred to as *Report of the President's Task Force on Foreign Economic Assistance.*

[2] *The Development of the Indian Economy* (Homewood, Illinois: Richard D. Irwin, 1962), p. 215.

as well as the donor countries to plan for substantial amounts of external assistance for a relatively short period rather than to proceed in terms of varying and uncertain amounts of assistance over an indefinite period."[3] Apparently this approach made sense to the President's Task Force on Foreign Economic Assistance, for in its 1961 report it stated: "We know that the loan support for such countries as India and Pakistan must continue at high levels for the immediate future if their efforts are to be successful. In these cases, it is possible to foresee the general level of activity which it would be in our interest to maintain." The report also endorsed the assumption that substantial amounts of assistance in the next few years offer the hope of a decided tapering off of all such aid in future years.[4]

Nevertheless, one gets the uneasy feeling that optimism has triumphed over realism. Certainly India and Pakistan have reached a stage of their development when they do indeed need large infusions of foreign capital and other forms of external assistance. Certainly their efforts have been impressive, and their goals clearly charted. Even with such assistance, in the needed amounts, however, there are grounds for doubt that the major targets — which are minimal targets — can be attained. If they are not attained, the results can be most serious. Even if they are attained, it does not follow that by the end of the present Plans, or the next ones, India and Pakistan will reach a relatively self-sustaining stage.

The demands of a developing society tend to multiply far beyond the capacity to meet them. The ultimate success of the planning efforts, as has been pointed out, depends not so much on economic factors as upon basic changes in the economic and social environment, in attitudes and customs, and also upon political stability and development. An environment conducive to growth does not yet exist in either India or Pakistan. In these circumstances, accentuated by the growing demands of a huge population which is increasing by more than 12,000,000 every year, one would be bold indeed to suggest that after five, ten, or fifteen years of planned growth the economies of these countries can be self-sustaining. They surely will still be unbalanced, weak, and inadequate, although they should be much stronger than those which now exist. They are moving in the right direction; but the basic questions remain unanswered: Are they moving fast enough? What hope do present trends and future prospects offer for survival as open societies, or even for survival at all?

These comments are advanced not to suggest that the outlook is hopeless — for real and impressive progress is being made — but rather to question

[3] Planning Commission, Government of India, *Third Five Year Plan* (New Delhi: Author, 1961), p. 107.

[4] *Report of the President's Task Force on Foreign Economic Assistance*, p. 48. The Report was even more specific and positive with reference to India: "In several significant cases, such as India, a decade of concentrated effort can launch these countries into a stage in which they can carry forward their own economic and social progress with little or no government-to-government assistance." *Ibid.*, pp. 15–16.

the assumption, apparently shared by recipients and donors, international economic agencies, and many economists, that if internal and external resources are made available in accordance with present plans, countries like India will become relatively self-sustaining in a short period of time. In all probability this is a dangerous chimera. It is particularly dangerous because if the goal of relative self-sufficiency is not achieved within this short period, disillusionment and hopelessness will set in, on the part of the peoples of the developing countries and of donor countries as well. In the annual battle with the Congress over foreign aid it may be necessary to seek support for large foreign aid appropriations on the ground that after a few more years of such appropriations, the need for them will no longer exist. Certainly, as the President's Task Force on Foreign Economic Assistance insisted, "the process of foreign aid should not be endless," but it will doubtless continue long after the "decade of development" which President Kennedy proclaimed. The 1970s and 1980s and subsequent ones will also be "decades of development." India and Pakistan may by then be able to get along more or less on their own resources, supplemented by normal international commercial activity, but this is by no means certain; and in the meantime other new states of the world will presumably reach a stage of growth where larger amounts of foreign assistance will be required.

Although the old adage, "It is more blessed to give than to receive," may still have general validity, it is particularly difficult for governments and for people either to give or to receive. Those who give often do so with bad grace, sometimes for the wrong reasons, and they expect more in the way of tangible and intangible returns from the recipients than they ever get.[5] Those who receive also often do so with bad grace, with doubts and suspicions, and they sometimes seem to assume that they are receiving only what is due to them or that the giver is making help available only for some very selfish or even Machiavellian reason.[6] Undoubtedly there are grounds

[5] In an address at the Conference on Tensions in Development in the Western Hemisphere, held in Bahia, Brazil, in August 1962, B. K. Nehru, Indian ambassador to the United States, voiced some of the standard complaints of recipient countries with regard to foreign aid: "Foreign aid is often rung out of unwilling hands with a lack of grace that is truly remarkable; it is often given the color of charity so that there is almost invariably resistance to the acceptance of it. Furthermore, it is on occasion overtly and often covertly sought to be used to ensure that recipient nations do not depart in their external political policies from the line taken by the donor country." Quoted in *India News* (issued by the Information Service of India, Washington), August 13, 1962.

[6] Spokesmen of recipient nations like to point out that donor nations give aid for reasons of their own national interest, selfish or otherwise. In his address at Bahia, for example, Ambassador Nehru said: ". . . . as yet there is no clear recognition that, in a world that has shrunk to small proportions, economic assistance is no more than a fact of good neighborliness. There is little understanding that prosperity like peace is indivisible, that the continuance of poverty among two-thirds of the world's population is a hindrance to the economic growth of the one-third that is comparatively prosperous nor a sufficient realization of the fact that economic discontents of the order now prevailing in the world are a threat to the continuance of the international orders." Quoted in *India News*, August 13, 1963. In his remarkably blunt address to a joint session of

for such reservations and suspicions, especially when foreign aid is used as a "cold war" weapon or when it is received in lieu of maximum effort on the part of the recipients.

For a variety of reasons, many of them political, there is a great deal of sentiment in the United States against foreign aid in general, and against aid to India in particular. It is obviously difficult to argue or to justify the case for large-scale economic assistance to India and Pakistan in dealing with those who are totally opposed to "foreign give-aways" under any circumstances.

Such an attitude, buttressed by a variety of rationalizations and prejudices, raises the whole question of the objectives of the American aid programs, in relation to national interests and the goals of foreign policy. Naturally they are regarded by some Indians as further proof that the United States is not genuinely interested in their welfare and development, and looks upon foreign aid as a cold war weapon and as a means to force needy nations to revise their policies according to the American image. In American relations with South Asia such doubts and criticisms should not obscure the underlying motives for the grant and receipt of aid, which are right and sound, and based on mutual interest. "Our new aid policy," declared President Kennedy in his foreign aid message to the Congress in March 1962, "aims at strengthening the political and economic independence of developing countries. . . . Our efforts to help them help themselves, to demonstrate and to strengthen the vitality of free institutions, are small in cost compared to our military outlays for the defense of freedom. Yet all of our armies and atoms combined will be of little avail if these nations fail, unable to meet the needs of their own people, and unable to stave off within their borders the rise of forces that threaten our security."

Obviously the main burden of development efforts must rest upon the governments and peoples of the developing countries themselves. Foreign assistance, however great, is only a part of a vast effort. In the case of India and Pakistan, however, it contributes the "extra margin" without which the success of the development would be very much jeopardized. It also makes important contributions in indirect as well as in direct ways. These facts were recognized in Pakistan's Second Plan:

> The importance of foreign assistance to the economy was greater than its magnitude might suggest. Although it amounted to only 4 per cent of gross national product, it financed a very substantial proportion of development expenditure and about one-third of the total imports of the country. In recent

the United States Congress, on July 12, 1961, President Ayub Khan said: "As far as the problem of aid is concerned — you have to give it to us — because it involves the fate of the world and also your own destiny. . . . Today we want you to assist us to develop. . . . You might say, 'We have heard this before' — that you are getting a bit tired of this story. . . . You today have world obligations, you cannot hide yourself from this position in the world no matter what you say. If you do, you do so at your own peril." Quoted in *The New York Times*, July 13, 1961.

years, nearly 10 per cent of the country's total foodgrain requirements were met through imports, made possible mostly by United States aid. The impact of external assistance on production and incomes, though not precisely calculable, was very considerable in the First Plan period. What is still less measurable is the continuing effect of external foreign assistance on the development effort in future years.[7]

Although massive assistance will create difficulties for the United States as a donor country and for the South Asian states as recipients, it is absolutely essential if the development efforts of India and Pakistan, which have now reached a critical stage, are to have any prospect of accomplishing even their minimal objectives. It is by no means certain that these objectives can be achieved even with large-scale American aid; but it is quite certain that they cannot be achieved if such aid is not forthcoming. The United States therefore has to give careful consideration to the consequences of a failure to provide substantial economic assistance to India and Pakistan in the coming years, as well as to the prospects for the useful employment of this assistance.

Economic Aid to South Asia: the Record

A brief summary of the nature and extent of foreign assistance to India and Pakistan since they launched their development programs may be helpful by way of illustrating some of the points made in the preceding discussion and by way of background for a consideration of the impact of foreign assistance, with particular reference to assistance from the United States.[8]

Broadly speaking, foreign aid was about 6 per cent of the total investment in the Indian economy during the First Plan, about 13 per cent during the Second, and about 25 per cent during the Third Plan. Aid from the United States under P.L. 480 is not included in these figures, and would add substantially to the percentages for the Second and Third Plans. During the period of the First Plan $794 million of foreign assistance were available, but only about $414 million, hardly more than half the available amount, were actually expended. Of this amount about $195 million of loans and about $88 million of grants came from the United States. For the Second Plan period somewhat more than two-thirds (about $1.870 billion)

---

[7] *The Second Five Year Plan* (*1960–65*), p. 87.

[8] Most of the figures cited in this section are taken from *ibid.*, or from *Third Five Year Plan*. See also *Proposed Mutual Defense and Assistance Programs FY 1964: Summary Presentation to the Congress* (Washington: Government Printing Office, April 1963), Table No. 2, "U.S. Aid to Foreign Assistance Act Countries, Obligations and Loan Authorizations, Cumulative July 1, 1945–June 30, 1962, and Fiscal Year 1962," pp. 169–171, and Table No. 3, "U.S. Economic Aid — Obligations and Loan Authorizations, Fiscal Year 1962, by Region and Country," pp. 172–173.

of the foreign assistance authorized ($2.645 billion, including a carry-over of $380 million from the First Plan) was actually utilized. The largest loans utilized were from the United States ($690 million) and the World Bank (about $607.5 million). Of the utilized grants of about $400 million, $185 million were made available by the United States.

The Third Plan estimates the foreign aid requirements at $5.46 billion. A substantial part of this amount has already been pledged, most of it by the "Aid-to-India Club," an International Consortium organized by the World Bank in an effort to provide extra assistance to India's Second Plan when the Plan ran into difficulties in 1957–58. The Consortium originally was made up of the World Bank, the United States, the United Kingdom, Canada, West Germany, and Japan, with observers from a few other countries and from the International Monetary Fund. In 1961 France and the newly formed International Development Association, and in 1962 Austria, Belgium, Italy, and the Netherlands also became members.

At a meeting in June 1961, shortly after India's Third Plan was officially launched, the members of the Consortium agreed to provide about $2.29 billion "to enable India to launch a Third Five Year Plan of economic development with confidence in the ultimate development of its objectives." Loan agreements covering $670 million of the $1.295 billion of promised assistance for 1961–62 were signed in 1961. The next two meetings of the Consortium, however, produced no more agreements. One was held in January 1962, shortly after India had sent troops into Goa, and some of the Consortium members, including the United States, were in no mood to consider India's needs from a strictly economic point of view. At the next meeting, in the following May, while the Kashmir question was again being discussed in

■ TABLE 3: India Consortium Pledge for the First Four Years of Third Plan
(Millions of Dollars)

	1961–64	1964–65	4-year total
Total	$3,417.0	$1,028.0	$4,445.0
U.S. Total[1]	1,415.0	435.0	1,850.0
AID	1,242.5	385.0	1,627.5
Ex-Im Bank	172.5	50.	222.5
Total Others	2,002.0	593.0	2,595.0
IBRD & IDA	695.0	245.0	940.0
W. Germany	463.5	95.0	558.5
U.K.	350.0	84.0	434.0
Japan	170.0	60.0	230.0
Six Others[2]	323.5	109.0	432.5

[1]Excludes P.L. 480.
[2]Austria, Belgium, Canada, France, Italy and Netherlands.

Source: **U.S. Foreign Aid in the Near East and South Asia** (Washington, D.C.: Agency for International Development, n.d.), p. 12.

the UN Security Council, the Consortium's members decided to postpone any further commitments for a few weeks. On July 30 they announced that they would pledge an additional sum of approximately $158 million for India's Third Plan, about half to be provided by the older members and the other half by the four new members.

Since 1962 the members of the Consortium have had less difficulty in agreeing on pledges for the third and fourth years of India's Third Plan. In each year the amount pledged has been over one billion dollars. In 1964 the agreement was reached at a meeting of the Consortium on May 27, the day of Nehru's death.

Other credits pledged to India include $777 million carried over from the commitments for the Second Plan, a Soviet credit of $500 million, a loan from the Export-Import Bank of $504 million, and smaller credits from Czechoslovakia, Yugoslavia, Poland, Switzerland, Italy, and the International Development Association. In addition, substantial quantities of agricultural commodities have been forthcoming from the United States under P.L. 480, and the major part of the rupee funds obtained from the sale of these commodities in India will be made available for development purposes. Extensive technical cooperation will be provided by the United States under the Technical Cooperation Agreement with India of January 5, 1962, by Colombo Plan members and several other countries, and by a number of private organizations, notably the Ford Foundation.

Pakistan has relied even more heavily than has India on external assistance. About 47.5 per cent of the expenditures for the First Plan came from this source, and about the same percentage, involving more than twice as much assistance, was needed for the Second Plan. During the First Plan period $1.2 billion were committed by foreign governments and agencies, and about $975 million were actually made available — $583.6 million for project and commodity aid, $340 million for food aid, and $52.1 million for technical assistance. Eighty per cent of the total amount of foreign assistance came from the United States. The only other large contributors were the World Bank ($76.86 million) and Canada ($62.8 million).

Most of the external assistance needed by Pakistan to finance the Second Plan was provided by the members of the same International Consortium which is giving heavy support to India's Third Plan. In June 1961 the members of the Consortium pledged $320 million dollars for Pakistan's Second Plan. Pakistan was disappointed with the amount pledged, because the estimated needs for foreign assistance for the first three years of the Plan (1960–63) were $945 million, and also because at the same meeting the Consortium pledged nearly $2.3 billion for India. One of the reasons for the more limited commitment to Pakistan at that time was a widespread feeling on the part of members of the Consortium that the estimates and targets submitted by Pakistan needed to be revised and made more firm. This was done by the Planning Commission in the latter half of 1961, and in January

■ TABLE 4: Pakistan Consortium Pledge for First Three Years of Second Plan
(Millions of Dollars)

	FY 1962–64	FY 1965	Total
United States*	$712.5	$212.5	$925.0
A.I.D.	(637.5)	(187.5)	(825.0)
Export-Import Bank	(75.0)	(25.0)	(100.0)
All Other Consortium	662.7	218.5	881.2
IBRD & IDA	(289.0)	(80.0)	(369.0)
Germany	(107.5)	(38.1)	(145.6)
Japan	(75.0)	(30.0)	(105.0)
United Kingdom	(70.4)	(22.4)	(92.8)
Canada	(57.0)	(23.6)	(80.6)
Others**	(63.8)	(24.4)	(88.2)
Total Consortium	$1,375.2	$431.0	$1,806.2

*Excludes P.L. 480.
**Belgium, France, Italy and the Netherlands.

Source: **U.S. Foreign Aid in the Near East and South Asia** (Washington, D.C.: Agency for International Development, n.d.), p. 18.

1962 the Consortium "endorsed" the Second Plan and recommended that its members make available the remaining $625 million. This result was achieved by the latter part of the summer, through agreements between Pakistan and individual members of the Consortium. In May 1963, the members of the Consortium pledged $425 million for the fourth year (1963–64) of the Second Plan. Again the United States pledged half of the total amount.

The assistance needed for the Second Plan was in addition to Pakistan's continuing food requirements and to the foreign exchange needed for the Indus Basin Development Program and for a special Works Program. In October 1961 a separate agreement between Pakistan and the United States — the first major agreement between the two countries after the Kennedy Administration assumed office — provided that Pakistan should receive foodgrains and certain other agricultural commodities during the next four years, under P.L. 480, to the value of $621.56 million.

American Economic Aid to India and Pakistan

By mid-1965 American economic aid to India had reached a total of nearly $6 billion, by far the largest amount of economic assistance to any developing country, and aid to Pakistan a total of more than $3 billion. These amounts are exclusive of substantial American contributions made available to the South Asian countries through multilateral agencies, such as the World Bank and the International Development Association, to which the United States is the largest contributor. United States bilateral aid is channeled through three main agencies, the Agency for International Development (development loans, grants for technical assistance, etc.), the Public Law 480 (Food for Peace) Program, and the Export-Import Bank (which makes "hard" loans). For some years India and Pakistan have been the largest recipients of American economic aid.[9] At the present time economic aid to India is running at approximately half a billion dollars each year, exclusive of P.L. 480 aid, and Pakistan is receiving nearly half as much, which means that it is getting a considerably larger relative amount of American economic assistance.

Aid to India began in 1951 with the passage by the Congress of the Indian Emergency Food Act, which made available to India credits of $190 million to import some 2,000,000 tons of wheat to meet a major food crisis. Later a series of "wheat loans" or grants were made to India, chiefly for the purpose of importing surplus foodgrains under Public Law 480. By December 31, 1961, the total amount of wheat loans and grants (which actually covered a few other agricultural commodities), including the 1951 wheat loan, was $2.7 billion, more than one-half of all American aid to India up to that time. A substantial portion of the rupee repayments under the wheat loans was made available to the Indian Government for development projects. About $275 million were used either to make loans to private enterprises in India or to support institutions which make such loans.

From 1951 to 1957 American grants and loans to India for development purposes — about two-thirds grants, and one-third loans — averaged around $50 million a year. After the Development Loan Fund was established in 1957, more loans than grants were extended, at a yearly average of about $100 million. Toward the end of India's Second Plan the level of development lending rose to about $150 million a year. Other kinds of American assistance included Export-Import Bank loans of $246 million, and substantial contributions to international financial agencies. Perhaps the grants from several American private agencies, including the Ford Foundation, should also be mentioned in this connection.

American aid to India, representing its share of the commitments agreed upon by the International Consortium, has been approximately $450 million

[9] For countries in a relatively advanced stage of development, like India and Pakistan, the main force of economic assistance will be development loans, "the heart of the new program of the Decade of Development," *Report of the President's Task Force on Foreign Economic Assistance*, p. 38. Since October 1959 dollar aid obtained through development loans must be used for purchase of goods and services of American origin. Until 1961 D.L.F. loans could be repaid in local currency, with a period of repayment extending from 15 to 20 years, and with interest rates varying generally from 3½ to 5¼ per cent. In accordance with a new approach adopted in 1961, development loans were made on a long-term basis, up to fifty years in some cases, with no repayment of principal in the early period of the loans, and with either no interest at all or interest at nominal rates (usually ¾ of 1 per cent) during the first ten years.

■ TABLE 5: United States Economic Aid to India, 1946–1964

(U.S. Fiscal Years — Millions of Dollars)

U.S. Overseas Loans and Grants — Net Obligations and Loan Authorizations

PROGRAM	Postwar Relief Period	Marshall Plan Period	Mutual Security Act Period					Foreign Assistance Act Period			Total 1946–1964
	1946–1948	1949–1952	1953–1957	1958	1959	1960	1961	1962	1963	1964	
• A.I.D. and Predecessor Agencies — TOTAL	—	57.3	342.5	89.8	137.0	194.6	200.8	465.5	397.2	336.5	2,221.0
Loans[a]	—	—	130.0	75.0	120.0	171.3	180.1	445.9	392.3	330.6	1,845.2
Grants	—	57.3	212.5	14.8	17.0	23.3	20.7	19.6	4.9	5.9	375.8
• Food for Peace — TOTAL[R]	—	0.6	362.7	63.5	229.7	550.2	316.1	275.2	276.1	294.4	2,368.6
Title I — (Total Sales Agreements)[R]	(—)	(—)	(354.6)	(50.0)	(237.9)	(616.9)	(332.8)	(278.3)	(293.3)	(292.9)	(2,456.7)
Less: (Planned for U.S. Uses)	(—)	(—)	(74.3)	(8.1)	(27.6)	(78.8)	(35.4)	(29.2)	(30.7)	(30.7)	(314.8)
• Title I — Planned for Loans and Grants[R]	—	—	280.3	41.9	210.3	538.1	297.4	249.0	262.5	262.1	2,141.6
104c — Grants for Common Defense	—	—	—	—	—	—	—	—	—	—	—
104e — Grants for Economic Development	—	—	54.0	—	37.5	253.6	140.4	100.8	100.8	100.8	787.9
104e — Loans to Private Industry	—	—	—	12.5	65.0	30.9	16.6	12.4	14.7	14.7	166.8
104g — Loans to Governments	—	—	226.3	29.4	107.8	253.6	140.4	135.8	147.0	146.6	1,186.9
Title I — Ass't from other Country Sales Agreements	—	—	—	4.0	—	2.1	—	—	—	—	6.1
Title II — Emergency Relief & Economic Development	—	—	4.9	—	—	—	0.3	3.4	—	7.8	16.4
Title III — Voluntary Relief Agencies	—	0.6	77.5	17.6	19.4	10.0	18.4	22.8	13.6	24.5	204.5
Title IV — Dollar Credit Sales	—	—	—	—	—	—	—	—	—	—	—
• Export-Import Bank Long-Term Loans	—	—	—	151.8	—	—	79.5	25.7	40.3	57.2	368.2
• Other U.S. Economic Programs	39.9[b]	190.8	—	—	—	13.6	—	0.4	1.0	1.7	233.8
TOTAL ECONOMIC	39.9	248.7	705.2	305.1	366.7	758.4	596.4	766.8	714.6	689.8	5,191.6
Loans	39.9	190.2	356.3	268.7	292.8	469.4	416.6	619.8	594.3	549.1	3,797.2
Grants	—	58.5	348.9	36.4	73.9	289.0	179.8	147.0	120.3	140.7	1,394.4

a Does not include $20.0 million loan in FY 1958 financed by Asian Economic Development Fund. This loan is included in NESA Regional data.

b Includes the utilization during FY 1946 of $29.2 million of lend-lease silver credits. During FY 1940–1946, a total of $160.7 million of such credits were extended to British India. After partition, Pakistan agreed to repay $38.0 million, but it is not possible to distribute the FY 1946 portion between the two countries.

R Data for FY 1961–1964 reflect revisions in aid from multi-year agreements.

TABLE 6. United States Economic Aid to Pakistan, 1946-1964

(U.S. Fiscal Years — Millions of Dollars)

U.S. Overseas Loans and Grants — Net Obligations and Loan Authorizations

PROGRAM	Postwar Relief Period 1946–1948	Marshall Plan Period 1949–1952	Mutual Security Act Period					Foreign Assistance Act Period			Total 1946–1964
			1953–1957	1958	1959	1960	1961	1962	1963	1964	
• A.I.D. and Predecessor Agencies — TOTAL	–	**10.6**	**330.3**	**92.9**	**162.7**	**198.6**	**124.2**	**240.1**	**174.3**	**213.9**	**1,547.6**
Loans	–	–	103.0	38.6	63.2	102.0	27.2	207.1	169.4	206.0	916.5
Grants	–	10.6	227.3	54.3	99.5	96.6	97.0	33.0	4.9	8.0	631.2
• Food for Peace—TOTAL	–	**0.1**	**169.5**	**67.1**	**72.3**	**99.2**	**41.4**	**159.5**	**185.4**	**163.8**	**958.6**
Title I—(Total Sales Agreements)	(–)	(–)	(118.9)	(65.4)	(85.9)	(114.6)	(45.2)	(168.0)	(155.4)	(155.4)	(908.8)
Less: (Planned for U.S. Uses)	(–)	(–)	(17.0)	(8.2)	(14.2)	(16.5)	(6.2)	(11.1)	(9.3)	(9.3)	(91.8)
• Title I—Planned for Loans and Grants	–	–	**101.9**	**57.2**	**71.6**	**98.0**	**39.0**	**156.9**	**146.1**	**146.1**	**817.0**
104c—Grants for Common Defense	–	–	74.3	5.0	–	–	–	–	–	–	79.3
104e—Grants for Economic Development	–	–	5.0	15.0	32.4	48.7	20.6	112.9	107.2	107.2	449.0
104e—Loans to Private Industry	–	–	–	6.4	3.1	8.2	2.5	8.5	7.8	7.8	44.3
104g—Loans to Governments	–	–	22.6	30.8	36.1	41.1	15.9	35.5	31.1	31.1	244.2
Title I—Ass't from other Country Sales Agreements	–	–	–	–	–	–	–	–	–	–	–
Title II—Emergency Relief & Economic Development	–	–	40.6	8.0	–	–	–	–	35.5	10.7	94.8
Title III—Voluntary Relief Agencies	–	0.1	27.0	1.9	0.7	1.2	2.4	2.6	3.8	7.0	46.8
Title IV—Dollar Credit Sales	–	–	–	–	–	–	–	–	–	–	–
• Export-Import Bank Long-Term Loans	–	–	–	–	–	3.5	6.4	37.9	–	–	51.0
• Other U.S. Economic Programs[a]	0.1	0.4	67.4[b]	3.2	–	–	–	1.1	2.3	1.9	73.2
TOTAL ECONOMIC	**0.1**	**11.1**	**567.2**	**163.2**	**235.0**	**301.3**	**172.0**	**438.6**	**362.0**	**379.6**	**2,630.4**
Loans	0.1	–	125.6	79.0	102.4	154.8	52.0	289.0	208.3	244.9	1,256.1
Grants	–	11.1	441.6	84.2	132.6	146.5	120.0	149.6	153.7	134.8	1,374.2

a See footnote b on table for India.
b PL 77 Wheat to Pakistan.

annually during the period of the Third Plan. American taxpayers — and Congressmen — may note with some concern that the average annual rate of aid to India has trebled with each Five Year Plan, and they may wonder how long this kind of escalation must continue.

American economic aid to Pakistan during this same period, as has been noted, totaled about $2.5 billion, and was similar in kind to the aid extended to India. In recent years most of the economic aid to Pakistan has been in the form of loans and food shipments under P.L. 480. During the period of the First Plan American aid for development purposes averaged about $80 million a year, and the value of the foodgrains shipped to Pakistan averaged somewhat less than $70 million a year. During the Second Plan, more than $200 million were made available each year for development projects and large amounts, perhaps up to $150 million, for foodgrains.

The Impact of Foreign Aid

No general conclusions can be reached regarding the effectiveness of foreign assistance to India and Pakistan, beyond the obvious statement that while some of the aid has undoubtedly not been well used, the net impact has been definite and constructive. Indeed, without substantial foreign assistance neither country would have been able to reach its present level of economic development. As much of the aid has been granted to support particular phases of the development programs, it can be evaluated only in relation to the value of the programs supported. Some has of course been allocated for purposes and projects which will have their full impact only in years to come. Some has gone for broad social purposes, such as education, community development, and malaria eradication, the results of which cannot be measured precisely. Unfortunately, because of shortages in India and Pakistan, a great deal of foreign aid has had to be used for food imports, which contribute little to overall development but are nevertheless essential for human survival.[10]

In his testimony on the Foreign Assistance Act of 1962, Ambassador J. K. Galbraith said that American aid has accomplished at least three things in India in the past ten years. In the first place, assistance in foodgrains had supplemented Indian agricultural production, and had helped to prevent substantial price increases, in spite of increased pressure on the food supply. Second, American aid had provided "the dollars for essential industries, or the hard currency for essential imports, . . . things which for the purposes of economic development could not be supplied from domestic sources." And third, it had eased the pressure on the masses of India's poor "for the

[10] The drain on foreign exchange for this program has been far less than it would have been because much of the food was made available by the United States under P.L. 480.

investment funds which enable them at the next stage to have an increased income."[11]

Undoubtedly the full impact of American aid is not to be measured primarily by immediate and tangible results. It is difficult to evaluate the relative contribution of aid for some social purpose *vis-à-vis* support for a specific industrial project. Soviet aid to India, for example, has been mainly for large impact projects in steel, oil, and heavy engineering. American aid has also gone into large projects, but much of it has been devoted to more diffuse but perhaps even more important social programs. Ambassador Galbraith referred to this point by citing an arresting example:

> One of the things we are doing in the south of India, the State of Kerala and the State of Madras — the State of Kerala is a state of strong left-wing orientation — is to provide Public Law 480 funds through a school-lunch program for the children. This isn't a steel mill, or heavy engineering plant, and it doesn't look like a very productive form of investment. I would go so far as to say, however, it is the best thing we do. It keeps the children in school because they come to school to get those meals. It is the finest form of truant officer that you can possibly invent. At the next stage you have a literate population which can learn machine skills, which will be more responsive to the improved agricultural techniques which will be more productive.[12]

All over South Asia even a casual traveler can find tangible results of foreign assistance and technical cooperation. Especially impressive are the huge impact projects which are largely supported by foreign aid. Giant examples are the Warsak Dam in West Pakistan, the Karnaphuli project at Kaptai in the Chittagong Hill Tracts in East Pakistan, and in India the three giant steel mills in the public sector at Bhilai, Durgapur, and Rourkela, all mentioned earlier.

Inevitably comparisons and contrasts are drawn between these huge projects. The Karnaphuli project, for example, by far the largest multipurpose hydroelectric project in East Pakistan, was criticized because of some flaws that developed in the construction of the sluiceway and especially because of the eventual costs, which were over $100 million (more than twice the original estimate) and which were more than double the costs of the Warsak Dam project in West Pakistan, which develops more electric power. Apparently the answer to such criticism is that prices rose considerably during the period of the construction, that the engineering problems involved were considerably more complicated than those at the Warsak site, and that the Karnaphuli Project was charged with many additional expenses, such as the rehabilitation of some 100,000 people whose lands were inundated by the fifty-mile-long lake created by the dam at

---

[11] *Foreign Assistance Act of 1962*, Hearings before the House Committee on Foreign Affairs, 87th Cong., 2d Sess., March 29, 1962 (Washington: Government Printing Office, 1962), pp. 583–584.

[12] *Ibid.*, p. 603.

Kaptai, and even customs duties on all machinery and equipment imported for the project. In this instance, too, the United States was indirectly involved in a dispute between India and Pakistan. When the Karnaphuli Project was first considered, the Government of India agreed not to raise objection to it, even though the lake to be created would flood a small piece of Indian territory. But India did object strongly when the project was officially inaugurated by President Ayub Khan in March 1962, on the ground that more land would be inundated than was contemplated and that Pakistan had failed to enter into agreements for adequate compensation of Indian nationals who would be compelled to move because of the rising waters.

A great deal of comment, favorable and unfavorable, has been made about the relative merits and costs of the three steel mills in the public sector in India. The Russian-built mill in Bhilai was the first steel mill in the public sector to reach maximum capacity, and there is widespread feeling in India that the Bhilai operation is by far the most satisfactory of the three. Both the Durgapur and Rourkela plants are being severely criticized on grounds of cost, efficiency, and overall suitability, especially the German-built plant at Rourkela, despite the Germans' high reputation for technical efficiency.[13]

A more difficult question to answer is whether the availability of foreign assistance in large amounts acts as a crutch for India and Pakistan, and encourages undue dependence, or unrealistic planning, or excessive expenditures, or a slackening of efforts at home. Even the most sympathetic observer can find all too many evidences of all of these unfortunate results. But one gets the impression that, despite the dead weight of inertia, especially in the countryside, the all-too-many examples of waste or misuse of funds, the seemingly excessive expenditures for public buildings — in short, despite the things that help to explain why India and Pakistan are under-developed societies — far more than meets the eye is going on in these countries. They are societies on the move. It would be extreme short-sightedness to oppose economic aid to India and Pakistan on the ground that the assistance rendered has not always been used to the best advantage.

The Bokaro Story

The United States Government, as has been pointed out, is reluctant to encourage public or private American aid for public sector enterprises, although in India and Pakistan much of the American aid inevitably is used to support the public sector activities under the development plans. A

---

[13] The difficulties at Rourkela stemmed, at least in part, from a technically more advanced and complicated plant. Moreover, much of the cost of the Bhilai plant was charged to social overhead, and hence was not an accurate measure of industrial efficiency.

special problem, however — and possibly a special opportunity — arose from the Indian request in 1960 for American assistance in erecting a fourth steel mill in the public sector at Bokaro in the state of Bihar. The American Government seemed disposed to favor the request; but in an on-and-off manner negotiations dragged on for months, and as time passed it seemed to become more and more reluctant. Perhaps it feared the reaction in Congress and in the country. The Bokaro venture would have represented the largest single American-supported public sector project anywhere in the world, and, according to original estimates, would have involved a financial commitment, presumably in addition to the regular United States aid program to India, of between $300 and $500 million. Later estimates were much higher.

The United States obviously did not want to get involved in such an ambitious and expensive project before being reasonably assured of its soundness and India's willingness to accept American technical advice and leadership as well as money. It was mindful of the inevitable comparisons with the highly publicized Russian accomplishments in supervising the construction of the steel plant at Bhilai, and of the criticisms that had been made of the plants built under British and German supervision at Durgapur and Rourkela. It seemed to have a rather poor opinion of the Hindustan Steel Corporation, the public enterprise in charge of the three steel mills in the public sector. Apparently it had some doubts about the feasibility of the Bokaro project, and about the extent to which India would permit American participation in the basic decisions regarding the project, its construction, and its operation. It feared that Americans involved might be blamed for difficulties which might arise from excessive Government control or red tape, and that American skills could not be put to effective use under such restrictions. In short, while it publicly favored support of the Bokaro project, it had all kinds of reservations and seemed to have a great deal of difficulty in making up its mind.

The Bokaro proposal would have been more palatable for the United States if some private participation had been definitely assured. When Ambassador Galbraith came to India in 1961, he publicly promised American support for a fourth steel mill, but from time to time he expressed the view that a limited equity stake would remove many American reservations and would provide greater incentives for participating American firms. The Director of the AID Mission in India was more insistent on the need for an equity interest for private American and Indian firms. Although the Government of India had permitted only non-equity participation by private Indian or foreign firms in the public sector steel projects, it did tentatively agree to consider a limited measure of private equity participation and it offered assurances that participating American companies and technicians would have ample scope "to make Bokaro a showpiece of Western aid."

Feasibility studies of the proposed plant at Bokaro, and extensive technical studies, were made over a period of some four years by a well-known Indian consulting firm. American experts also studied and restudied the proposal. Still no definite decision was made. At length, the Agency for International Development offered to finance a complete technical and economic survey of the project by a team of experts sent out by the United States Steel Corporation, after which the United States Government would determine whether it was willing to support the construction of the Bokaro plant. India agreed to this proposal, and in the summer of 1962 the United States Steel team began its study. After a thorough investigation in India over a period of some six months, at a cost of $686,000, the team submitted its report in March 1963. While the massive report has not been made public, its general nature and findings have been indicated by AID and other government officials and by Indian and American newspaper comments, which have not been contradicted. "The seven-volume study made no recommendations. Instead, it raised a long series of complex technical questions about the sources of ore, power, qualified labor and management. None of these questions was regarded as unanswerable by American aid officials."[14] The report was praised as useful and constructive; its net effect, however, was to provide ammunition for members of Congress and others who were seeking reasons for opposing American aid to the Bokaro project.

The Indian Government had been quite patient with American delays and with the insistence on further surveys of the whole proposal. By early 1963, however, it finally began pressing for a quick decision. The Bokaro project had assumed greater urgency, not only because the long delay in starting it had created a serious lag in planned steel production in the next few years, but also because of the new defense needs occasioned by the enlarged crisis with China.

If the report of the United States Steel technical team created doubts regarding the Bokaro project, another report submitted in the same month raised fresh apprehensions in both India and the United States. The Clay Committee included a sentence in its much discussed report which suggested that the United States should be wary of giving assistance to public sector projects: "We believe the U.S. should not aid a foreign government in projects establishing government-owned industrial and commercial enterprises which compete with existing private endeavors."[15] Many persons in India and in the United States interpreted this sentence as an indirect warning against an American commitment to the Bokaro venture, which General Clay later confirmed. Others, however, pointed out that the Clay Committee had recommended that special attention and assistance must

[14] Joseph Lelyveld, "Shift on New Indian Steel Mill Poses Questions on Foreign Aid," *The New York Times*, September 3, 1963.

[15] *The Scope and Distribution of United States Military and Economic Assistance Programs*, Report to the President of the United States from the Committee to Strengthen the Security of the Free World (Lucius Clay, Chairman) (Washington: Department of State, March 20, 1963), p. 5. Hereafter referred to as the Clay Report.

be given to India, and that the caveat about American aid to "government-owned . . . enterprises" would probably not apply to the Bokaro project, for this project was in no way competitive "with existing private endeavors" in India.

In the meantime the Government of India had made a number of significant concessions to satisfy certain American reservations. In his testimony before the House Committee on Foreign Affairs, David E. Bell, Administrator of AID, mentioned some of the Indian concessions.[16] These included agreement that if the steel mill at Bokaro was built with American assistance "it would be established as a separate corporation, not as part of the present Hindustan Steel Corp."; that "it would be managed by a board of directors who would include not only public officials but also private citizens"; that it would pay the same taxes as a private company; that "there would be a commitment from the beginning that a share in the ownership would be sold privately"; and that "there would be an American management contract established which would be entered into so that an American firm would set this up and run it for at least five years, train the Indian management, train the Indian labor, and get the plant running." Mr. Bell then endorsed American support to Bokaro by stating: "If all those conditions were met" — as the Indian Government had agreed — "it would seem to me to be a sensible thing to do." He also pointed out that leaders of private industry in India were in favor of the proposed fourth steel mill in the public sector, if only because "There is no alternative under Indian terms today by which you could get a mill of any size started privately."[17]

While Mr. Bell spelled out the significant Indian concessions and his favorable attitude, he also gave a clear indication that the long-postponed American decision on Bokaro would be subject to further delays, which would in effect amount to a negative decision. The bases of further postponement which he cited were technical — for example, "the resources of raw materials have to be demonstrated before there is going to be a funding proposition to be looked at" — but he stated that whereas the United States Steel team estimated that it would take two years to "prove" that the

---

[16] *Foreign Assistance Act of 1963*, Hearings before the House Committee on Foreign Affairs, 88th Cong., 1st Sess., May 22, 1963 (Washington: Government Printing Office, 1963), pp. 1119–1121. Hereafter referred to as *Hearings on Foreign Assistance Act of 1963*.

[17] In a letter published in *The New York Times* on June 9, 1963, and also in *The Washington Post* on June 20, 1963, Bharat Ram, then President of the Federation of Indian Chambers of Commerce and Industry, wrote: "The installation of the Bokaro steel plant is a hope strongly held by Indian enterprise, because on it will depend the utilization of the capacity of the engineering industry, its expansion, and the competitive position of private enterprise — in short, the future strength of the Indian economy." G. L. Bansal, Secretary-General of the Federation, suggested that the American failure to support the Bokaro project could hurt the private sector in India, instead of help it. "Those of us who are in the private sector," he remarked, "were really banking quite a lot on this big thing being built by the Americans. I am one of those Indians who personally feel let down." Quoted in Lelyveld, cited.

necessary raw materials — iron ore, coal, limestone, etc. — would be available, staff members in AID thought that "it would not take that long."[18]

Many members of Congress were even more troubled than Mr. Bell by some of the technical questions and the cost estimates. The estimates, based on the cost of a mill with a capacity of four million tons, capable of producing one million tons at first, indicated that the United States would be asked to provide over half a billion dollars for Bokaro in the first six years of the project and at least $379 million more before the plant was completed. But apparently the main objections in the Congress were political, along the lines of the reservations indicated in the Clay Report.

It was soon clear that the Congress would not approve an appropriation for Bokaro in the budget for fiscal 1964. In fact, in August 1963 the House put a rider on the foreign aid authorization bill, specifically aimed at any commitment to Bokaro, forbidding any allocation of more than $100 million to a public sector project without specific Congressional authorization.

The action — and the attitude — of the Congress placed the Kennedy administration, strongly on record in favor of support to the Bokaro project, in an embarrassing dilemma. Undoubtedly the administration was relieved when, on September 11, 1963, the Government of India announced that it was formally withdrawing the Bokaro project from the list of projects for which it was seeking American aid, in order to avoid "further embarrassment to administrations of both countries." C. Subramaniam told cheering members of the Lok Sabha that the Indian Government was determined to proceed with the construction of the mill "with such assistance from friendly countries as we can get." In October, in an address to officials and engineers at the Russian-built Bhilai steel works, Mr. Subramaniam announced that the Bokaro plant, and presumably all future steel plants in the public sector, would be built by India itself, that it would be in production by 1967 with an annual capacity of 1.5 million tons, which would be raised to 4.5 million tons by 1971–72.[19]

The news of the collapse of the Bokaro negotiations, as a result of the recalcitrance of the American Congress and the technical morass into which the negotiations floundered, was received more in sorrow than in anger in India, and apparently did not seriously jeopardize Indo-American relations or the working relationship that had been developed between the two governments on many fronts. For India it created real problems of finding the necessary technical and financial support for Bokaro and other steel plants in the public sector, and the long negotiations with the United States delayed the start on Bokaro, regarded as vital to the development program.

Demonstrating again "a shrewd instinct for flashy foreign aid programs that pay off in maximum propaganda at minimum cost,"[20] the Soviet Union

[18] *Hearings on Foreign Assistance Act of 1963,* May 22, 1963, p. 1120.

[19] Quoted in *India News,* October 11, 1963.

[20] Conrad Fink, "Red Aid Pays Off in Propaganda," AP dispatch from New Delhi, May 3, 1964; in *The Philadelphia Inquirer,* May 4, 1964.

stepped in to fill the foreign aid gap created by the withdrawal of the United States promise — or assumed promise — of aid, as it had in 1956 when the United States withdrew from the Aswan High Dam project in the U.A.R. On May 1, 1964, the Government of India announced that the Soviet Union had agreed to assist in financing and building the proposed steel mill at Bokaro by a loan of $350 million, and presumably by further assistance in the future. It seemed to assure that the Bokaro project, so long delayed because of the negotiations with the United States, would at last be undertaken speedily. As C. Subramaniam informed the Indian Parliament, "Bokaro is not the only steel project which we propose to build in the immediate future."

The Government of India has already entered into agreements with an Anglo-American Consortium of private engineering and construction companies regarding a fifth steel plant in the public sector.[21] India needs to increase its capacity for steel production, and it needs the assistance of "friendly countries," definitely including the United States, in realizing this objective, so basic to the success of the entire development effort.

The United States must weigh the political and economic implications of its failure to aid India directly at a critical time in a critical sector of that country's development efforts after it had taken so long to make up its official mind, and after responsible American spokesmen, including the President of the United States himself and the American ambassador, had publicly endorsed United States aid for the Bokaro project. The Bokaro story is not one of which the United States has reason to be proud.

Foreign Aid and the Oil Impasse in Ceylon

Between 1962 and 1965 Ceylonese relations were complicated by the impasse between the Government of Ceylon and American and British oil companies, some of whose properties have been expropriated, and by the arrangement for the import of oil and other petroleum products from the

[21] In October 1964 the Consortium, consisting of Koppers International, Blaw-Knox International Company, International General Electric Company, and International Investment Company of the United States, and Davy and United Engineering Company, Wellman Smith Owen Engineering Corporation, and Woodall-Duckham Construction Company of the United Kingdom, presented a three-stage proposal to the Government of India, and in January 1965 it signed an agreement with the Indian Government for the first stage, calling for a recommendation of at least two sites for the steel plant and of Indian participation in the design, engineering, and construction of the plant. "Subject to a decision on the site and the adequacy of the Indian participation proposals, the Consortium are to prepare, within nine months thereafter, a detailed project report for the selected site. . . . The Consortium hope to submit a financing plan for the project within six months of the submission of the detailed project report. It is expected that a major portion of the foreign cost will be found by the Consortium from private financing institutions abroad and not Governmental sources." Anglo-American Consortium," *Foreign Affairs Record* (New Delhi), January 1965, p. 1.

Soviet Union and other Bloc countries, as well as the U.A.R. In this case foreign aid was used as a coercive instrument of foreign policy.

Under the Hickenlooper Amendment to the Foreign Assistance Act of 1962 [Section 620 (e)] the President is obligated to suspend aid to any recipient country which, within a period of six months, does not take "appropriate steps" to reach an agreement with the American companies whose property has been "nationalized, expropriated, or otherwise seized." No agreement between Ceylon and the oil companies regarding the expropriated properties was reached within the stipulated time. Hence the Hickenlooper Amendment, which had been aimed primarily at Brazil, was first invoked against Ceylon. In January 1963 the United States Government informed the Government of Ceylon that all American aid would be terminated as of February 1st, and would be suspended until the President was satisfied that "appropriate steps" were being taken to reach a settlement with the oil companies. Until 1965, when the government headed by Mrs. Bandaranaike was forced to resign after a national election, little progress was made in resolving the oil controversy and United States-Ceylonese relations were adversely affected in many tangible and intangible ways.

Monetarily the stakes were not high, for the investments of the American oil companies in Ceylon and the amounts of American aid to that country total only a few million dollars; but the principle was important to all parties concerned. The American Government felt that it must protect American companies from the risks of expropriation without compensation.

This was a test case not only for the application of the Hickenlooper Amendment but also for the effects of the suspension of American aid to a country with which the United States is on friendly terms. It was a highly dubious procedure at best, and raised questions about the basic purposes of foreign aid and about the desirability of bringing this kind of pressure, amounting almost to sanctions, to bear upon a friendly government, at the almost certain cost of resentment and retaliation. Surely a more suitable means may be found to resolve problems arising between a foreign government and private American concerns.

Special Problems

Among the many matters to which the United States should give careful consideration the following may be singled out for special mention:

1. *The relative amounts and priorities of aid allocations within and between South Asian countries.* The main problems here are the selection of the kinds of projects or of the areas of development for which assistance is to be given, and the relative amounts of assistance made available to India and Pakistan.

Although India has nearly five times as many people and its current development program is approximately five times as large as that of Pakistan, it receives only a little more than twice as much economic assistance from the United States as does Pakistan. Since, as compared with Pakistan, both its capital needs and its capital absorptive capacity are greater, this proportion of American assistance seems to be out of balance. The conclusion might be drawn that India is "entitled" to considerably more aid or Pakistan to considerably less. On the other hand, Pakistan is more dependent than is India upon foreign assistance to finance its development program, and for more than a decade it has been a military ally of the United States.

Possibly aid to India and Pakistan should be given without regard either to relative amounts or to the nature of the political relationship that each has to the United States. But in view of America's interests in both countries, the unhappy state of their relations with each other, and the need for a more integrated American approach to South Asia, the United States must seek to preserve some kind of reasonable balance in its aid to each of the unfriendly neighbors.

In some instances it may be felt to be necessary to use foreign assistance as a device to reward friends and to penalize unfriendly governments. This is a dubious policy at best, and certainly should not be applied to India and Pakistan. Both countries are friends of the United States, and both are entitled to special consideration.

2. *The soundness of the development programs and the extent to which the United States should become involved in the planning process in each country.* Obviously these considerations are delicate ones, but the United States can hardly avoid them. It cannot, in good conscience, justify support of development programs with which it is unfamiliar, or of which it disapproves. It must have good grounds for believing, on the basis of its own appraisals, that the planning is sound, and that American aid will be used effectively in contributing to the overall objectives.

American specialists have been provided to both India and Pakistan, both by the American government and under international and private auspices, for assistance in many aspects of development planning and implementation. Specialists have worked intimately with the members and staff of the Planning Commission of Pakistan, for example, and have in fact played far more than an advisory role. This is the kind of involvement which could lead to great embarrassment if things went wrong, but which thus far has been welcomed in Pakistan. Undoubtedly Pakistan has been more willing to use these specialists in the central agency of the planning activities because they have been private American citizens provided by a great American university under the sponsorship and financial support of the Ford Foundation, which has a high reputation for disinterested service in the subcontinent.

3. *The appropriate forms, channels, and conditions of aid.* As already mentioned, in recent years the preference of the administration, strongly

backed by Congress, has been to favor loans rather than grants in its foreign assistance programs. Professor John P. Lewis has questioned this preference as far as India is concerned — and the same reasoning is even more applicable to Pakistan — on the ground that "such a policy line makes no sense if one means conventional loans at conventional terms. Such loans cannot begin to do the needed job." Thus "in the Indo-American program the choice between grants and loans reduces, in practice, to the question of how far the pro-loan bias can safely be indulged in the light of the Indian economy's probable future capacity to service ordinary international loans." Since grants are "political anathema in Washington," and since hard loans "cannot begin to do the needed job," the bulk of assistance to the South Asian countries is now extended in the form of "soft" loans, repayable either in local currency or in dollars on very easy terms. Such loans, in Professor Lewis' view, are "camouflaging devices," and may in fact be "scarcely distinguishable from grants," but they help to save face in New Delhi and Karachi as well as in Washington, and hence should probably continue to be the main type of assistance to India and Pakistan, so long as they do not raise more problems than they solve.[22]

Most of the aid that has flowed into South Asia has been as a result of bilateral agreements. The major multilateral source of assistance has been the International Bank for Reconstruction and Development, but this agency makes only "hard" loans, which probably should not be classed as "foreign assistance" at all. The amounts available from the Bank are limited, and the conditions of loans, repayment, and interest are such that a developing country cannot incur too heavy an obligation to the Bank without further straining its limited resources. If the newer International Development Association, the Bank's "soft-loan satellite," had sizable funds at its disposal — which it does not now have — it could be the major channel of multilateral aid. The International Consortium of Nations, organized through the efforts of the World Bank, is not so much a channel of aid as an agency for negotiation between potential donor countries and India and Pakistan, and any commitments made in the course of these negotiations are made by individual members and must be spelled out in bilateral agreements.

The channeling of aid through multilateral agencies would obviously remove many of the difficulties and embarrassments of bilateral aid. In an address to the Governors of the International Bank and the International Monetary Fund in Washington on September 20, 1962, on the eve of his retirement as President of the Bank, Eugene Black said: "My most serious criticism of bilateral aid programs is their susceptibility to political influences, whether overt or otherwise. At its worst, aid is offered or exacted as a price in political bargaining that takes no account of the actual economic requirements of the recipients. But, even at best, there is always the risk

[22] John P. Lewis, *Quiet Crisis in India: Economic Development and American Policy* (Washington: The Brookings Institution, 1962), pp. 309, 312.

that political influences may misdirect development aid, since they may bring in considerations that are irrelevant to the real needs."

Coming from such a source, these observations are doubly impressive, as they reflect a point of view often advanced by spokesmen of developing nations. The fact is, however, that there is virtually no prospect of a major shift from bilateral to multilateral assistance, and it is also probable that such a shift would be unwise. In any event, it would be politically inexpedient, and might result in a drastic curtailment of the amounts of foreign assistance that would be available for developing nations. Certainly the major source of foreign assistance, the United States, is not likely to consent to channeling the bulk of its assistance through multilateral agencies, in which its voice, however powerful, may be muted in the babel of contesting aspirants for assistance. The American Congress is dissatisfied with the degree of control it exercises over the Agency for International Development, and it is hardly likely to be more generous in voting appropriations to international aid agencies. Many leaders in the developing countries are in fact in favor of the continued reliance on bilateral aid, for, whatever their theoretical preference for receiving aid through multilateral agencies, they realize that they stand a better chance of getting what they need.

Recipient countries naturally want aid "without strings," by which they usually mean without political conditions. This obviously raises all kinds of delicate questions. Governments are not eleemosynary institutions, and they do not make large sums of money available for other nations unless they feel that it is in the national interest. Hence political considerations are a major motivation of the extension of foreign aid. This does not mean, however, that the existence of such considerations imposes unacceptable "political strings" on recipient nations. Presumably this is an area in which the national interests of donor and recipient countries coincide. The United States has asked for certain broad assurances from recipient countries, especially since the Mutual Security Act has been on the statute books, in an effort to ensure that its aid will not be misused, either politically or economically. On the economic side the Congress insists that the United States must maintain some broad checks on the use of American aid.

Two of the conditions on which American aid is extended have been particularly irksome to recipient countries. These are the project tying and the country-of-origin tying conditions. Most of the recipient nations would prefer to have non-project aid, which could then be used, largely as determined by their responsible planners, in areas where it is most needed, instead of for specific projects, approved only after long and sometimes frustrating negotiations. The country-of-origin tying, which has been insisted upon by the United States more strongly in recent years, is even more annoying to recipients. The "Buy American" or "Ship American" provisions were inserted into foreign aid legislation for reasons which are extraneous to the purposes of foreign aid. They are in effect a program for subsidizing certain American private interests. Because American prices are generally higher than those in many other countries, this condition means that American aid will not go so far as it would if orders could be placed where the price and other considerations are more favorable, if lower-cost shipping could be used to bring the products to be imported to the recipient countries, and if these countries would have greater freedom in obtaining the equipment and supplies that they need for development purposes.

For the time being, however, most developing nations realize that they must live with these special conditions (which are not peculiar to the United States), although they do not like them.

4. *The best ways to use the counterpart funds that have accumulated.* This problem is particularly serious, and potentially quite disruptive, especially in India. Huge blocked rupee funds, credited to the United States Government, have accumulated in India and Pakistan as a result of repayment in local currency of old-style Development Loan Fund "soft" loans and especially of sales of surplus foodgrains provided under P.L. 480 loans. Professor Lewis has estimated that by the end of the Third Plan (i.e., in 1966), United States rupee holdings in India "are likely to have an aggregate value of Rs. 800 crores or 900 crores," which "might be equivalent to, say, one fifth of the total Indian money supply."[23] This estimate, startling as it is, was too conservative. By January 1964, more than two years before the end of India's Third Five Year Plan, the blocked rupee holdings of the United States government had exceeded 1100 crores of rupees ($2.3 billion).

As Professor Lewis points out, "there appears to be nothing seriously improper about these arrangements," but "the trouble is that they produce friction between the two governments and, in the case of the Indian government, anxieties that threaten seriously to impede the smoothness of the aid relationship." He mentions five issues involved in these blocked rupee funds, "ranked in descending order of prominence but ascending order of importance: (1) the allegedly inflationary effects of expenditures of blocked rupees, (2) the extent to which the operation of the rupee funds delegates to a foreign government control over indigenous development activities, (3) the sheer administrative nuisance of the arrangements, (4) the progressive accumulation of United States rupee holdings that present procedures seem to assure, and (5) the mounting dangers of proprietary delusion as this accumulation proceeds."[24]

About 15 per cent of the rupee proceeds from the sale of P.L. 480 imports is available to the United States for meeting its rupee expenses in India. Another 5 to 11 per cent is available in the form of "Cooley loans" to American firms or their affiliates for their business activities in India or to any firms whose operations will promote the marketing of American farm products in

[23] Lewis, cited, p. 324.
[24] *Ibid.*, pp. 317–318.

India. The rest of the blocked rupee funds — between 70 and 80 per cent of the total — may be loaned or granted by the American Government to the Indian Government for development purposes. At present the proportion of grants and loans is about 50-50, although previously most of the rupees were made available as loans. The distinction may prove to be largely an academic one, for the loans are soft ones, and the proceeds will be used mostly as a revolving fund for further use for Indian development.

The disadvantages of allowing the blocked rupee funds to accumulate at the present rate, and of maintaining the fiction of repayment obligations on the part of the Indian Government, are becoming increasingly apparent. Both the American and Indian Governments, for reasons which do no credit either to their efficiency or to their tactics, have been slow in agreeing on the use of these funds for development. Immediate efforts should be made to channel larger amounts of these funds into development projects and non-project supporting assistance, and to reach agreement on the use of much larger funds for programs of Indo-American cooperation in educational as well as economic fields. The release of these funds, however, has to be made cautiously, so that they do not lead to inflation, or upset the value of the rupee, or distort the development program.

American Attitudes Toward Soviet Aid to South Asia

Next to the United States, the largest supplier of economic aid to India has been the Soviet Union, which also has given far more aid to India than to any other non-Communist underdeveloped country. Soviet aid has been slightly less than one-fourth the American figure, but it has been extended only since 1955. It has been largely in the form of loans, usually repayable in local currency or in commodities in twelve annual instalments at 2.5 per cent interest, with payment to begin only upon the completion of projects for which the loans are made. Emphasis is placed upon impact projects, and very few conditions or formalities are insisted upon, in marked contrast to the hesitant and more rigid American approach. The leaders of the Soviet Union do not have to obtain approval for foreign aid funds from a vigilant and suspicious legislative body, and they are more concerned with the political than with the economic aspects of their aid program. The Soviet leaders have been careful to see to it that the technicians they send into India are highly competent and that they confine themselves strictly "to their proper fields of activity." The same observation cannot be made of the oversized Soviet diplomatic mission in India.

The United States is understandably concerned about the effects of large-scale Soviet aid upon India at this critical stage. It suspects the motives of the Soviet Union and fears that economic aid may be the entering wedge for political penetration.[25] Thus far, however, the visible effects of Soviet penetration in India are slight, and they are not due primarily to Soviet technicians and Soviet economic aid. After all, the leaders of India have publicly espoused a democratic approach and have publicly rejected the way of forced progress through regimentation. For every contact which it has with the Soviet Union India has a thousand contacts with the non-Communist world, of which it is a part.

The American attitude toward Soviet aid to India, involving as it does some causes for concern and an inevitable competition between the two giants of the modern world, should be a calm and sophisticated one. As the President's Task Force on Foreign Economic Assistance observed:

> It is important that the United States, in its desire to offset these dangers, not engage in a frantic competition to outbid the bloc's offers of aid to seek to prevent countries from accepting aid that will help them. To react this way would involve us in waste, draw us into an undignified posture, and open us to the charge of not being sympathetic to the economic development of other countries except on our own political terms. The size and effectiveness of the Communist effort are reasons for concern and self-examination but not alarm. They emphasize the need for the United States to make its aid as effective as possible, timely, vigorous, and responsive to short-term as well as long-term considerations.[26]

To the extent that Russian and other Communist-bloc aid helps to further the Indian development efforts, it is something which the United States should certainly not oppose. In fact, in some respects it should welcome Soviet willingness to share the burdens of foreign assistance to India, whatever the motives of the Soviets may be. Possibly at this particular period, when the United States and the Soviet Union are unable to reach firm understandings on most issues in dispute between them, South Asia might be in small measure an area of agreement between them.

American Economic Aid to South Asia: Patterns for the Future

Political as well as economic considerations must enter into the American aid program, and determine its size, nature, and priorities. On any basis there is ample justification for making India and Pakistan the major recipients of economic assistance. These two new nations are the giants of the underdeveloped world outside of the Communist orbit. They have as many people as all of Latin America, Africa, and the Middle East combined. They have well-formulated development programs, which have been subjected to close analysis by economists and other specialists. With several years of experience in planning, they have made substantial progress, in spite of many

[25] *Report of the President's Task Force on Foreign Economic Assistance,* pp. 187–189; note particularly the chart, "Other Aspects of the Bloc Offensive," p. 188.
[26] *Ibid.,* p. 189.

difficulties and handicaps. They could not have made as much progress as they have, which is little enough in view of the vast needs they must meet, if they had not had extensive assistance from the United States and other friendly countries, and from international agencies. They cannot continue their planned progress, at an accelerated scale, without even more outside assistance, at least for some years to come. In short, they must move forward with their Plans, for failure to do so will have the most serious consequences, not only for these two great nations and one-sixth of the human race, but for the prospects for peace and stability in the world as a whole.

At least since President Truman's famous "Point Four" speech in January 1949, the United States has been publicly committed to support the efforts of developing nations to establish a better economic base for their continued existence and progress. Yet every year the desirability of this commitment is questioned in the annual debates on the President's request for appropriations for foreign aid, which, after many bitter things are said, the Congress has approved with some cuts in total amounts. As the years pass American impatience with foreign aid grows, reflecting a lack of understanding of the long-time nature of this need and of the importance of American assistance. This impatience is fed, no doubt, by economic difficulties facing the wealthy United States in its foreign economic relations, especially by the continuing drain on its gold reserves and balance-of-payments problems, and also by dissatisfaction with the results and with the reactions in the developing countries to American aid and policies.

Some Americans are totally opposed to foreign aid, either on principle or because they think it does more harm than good. It is hard to believe that they have weighed carefully the consequences of a failure by the wealthiest democratic nation to give assistance out of its abundance to nations that are struggling upward under the most adverse circumstances. Other Americans think that present aid programs are inadequate to offer hope of achieving the professed objectives, and therefore should be greatly increased.

On the whole, the present levels of foreign assistance from countries like the United States which are making large amounts available for such purposes are about as high as one can reasonably expect. Other developed countries that are not presently contributing to development efforts at a similar level might well increase their contributions. In any event, even more important than larger sums of money is the growth in the capacity of the developing nations to plan wisely and to use resources, foreign or domestic, effectively, and in the willingness of the donor nations to place foreign aid on a more sustained and more assured basis and to make it available for the right motives.

All of these observations would seem to argue for the continuance of aid to India and Pakistan along the existing lines of policy and of implementation. The Clay Committee, which expressed the belief that "we are attempting too much for too many" and that "a higher quality and reduced quantity of our diffuse aid effort in certain countries could accomplish more," nevertheless singled out India as a country which should continue to receive "special attention" from the United States, and recommend that "in the interest of our own and free world security, economic and military assistance to India, as well as to Pakistan, must continue under present circumstances."[27]

To the extent that the United States helps the major countries of South Asia, with one-sixth of all the world's people, to attain their development goals it will be furthering American national interests as well. In South Asia, more than in any other part of the underdeveloped world, the United States has an opportunity by enlightened statesmanship and concrete measures to promote what the Congress in the Foreign Assistance Act of 1962 declared to be "a primary necessity, opportunity, and responsibility of the United States, and consistent with its traditions and ideals," by helping "to make a historic demonstration that economic growth and political democracy can go hand in hand to the end that an enlarged community of free, stable, and self-reliant countries can reduce world tensions and insecurity."

[27] Clay Report, p. 8.

CHAPTER SEVEN

The Foreign Policy of India and Pakistan: An Overview

INDIA AND PAKISTAN ARE PLAYING ROLES in world affairs which are out of keeping with their present power but not with their potential significance. They are in many respects weak states, with relatively little economic, political, or military strength. Their vast populations, at existing standards of living, levels of literacy, and lack of national cohesion are probably sources of weakness rather than of strength at the present time. Each is having difficulty in achieving minimally tolerable levels of political and economic development; each is in fact faced with grave problems of survival. Forced to concentrate on such basic problems, both countries are further handicapped by the strains and stresses in their mutual relations.

If considerations of this kind suggest weakness rather than strength, other considerations help to explain the present importance and future potential of India and Pakistan. As the giants of the underdeveloped world outside of the Communist orbit, occupying the clearly delimited Indian subcontinent, they command special attention among all the emerging nations. It would of course be absurd to consider either country as the voice of Asia and Africa; but there can be no doubt that the two major South Asian states do occupy a position of special significance among the more than fifty states of the two continents and that on many issues they do reflect widely held views in the underdeveloped world. Spokesmen of both countries deny that they are seeking to give leadership to the Afro-Asian world — Nehru in particular was quite insistent on this point — but they obviously want their countries to play an active role in world affairs, and they are consciously trying in every possible way to enhance their international influence and prestige. Because of the mutual antagonisms and differences of policies, the two countries often compete with each other in international diplomacy, but on most international issues, such as those brought before the various organs of the United Nations, their views often coincide.

161

Except for a few generalizations of this sort, it would perhaps be misleading to link India and Pakistan so closely in examining their roles in the world.
Thus far India has been much more active and influential than Pakistan. It is
a larger and in most respects a more powerful nation; it has had a more experienced leadership; its representatives have been more numerous and more
conspicuous in almost all international activities. Its enhanced status as
the leading nation of the nonaligned world has at the same time created
special criticisms and difficulties. Often critical of the special attention which
other nations give to India, Pakistan has sometimes charged that this attention can be attributed solely to considerations of power politics, which
encourages India to "play both ends against the middle" and to maintain a
position of "international busybody" without responsibility.

Conditioning Factors

Speaking in the Lok Sabha in 1958, Prime Minister Nehru thus summed
up the conditioning factors of India's foreign policy, in words which could be
applied with equal validity to Pakistan: "Our foreign policy . . . is a policy
inherent in the circumstances of India, inherent in the past thinking of India,
inherent in the whole mental outlook of India, inherent in the conditioning of
the Indian mind during our struggle for freedom, and inherent in the circumstances of the world today."[1] And as Keith Callard has observed, "The determinants of Pakistan's outlook upon the world lie largely in the years
before 1947,"[2] a comment that can be made of India as well.

For India three pre-independence factors are still quite operative: Hindu
traditions and values; what Nehru called "the conditioning of the Indian
mind during our struggle for freedom"; and as an important aspect of the
latter the influence of Mahatma Gandhi on external as well as internal policies. For Pakistan the special background factors are: the influence of Islam
upon Pakistan's foreign policy; the course of Muslim nationalism, and the
events leading to the demand for a separate state of Pakistan; and, as an
important aspect of the second factor, the two-nation theory and other ideas
of Mohammed Ali Jinnah.

There is a tendency in Western countries to underrate or even to ignore
these pre-independence factors. This is a great mistake, and can lead to
some very erroneous conclusions regarding the motivations and the assessment of the foreign policy of India or Pakistan. On the other hand, it is pos-

[1] Statement in the Lok Sabha, December 9, 1958; quoted in Jawaharlal Nehru,
India's Foreign Policy (New Delhi: The Publications Division, Ministry of Information
and Broadcasting, Government of India, 1961), p. 80. This volume of more than 600
pages contains an excellent selection of speeches by Prime Minister Nehru on questions
of foreign policy between September 1946 and April 1961.

[2] *Pakistan's Foreign Policy: An Interpretation* (New York: Institute of Pacific Relations, 1957), p. 1.

sible to exaggerate the impact of such factors. Certainly India's behavior in world affairs cannot be explained wholly on the basis of ancient Hindu traditions and values, or the teachings of Mahatma Gandhi. Unconsciously as well as consciously, the leaders of post-independence India have been influenced by such factors, but it would be impossible to run a modern state in the world of the second half of the twentieth century along such lines. The leaders have in fact followed a pragmatic approach, which can be explained more easily by their own appraisals of Indian national interests under the existing circumstances. The leaders of Pakistan since independence have mostly been men of politics and not of religion; and although Pakistan has been avowedly an Islamic state and its policies have been professedly conducted with this fact constantly in mind, more immediate factors and considerations account for the course of events.

Remarking that "an easy-going tolerance and an assumption that there is some good in everybody, are characteristic Hindu attitudes," Mrs. Beatrice Pitney Lamb writes: "Many observers have noted that Hindus value highly the process of meditation and conciliation, admire the successful mediator, and believe that all disputes can and should be settled by mutual agreement. This optimistic view of the possibilities of peaceful settlement seems likewise to trace back to the fundamental assumption of the underlying unity of reality."[3] Indians close to the conduct of foreign affairs have expressed the same point of view. Mrs. Lakshmi Menon, who has been for some time the second ranking official in the Indian Ministry of External Affairs, has stated: "Even if our cultural and historical traditions do not provide a direct answer to the choice of our policies they do produce a mental and spiritual climate which favours a policy of nonalignment and peaceful co-existence."[4]

"In the position taken by the Indian National Congress on many issues of international import during the sixty-two years of its existence prior to independence may be found the immediate roots of the foreign policy of independent India. . . . A study of the resolutions passed by the . . . Congress will reveal that the Congress took a deep interest in certain external questions from its inception, and that it based its position on certain fundamental principles which still shape the foreign policy of India today."[5] India has, in fact, a remarkable continuity in foreign policy, which dates back many years prior to independence. As early as 1927 the Congress established a Foreign Department, with Jawaharlal Nehru at its head. Thus Nehru was in a very

[3] *India: A World in Transition* (New York: Praeger, 1963), p. 114.

[4] "Our Policy," *Seminar* (New Delhi), No. 19, March 1961, p. 18. See also A. Appadorai, "Traditional Values in the Direction of Peace," *Comprendre* (Venice), No. 20, 1959, pp. 4–5. This is a special issue of *Comprendre* (published by the Société Européenne de Culture in Venice) on "L'Inde dans le Dialogue des Civilisations."

[5] Norman D. Palmer, *The Indian Political System* (Boston: Houghton Mifflin, 1961), pp. 238–239. The main resolutions on foreign policy of the Indian National Congress may be found in N. V. Rajkumar, ed., *The Background of India's Foreign Policy* (New Delhi: All-India Congress Committee, 1952). See also Bimla Prasad, *The Origins of Indian Foreign Policy* (Calcutta: Bookland Private Limited, 1960).

real sense the chief spokesman and architect of India's foreign policy for more than a generation. In a letter to the Presidents of the Pradesh Congress Committees in July 1954 he wrote that the background of India's foreign policy "has been conditioned by our struggle for freedom under Gandhiji's leadership which taught us peaceful methods and tolerance. . . . Our present foreign policy flows from that background and naturally works for world peace and avoidance of war."

Gandhi, as has often been pointed out, harked back to ancient Hindu traditions, and reinterpreted them to support policies of positive action. "What . . . I have done," wrote Gandhi, "is to put a new but natural and logical interpretation upon the whole teaching of the Gita and the Spirit of Hinduism."[6] Gandhi, who took a deep interest in world affairs, held that his teachings were as applicable to the world as to India. Critics often charged that they were so nebulous that their application would be difficult even for those who understood and believed in them, and that some of the methods which he employed most successfully, including nonviolent noncooperation, could hardly have worked if he had had to contend with a Hitler or a Stalin. But to Gandhi nonviolence was not simply a technique but a moral imperative.

Independent India is obviously not being run along Gandhian lines, and retains few Gandhian features. Even though he would surely disapprove of or only reluctantly acquiesce in the basic approach and the specific policies of independent India, almost every one of the leaders have come under his influence and that influence is still felt, if only as a goad to the Indian conscience.

Pakistan is the result of the demand of the Muslim League, supported eventually by a majority of Indian Muslims, for a separate state, and Islam is the ideological, as well as the religious, basis of its existence. Ayub Khan declared in a major address on foreign policy in August 1961: "As far as the ideological integration is concerned, that really means that the Islamic way of life should be the life-pattern of the Muslims of Pakistan. It was on that basis that Pakistan came into being, and it is on that basis alone that it can survive, progress and become strong."[7] To be sure, Islam dominates the life of the country to a greater degree than it does Pakistan's foreign policy, for it is difficult to decide what an Islamic approach to foreign policy really is.

One would expect that Pakistan would have particularly close ties with other Muslim states. Actually, this is not the case, although Pakistan is associated with Turkey and Iran in the Central Treaty Organization. Its relations with its neighbor, Afghanistan, have often been very strained, and its relations with the members of the Arab League are either quite cool, as with the United Arab Republic, or at least not particularly intimate. In his foreign

[6] *Hindu Dharma* (Ahmedabad: Navajivan Publishing House, 1950), p. 177.

[7] Mohammed Ayub Khan, "Essentials of Pakistan's Foreign Policy," *Pakistan Horizon* (the organ of the Pakistan Institute of International Affairs), Fourth Quarter 1961, p. 263. Hereafter cited as "Essentials of Pakistan's Foreign Policy." This article is a condensation of President Ayub's address to the Pakistan Institute of International Affairs on August 25, 1961.

policy address of August 1961, Ayub Khan explained this lack of close affinity with other Muslim states on the ground that "the upsurge in other Muslim countries is, by and large, racial, linguistic, territorial, anti-imperialistic, and anti-colonial. It is not to any large extent religious."[8]

In the struggle for independence in India many Muslims cooperated with the Indian National Congress. Jinnah himself was a member of the Congress until about 1920. Inevitably, however, the Congress was dominated by Hindus.

A kind of Muslim nationalism developed alongside the mainstream of Indian nationalism, particularly after 1906, when the British Government granted a Muslim request for separate electorates and the Muslim League was formed. For a time the League worked rather closely with the Congress, especially during and immediately after World War I. But Jinnah and Gandhi could not agree, and more and more the haughty leader of the Muslim League sought to further his ends by an independent course.

The final parting of the ways came in 1937, when the Congress, having participated in the provincial elections, refused to include Muslims in its ministries unless they were members of the Congress, or would join the party. In 1940, in the famous Lahore resolution, the Muslim League for the first time officially advanced the demand for a separate state. Various efforts to bring the Congress and the League into agreement on some kind of federal or confederal pattern for an independent India failed one by one, and eventually, in 1947, the British Government decided to create two independent states. The Indian National Congress reluctantly concluded that partition was the inescapable price of independence.

Partition was of course the end result of many circumstances, but the man mainly responsible for it was Mohammed Ali Jinnah, the dominant leader of the Muslim League for many years. As Governor General of Pakistan for a year before he died, Jinnah set the pattern for the domestic and foreign policy of the new country and left an indelible stamp on its national life and thought.

Jinnah was a vocal advocate of the two-nation theory, which was and still is anathema to the leaders of the Congress and the Government of India. According to this theory, Muslims and Hindus form not just two religious groups but two nations. As a religious group India's Muslims were outnumbered by the Hindus, before independence, in the proportion of something like three to one, but as a nation they were entitled, Jinnah insisted, to equality of treatment in all respects with the Hindus. Not only should the Muslim League be accorded equal representation and consideration at all conferences with the Indian National Congress, but also Pakistan should be treated on terms of complete equality with India. His successors have been just as adamant on equality of status with India.[9]

---

[8] *Ibid.*

[9] See Callard, *Pakistan's Foreign Policy*, p. 8.

Basic Principles

One British commentator has expressed the view that India does not really have a foreign policy; it has only a foreign commentary. Apparently many people in other countries, including officials and other informed persons who should have known better, were persuaded by the frequent references by Indian spokesmen to the Gandhian traditions of nonviolence and interest in peace that India would under no circumstances resort to force, even to promote its own interpretation of its national interests. Hence the use of force, whatever the justification, in Goa, was widely regarded as a betrayal of professed principles. Yet few persons in India or other non-Communist countries criticized India's military resistance to the Chinese attack in October–November 1962, except on grounds of inadequacy and inefficiency.

Most of the basic principles of India's foreign policy were enunciated in resolutions of the Indian National Congress prior to independence. As stated briefly in a resolution adopted shortly after independence: "The foreign policy of India must necessarily be based on the principles that have guided the Congress in past years. The principles are the promotion of peace, the freedom of all nations, racial equality and the endings of imperialism and colonialism. In particular, the Congress is interested in the freedom of the nations and peoples of Asia and Africa who have suffered under various forms of colonialism for many generations."[10] In an address at Columbia University on October 17, 1949, during his first visit to the United States, Prime Minister Nehru summed up the objectives of the foreign policy of India in a single sentence: "The main objectives of that policy are: the pursuit of peace, not through alignment with any major power or group of powers but through an independent approach to each controversial or disputed issue, the liberation of subject peoples, the maintenance of freedom, both national and individual, the elimination of racial discrimination and the elimination of want, disease and ignorance, which afflict the greater part of the world's population." On innumerable occasions Nehru reiterated these same principles. From these statements, typical of many similar pronouncements of other Indian spokesmen, some of the bases of India's foreign policy clearly emerge. These would include the following: (1) a growing role for India in world affairs, an active participation in international organizations, except for military alliances; (2) a demand for the recognition of Asia as a new and vital force in the world arena, and of India as occupying a position of special importance in Asia, without aspiring, however, to a role of leadership, for this would involve the domination of other Asian countries; (3) anti-colonialism, the liberation of subject peoples, freedom of all nations (this would apply particularly to Asia and Africa); (4) anti-racialism, the

[10] Quoted in Rajkumar, cited.

demand for racial equality and the elimination of racial discrimination everywhere in the world; (5) nonalignment with "power blocs," which is defined as a positive and not a negative approach, one which makes possible a position of independence in foreign policy, and which is opposed to participation in military alliances and pacts of any kind; and (6) the promotion of world peace, peaceful coexistence, the reduction of international tensions, and an emphasis on *Panchsheel* (the five principles of peace). These aims are designed to create an international atmosphere in which India can concentrate on more immediate objectives of paramount importance, such as internal integration and unity, economic development, and military security and defense.

Moderation appears to be the keynote of India's foreign policy, and on the whole India has exercised a moderating role in world affairs. For example, as the elder statesman of the nonaligned nations represented at the Belgrade Conference in September 1961, Nehru exerted a restraining influence on some of the younger and more impetuous leaders of other nonaligned countries. His bold decision to send Indian troops to bolster the United Nations forces in the Congo came at a crucial time for UN operations in that troubled new country, and it served to restrain some African leaders who were threatening to boycott or obstruct the UN's efforts in the Congo.

Relations with India have been the main preoccupation of Pakistan's foreign policy. Its objectives *vis-à-vis* India have centered on security and defense, on the resolution of a long list of disputes, especially the Kashmir dispute, and on gaining equality of status with India in every possible way. Since Pakistan entered into a mutual defense agreement with the United States and became a member of both SEATO and CENTO, in 1944–55, it has inevitably been more directly involved in the "cold war" and in international affairs generally; and since it has at long last come under the control of a strong and confident regime, with wide popular support, it has asserted itself more strongly — some would say more aggressively — in world affairs.

In contrast to the plethora of pronouncements on foreign policy by Nehru and other Indian leaders, authoritative statements of the foreign policy of Pakistan are relatively few. In the National Assembly of Pakistan on February 22, 1957, Prime Minister H. S. Suhrawardy made perhaps the most significant statement on foreign policy by any Pakistani leader prior to 1958. He insisted that Pakistan desired to live on terms of friendship with all nations, including the Communist countries. At the same time he vigorously defended Pakistan's membership in SEATO and CENTO on grounds of their contribution to Pakistan's security. "We are not big enough," he declared, "we are not strong enough to defend ourselves. We have to ask for military assistance from others, because we have not got the resources." "Everything that we do," he said at the beginning of his lengthy speech, "must be directed toward the policy of maintaining our independence in the real sense of the term and our territorial integrity." This understandable, if rather egocentric, approach to foreign affairs has been continued by Ayub Khan, although with some changes in emphasis and in style.

Much of Ayub's major address on foreign policy in August 1961 was devoted to Indo-Pakistan relations. He summed up Pakistan's objectives *vis-à-vis* India in this concise sentence: "I maintain that while wanting to live in peace with it, we should continue to lean against India till such time as a solution of our problems with it [referring particularly to Kashmir] has been found." Pakistan, Ayub declared, had no alternative to seeking outside cooperation in the realm of military security; and the same was true with regard to foreign economic assistance: "We have to rely on outside assistance. There is no need of being ashamed of it. It is a hard fact of life."[11]

In another major statement, a speech to the National Assembly on June 27, 1962, Foreign Minister Mohammed Ali listed the following "seven pillars of our foreign policy":

1. Ensuring security;
2. Maintaining political independence;
3. Preserving territorial integrity;
4. Increasing prosperity;
5. Enhancing international prestige;
6. Promoting peace;
7. Establishing friendly relations with all countries by
   a. bringing about greater stability, strength and prosperity at home; and
   b. by playing a more active and vigorous role abroad.

Actually, the first four of these so-called "pillars" are objectives not so much of foreign policy as of national policy generally, for they involve the immediate issues of survival and development. The Foreign Minister did refer more specifically to relations with Afghanistan, China, the Soviet Union, and the United States. He dismissed India in four sentences, avowing that while "we extend the hand of friendship, the foreign policy of India, in so far as Pakistan is concerned, is aimed at isolating and strangulating us." His views on membership in regional security arrangements reflected the growing disillusionment in Pakistan regarding these arrangements. "These pacts," he said, "have served a useful purpose at a time when we were apparently friendless and alone. We are, however, not fully satisfied with these pacts, although it cannot be denied that they have afforded us some protection." In any event, he insisted, they "have no aggressive designs whatsoever," and they "have not ruled out friendly relations with the Communists or neutralist countries."[12] It is significant and rather ironical that these rather qualified references were made by the man who was Prime

---

[11] For President Ayub's address, see "Essentials of Pakistan's Foreign Policy," pp. 263–271.

[12] The text of Mohammed Ali's address is available as Press Release No. 33, July 5, 1962, issued by the Embassy of Pakistan, Washington.

Minister when his country entered into the military alliance with the United States and joined SEATO and the Baghdad Pact (later known as CENTO).

Even a brief analysis will reveal a remarkable similarity in the professed bases of the foreign policy of India and Pakistan. The major differences are those of outlook and approach, rather than of objectives. The contrast between the two-nation theory of Jinnah and the emphasis of the Indian National Congress and of independent India on the concept of the secular state is very real. The fact that in almost every respect India is a more powerful state than Pakistan conditions their unhappy relations with each other, and their respective roles in international affairs. Aside from their mutual antagonisms, the major difference seems to arise from the fact that Pakistan is an aligned country, whereas India follows a policy of nonalignment. Actually, as we shall see, this has never been as great as it at times appeared. Divergent political evolution, economic policies, and leadership also inevitably tend to shape and color the foreign policies of the two countries.

Role in International Associations

For obvious reasons India has played a more conspicuous and active role on the world's stage than has Pakistan, but both countries have deliberately sought to be active participants in international affairs, in multilateral organizations, associations, and conferences, as well as in bilateral diplomacy.

In the United Nations

Although it was still under British rule, India was a member of the League of Nations. "India's official representatives in the League and in other international organizations before 1946 were nominated by the British Government. . . . Although they took an independent stand on many minor matters, on vital issues of international policy these 'Indian' delegates did not reflect India's views as much as those of the British Government. Occasionally they even went against the spirit of the predominant opinion in India."[13] Many Indians regarded it as a league of "white nations" only, and hence an organization dominated by Western imperialist powers. They objected to the provisions regarding mandated territories, and they felt that the provisions in the Covenant for changes in the *status quo* in dependent territories were quite inadequate. They were interested, however, in many of the nonpolitical activities of the League, and in the growing crisis in international affairs after 1933 they hoped that the League could be helpful in resisting aggression and Fascist expansionism. They seemed to feel that

[13] *India and the United Nations,* Report of a Study Group set up by the Indian Council of World Affairs, prepared for the Carnegie Endowment for International Peace (New York: Manhattan Publishing Company, 1957), p. 4.

"although the League had not made the world a better place to live in, the conditions around us would have been worse but for the League."[14]

At the San Francisco Conference in 1945 which drafted the United Nations Charter, the British Government nominated an able moderate statesman, Sir Ramaswami Mudaliar, to represent India. Sir Ramaswami joined with representatives of other less powerful states in efforts to broaden and liberalize the Dumbarton Oaks Proposals, to give greater attention to economic and social matters, to bring all dependent territories under the international trusteeship system, and to reduce the special rights of the great powers.

India became a charter member of the United Nations. Pakistan, which was held to be a new state and not a successor state to the former undivided India, became a member in September 1947. Although neither country would agree to this comment with respect to the other, both have been faithful members of the United Nations and have taken an active and constructive part in almost all phases of its work.

Representatives of both countries have held high posts in all the main organs of the United Nations, and in its specialized agencies. Madame Pandit was the first Asian — and thus far the only woman — to be elected President of the General Assembly. An eminent Pakistani, Zafrulla Khan, was President of the Seventeenth General Assembly. Both India and Pakistan have at various times been members of the Security Council, the Economic and Social Council, and the Trusteeship Council, and their representatives have therefore been called upon to serve as chairmen of all these bodies. Distinguished nationals of both countries have served on the International Court of Justice.

India, in particular, has made a great and almost unique contribution to the work of the UN through its generally moderating influence with its fellow Afro-Asian states, particularly in recent years, and through its tireless efforts to reconcile different points of view and to develop a "climate of peace." At times the United States — and doubtless the Soviet Union too — has felt somewhat irritated by the efforts of India's representatives to offer the great powers an unlimited supply of free advice and to mediate great power disputes. But on the whole India has made a genuine contribution to the lessening of international tensions and to the reconciliation of international differences.

In their careful study, *The Diplomacy of India,* Ross N. Berkes and Mohinder S. Bedi profess to detect a number of significant changes in the Indian approach to the problems brought before the United Nations. Among these changes are "the transformation of India's performance from that of a radical Power to that of a conservative Power," an increasing tendency to attempt to particularize general issues (which helps to explain

[14] *Ibid.,* p. 12.

India's obsession with the banning of nuclear tests), and a growing willingness to try to function as both partisan and mediator on issues which India feels are important to human as well as to national survival.[15] The latter trend is well illustrated by the more active role which India has been taking in disarmament negotiations.

In spite of their differences in foreign policy, India and Pakistan have shown substantially the same approach to and evaluation of the limitations and potentialities of the UN. Study of the voting record in the various organs, agencies, and committees of the UN reveals that on most of the issues India and Pakistan have taken essentially the same positions.[16] Their relative degree of interest in the various questions that have come before the UN is also strikingly similar. Naturally, they are most vitally interested in the Kashmir question. Other areas of special interest to both are the welfare of dependent peoples, colonialism, economic development in and assistance to underdeveloped countries, racial equality and the elimination of discrimination, and human rights generally. On almost all questions which fall within the broad categories the position of India and Pakistan is virtually the same. Again, except for the Kashmir question, both countries seem to be more concerned with the nonpolitical than with the political functions of the United Nations, although both share a deep interest in the maintenance of international peace and security.

On the maintenance of peace and security rather important differences in the position of India and Pakistan can be found, as would be expected from their general orientation in foreign affairs. Pakistan is somewhat more in favor of efforts to give teeth to the United Nations than is India. Pakistan, for example, voted for the Uniting for Peace Resolution, whereas India abstained. India was the only one of thirty-eight states replying in 1951 to an inquiry by the Collective Measures Committee, provided for in the Resolution, which frankly expressed "clear opposition both to the principle and to the resolution."[17] When, in an exchange on this subject, the American representative declared that the United States regarded collective measures and the pacific settlement of disputes "as inseparable parts of collective security under the United Nations Charter," the Indian delegate sharply disagreed, endorsing a statement by an Indonesian representative that "The implementation of a General Assembly resolution for recourse to collective measures might create a situation likely to develop into world war and to precipitate the very thing that the United Nations was intended to avoid."[18]

---

[15] *The Diplomacy of India* (Stanford University Press, 1958), pp. 203–207.

[16] See Gertrude C. Boland, *India and the United Nations: India's Role in the General Assembly, 1946–57* (unpublished doctoral dissertation, Claremont Graduate School, 1961). This dissertation is a detailed study of roll-call votes in the General Assembly from January 1946 to September 1957.

[17] Berkes and Bedi, cited, p. 7.

[18] UN General Assembly (6th Sess.), *Official Records: First Committee,* January 1952 (New York: Author, 1952), p. 130. The document under consideration at the time

Here India's whole approach is obviously conditioned by its "climate of peace" psychosis: "In regard to the most important question, the maintenance of international peace and security, India believes that the responsibilities and functions of the United Nations will be better exercised and performed through concentration on the pacific settlement of disputes rather than on any other methods, for it is feared that emphasis on the military functions of the United Nations will tend to disrupt rather than strengthen the Organization."[19] Likewise, India is not keen on pushing Charter revision, much as it would like to see the UN changed in a number of respects. It has opposed all proposals for the abolition or even limitation of the use of the "veto" by the permanent members of the Security Council.[20]

Although it prefers to avoid the use of force, even for worthy international ends, India has participated in two of the three operations in which forces under the UN flag have been employed to resist aggression, or to preserve the peace, or to avert internal civil war. India provided contingents for the United Nations Emergency Force in the Gaza strip, although the U.A.R. and other Arab states, and other members as well, were opposed to this Force, and it provided the bulk of United Nations forces in the Congo, in a situation in which the Soviet Union and the United Kingdom and other members were opposed to the UN's efforts. In the Korean crisis, India did not provide any units and generally disapproved of many of the actions of the UN Command, but did vote in favor of the Security Council resolution of June 25, 1950, which declared North Korea the aggressor and called upon all UN members to cooperate in resisting the aggression. It accepted the Chairmanship and provided the custodial force of the United Nations Reparation Commission, which in June 1953 was given custody of all Korean prisoners of war who did not exercise their right to be repatriated.

Unlike India, Pakistan has advocated a regular United Nations peace force.[21] This was suggested by Feroz Khan Noon at both the Eleventh and the Twelfth Sessions of the General Assembly, and it was also proposed by Ayub Khan and Mohammed Ali.

Both India and Pakistan feel that in its present form the United Nations is a rather ineffective organization. But India would rather have it continue as an ineffective organization than become a stronger body, for this could be done only by antagonizing one or more of the great powers that are mem-

---

was the Report of the Collective Measures Committee, UN General Assembly (6th Sess.), *Official Records: Supplement 13, Report of the Collective Measures Committee*, A/1891 (New York: Author, 1952).

[19] *India and the United Nations*, cited, p. 213.

[20] "It is fully realized that the veto very often makes the United Nations ineffective; but India prefers an ineffective organization, representing all the major political elements in the international community, to an effective organization which may grow into an instrument of one power bloc." *Ibid.*, p. 209.

[21] K. Sarwar Hasan, *Pakistan and the United Nations* (New York: Manhattan Publishing Company, 1960), pp. 295–299.

bers of it or by an agreement among the great powers which might be dangerous for weaker members, whereas Pakistan would like to see it become an organization with real vigor and "teeth." Neither country seems to think that the UN can be very helpful in resolving disputes in the South Asian area, but both continue to believe that it is more useful than useless. Nehru seemed to have more faith in the future of the UN than does Ayub Khan. Perhaps because of his military background and impatience with the endless complexities and delays of multilateral diplomacy, Ayub Khan has generally taken a dim view of the UN, even though he has frequently called for its strengthening.[22]

Other differences between the positions taken by India and Pakistan in and toward the UN could easily be found, but these would be greatly outweighed by the similarities in views and in votes, always excepting anything relating to Kashmir. The two countries have voted more often with than against each other, and they have frequently differed from both the United States and the Soviet Union. Between 1947 and 1957, for example, on roll-call votes in the General Assembly India's percentage of agreement with the Soviet Union and the United States was only 49.3 and 39 per cent respectively.[23] In cases in which India and Pakistan take opposing positions, the United States has not always taken the same side as its ally, although its votes on resolutions relating to Kashmir have generally been more acceptable to Pakistan than to India.

In the Asian-African Group

India was largely responsible for the formation of the Asian-African Group, which now, with more than fifty-five members, is by far the largest of the four main caucusing groupings in the United Nations. It includes all the Asian and African members of the UN, except Nationalist China, Israel, and South Africa. Mrs. Vijayalakshmi Pandit has stated that it originated at the Asian Relations Conference in New Delhi in 1947. During the debates in the Third and Fourth Sessions of the UN General Assembly, in 1948 and 1949, the representatives of the Arab League states, plus India, Pakistan, Afghanistan, and Burma, supported by the Communist bloc and some Latin American states, joined forces to defeat an Anglo-French "package deal," supported by the United States, for the disposition of the former Italian colonies. The more formal organization of the Arab-Asian Group, as it was then called, dates from late 1950, when, under the leadership of Sir Benegal Rau of India, the thirteen Arab and Asian members of the UN were organized

---

[22] In an interview with a correspondent of the American Broadcasting Company, broadcast over ABC's radio and television networks on January 6, 1963, Ayub declared: "The United Nations as it is is a sinking bank. It cannot meet its bills and several countries are not prepared to pay their share for the maintenance of the commitments that the United Nations has taken in several places."

[23] See the analysis of roll-call votes in the General Assembly during the period in Boland, cited, p. 51.

to support India's unsuccessful efforts to effect a cease-fire in Korea. It became much stronger and more prominent in UN affairs after the historic Bandung conference of Asian and African states in April 1955.

A loosely organized association with a rotating chairman, the Group has been the voice of Asia and Africa in the UN General Assembly, particularly on questions relating to colonialism, economic assistance to underdeveloped countries, racial discrimination, and human rights. It has played an increasingly active role in a changing United Nations, in which its members alone constitute more than half of the total membership, and therefore possess at least a veto power in the Assembly. On issues on which they can unite and can also get the support of other UN members, such as the Communist bloc, they can usually muster a two-thirds vote.[24]

From the beginning India has been a far more influential member of the Asian-African Group than has Pakistan. India is a nonaligned country, and all but Pakistan and six other members of the Group are also nonaligned. India is the largest of the underdeveloped countries, and virtually all of the members (Japan being the only obvious exception) are underdeveloped. This is not to say that India always gets its way. Even when the Group consisted of a few Arab and Asian states, some members, notably Pakistan and Egypt, often refused to follow India's lead. The Group is now dominated by the new African states, which in turn could be divided into many sub-groups. Some of these African states seem to look to India for leadership, but more of them look elsewhere.

Increasingly the Asian-African Group is taking on a "neutralist" tinge. On those issues on which it can reach a large measure of agreement, it usually takes positions at odds with the views of the United States.

The Communist bloc members of the United Nations have been able to accommodate themselves more readily to the aspirations and sensitivities of most members of the Asian-African Group. Studies of voting records in the General Assembly reveal that the incidence of agreement in voting between the Soviet Union and the majority of the members of the Asian-African Group has been less than 50 per cent; but the United States has voted with the Asian-African majority on even fewer occasions. This applies to questions relating to colonialism (a very wide area indeed), assistance to underdeveloped countries, opposition to atomic and hydrogen bomb tests, admission of Communist China to the UN, and ways to peace generally.

In the Commonwealth

Contrary to the prevailing assumption, based on statements by its leaders and on the anti-British feeling stirred up during the freedom struggle, India chose to become a Dominion in the Commonwealth upon independence. In

---

[24] See Norman D. Palmer, "Changing Balance of Power: The 'Neutral' Nations in the United Nations," in J. S. Bains, ed., *Studies in Political Science* (Bombay: Asia Publishing House, 1961), pp. 38–76.

1949 an agreement was reached at a conference of Commonwealth Prime Ministers whereby India, which announced that it planned to become a Republic, could nevertheless remain within the Commonwealth. Nehru became a stout champion of the Commonwealth tie, from which he maintained India derived substantial benefits without incurring any restrictions on its freedom of action. Most Indians who had any feelings on the subject seemed to go along with his views, with varying degrees of enthusiasm. Serious reappraisal developed at the time of the Suez crisis in 1956, when feeling against Britain was so strong in India. Paradoxically, "the significant result" of the reappraisal following the British actions in Egypt (which were taken without consultation with any Commonwealth countries or with the United States) "was not merely a re-affirmation of India's continued membership of the Commonwealth — which was perhaps never seriously in doubt — but the fact that it was done after a public debate which clarified or underlined the real nature of the Commonwealth and the reasons for India's membership in it in the minds of millions of Indian people."[25]

Now that South Africa has withdrawn from the Commonwealth, India is on good terms with all the members, with the conspicuous exception of Pakistan. Its generally close and friendly relations with the United Kingdom is one of the miracles of postwar international relations. Thousands of Englishmen are still in India, and thousands of Indians, mostly students and immigrants, are in England. Some 80 per cent of foreign private investment in India has been made by English interests.

But although relations between India and England are generally cordial, some serious differences have developed which have inevitably had their effects on Indian attitudes toward the Commonwealth. These include the Indian reactions against the Commonwealth Immigration Act of 1962, which they attribute to "the rising crescendo of colour consciousness in Britain," a development which alarms them immensely; the indignation in India over the strong criticisms in Britain of the move into Goa; differences between India and Britain in the Congo; Indian resentment over Britain's support of the resolution on Kashmir in the UN Security Council in June 1962; and India's concern over the consequences to it of Britain's proposed association with the European Economic Community.

That Britain's role in any steps leading toward a united Europe would continue to be peripheral rather than central was confirmed by the divisions within Britain itself on this issue and by de Gaulle's rejection of Britain's bid to join the Common Market in January 1963. There was little regret in Commonwealth countries over these developments, although there were many expressions of resentment at de Gaulle's arbitrary behavior. India had already experienced a new upsurge of attachment to the Commonwealth and toward Britain as a result of the strong sympathy and the prompt

[25] M. S. Rajan, "India and the Commonwealth," *India Quarterly*, January-March 1960, pp. 32, 36–37, 47.

dispatch of military assistance by Britain and Canada after the unexpected Chinese assault on India in late October 1962.

Pakistan, too, has been a consistent supporter of the Commonwealth, despite disappointment with the lack of support on issues of greatest concern to it. At an early stage it was alienated from Britain by what it regarded as anti-Pakistan actions and attitudes of British representatives in the subcontinent, notably Lord Mountbatten and Sir Cyril Radcliffe, and as an inadequate amount of British assistance in dealing with the pressing problems immediately after independence. Its interest in the Commonwealth increased gradually, especially after it became associated with Britain and two other Commonwealth members in SEATO and with Britain in the Baghdad Pact in 1954 and 1955. Most Pakistanis, like most Indians, reacted strongly against the British participation in the Anglo-French-Israeli military operations against Egypt in 1956, and some questioned the desirability of remaining in any associations of which Britain was also a member.[26] Prime Minister Suhrawardy, however, stoutly rejected all proposals for abandoning the Baghdad Pact or the Commonwealth.

In recent years Pakistan has blown hot and cold over its membership in the Commonwealth and over its ties with Britain. The fact that Queen Elizabeth and Prince Philip visited Pakistan as well as India in 1961 was a boost to Pakistan's pride and tended to strengthen support of the Commonwealth. Pakistan shared India's indignation over the Commonwealth Immigration Act, but it took a quite different and favorable view of Britain's reactions to the Indian occupation of Goa and of the British vote on the Kashmir question in the Security Council, in June 1962. Officially, at least, it took a more favorable attitude toward the prospect of British participation in the European Common Market, although many Pakistanis shared Indian apprehensions of the consequences of this step upon their trade with the United Kingdom.

In 1962 Foreign Minister Mohammed Ali declared: "We continue to be a member of the Commonwealth of Nations, which we regard as a partnership of equals. It is a unique example of international cooperation which we find useful in our own national interest."[27] In another major speech on foreign policy, Mohammed Ali gave a clear indication that the very act which had given India a new appreciation of the United Kingdom and of the Commonwealth tie had had precisely the opposite effect in Pakistan. British military aid to India, he asserted, was "an act hostile to Pakistan. . . . While rushing to the aid of one Commonwealth country, they should have considered to what extent their action was likely to affect the safety

[26] "There is no doubt that if the invasion had not been halted, this demand would have been irresistible." Sarwar Hasan, cited, p. 183.

[27] Address in the National Assembly, June 27, 1962; Press Release No. 35, July 5, 1962, issued by the Embassy of Pakistan, Washington.

and security of another Commonwealth country."[28] But he did not suggest that the British action, of which Pakistan disapproved, had in any way turned Pakistan against the Commonwealth.

Thus the official view in both India and Pakistan is that membership in the Commonwealth is in the national interest, and brings more advantages than disadvantages. That the two South Asian neighbors find it possible to cooperate with each other in the Commonwealth and with Britain is a commentary on the flexible nature of the ties and on the good sense of the leaders and people of the two Asian countries. The Commonwealth has evolved from an association of white nations to a multi-racial association. It can be an important agency for cooperation and understanding not only between Britain and its former dependencies but between the Western world and the developing countries, during the difficult transition period that lies ahead.

The "New Realism"

The international behavior of India and Pakistan is a reflection of a profound and encouraging fact, namely that in spite of their many differences and their mutual distrust and suspicions, the similarities in the bases, objectives, and policies of the two countries in foreign affairs are far greater than the differences. These similarities are becoming more marked in the present period of foreign policy reappraisal in which both countries are engaged.

The United States should re-examine its own approaches to India and Pakistan to ensure that they are consistent with this trend, for surely one of its basic objectives in the subcontinent of South Asia is to be a force for cooperation. At the same time it should not be too optimistic about apparent similarities, for some of them occur in the less healthy aspects of what has been called the "new realism." Moreover, the differences in foreign policy between India and Pakistan are less significant than differences in domestic politics and economic policies, and in these more basic spheres of national life the two South Asian neighbors seem to be moving farther apart.

What may be described as a "new realism" has been manifest since 1959. It can be dated from rather specific events: in Pakistan from the October "revolution" of 1958 and the commencement of the Ayub Khan regime, and in India from the Chinese moves in 1959 in Tibet and along India's northern frontiers. It has been visible in several ways: in a more realistic approach to international developments and to foreign policy generally; in a new,

[28] Address in the National Assembly, November 22, 1962. For complete text see *Pakistan News Digest* (Karachi), December 1, 1962.

rather surprising, and somewhat unhealthy emphasis on *realpolitik;* in deeply felt and publicly expressed disillusionment with the attitudes and policies of other countries.

The new realism has both healthy and unhealthy aspects, which in many respects tend to be self-defeating and contradictory. It is obviously all to the good that India and Pakistan have undertaken a more realistic approach to foreign policy, but it is rather unfortunate that they have found this franker facing of the problems so upsetting and disturbing that they have fallen back on *realpolitik,* disillusionment, and egocentrism. As a result both countries, for different reasons, are in a sensitive, prickly, and even sulking mood.

An extreme expression of the new realism in Pakistan was voiced in an editorial in the *Dacca Morning News* of January 7, 1962, entitled "Power-intoxicated India." After referring to "the full-blooded threats of Indian warmongers," the editorial concluded:

> It was time we spelled out our policy towards India in more realistic and rather stern terms . . . . Our problem-neighbor understands only strong language and unless we fling its threats back in its teeth it would not serve any useful purpose. Nor is it worthwhile to place any undue reliance on allies or on the effeminate [*sic*] offices of the U.N. President Ayub hit the nail on the head when he asserted the other day that if India attacked Pakistan we shall not depend so much on CENTO and SEATO as on our own armed forces and the whole nation which has to stand on guard against aggression. Whatever the basic postulates of our foreign policy in the past, we must reorient our thinking to meet the new dangers and prepare ourselves afresh with one sole objective: the survival of Pakistan in the midst of its enemies.

Ayub Khan reflected the prevailing disillusionment in Pakistan when he described Pakistan's allies as a "necessary evil." He is obviously disappointed with their position on the Kashmir question, and he now entertains grave reservations regarding the usefulness and vitality of both SEATO and CENTO. He is sensitive to what he regards as the favored treatment of India by other countries, even by Pakistan's allies, which he attributes to the fact that India is a larger country and to other power-political considerations. He has taken several steps, including strong measures against Afghanistan, an insistence on the reopening of the Kashmir dispute in the UN Security Council at an unusually awkward time for India, violent objections to Western military aid to India after the Chinese attack, and the conclusion of several agreements with Communist China, which have created additional problems for his major allies, the United States and the United Kingdom. He has assured his people that come what may, he will see to it that "justice" is done in Kashmir, although he has not indicated how he hopes to force the kind of concessions he has in mind. He has helped to instill new confidence and self-reliance into his fellow-countrymen, but he has also, consciously or unconsciously, helped to strengthen the prevalent feeling that Pakistanis must rely on their own resources, with precious little help or sympathy from others.[29]

Nor is India wholly immune to charges of *realpolitik*. Even some of its friends criticized its military move into Goa as a violation of its professed principles and objectives in foreign policy, as well as of international law and the United Nations Charter. Obviously, the Goa action was not regarded in India in this light; rather it was held to be a deplorable necessity because the great powers, either through the United Nations or through military alliances or by direct negotiations, had failed to compel a stubborn colonial country to yield to the inevitable. It was an act of liberation, not of aggression. If aggression occurred, it was committed by Portugal in refusing to get out of Goa. The tone and vehemence of the American and British criticisms of India's move into Goa shocked and startled many Indians, and left them in a bitter and resentful mood. This mood was modified somewhat in the following months, as both India and the Western powers had sober second thoughts about Goa. It was, however, stirred up again by certain other developments in 1962, notably by the support by the United States and the United Kingdom, against the known desires of India, of the resolution introduced in the Security Council in June 1962, calling upon India and Pakistan to resume direct negotiations regarding Kashmir.

The change in the Indian attitude toward Communist China has been the most obvious feature of India's new realism.[30] When the Chinese attack came, the disillusionment of most Indians was transferred from the Western powers to China, to the nonaligned states, to a certain degree to the Soviet Union, and to their own policies and leaders. Nothing has done more in recent years to create good will toward the United States and the United Kingdom in India than the prompt extension of military assistance to India in its hour of peril.

Changing Patterns of Alignment and Nonalignment

The most obvious difference between their foreign policies is that Pakistan is an aligned country and India is not. The difference, however, has never been as great as it would appear. Except on the level of official policy, alignment and nonalignment have little meaning in South Asia. While India clings to a policy of nonalignment, at least in name, it has recently undertaken many actions which its own leaders would have characterized in the past as inconsistent with nonalignment. While Pakistan has been an officially aligned nation since 1953–54, it has been very critical of its alliances, and it has not hesitated to take unilateral actions, such as its negotiations with China on border questions and other matters,

---

[29] See Norman D. Palmer, "Pakistan's Mood: The New Realism," *Current History*, November 1962, and "New Directions for Pakistan," *Current History*, February 1964.

[30] See below, pp. 259–263. See also Norman D. Palmer, "Trans-Himalayan Confrontation," *Orbis*, Winter 1963, pp. 513–527.

which are looked upon with extreme suspicion by the United States and its other allies. Alignment was never really popular in Pakistan — indeed, the sentiment for "neutralism" stemmed from the same roots and was about as strong among Pakistanis as among Indians. Recently there have been growing evidences of a trend away from alignment to a more independent position.[31] Ayub Khan is under considerable pressure inside Pakistan to turn his back on Pakistan's "incredible allies," to withdraw from SEATO and CENTO, to seek even closer relations with the Communist countries, and to abandon the policy of alignment. While he shares the prevailing disillusionment, Ayub has denied that there has been any basic change in Pakistan's foreign policy, and he has re-affirmed the policy of alignment.[32]

The Chinese moves in 1959 led many Indians to question the basic validity of the nonalignment policy. Although he maintained stoutly that the Chinese violations of *Panchsheel* and of India's borders did not in any way undermine India's basic approach to world affairs, Nehru did not underrate the seriousness of the Chinese moves.

Indians were considerably taken aback by the lukewarm support, or even absence of support, or, in a few instances, actual criticisms, from other nonaligned countries when their country was in grave peril because of the Chinese attack; they were puzzled and rather troubled by the equivocal stand of the Soviet Union; and they were happily surprised by the strong support, of a moral and tangible nature, which came from the aligned nations of the West. Nonalignment, it seemed, had lulled India into a state of dangerous somnolence and into a false sense of security, had led India to shun and criticize countries on which it would have to rely, and to court countries which would turn against it. If India had been a member of SEATO, some Indians claimed, the Chinese would never have dared to attack.

Nehru resisted all pressures to abandon the policy of nonalignment, although he did take, with obvious reluctance, steps which in the past he would have regarded as inconsistent with his basic approach. When asked

[31] See Norman D. Palmer, "New Directions for Pakistan," *Current History*, February 1964, pp. 71–72. At a news conference in Karachi on February 19, 1964, Pakistan's Foreign Minister, Z. A. Bhutto, said frankly: "We do not know how it is possible to be aligned and nonaligned. Some countries are very good experts on being both aligned and nonaligned." *Pakistan Affairs* (issued by Embassy of Pakistan, Washington), March 16, 1964.

[32] When he was asked by a correspondent of the American Broadcasting Company, in an interview broadcast in the United States over ABC's television and radio networks on January 6, 1963, whether there was "any chance of Pakistan . . . joining the bloc of nonaligned countries," Ayub replied: "I do not think so. I do not think so. No. No. I do not think so. Unless some very unfavorable situation which I cannot predict — I cannot visualize or mention — I do not see such a thing happening. We have no intention of putting ourselves in a position where we want to blackmail anybody or anything like that. All we want to make certain is that our safety and security is not in danger, and if our friends do see to that there should be no necessity of changing, or forcing us to change, our stand."

in a television interview not long after the Chinese struck whether this portentous event had not raised doubts about the validity of nonalignment, Nehru said: ". . . you are right to say that it does introduce an element of confusion in regard to our policy. But we want to pursue that policy as far as we can. Of course, if we are attacked, we have to defend ourselves and we take such help as we can get. But still we do not want to join any military bloc and that, in essence, is nonalignment."

The fact is that both India and Pakistan are, and have been, carrying on pragmatic policies in accordance with their leaders' interpretations of the national interest, and neither a professed devotion to either alignment or nonalignment has stood in the way of whatever measures these leaders have deemed necessary under changing circumstances.

Today the value and validity of alignment and nonalignment in South Asia are being questioned as never before, and while neither Pakistan nor India has abandoned its long-standing approach, their respective policies will never be the same again. They will be subject to more searching scrutiny and questioning, and will be judged by the extent to which they contribute to basic security and development.

The Role of the United States

The United States would also do well to take a more pragmatic approach to all South Asian countries, and not to praise or criticize them in accordance with their willingness or unwillingness to take an aligned position. Many articulate elements in the United States — newspaper editors, columnists, members of Congress, and various pressure groups — are insisting that India should officially abandon its "neutralist" policy and join the Western-led collective security system as a price of American assistance in the present emergency. This is a short-sighted view, and it could be a disastrous one.

Since India and Pakistan are in a state of transition and reappraisal, with a new appreciation of external and internal perils, the United States is faced with the necessity, which can be turned into an opportunity, to reappraise its relations with the two countries and seek a firmer footing for them. It faces the particularly delicate task of convincing Pakistan that alignment is worthwhile, and that its interests are not being neglected or jeopardized; at the same time it is trying to establish a new relationship with India and to assist that country in achieving greater military as well as economic strength, without caviling about India's continued adherence to nonalignment.

At the moment, the relations of the United States with its greatest Asian ally, Pakistan, are less satisfactory than are those with the leading Asian "neutralist," India. Pakistan feels that its ally really pays much more attention to India than to it, and, further, that in any showdown between the two the United States would probably back India. "Over the last decade," wrote Ayub Khan in 1963, "the policies of the United States have undergone a change which has operated progressively to the disadvantage of her ally, Pakistan, vis-a-vis neutral India." He seemed particularly disturbed over two aspects of recent United States policy: first, "over the decade the distinction in American eyes between an ally and a neutral has become increasingly blurred to a vanishing point"; and secondly, the provision of American military assistance to India after the Chinese attack in October 1962 — which he called a "border clash" — was "on a scale which to us seemed totally unjustified by the requirements of the situation." "A massive Indian military buildup," he warned, "would . . . imperil the existing precarious balance of power in this area. It would increase the existing sense of insecurity among India's smaller neighbors, which could force them to courses of action that might undermine the West's position throughout South Asia."[33]

In the present situation it is particularly important that the United States should not neglect Pakistan. Much damage has been done to relations between the two countries, and hence a major effort to restore them to a new level of understanding and confidence is needed. This calls for effective steps to restore a deteriorating alliance and to convince sensitive Pakistanis that the United States is not neglecting Pakistan's needs and interests in its present absorption with India's defense and other needs. It should give every consideration to Pakistan's views, and it should explore the possibilities of giving Pakistan some more definite assurances or guarantees against attack from India or any other country.

If Pakistan is becoming increasingly dubious of the value to it of SEATO and CENTO, this is due in part to uncertainty regarding America's own assessments of their value and the degree of American willingness to support them. The United States should make up its own mind about the value, or lack of value, of these alliances and should inform its allies of its views. It should also solicit the views of Pakistan, and should give concrete evidence that it does not take Pakistan too much for granted. On the other hand, it should not hesitate to express its concern over those recent trends in Pakistani policies and attitudes which seem detrimental to American interests and objectives.

In the case of India the United States has an unprecedented opportunity to establish a new and deeper relationship. Indo-American relations reached a new high after the prompt American military assistance to India at a time of grave peril. They have continued to be high, although they have experienced ups and downs since October 1962, as they did in previous years.

The limitations of nonalignment are now more clearly understood in India, and at the same time the Western powers have been brought to redefine

[33] "The Pakistan-American Alliance: Stresses and Strains," *Foreign Affairs*, January 1964, pp. 198, 200, 209.

the nature and purposes of their alliances. A different kind of alliance seems to have developed between India and the Western nations which have come to its aid in an economic, and more recently military, way. An alliance without formal ties, it is compatible with both alignment and nonalignment. Springing from an emergency, it is based on a greater awareness of "the realities of the modern world" and of the steps that free peoples must take to protect their freedoms and ensure their survival.

Again it is important to remember that United States policies toward India and Pakistan should not conflict with each other; wherever possible, the United States should look at South Asia as a whole and make every effort to promote cooperation within the area. The course of United States-South Asian relations will be greatly affected by such immediate matters as the tensions existing between India and Pakistan on Kashmir, in which the United States is involved, and by the extent and nature of American economic assistance to all the countries of the area and of military assistance to India and Pakistan. In these sensitive matters effective assistance to one country may be regarded as an unfriendly act by another, and any large-scale assistance on a regional basis is apparently ruled out by the state of inter-regional relations. Moreover, the problem of extensive economic and military assistance to India and Pakistan is perhaps more a matter of internal American politics than of United States-South Asian relations, for in South Asia itself the need for such assistance is painfully apparent; and the question of military assistance to India and Pakistan can hardly be avoided, until and unless some better way is found to assist these countries to develop an adequate defense posture.

CHAPTER EIGHT

Problems of Security
and Defense

EVEN MORE THAN IN FORMER TIMES, security in the atomic age is at best a relative matter and at worst a will-o'-the-wisp which constantly eludes the hardiest and most earnest pursuer. Possibly the least secure nations today are those great powers which are economically, technologically, and militarily the most powerful, whereas the most secure may be those relatively small, remote, and underdeveloped states which have not yet become involved in the maelstrom of international affairs or have not yet even entered the twentieth century in any real sense.

India and Pakistan lie in between these two extremes. Speaking in the Indian Parliament on December 21, 1950, Nehru said: "India is more secure than 90 per cent of the countries of the world, not on the basis of her armed strength, but judging from the present world situation, the danger to India in the near future is far less than that threatening more powerful and advanced nations." Presumably most Indians shared this feeling, although they had growing doubts about India's security as the international situation became more alarming and as the "cold war" was brought closer to India's borders. In any event, the Chinese attack in late 1962 gave Indians a sense of imminent danger which they had not had before, and which most Pakistanis apparently do not share.

Approaches to Problems of Defense

As relatively weak states with large populations and of rather large size and strategic importance, India and Pakistan have special problems of survival in an era characterized by man's limited ability to use wisely the unlimited power he has unleashed. All nations and peoples presumably have a stake in preserving the peace, but Indians and Pakistanis feel that

184

they have a special commitment, for without peace they cannot possibly lay the bases of a tolerable existence for their growing millions, and they would become more or less helpless victims in any atomic conflict. Hence the strong emphasis on the necessity for peace has a starkly practical as well as an idealistic aspect, mixed, to be sure, with some ingredients of unreality and moral preachment.

There is little that India can do militarily to achieve greater security against the danger of atomic warfare. India is not, and officially does not wish to be, a nuclear power. Its defense forces and defense strategy are not designed to meet an atomic attack, or to fight an atomic war. In such an event, its first object will undoubtedly be to keep out of the contest, and it will be forced to rely on assistance from outside if it comes under attack. Its main defense against such a dire eventuality must be on the diplomatic level. For this reason, among others, it has sought to reduce international tensions and to act as a mediatory and mollifying force in the councils of the nations.

Pakistan, an even weaker state than India, can also do little, except through its international diplomacy, to prepare itself for a possible nuclear war. By choice it is associated with SEATO, with CENTO, and with the United States in four mutual security arrangements. The majority of its people have always had grave doubts of the wisdom of these commitments, and its present leaders, most of whom are military men, seem now to share these doubts. The prevailing Pakistani point of view seems to be that its willingness to "stand up and be counted" has not strengthened its position *vis-à-vis* India, its main security concern, and at the same time has had adverse effects on its internal development and on its international position, chiefly by incurring the hostility of the Communist states. The revelation that the American U-2 had taken off from a Pakistani airfield on its ill-fated flight over Soviet territory in May 1960, and Khrushchev's blunt warning to Pakistan, came as a shock to most Pakistanis and reminded them that because of their alliance with the United States they might be directly and fatefully involved at an early stage in any Soviet-American conflict.

The leaders of India and Pakistan are quite aware of the geopolitical importance of South Asia under present world conditions, and of the inherent dangers. While they are not able to do much by themselves to guard against these dangers, they realize that they are far from disinterested spectators of the current world drama, and they will do all they can by diplomacy and other nonmilitary means to help to prevent a global holocaust, in which they might be involved despite all efforts to remain relatively immune. Nevertheless, India and Pakistan are primarily concerned with more immediate and less global dangers and threats. Since the character of their armed forces depends upon the missions for which they are designed, subject to very serious financial limitations, it is important to bear in mind that leaders of both countries are thinking in terms of non-nuclear war, as far as defense preparations are concerned.[1]

Because of developments at home and abroad since 1959, both India and Pakistan have changed their approach to defense as well as foreign policy. The crisis in Sino-Indian relations has forced India to look to its northern borders, to take special measures for defense, to re-examine many aspects of its policies, and to consider a number of unpleasant eventualities. Pakistan is currently in a disillusioned frame of mind with regard to all kinds of security pacts, and its spokesmen are now taking the position that they must rely only upon themselves and look to their own resources for promoting their deepest interests and protecting themselves against India and other potential foes. Since its own resources are patently inadequate for such purposes, Pakistan is faced with a real dilemma, which involves far more than security considerations.

Defense Against Whom?

Throughout the years of their independence the main security concern of India and Pakistan has been defense against each other. The continuing unfriendly relations of the two neighbors have been a grave handicap to their efforts at unification and development, even to their survival as independent states.

The reason why Pakistan considers India a threat is fairly obvious. India is a larger and, in almost every respect, a much more powerful state. Pakistanis have never been impressed with the image of India as a state dedicated to nonviolence and peace.[2] They are convinced that many Indians do not even concede Pakistan's right to independent existence and favor the reunification of the subcontinent, if necessary by force. They remember the military operations in Kashmir in 1947–48, the massing of Indian troops along Pakistan's borders, the forceful means employed by India in Junagadh, Hyderabad, and Goa. They tend to interpret strong statements by Indian spokesmen — such as Sanjiva Reddy's promise in January 1962 that India would "vacate the aggression" in Kashmir — as constituting threats directed against Pakistan. Immediately after India's military take-over in Goa, *Dawn*, the leading Pakistani newspaper, stated: "Pakistan faces exactly the same

---

[1] In the opinion of a well-known ICS Officer, a former Secretary of the Indian Ministry of Defense, "Our armed forces must be capable of defending our territory against a possible attack by a strong power of a second class variety using conventional weapons." H. M. Patel, "Realities of the Situation," *Seminar* (New Delhi) No. 35, July 1962, p. 23.

[2] Speaking in the General Assembly of the United Nations on September 30, 1963, Z. A. Bhutto, Foreign Minister of Pakistan, charged that "In the last fifteen years, India has committed aggression no less than five times." This same charge was made by Aziz Ahmed, then Pakistan's ambassador to the United States, in an address at the Naval War College, Newport, R. I., on May 14, 1963, and it has been repeated by many other Pakistani spokesmen.

danger as Goa did and as soon as India feels strong enough to do so she will try to wipe out Pakistan."[3] This kind of warning is common in the excitable Pakistani press. It was undoubtedly uppermost in many Pakistani minds when India and Pakistan became involved in a full-scale war in the fall of 1965.

India's reasons for alarm about Pakistan are more difficult to state, but are perhaps equally compelling. Pakistan is a hostile neighbor; its present armed strength, fortified by the alliance with the United States and by American military aid and by its membership in military pacts, is formidable; and its leaders, its press, and other channels of opinion are constantly agitating for a resolution of the Kashmir question in ways unacceptable to India and are often threatening to resort to forceful measures, if necessary, to see that "justice" is done in Kashmir. Most Indians would agree that Pakistan is a potential threat; they remember all too vividly the tribal invasion of Kashmir in 1947, and the presence of regular units of the Pakistan armed forces in that disputed area in 1948, the repeated calls for a *jihad* against India by some of the more fanatical Pakistanis, the frequent statements by responsible spokesmen of Pakistan which may easily be interpreted as threatening in tone. They are also aware that in Pakistan the military are still in control, whereas in India the military are subordinate to the civilian authorities. India has long believed that it has to consider the possibility of the use of force against it by Pakistan, as a gesture of frustration over Kashmir or as an attempt to preserve national unity in a deteriorating situation by foreign ventures. In 1965 this fear became a reality.

Since the Chinese moves in 1959, and especially since the military invasion of the North East Frontier Agency and Ladakh, Indians have suddenly awakened to the existence of another, and perhaps even a greater, threat to the north. Their Himalayan borders have become "live frontiers"; and while they are still partially protected from the full might of China by forbidding terrain, vast distances, and many other restraining factors, they must seek policies and defense measures against further pressures which will be more effective than the *Panchsheel,* whose open and contemptuous violation by China has come as a great shock to them.

At present India does not regard the Soviet Union as a major threat. Indeed, it seems to hope that the senior partner of the Communist world will act as a modifying and restraining influence on the Chinese Communists. Many Indians realize, however, that at some future time the Soviet Union may decide to put real pressure on India, instead of upon China. The great land mass of Soviet Asia extends to within a short distance of Indian territory, and they would by themselves be almost helpless against a major Soviet push or atomic attack.

Pakistan has more immediate reason to be concerned about Soviet inten-

---

[3] "A Warning to Pakistan" (Editorial), *Dawn,* December 20, 1961.

tions regarding it, for, as has been pointed out, it has already incurred open Soviet displeasure by its policy of alignment. At the moment Pakistan seems to be engaged in a mild flirtation with both Communist China and the Soviet Union, for reasons that are obviously devious and complex; but while Pakistan would regard China as an immediate threat only if it undertook a major thrust into the subcontinent, it has to give some serious attention in its defense planning and preparations to the possibility of further difficulties with the Soviet Union.

Pakistan undoubtedly regards its unfriendly neighbor, Afghanistan, as a threat because of the agitation of the Afghan government for a separate Pakhtunistan, to be carved completely out of Pakistani territory, and especially because of Soviet activities in Afghanistan. These include assistance to the Afghan army, the development of trade routes from Afghanistan through the Soviet Union, agitation among the Pathans and other tribesmen in sensitive areas close to or even on Pakistan's side of the Durand line with, no doubt, subsidies and the supply of arms, and other actions which may turn Afghanistan into a Soviet satellite. (Some Pakistanis believe that this has already occurred.)

Ironically, both India and Pakistan, which often assert their desire to live on friendly terms with all nations and frequently exhort the great powers to settle differences by peaceful means, are on rather bad terms with almost all of their near neighbors. This unhappy situation greatly complicates the security problems of both India and Pakistan.

The Defense of South Asia: Basic Considerations

Although there are many historical and geographic constants in South Asian defense considerations, the present defense policies of India and Pakistan must be designed to meet the new circumstances which independence, accompanied by partition, created.

British Defense Policy

Except among the so-called "martial races" in recent times, India lacks an impressive military tradition. Even though in the Hindu hierarchy the Kshatriyas — the rulers and warriors — were high-caste Hindus, outranked only by the Brahmins, and even though the Indian subcontinent was frequently subject to invasions and to internecine struggles, relatively little attention was given to the art of war. Some military traditions were instilled into the Indian members of the British Indian army, but the people were little involved in any military affairs. During the Second World War, when the Indian National Congress refused to participate in the war effort, some 2,000,000 Indians fought under British command in almost all of the theaters of military operations.

After the mutiny of the Sepoys (i.e., Indian mercenaries) in 1857, the main recruiting ground for the native members of the British Indian army was in areas which are now mostly in West Pakistan — among the Sikhs, Punjabis, Rajputs, Pathans, Baluchis, and others who had generally remained loyal during the trying days of 1857. Despite the greater population of East Pakistan, the number of Bengalis in the armed forces of Pakistan is no more than 15 per cent. Punjabis and Pathans, in particular, not only dominate the armed forces, but also the politics, the administration, and to a lesser extent the business and intellectual life of the entire country. President Ayub Khan, it may be noted, is a Pathan and a professional soldier.

From Britain's point of view the problems of security and defense in South Asia were far greater than those of the maintenance of law and order and imperial rule in the subcontinent itself; for South Asia was the fulcrum of British power in all of Asia. It was the center of a pattern of defense and power which included the great bastions of Hong Kong and Singapore to the east and Aden and the Suez Canal area to the west.

British policy for the defense of India's land frontiers was based on three cardinal objectives: (1) to maintain substantial military strength in the more vulnerable parts of the frontier, chiefly in the North West Frontier Province and Baluchistan, and to keep the tribal peoples of this area pacified or under control by a judicious mixture of concessions, bribes, "divide and rule" tactics, rewards for cooperation and punishments for too vigorous opposition, and firmness and resolution at all times; (2) to encourage the establishment of a string of buffer states all along the periphery of the subcontinent and to maintain influence, and, wherever possible, friendly relations with them; and (3) to prevent, by balance-of-power diplomacy and if necessary by forceful means, Tibet or any other contiguous territory from coming under the control of a strong power, notably Russia.

Lord Curzon, when Governor-General of India, made a classic statement of the British approach to the defense of India:

> India is like a fortress, with the vast moat of the sea on two of her faces and with mountains for her walls on the remainder; but beyond these walls, which are sometimes by no means of insuperable height and admit of being easily penetrated, extends a glacis of varying breadth and dimension. We do not want to occupy it, but we also cannot afford to see it occupied by our foes. We are quite content to let it remain in the hands of our allies and friends, but if rival and unfriendly influences creep up to it and lodge themselves right under our walls, we are compelled to intervene because a danger would thereby grow up that would one day menace our security. That is the secret of the whole position in Arabia, Persia, Afghanistan, Tibet, and as far eastwards as Siam. He would be a shortsighted commander who merely manned his ramparts in India and did not look beyond.[4]

[4] Quoted in J. C. Kundra, *Indian Foreign Policy, 1947–1954: A Study of Relations with the Western Bloc* (Groningen, 1955), pp. 32–33.

New Elements in the Security Picture

British withdrawal forced India and Pakistan to consider immediately their defense needs and organize at least minimum defense forces. Both countries inherited from the British the nucleus of a defense force, plus valuable military training and traditions; but partition led to the withdrawal of most of the British officers and other personnel, and to the division of the British Indian army and of military stores and equipment. A difficult process at best, this was made doubly hard by the circumstances attending partition and the strained relations between the new states. The bulk of the armed forces had been recruited in the Punjab, the very area where the post-partition riots and bloodshed were most extensive. The division of forces took place at a time when they were badly needed to maintain law and order, and when the discipline and loyalty of the troops were being seriously tested by the news that relatives and friends were being driven from their homes and even butchered.

Under British guidance, and in accordance with arrangements worked out between the leaders of the Indian National Congress and the Muslim League, the army and equipment were divided. Personnel were given a free choice of continuing to serve under the British, henceforth outside of India, or in the armed forces of the country of their choice, or of resigning with the usual pensions and payments. Most, but not all, of the Muslim soldiers opted for Pakistan. Of the ten Gurkha regiments, four were transferred to the British, under an agreement between Britain and Nepal, and the remaining six were attached to the new Indian army.

Under these unfavorable circumstances the British Indian army entered the pages of history, and the new armed forces of India and Pakistan came into being, with much more wrangling in the bitter aftermath of partition. An even more serious situation developed when India and Pakistan became involved in armed hostilities as a result of the tribal invasion of Kashmir, the dispatch of units of the Indian army to resist these invaders, and the involvement of regular units of the Pakistan armed forces, at least as early as May 1948, in Kashmir. As a result of the good offices of the United Nations Security Council and the UN Commission for India and Pakistan, the warring neighbors were persuaded to agree to a cease-fire, effective in January 1949; but Kashmir has been an area of danger ever since 1947, and was again a battleground in 1965. Because of strained relations between India and Pakistan, the grave security problem inside the subcontinent still continues, and indeed in recent months has become even more serious. Thus the main defense problem of South Asia since independence has been an internal one, although a new and potentially greater threat has materialized to the north.

Since independence India and Pakistan have been able to do no more than man the "ramparts in India." Beyond their borders they have been rather disturbed by certain events which have added to their security concerns. Among them have been the establishment of a strong Communist regime in China; the take-over of Tibet, which gives the troublesome Chinese Communists a foothold on "the roof of the world" where they have been building roads and military installations, including airfields within easy striking range of Indian centers; and the Chinese pressures along the Himalayan borders and incursions into territory which India insists is a part of the Indian Union. There is increased Chinese influence in Burma and elsewhere in Southeast Asia. The rapid development of those parts of Soviet Asia just to the north of the subcontinent brings Russia closer to South Asia, and there are many evidences of Soviet activities in Afghanistan.

Circumstances of history and of geography have made Pakistan's overall problems of security and defense particularly difficult and complex. "There are no strategic frontiers between Pakistan and India and therefore the defense of the Indo-Pakistan subcontinent has to be considered as a whole."[5] Moreover, on partition Pakistan inherited the traditional frontier problem of the Indian subcontinent. Since Pakistan controls the historic western passes, through which past invasions of the subcontinent have usually come, Pakistan may be called, from the point of view of conventional security considerations, India's first line of defense. Conversely, it may be said that India is vital to Pakistan's defense, for only in Indian territory can Pakistan find its territorial defense in depth. Moreover, East Pakistan must be defended by India against a thrust from the east or north, or it can hardly be defended at all. Both countries have a common interest in keeping potentially hostile powers as far away as possible, and especially in guarding the mountain perimeters and the Indian Ocean avenues of access. Unfortunately, the compulsions toward cooperation in common defense are outweighed by frictions between the two neighbors.

Pakistan's defense problems are, in fact, almost insuperable. In January 1956, General Ayub Khan, then Commander-in-Chief of the Pakistan army, summed up the dilemmas of Pakistan's defense:

> The defense of East Pakistan does not lie in that part of the country. So long as the western base is not strong, it remains indefensible. In spite of the great length of territory in West Pakistan, there is no depth in the area. . . . Since there are no grounds to be given, we have to spring to action immediately in case of a war. Our battles will have to be crucial in the first months.[6]

Against India, which it regards as the greatest threat, Pakistan, the weaker power, has almost no natural protection.

[5] Aslam Siddiqi, *Pakistan Seeks Security* (Lahore: Longmans, Green, 1960), p. 49.
[6] Quoted in *Dawn*, January 18, 1956.

Defense of the Indian Ocean

Though, quite naturally, India and Pakistan give primary attention to the defense of their land frontiers, they must also consider the defense of their sea frontiers. In his *Problems of Indian Defence,* K. M. Panikkar declared: "If the mastery of the Indian seas is established by a hostile power, its pressure would be relentless, since India's economic life is dependent on maritime trade. . . . Attack from the sea is more dangerous to the freedom of India than any threat from across her land frontier."[7] At the moment the problem is not pressing; but Indians and Pakistanis cannot forget the alarms of World War II when British naval losses off Singapore and naval priorities elsewhere left the Indian Ocean highly vulnerable until American sea power intervened.

At present effective control of the Indian Ocean area rests with the American and British navies and air arms; but there are no American naval bases in the area itself, and the British have lost their main bases in South Asia, including Trincomalee in Ceylon, although they still have bases in Singapore and Aden and are developing others in the western part of the Indian Ocean. Fortunately for South Asia the United States and Britain pose no threat. The small Indian navy is powerful enough to exercise a local predominance in the Indian Ocean (a disquieting fact for Pakistan, for in the event of an Indo-Pakistan conflict the Indian navy could probably cut the only supply lines between West and East Pakistan for heavy and bulky items on the long journey around the Indian peninsula).

The only other country which could present a real challenge in the area at the present time is the Soviet Union, through the use of long-range planes, guided missiles, and submarines. Indians and especially Pakistanis are not unaware of traditional Russian interests in the Indian Ocean area and of their revival under the Soviets. In 1960 President Ayub Khan wrote: "As a student of war and strategy, I can see quite clearly the inexorable push of the north in the direction of the warm waters of the Indian Ocean." This push," he warned, "is bound to increase if India and Pakistan go on squabbling with each other." "If, on the other hand," he added, "we resolve our problems and disengage our armed forces from facing inwards as they do today, and face them outwards, I feel that we shall have a good chance of preventing a recurrence of the history of the past.[8]

Military Planning and National Policy

Absorbed in the independence struggle prior to 1947, Indian leaders gave little thought to questions of military policy and strategy. In any event,

---

[7] (Bombay: Asia Publishing House, 1960), pp. 130–131. See also the same author's *India and the Indian Ocean* (London: George Allen and Unwin, 1945), p. 83; and Siddiqi, cited, p. 54.

[8] "Pakistan Perspective," *Foreign Affairs,* July 1960, p. 556.

under the influence of Gandhian ideas the whole tenor of their thinking was different. After independence problems of defense were immediate and compelling. India and Pakistan had to achieve internal order and integration and to defend themselves against each other. Later the impact of the cold war reminded them that to a greater degree than they cared to admit their defense and security, perhaps their whole future, depended upon developments over which they had little, if any, control.

The mission of the Indian army is to defend the frontiers and meet any outside attack. As the Chinese invasion of late 1962 demonstrated, however, the Indian army is not capable, in view of its present size, training, and equipment, of filling this role. In the past, the army was geared almost exclusively for possible trouble with Pakistan, and even today, in the aftermath of the Chinese invasion, major units continue to be stationed in Kashmir and elsewhere along the borders, still pointed toward Pakistan and not toward the north. Six new divisions, however, are being trained and equipped for mountain operations. The mission of the air force is to maintain control of the air space over India and to provide support to the army in its various theaters of operations. It also has a limited capability to take the offensive against any attack from Pakistan, the Indian Ocean area, or immediately north of the Himalayas. It is not adequate to protect the major cities of India from air attack from either China or the Soviet Union. The mission of the navy is to protect the coastline of the country.

One gets the impression that many Indians accept the fact of India's limited capacity to defend itself against any major attack, including any kind of nuclear attack, but that Indian military planning gives little attention to such an eventuality. Romesh Thapar, editor of a well-known Indian magazine, *Seminar,* has insisted that "the starting point of any . . . reassessment must be a willingness to recognize the fact that any major conflict on our soil, whether prompted by Pakistan or China, willy-nilly would involve the nations of the world. If this is accepted, then the role of our armed forces is primarily to cushion the initial shock until such time as help arrives."[9] There is little evidence that the reassessment that must be going on is based on any such premise.

It is very difficult to determine who does the serious military thinking and planning in India, and how much is actually done. Prior to October 20, 1962, neither the Prime Minister nor the Defense Minister took a great interest in such matters, and their approach seemed to be essentially a nonmilitary one. In theory, at least, "the Defense Committee of the Cabinet, presided over by the Prime Minister, . . . decides all matters of policy relating to defence." A Defense Minister's Committee makes "final and binding" decisions on more technical questions.[10] Questions of defense are often discussed in the Parlia-

[9] " 'Leaks' and 'Scoops'," *The Economic Weekly* (Bombay), May 26, 1962, p. 834.
[10] Jaswant Singh, ed., *Indian Armed Forces Year Book, 1960–61* (Bombay: The Commercial Printers and Publishers, 1961), p. 615.

ment, but seldom in a very detailed or informed way. Shortly after the Chinese attack, Nehru announced the formation of a National Defense Council, consisting of a six-member emergency committee of the Cabinet, the chiefs of staff, and a number of retired generals and prominent private citizens. Presumably military policy is now made by the Prime Minister and the Defense Minister in consultation with the new National Defense Council, with some reference to the Cabinet and the Parliament.

In the country generally the discussion of such questions is limited and usually vague. Indeed, there seems to be an "increasing confusion among M.P.'s, editors, special correspondents and other opinion-makers on matters connected with defense."[11] India has almost no military journalists or military historians whose views on defense problems are widely circulated and read, and except for the contributions of the late Sardar K. M. Panikkar[12] there is almost no significant writing on overall problems of Indian defense.

For reasons of history and circumstance Pakistan has given more attention to military matters than has India, and has achieved a closer integration of its military and foreign policy. Whereas, at least until recently, Indian military men have remained behind the scenes, clearly subordinate to the civilian authorities, in Pakistan the army and air force have been very much to the forefront, especially since October 1958. Ayub Khan, who professed to have little knowledge of or interest in politics, has had to run a country as well as control a military establishment. Presumably he and his closest military associates do the thinking and planning for the country in defense matters, and for most other matters as well. Thus, while the leaders of Pakistan seem to be far more conversant than the Indian leaders with strategy and defense, and far less at home in the fields of politics, there is even less public discussion in Pakistan than in India of defense problems, or indeed of any public issues, except by way of parroting the views of those now in power.

The Armed Forces of India and Pakistan

No accurate estimate of the defense capabilities of India and Pakistan can be made; there are clearly too many intangible, and too many unknown, factors. In part this is due to the unavailability of precise information about the exact size, composition, organization, deployment, equipment, and morale of the armed forces of the two countries. To a more significant

---

[11] Thapar, " 'Leaks' and 'Scoops'," p. 835.

[12] See, for example, the following writings of Panikkar: "The Himalayas and Indian Defence," *India Quarterly* (the organ of the Indian Council of World Affairs), April-June 1947; *Geographical Factors in Indian History* (Bombay: Asia Publishing House, 1955); *India and the Indian Ocean*, cited; and *Problems of Indian Defence*, cited.

degree it is due to the larger aspects of the defense equation, for, as Dwight D. Eisenhower once observed, the armed forces are only "the cutting edge" of a defense establishment, which rests ultimately upon the more fundamental determinants of "national power."

Factors Affecting Defense Capabilities

The responsible leaders of India and Pakistan are well aware of the broader aspects of defense policies and needs. This is as true of the civilian leaders of nonaligned India, who profess to abhor any "warlike" approach to peace, as it is of the military leaders of committed Pakistan, who have been trained to consider realistically the whole range of defense problems and capabilities. As Prime Minister Nehru said in the Rajya Sabha on December 8, 1959, "The basic factor in defense is the industrial growth of the country, and all the armies in the world without an industrial background cannot function adequately." Major-General E. Habibullah, a former Commandant of the National Defense Academy, wrote in 1962: "If the canvas of India is to be seen as one whole, then the center of emphasis on it is not defence but what is to be defended. Only when people are conscious of what they can defend can defence itself be ensured."[13]

Many of the details regarding the armed forces and the defense organization of the two countries are of course unavailable. There is also considerable disagreement regarding the relative strength and effectiveness of the armed forces. India started with a larger army, navy, and air force than Pakistan, and it has consistently spent much more on them. Even before October 1962 it was spending about three times as much (amounting to about twice the total revenue of Pakistan), and since the Chinese attack its military expenditures have nearly doubled. It also has greater resources and greater military potential. Its army and navy are much larger and its air force is larger, although not so well equipped. On the other hand, under the control of the military Pakistan has given relatively more attention to military defense than has India. Since 1954, Pakistan has received a great deal of military assistance from the United States, which has defrayed a large share of the total defense budget. Even with this aid Pakistan's military strength is far less than India's, although man for man the Pakistan armed forces are probably superior to India's.

The Indian Army

According to estimates in March 1962, the Indian army consisted of "fewer than 600,000 men," with "ten regular divisions — one armored — and an independent armored brigade." In addition, India had "at least twenty-five battalions of locally recruited militia," and reserves of half a million.[14] The

---

[13] "Facing Facts," *Seminar*, No. 35, July 1962, p. 28.
[14] "If Red China Pushes India Too Far," *U.S. News & World Report*, March 12, 1962, p. 72.

militia are mostly members of the Territorial army, and the reserves are mostly in the Lok Sahayak Sena (formerly the National Volunteer Force) and the National Cadet Corps. In 1963, for the first time, participation in the NCC program was made compulsory for every college and university student under twenty-six years of age, unless special exemption is granted. In that year the NCC reached a strength of about one million.

In the course of two years the army was increased by "at least 25 per cent." The enlarged crisis with China after October 1962 led to further expansion of the army, although it is well below the million-man force which was frequently mentioned as a minimum target in the frantic days following the attack, and to many other steps to strengthen India's military capabilities. At the time of the outbreak of fighting between India and Pakistan in the fall of 1965 it was reported to have at least sixteen divisions and a total strength variously estimated at between 820,000 and 870,000 men.

The army is still composed entirely of volunteers, recruited from all parts of India, but still with a preponderance of Sikhs, Punjabis, Raiputs, and other "martial races." Recruits are often good physical specimens, but most of them are illiterate and lacking in basic skills. They receive about thirty-two weeks of basic training before they are assigned to some army battalion.

The Indian army is still very British in its organization, traditions, and outlook. Its senior officers were almost all graduates of Sandhurst, of whom there are now only a handful in service. The rest were trained at the Indian Military Academy at Dehru Dun, most of whose cadets now come from the National Defense Academy near Poona, where some 500 young men are trained each year as potential officers for all three branches of the armed forces. Senior officers get additional training at the Staff College at Wellington and the new National Defense College in New Delhi (for senior officers of the three branches of the armed services). Junior officers are less well trained, and are less familiar with the English language or with the traditions of the service. "India's best men are not now seeking army careers, as they used to. From the potential officer's point of view the regular army is now a rather ill-paid and slightly shameful part of the body politic, much as it was in the United States before 1941."[15] The enlisted men, however, are still of high quality and good morale.

Military equipment is inadequate and often outmoded — "the weak point" of India's armed forces.[16] The army still uses equipment dating back to World War II or even, as in the case of the Enfield rifle, to World War I. It has been the policy of the Indian government — especially after Krishna Menon became Minister of Defense in 1957 — to manufacture as many of

[15] John Masters, "The New Indian Army," *The Saturday Evening Post*, April 1, 1961, p. 72. The author of this much-discussed article, who is well-known as a novelist, served with the British Indian Army before and during World War II.

[16] *Ibid.*, p. 71. See also H. M. Patel, *The Defence of India*, R. R. Kale Memorial Lecture, 1963, at the Gokhale Institute of Politics and Economics, Poona (Bombay: Asia Publishing House, 1963), pp. 25–29.

the needed weapons and military equipment and supplies as possible. The Defense Production Organization, which is associated with the Department of Defense, operates about twenty-five arms plants in various parts of the country and also factories for the manufacture of military supplies.

"In sum," according to John Masters, "the Indian Army of today is first class in its senior leaders and its enlisted men, something less than first class in its junior officers and its overall morale, and third class in its equipment and political direction."[17]

In spite of the emphasis on defense production, India must depend for a long time to come on outside sources for "all except the simplest defense items." This raises grave problems of foreign exchange, replacements and spare parts, standardization of equipment, availability of equipment when needed, the world political situation, and control of the sea lanes. Nevertheless, if the Indian armed forces are to be provided with modern weapons and equipment, most of these will have to come from countries where defense production is more advanced. This need has been dramatized by the supply of F-104 jets and Sidewinder missiles to Pakistan.

As the short-lived war with China in October–November 1962 demonstrated, the army is ill-prepared for operations along its northern borders, but it is devoting much effort to improving its capabilities in this respect. Indian soldiers are building roads toward the frontier in Ladakh and the North East Frontier Area, and they are training for high altitude operations. Deficiencies in logistics and in transport were also apparent in the Goa operation, when it took the Indian army more than a month to mobilize along the borders of Goa and to undertake other troop movements.

The Indian army must be reorganized, re-equipped, and expanded before it will be ready to meet another major attack from the north. Estimates indicate that this will require an energetic build-up over a period of at least two years, and that the costs of the military build-up will be well over a billion dollars. Most of the sophisticated weapons and equipment must come from the United States and other major military powers, and since India does not have foreign currency to pay for these "unproductive" materials, they must be provided either on a grant or on a long-term basis. "It will be a major strain on the Indian economy to produce even the clothing, food, and housing for a force larger than the present . . . army, let alone meet the costs of arms and equipment needs."[18]

The Indian Air Force — and Russian MIGs

Although the main mission of the Indian air force is still to give tactical and strategic support to the army, it is gradually developing more of an identity of its own, and it is being equipped and trained to perform larger functions. One of the great handicaps of the air force is its almost exclusive

[17] Masters, cited, p. 72.
[18] *U.S. News & World Report,* December 10, 1962.

reliance on other countries for its aircraft and for most of the more complicated equipment. While most purchases of planes and equipment are made in Britain, there have been extensive purchases from other states as well. This introduces special problems of procurement, maintenance, training, replacement of spare parts, and effective operation. The air force has "British Canberras, Vampires, and Hunters, French Ourgons (Toofanis) and Mystères, American Fairchild Packet and Bell helicopters, Russian AN-12 transport planes and MI-4 helicopters."[19] It also has Liberators, Dakotas, Ilyushins, Devons, Otters, Viscounts, and trainers, plus several types manufactured in India. It had some American C-119 transport planes, but since these had too low a ceiling and were not suitable for the purposes for which they were used, they were transferred to the Indian Airlines Corporation. India now manufactures some military aircraft, including the AVRO 748 transport, under arrangements with the British, Gnat and Vampire fighters, and the HF-24, India's first supersonic fighter. The HF-24 is now operational, but it can be manufactured only in small quantities, and its performance cannot compare with the most modern jet fighters.

Since the first F-104As were delivered by the United States to Pakistan, along with Sidewinder missiles, India has been determined to match or surpass the formidable increase in Pakistan's military strength by equipping some of its own jet squadrons with aircraft of comparable performance, and by insuring a continued supply by domestic manufacture. This search led it to contemplate the purchase of MIG-21 jet fighters from the Soviet Union, and to make arrangements with the Soviets for local manufacture of these planes and of guided missiles.

The proposed MIG deal evoked a great deal of criticism in the United States, at a time when aid to India was under consideration in Congress. The United States is understandably concerned over the prospect of Indian dependence on the Soviet Union for its modern jet aircraft and missiles, and especially over the manufacture of Russian planes and missiles in India. On the other hand, as the Indians point out, the United States is in a weak position on this issue, for it has virtually forced India to seek modern jets and missiles by supplying such items to Pakistan and, even if certain legal obstacles could be removed, India would probably not be able to obtain similar planes and Sidewinders from the United States except under conditions which it would be reluctant to accept.

The British, also, will probably be unable to meet India's needs. Negotiations with the Soviet Union were initiated in part because a British firm, Bristol-Orpheus, which has been supplying India with engines for the Gnat and HF-24 Mark I fighters, informed the Indian Government in 1961 that it would not be able to proceed with the development of Bors-12 engines,

[19] K. Rangaswami, "Production of Jets and Missiles," *The Hindu Weekly Review*, May 14, 1962. See also Jaswant Singh, cited, p. 665.

which India had ordered for use in the HF-24 Mark II, unless India would bear the entire cost of development, estimated at some £5 million. This unexpected difficulty led the Indian Government to seek suitable jet engines in other markets, and to link this search with arrangements for the purchase of the most modern type of jets and for their manufacture, with the cooperation of the producing country, in India. Serious consideration, it was reported, was given to the British P-1 Lightning, the French Mirage III, the American F-104A, and the Soviet MIG-21. The American jets were not available to India. Indian experts seemed to have some doubts regarding the suitability or availability of the British or French types. Neither Britain nor France showed much interest in assisting in the manufacture of jets in India, under licensing arrangements.

Under these circumstances it was difficult for the Indian Government to turn down Russia's long-standing offers, although India had, for political and other reasons, refrained from taking them up. Krishna Menon, then the Defense Minister, favored acceptance of the Soviet offer. Possibly the fact that this arrangement would irritate and alienate the Western powers was in Mr. Menon's mind an argument in favor of the proposed arrangement. He also argued that the Russian terms were attractive, and that the MIG-21 was particularly suited to India's needs and conditions.

Apparently the Soviet offer was indeed an attractive one. Russia, it was reported, would provide all the MIG-21s India wanted in the near future (perhaps enough for two squadrons), at a price about half that quoted by Western manufacturers of comparable planes, with easy terms of payment over a long period of time, in rupees or goods and not in rubles or other foreign currency. Furthermore, the Soviet Union would assist India to develop facilities for the manufacture of MIG-21s and guided missiles, by providing technicians, financing, engines, and supporting assistance. Certainly this was an offer which no Western country could or would match, and it seemed to provide the only way for India to develop as modern an air force as Pakistan. In May 1962 the Indian government announced that the Soviet Union would supply some MIG-21s and would help to build several factories in India.

The Chinese attack on India increased India's need for modern jet fighter planes, and raised new doubts about Russia's willingness to make good on its past offers. It had already supplied China with an unknown number of MIG-19s, some of which were based at airfields in Tibet. Would it now supply even more modern MIGs to India and help it to manufacture them, a concession which it had not made to China? Would the Western powers continue to extend military assistance if India relied on the Soviet Union to supply modern jets, and would the Soviet Union renege if India became a major recipient of Western military aid? For a time after the Chinese attack the Soviet Union seemed to be stalling in the fulfillment of its promised commitments. It notified India that it was compelled to postpone deliveries of MIGs promised in December. Many Indians criticized their government for continuing to believe that the Soviet Union could be relied upon to fulfill its commitments. Nehru, however, insisted the Russian promises would be redeemed.

Four MIGs were delivered in Bombay in February 1963, and three more by October. Two of these were destroyed in a mid-air collision in December. Only a few — perhaps less than one squadron — are now in service. Late in 1963 project reports were completed for an airframe factory at Nasik, Maharashtra, and an engine plant at Koraput, Orissa; and plans were being discussed to build a factory at Hyderabad to manufacture guided missiles and electronic equipment. In August 1964 an Indian mission headed by Defense Minister Y. B. Chavan went to Moscow to renew a request, turned down earlier in the year, that the Soviet Union help India to build a ground-to-air missile factory. The U.S.S.R. has already shipped some ground-to-air missiles to India.[20]

Thus plans are well advanced for Soviet assistance in manufacturing MIGs and missiles. But there are still signs that the Soviets are vacillating, and that India is none too happy with the deal. The original cost estimates reportedly have jumped from $143 million to $336 million, the Soviet terms of payment are apparently more severe than India had expected, and construction of the proposed plants seems to be lagging.

For political reasons the Soviet Union may give India some limited assistance in meeting its needs for modern jet fighters; but from India's point of view this assistance may prove highly undependable, and perhaps politically unwise as well. The Indian air force and the Finance Ministry are not enthusiastic about the arrangement, apparently because they are concerned about the possibility of undue Soviet influence, about the reaction of the Western countries which are the main suppliers of military as well as economic materials and aid, and about the danger that the Soviet Union may not honor its commitments, especially if Sino-Soviet relations take a turn for the better. Even if the Soviet Union does assist India in building facilities for the manufacture of MIG-21s or later models, no significant domestic production can be expected for many months, and the models that may be produced may be obsolete by the time they are available.

The United States, the United Kingdom, and other Western countries that are now providing substantial military assistance to India can hardly criticize these negotiations until and unless they can assure India of a larger and more dependable source of modern jet fighters and assistance in making them under terms comparable to those offered by Russia, or, failing this, of some alternative arrangements which India will accept as equally or more satisfactory.

[20] Thomas F. Brady, "Figures on Soviet Arms for India Indicate that US Sends Less," dispatch from New Delhi, May 12, 1964; in *The New York Times*, May 13, 1964.

The Indian Navy

Like the air force, the Indian navy has been a subordinate branch of the armed forces, and it is still small and rather weak. At the time of independence the navy consisted of a few destroyers, frigates, mine-sweepers, tankers, and other auxiliary vessels. With the help of the British, who have supplied ships, officers, and technical specialists and have helped in training officers of the fledgling navy in Britain and in developing training institutions in India, the navy has been greatly strengthened and improved. Now with two cruisers, an aircraft carrier, three destroyers, several frigates, a great variety of auxiliary vessels, and some aircraft, it is capable of carrying out its limited defensive mission.

In the opinion of K. M. Panikkar, who took a special interest in the navy, India's main naval weaknesses are that it does not have submarines in an age when the emphasis is changing to underwater vessels, that it is almost wholly dependent on other countries for ships (and, he might have added, for almost all of the sophisticated and expensive equipment which modern ships require), and that India's coastline is exposed and vulnerable, for "the seas that wash her shores are not closed or regional seas." Obviously, as Panikkar points out, India "cannot build a navy for the nuclear age."[21] Again, in a conflict with a nuclear power with a large naval force, it would have to rely on outside assistance and support from other nuclear powers.

Pakistan's Armed Forces

The Pakistan army, less than one-third the size of India's, has substantially the same organization, traditions, strengths, and weaknesses. Its main fighting units are six regular divisions, one armored division, an armored group, and a few independent brigades. It is better equipped than the Indian army, especially with tanks, because of military assistance from the United States; its logistical capability is superior; and its morale, especially among junior officers, may be higher. Its leadership and training are substantially better, unit for unit, than the Indian army.

Pakistan's army is even less truly a "national" army than is India's. Although some 55 per cent of the people of Pakistan live in the East "wing," they provide less than 15 per cent of the army. None of the highest ranking officers is an East Pakistani. The Bengalis lack a military tradition, and the present military leaders of Pakistan seem to have a low opinion of their military prowess. But in view of the sensitivities of East Pakistanis over any discrimination against them, they will undoubtedly insist on larger representation in their country's armed forces.

Like India, Pakistan has established a number of institutions for the training of its military personnel, including the Military Academy in Kakul, the

[21] Panikkar, *Problems of Indian Defence*, pp. 107–113.

Officers Training School in Kohat, and the Army Staff College in Quetta. Similar institutions exist for the air force and the navy, and senior officers from all three services, plus selected civil servants, are assigned to the National Defense College in Karachi. Pakistan, like India, also sends many of its officers abroad for special training and experience, and liaison between American and Pakistani officers and institutions has been particularly close.

Pakistan's navy, consisting of one light cruiser, five destroyers, one submarine (obtained from the United States in 1963), and a few frigates, smaller warships, and supporting vessels, is far weaker than India's — a matter of understandable concern to Pakistan, for in the event of conflict the Indian navy could cut the sea lanes and blockade West and East Pakistan.[22] For some time Pakistan has wanted at least one aircraft carrier and a strengthened navy. Since it gets oil and other supplies from Arabia and the Persian Gulf area, and has special ties with Iran, it is inevitably concerned in the control of the Persian Gulf, and would like to exert more naval influence in that region.

Thanks to its fine traditions, excellent personnel, the emphasis given it, and the substantial amount of modern planes and equipment supplied by the United States, the Pakistan air force is comparable in effectiveness and strength to India's, although it is smaller. The United States has supplied it with B-57 jet bombers, F-86 Sabrejets, F-104A supersonic Starfighters, Sidewinder missiles, transport planes, helicopters, and supporting equipment and supplies. It has trained several scores of Pakistani airmen in the United States, and it has helped to establish training centers and programs in Pakistan. It has also assisted in the financing and construction of airfields and other installations.

The exact number of F-104As supplied by the United States is of course a military secret. It is doubtless much smaller than the Indians think, and much larger than the Americans and Pakistanis will admit. In 1961, Chester Bowles, while in India on official business, was reported to have informed the Indian authorities that only 12 F-104As were being delivered to Pakistan. In *The Times of India* of January 16, 1962, Prem Bhatia expressed the view that while "this estimate was correct at the time, deliveries of this powerful aircraft continue to be made and Pakistan will be in a position in the next two or three months to have at least two F-104 squadrons in service.[23] In all probability this represents about the present strength of F-104A units in the Pakistani air force.

[22] Admiral H. M. Siddiq Choudhri, the first Pakistani to command the Pakistan Navy, once declared that "the defence of East Pakistan has to be based on water." Quoted in Siddiqi, cited, p. 54.

[23] See also Selig S. Harrison, "South Asia and U.S. Policy," *The New Republic*, December 11, 1961, pp. 11–16.

Disposition of the Armed Forces

The disposition of the armed forces of India and Pakistan indicates the main defense concerns of the two countries. Most of Pakistan's army is stationed in the Punjab, especially in and around Lahore and Rawalpindi, the temporary capital of the country as well as its military headquarters, and in what used to be known as the North West Frontier Province. The army therefore can be readily activated in the event of trouble with either India or Afghanistan. Since relatively weak forces are stationed in East Pakistan, and since Ayub Khan himself has said that "the defense of East Pakistan does not lie in that part of the country," Pakistan's military strategy for the defense of its territory is to concentrate its strength in West Pakistan and to move rapidly and in force against India in the event of hostilities. If the Chinese moved into the plains of Assam, as they threatened to do in November 1962, and if the Indian armed forces could not check them, East Pakistan would be at their mercy.

On a state visit in 1961, Ayub Khan showed the President and other officials of the American Government a map purporting to reveal the disposition of the Indian armed forces, in support of his oft-repeated contention that even after the Chinese moves in 1959 some 85 per cent of India's armed forces were concentrated along Pakistan's borders. The map indicated that most of the Indian army was in Kashmir and the Punjab, close to Pakistani territory, with other concentrations in Rajasthan and Gujerat, and in West Bengal and Assam. Sizable forces were also located in central India, and in the disaffected Naga area.

Nehru, Krishna Menon, and other Indian spokesmen have pooh-poohed the Pakistani charges that from 75 to 85 per cent of India's armed forces are close to Pakistan's borders by insisting that their forces are not pointed in any direction in places like Kashmir, the Punjab, and Assam, but are available for any emergency. Ambassador Galbraith has expressed the view that "the figures are meaningless." But even if they are used in a rather misleading way they do indicate the almost paranoiac concern of both countries about any moves, and the basic intentions, of the other. When India was preparing for the move into Goa, one of its precautionary measures was to dispatch further units to the borders of West Pakistan. Even when Indian troops, inferior in numbers, weapons, and equipment, were falling back or were being overwhelmed by the advancing Chinese forces in 1962, the bulk of the Indian armed forces remained in Kashmir and the Punjab, facing Pakistan, instead of being rushed to the North East Frontier Agency or Ladakh. Today, however, the new mountain divisions, numbering at least six, are in Ladakh, Sikkim, NEFA, in high altitude locales, ready to meet any attack from the Chinese to the north.

Basic Defense Needs: Some Questions and Criticisms

India's defense expenditures were increased by approximately 10 per cent for the fiscal year 1962–63, when they amounted to some $700 million. In 1962, prior to the Chinese invasion, India and Pakistan together were spending around $900 million a year on their military establishments. India's annual defense expenditures alone are now nearly double this amount.

Several crucial questions inevitably arise: Do India and Pakistan have the right kind of defense forces? Are they adequate for the minimal defense needs of the two countries? Are they larger than they should be? Since obviously the defense needs of the two countries would be quite different if they were not at odds with each other, their strained relations must be taken as an overriding factor in the total defense equation. The military deficiencies of the two countries are obvious, as are the basic weaknesses of the political, social, and economic structures. Unfortunately, India and Pakistan are engaged in an arms race, which has been occasioned in part by American military aid to Pakistan since 1954 and to India since late 1962, and by Pakistani apprehensions about the Indian military build-up after 1962.

At the present time, at least, India has no intention of trying to become a nuclear power, or to equip itself with unconventional weapons, except to a very limited degree. It is placing its main reliance on an enlarged and better equipped army and air force — still far inferior to China's.

China's explosion of a nuclear device in the Takla Makan desert in Sinkiang in October 1964, and again in May 1965, and the clear evidences that China is developing a nuclear capability, led many Indians, including influential members of the Congress Party, to demand that India too must develop an atomic arsenal. This demand was firmly resisted by Prime Minister Shastri, but it will be raised again and again if relations with China continue to be strained or if the proliferation of nuclear weapons spreads to other countries of Asia.

Several of India's greatest soldiers have expressed the view that the present defense establishment is inadequate for even minimal needs. "In my opinion," wrote General Thimayya in 1962, "the present strength of the army and air forces of India . . . [is] even below the 'minimum insurance' that we can give to our people." To meet the new threat from China General Thimayya felt that India needed large numbers of lightly equipped infantry for Himalayan operations, and "a strong organised force with heavy fighting equipment, including tanks, armoured cars, artillery, etc., to defeat the enemy after he has penetrated the Himalayan main ranges."[24]

In 1962 Major-General Habibullah complained: "We content ourselves

[24] General K. S. Thimayya, "Adequate 'Insurance'," *Seminar*, No. 35, July 1962, pp. 13–15.

with obsolete weapons and make provision to build them in our country, without attempting to have modern weapons and to effect the economies which they would bestow. It is not only in weapons but in organization, logistics and training that we are in a dangerous state of bliss and profligate waste." He would "abandon the tank, the surface navy, and the fighter and bomber forces," and "invest and train in defensive guided weapons." He would completely reorganize the "territorial and NCC forces and the ordnance and supply system." He believes that "the best possible . . . use of India's present type of manpower potential would be on a local infantry basis, backed by horsed or other mobility easily fitted into an agricultural social structure." General Thimayya too would like to organize the Indian people for possible auxiliary service. The "whole nation" should be "trained as territorials and militiamen to operate as guerrillas and commandos." General Cariappa, among others, would introduce compulsory military training immediately.[25] Some Indian students of military affairs would deliberately turn their back on "the mirage of modern forces" and place their main reliance on a mass army, professionally trained and led.[26]

Indian Communists, of course, criticize the whole approach to defense problems and argue that what is needed is a "people's army," presumably modeled along Communist lines and subject to thorough political indoctrination and control. Many Indians, reflecting the Gandhian views on nonviolence, still seem opposed to military forces or defense expenditures; despite recent Chinese behavior, they would rather rely on the *Panchsheel,* and not on arms.[27]

Some Indians believe that a smaller army than India now possesses, more highly trained and equipped with the most modern weapons required for conventional and limited warfare, would be in every way a better investment.[28] It is difficult to see, however, how India could fulfill its present

[25] Habibullah, "Facing Facts," cited, pp. 24–31; Thimayya, "Adequate 'Insurance'," cited, pp. 13–15; and General K. M. Cariappa, "Our Defense Against China's Threat Today," *The Radical Humanist,* June 20, 1965, p. 298.

[26] In an article in a magazine of the Indian defense forces, *Sainik Samachar,* in early 1955, Lt.-Col. D. K. Palit suggested the reorganization of the Indian armed forces as a mass army with a militia of three to four million men, directed and led by a small and highly-trained group of professional military personnel. The opening article of the July 1962 issue of *Seminar,* devoted entirely to "India's Defence," posed this question: "Have we fully assessed the possibility of building a huge militia, trained and led by a hard core of professionals and equipped with weapons which we cannot produce locally?"

[27] H. M. Patel has expressed the opinion that "Were it not for our strained relations with Pakistan ever since Independence, we might well have adopted the rather tempting policy of more or less total disarmament." "Realities of the Situation," *Seminar,* No. 35, July 1962, p. 20. It is doubtful that under any conceivable circumstances the Indian Government would actually have adopted such a policy.

[28] "It is not a quantitative army that we require, but a qualitative one built around the most powerful weapons available. . . . I am not talking here of modern warfare, I.C.B.M's etc. but of warfare with what are today known as conventional weapons. . . . If she [India] has an army of 350,000 men and a proportionately strong navy and air force,

commitments with an army of, say, 350,000 men, unless relations with Pakistan and/or China take a decided change for the better. Its present army, more than double this size, is already heavily overcommitted.

Pakistan's forces are even more overcommitted, for they have the almost impossible task of guarding the land and sea frontiers of a divided country, with little natural protection against India, with undependable tribesmen in the North West Frontier region and with a hostile Afghanistan, backed by the Soviet Union, just beyond. For more than three and a half years they had the responsibility for enforcing martial law in Pakistan, and if the present experiment in the operation of constitutional government fails they may again have similar responsibilities.

The Common Defense of the Subcontinent

On occasion both Indian and Pakistani spokesmen have advocated some sort of mutual cooperation in the common defense of the subcontinent; but it is hardly surprising that nothing has come of these proposals. On the official level, at least, they have been advanced more frequently by Pakistanis than by Indians. Often they have been linked with the condition that India honor its pledge to hold a plebiscite in Kashmir. To all such proposals India has reacted negatively, either on the ground that they are inconsistent with India's approach to foreign policy and security or that they are simply tactical moves by Pakistan.

Shortly after independence Nehru offered to enter into a "no-war declaration" with Pakistan, an offer repeated on numerous occasions in later years. Pakistan has never responded enthusiastically, apparently on the ground that it would be virtually meaningless and might be regarded as a substitute for efforts to resolve the issues in dispute, especially Kashmir, for only then, in Pakistan's opinion, can peaceful relations be possible.

The Chinese actions in 1959 seemed to demonstrate conclusively that the security of the subcontinent was of more than academic concern. In April, while India was in a state of excitement because of the Chinese take-over in Tibet, Ayub Khan called attention to the need for India and Pakistan to resolve their differences and to cooperate in the defense of the subcontinent. He even offered to "consider joint cooperation without having pacts or treaties," or without even having "some sort of paper agreement."[29] This sug-

---

trained and equipped to the highest standards, her own purposes of defence will be more than amply served provided the army is backed by organizations like the national cadet corps and territorial forces which would enable it to be expended at will at a time of crisis." Panikkar, *Problems of Indian Defence,* pp. 7–8.

[29] Quoted in Sharif Al-Mujahid, "Indo-Pakistan Confederation," *Dawn,* October 27, 1961.

gestion was welcomed by some persons in India, including Jayaprakash Narayan and General Cariappa, but it was coldly received by Nehru, whose standard retort to all proposals for joint defense was: "Defense against whom?" By 1959 the answer to this question seemed obvious, but even then Nehru was reluctant to admit that China was a real threat. "We don't want to have a common defense policy, which will be almost some kind of military alliance," Nehru said in reply to Ayub Khan's offer. He even intimated that "the real motive was not joint defense, but Kashmir."[30] Ayub Khan indignantly denied this charge, and declared that if India cooperated with Pakistan in the joint defense of the subcontinent it would not compromise in any way India's basic policy of nonalignment. Nehru remained unconvinced.

That Ayub's offer of joint defense of South Asia was not unconditional and was in fact related to the Kashmir dispute, was indicated by his comments at a press conference in December 1961. He said that "joint defense" was perhaps not the right term to apply to his offer, that "what he had offered to India was that Indian and Pakistani forces should combine to combat aggression and to withdraw forces from borders without fearing each other"; and he added that "Pakistan would offer joint defense to India in case of foreign aggression on the subcontinent provided India comes with clean hands to solve the Kashmir issue."[31] As an Indian commentator wryly observed, "This made many in India wonder whether Pakistan wanted joint defense or Kashmir!"

Some leading figures in India, such as Vinoba Bhave and Jayaprakash Narayan, would favor some kind of common defense measures, but Bhave at least would insist on a basic realignment of Pakistan's foreign policy as a precondition. In October 1959 Bhave wrote: "I am happy that General Ayub Khan has made an offer of common defense. But I would like to add that common defense is not possible without a common foreign policy. India is following a policy of nonalignment. Hence, if Pakistan continues to remain a member of other alignments like the Baghdad Pact, how can there be a common defense?"[32] That Pakistan, and not India, should change its orientation in foreign policy is quite contrary to a typical Pakistani view that "reconciliation" between the two "is impossible unless there comes about a radical change in the Indian mental image of Pakistan."

[30] Quoted in *The Times of India,* May 5, 1959.

[31] Apparently Ayub's offer is not an open one. In April 1963, replying to a question whether he could foresee any conditions in which he would again offer joint defense with India as he did in 1959, the President said: "A lot of water has flowed down the bridge since then and, unless the situation changes completely, the question of offering joint defence does not arise." Interview in Rawalpindi with Sol. W. Sanders, Regional Editor, *U.S. News & World Report,* late April 1963, as summarized in *Pakistan News Digest,* May 15, 1963.

[32] *Bhoodan,* October 21, 1959; quoted in Louis Fischer, " 'Indo-Pakistan': A Federation to Meet China," *The New Leader,* January 16, 1961, p. 11.

The United States and the Defense of South Asia

For better or for worse, the United States decision to extend military assistance and enter into a mutual security agreement with Pakistan was a major intrusion of American power and influence in South Asia and in an even wider area as well.[33] No single decision has done more to involve the United States in the affairs of the subcontinent. It was a calculated move, related to the failure of the efforts to create a Middle East Defense Organization, to create at least some minimal strength in the weak arc peripheral to the Communist states in Europe and Asia. Between Turkey and Formosa the American planners must have seen little but weakness and, inferentially, an area of temptation and opportunity for the Soviet Union and Communist China. With most of the nations in the area firmly dedicated to policies of nonalignment, it seemed only logical for the United States to give direct military assistance to those states which were willing to join anti-Communist security arrangements with the Western powers. Thus the arrangements with Pakistan were wholly in keeping with the overall assessment and the mutual security policies of the United States. They were generally approved by the American people, in spite of their adverse effects on Indo-American relations.

Some critics have charged that a major consideration influencing the United States decision was the desire to provide more effective counterweights to India in the whole area from Turkey to Indo-China. An India definitely more powerful than any other state or coalition of states in the area, so it was argued, might be undesirable for American national interests. By building up Pakistan there would be less prospect that Indian influence would prevail in a strategic and generally weak area, and the Communists would be faced with a more formidable potential opposition than that offered by nonaligned states.

If this was a basic consideration, it was never advanced as a major reason for entering into the arrangements, whose justification may be sought in more obvious lines of American policy. If the major objective was to build up areas of strength between Turkey and Indo-China, the American policies were at best only partially successful. This fact is hardly surprising, in view of the uncertain political, economic, and social situation in Pakistan and other states which were brought into SEATO and CENTO. On the other hand, possibly the security arrangements, however disappointing they have proved to be, were better than none at all. Pakistan is probably a much

---

[33] Two months before it was announced Hanson Baldwin, the military editor of *The New York Times*, wrote: "The United States-Pakistan arms agreement . . . introduces an entirely new factor into the politico-military equation of the whole vast area stretching from the Mediterranean and Suez to the Red River Valley in Indo-China and the Strait of Malacca." *The New York Times*, December 20, 1953.

stronger state because of the substantial American military aid and other assistance stemming from the relationship.

The United States has derived some real benefits from this relationship. It has secured an important Asian ally, and it has been able to establish on Pakistani soil facilities for intelligence-gathering, communications, and other needed services which are hardly less valuable to it in peacetime than in the event of an armed conflict with the Soviet Union. Two of the more undesirable consequences have been the American involvement in the unsatisfactory internal situation of Pakistan, with perhaps some unintended support to the military rulers and to nondemocratic practices and policies, and the unfortunate effect of the American military efforts on Indo-Pakistan and Indo-American relations.

The wisdom of the decision is still being debated. With the advantage of hindsight, one may question whether the military ties with Pakistan have been worth the cost, in monetary or other terms. They have been a great disappointment to Pakistan, which expected that the military association would carry with it strong American support in other matters, such as the Kashmir dispute. Pakistan often contrasts the unequivocal support which the Soviet Union has given to India in the Kashmir dispute with the in-between position, which it usually interprets as a pro-Indian position, of the United States on the same question. It expected that its membership in CENTO and SEATO would assure it of further outside support. Instead, many Pakistanis complain, they have incurred the hostility of the Communist states and the disapproval of the nonaligned countries without gaining the expected compensations and security. The substantial American economic assistance to India has been severely criticized in Pakistan, on the ground that it indirectly enables India to build up its military strength and encourages India and other "neutral" nations to pursue a policy of "fence-straddling" and of getting "the best of two worlds," without commitments or risks. American military assistance to India after 1962 has raised new alarms in Pakistan, and new doubts about the value of its alliances. Conversely, American military assistance to Pakistan has been a source of constant irritation and alarm to India.

In short, in the existing situation direct military aid may be doing more harm than good, and America's military and economic interests may be in conflict. A possible way out of this real dilemma may already be in the making. The United States has already ceased its direct "supporting assistance" to Pakistan, on the ground that it is no longer needed, and has promised to provide equivalent amounts to supplement the economic aid programs. The next step might well be to cease military aid as such, and to provide Pakistan with sufficient economic aid so that it can still maintain an adequate military establishment. Somehow or other, economic aid has to be linked with the size of a nation's military establishment, for, except in certain emergency situations, it makes no sense to provide economic aid to a nation which is spending an undue proportion of its resources and national effort on military preparations. But this is obviously a sensitive question, and the criteria for the proper levels of military preparedness are hard to determine.

In a sense neither India nor Pakistan can afford to allocate a rupee for military purposes, for their resources are inadequate to meet their needs for economic and social development. On the other hand, with real security problems, both countries must divert some of their limited resources to the unproductive but essential tasks of security and defense. To some degree the United States, by extending aid of any kind, contributes to these efforts. But in general, except in areas where special conditions or obligations exist (as in Korea, Formosa, and Indo-China), it would be wiser to extend its assistance wholly, or almost wholly, in the form of economic assistance, which should be sizable enough to enable the recipient countries to meet certain vital security needs. In South Asia, in particular, this approach would seem most appropriate, and would help to resolve some of the dilemmas of United States policy in recent years. It would also seem to be more in tune with the changing attitudes and conditions of this important segment of the non-Communist world. In this way the United States might be able to effect a better reconciliation of its policies toward both India and Pakistan, without jeopardizing its special interests and commitments *vis-à-vis* both countries.

The kind of orientation in American policy toward South Asia which may produce better results than the divergent policies of the past decade was suggested in part by Selig S. Harrison in late 1961:

> In essence the idea is to move toward the indirect form of defense support implicit in economic aid to India. Increased funds loaned and granted for development and for general budgetary support would release other funds for military spending. The distinction between direct and indirect military aid may seem academic, but it makes an enormous political difference that in the Indian case, the Indians shop for themselves in world arms markets and have to make the hard financial choices determining the purchase of one kind of hardware as against another. The decisions are theirs, and because the hardware has to be paid out of limited resources with its cost added onto the national debt, the fact that they have it is blamed on them. In Pakistan, the onus is on the US for each and every gift parcel to reach the Ayub armory — in the eyes not only of the Indians and the Afghans but of the anti-government dissidents who may someday rule Pakistan.
>
> . . . the difficult question is not whether the US should broaden its general commitment to a strengthened Pakistan. It is whether the commitment to her security can be fulfilled while phasing out the end of a program of direct military aid grants which seriously complicates intra-regional tensions as well as US-South Asian relations. . . . And in the long term, the commitment of the US to Pakistan's security and growth should be broadened — not weakened — as part of an integrated approach to the region.[34]

[34] "South Asia and U.S. Policy," *The New Republic*, December 11, 1961, p. 16. See also the same author's article, "India, Pakistan and the United States — III: Undoing a Mistake," *The New Republic*, September 7, 1959.

The question of American military aid to Pakistan cannot be divorced from the larger questions of American attitudes toward the alliance with Pakistan and toward SEATO. The United States should reassess the value of these arrangements in the light not only of the prevailing conditions and attitudes in the area, but also the impact of recent technological developments on alliances and overseas bases. This does not mean, however, that the United States should desert its allies or fail to honor its commitments to them. Even if a reappraisal leads to the conclusion that it was unwise to enter into SEATO and the Pakistan alliance in the first instance, or that under present circumstances they are more of a liability than an asset, it does not follow that the United States should take immediate steps to divest itself of such commitments. As Morton Kaplan has observed, often, primarily because of what is at stake in the East-West contest, "it is not wise to scrap alliances which it was unwise to form."[35]

The United States and Pakistan should engage in a joint reassessment of their military alliance and the program of American military assistance. In all probability, the proper conclusion should be to continue their military associations, and to join hands in efforts to reinvigorate SEATO. As for abandoning direct military aid, whatever merit Selig Harrison's proposal may have had in the past, it can hardly be regarded as immediately feasible in view of the developments since the Chinese attack in 1962. The United States cannot consider seriously the abandonment of military aid to its ally, Pakistan, while it is extending such aid to India. If such assistance to Pakistan since 1954 altered the South Asian balance in favor of Pakistan, then assistance to India in 1962 and after will tip the balance in India's favor. If it was a "mistake" to provide such assistance to Pakistan, will it also be regarded as a "mistake" to help India rebuild and re-equip its armed forces?

The ideal solution would be for India and Pakistan to agree on joint measures of defense and on joint military assistance needs, and for the United States then to assist both countries, through some kind of coordinated defense set-up, to meet these needs. Such a solution seems to be quite unlikely, although it is often proposed in the United States and Pakistan and more rarely in India. Failing this, the United States should probably continue to give military assistance to both India and Pakistan, with careful attention to external and internal defense needs and to the impact of this assistance on the delicate balance of power in the subcontinent, and indeed in Asia as a whole.

If the United States could be certain that a basic change in Pakistan's foreign policy would lead to effective Indo-Pakistan cooperation for the common defense, it might well cease its military aid to Pakistan and might indeed urge that country to dissociate itself from all security pacts. But this would be a bold and rather foolhardy conclusion to draw on the basis of the

[35] *United States Foreign Policy in a Revolutionary Age* (Princeton: Center for International Studies, 1961), p. 20.

evidence at hand, and in any event the decision should be made only after a careful weighing of many other factors.

During the open warfare which broke out between India and Pakistan in the fall of 1965, American weapons and military equipment were used on a large scale by Pakistan and apparently on a smaller scale by India as well. The use of these arms clearly violated the conditions under which they had been given. Thus the Indo-Pakistan conflict highlighted the risks and disadvantages of American military aid to unfriendly neighbors, and resulted in the suspension of this aid to both countries. Almost simultaneously, however, renewed Chinese military pressures against India, especially in and near Sikkim and the vulnerable main access routes from Tibet into the Indian plains, were reminders of the inadequacy of India's defenses against possible Chinese aggression. These pressures also underscored the need for a further military build-up, either unilaterally or jointly with Pakistan, if Pakistan would recognize the danger from China, and if the two South Asian neighbors would join against a common danger instead of sapping each other's strength in fratricidal strife.

If the "emergency" with China becomes less serious, and as soon as the United States concludes that India's armed forces have been built up to adequate force levels and have been properly retrained and re-equipped, the United States should then consider the desirability of decreasing and perhaps ending its military assistance to both India and Pakistan. Naturally this step should be taken in full consultation with both countries, and not by way of disengagement from South Asia. The United States will continue to be deeply involved in the economic, political, and social development of that vital part of the world. Its concern with the security of that area will remain, but its contributions to that end will then be made in ways that will be less likely to add to tensions in Indo-Pakistan relations and to conflict with other aspects of America's South Asian policy.

CHAPTER NINE

India and Pakistan: Problems of Coexistence

INDIA AND PAKISTAN WERE BORN IN BITTERNESS, a mood which has persisted through all the stages of emerging nationhood. It has created an atmosphere of mistrust which has poisoned relations between the two nations, warped the minds and the actions of leaders and peoples, imposed added burdens on struggling economies, jeopardized the chances of national survival, and colored the approach of both nations to world affairs generally.

When Prime Minister Nehru was once asked by the Indian journalist, Frank Moraes, to name the diplomatic post abroad which he considered to be most important, he replied unhesitatingly: "Karachi." This prompt response pointed up the most important aspect of the foreign relations of both India and Pakistan, namely their relations with each other.

In a sense Indo-Pakistan relations might be considered as belonging to the realm of domestic rather than foreign affairs; for Indians and Pakistanis are essentially the same people, sharing a common historical experience and to a large extent a common culture, living in the same geographically confined subcontinent, with few natural barriers between them, and facing common problems. Indians and Pakistanis know each other very well — perhaps too well. They know their respective strengths and weaknesses, their faults and foibles. On the whole, despite communal feelings, they lived together in the past not as one people, but as neighbors and, for the most part, as friends.

India has more than half as many Muslims as has Pakistan. Even today members of the same families live in both countries, although they seldom see each other.[1] Older members of the civil service, the armed forces, college

---

[1] Dr. Zakir Husain, a distinguished Indian Muslim and prominent educator, is now Vice President of India; his brother, Dr. Mahmud Husain, is a distinguished Pakistani educator, a former Minister of Kashmir Affairs and Minister of Education in Pakistan. Two brothers named Beg once occupied identical posts in the Foreign Offices of India and Pakistan. A prominent official of the Indian Ministry of External Affairs told the

and university faculties, the business community, and almost all other professions in both countries were close associates hardly more than two decades ago. These ties of memory, of past experience, and often of blood relationship are still close.

The similarities in outlook, situation, and problems in India and Pakistan are as impressive as their differences, in spite of the unhappy state of their formal relations. In both the dominant approach is secular, and this fact is probably more important than differences of religion, political structure and orientation, or foreign policy. Even in foreign policy the differences may not be as great as they appear, for there is an underlying similarity in approach and outlook, and the official foreign policies are not so far apart, except in relation to each other, as they have been in the past.

Most Indians and Pakistanis share a fervent desire to improve their mutual relations. All responsible leaders of both countries have consistently gone on record in favor of a reconciliation of minds and hearts, as well as of policies. Unhappily Indo-Pakistan relations have generally not been friendly. The things which divide have predominated over the things that unite.

Although at the moment India and Pakistan seem to be unable to get along with each other, in a more fundamental sense they cannot get along without each other. Each country has a great stake in the stability, strength, and progress of the other, a fact rather generally recognized, and often proclaimed, in both countries. "A weak India," said Ayub Khan in October 1960, "will be no solace or strength to Pakistan."[2] "For India," declared an influential Indian newspaper, *The Hindu*, on February 13, 1962, "the maintenance of stability in Pakistan is important." Unfortunately, each country seems to harbor deep-seated suspicions and to question the *bona fides* of the other; and each charges that the other country is deliberately trying to weaken it in every possible way.

Bases of Distrust

Pakistan has been noticeably sensitive about its position *vis-à-vis* India. Before partition Jinnah maintained that the Muslims of India constituted a separate "nation," and that, therefore, even though greatly outnumbered, they should be treated on terms of complete equality; likewise, the Muslim

author that on one occasion when he arrived in Karachi on official business he was officially welcomed by his own uncle, a high officer in Pakistan's Ministry of External Affairs!

[2] Broadcast to the nation on the eve of the second anniversary of the "revolution," October 26, 1960. *Speeches and Statements by Field Marshal Mohammad Ayub Khan, President of Pakistan*, vol. III, July 1960–June 1961 (Karachi: Pakistan Publications, n.d.), p. 42.

League should be treated on the same basis in relation to the Indian National Congress. Since independence Pakistan has been sensitive to any discrimination against it in favor of India. "The primary aim of the foreign policy of Pakistan," wrote Keith Callard, one of the most astute Western students of the politics and foreign policy of that country, "is equality of status with India."[3] Pakistan seldom achieves this status in international affairs, except in a formal sense.

Ever since its independence, when, over its protests, India was recognized as the successor state entitled to a seat in the United Nations while Pakistan was required to apply for membership in the UN, Pakistan has had a serious problem of identity, and it is still sometimes associated in the thinking of many people in other parts of the world with India. Pakistan has had no world leader as well known as Nehru, and its own internal difficulties have handicapped it in establishing an international identity and impression.

Pakistanis insist that Indians have not yet really accepted the fact of Pakistan, and that the Indian government is doing everything in its power to jeopardize the independent existence of Pakistan. Pakistanis accept without question the existence of India, but they often charge that the secular state approach is a façade and that India is really a Hindu state. Indians discount Pakistani fears of India and often speak disparagingly of the capacity of Muslims to run a modern state or to do anything else really well.

In 1959–60 a marked improvement in Indo-Pakistan relations seemed to have set in. With the accession to power of Ayub Khan in October 1958, Pakistan had a strong leader who could deal on equal terms with Nehru, and Pakistanis gained a needed boost in confidence and morale. The Chinese suppression of the revolution in Tibet in the spring of 1959 and the moves along India's northern borders confronted India with a situation which seemed more ominous, at least immediately, than any threat from Pakistan, and led many Indians and Pakistanis to think in terms of common interests in the defense of the subcontinent. In late 1959 and early 1960 agreement was reached on most of the remaining border issues, which had been a long-standing source of tension, and on the canal waters dispute, truly a matter of life or death for several million Indians and many more millions of Pakistanis. The signing of the Indus Waters Treaty in Karachi in September, and the apparent amity in the talks of Nehru and Ayub Khan seemed to presage a new and happier era in Indo-Pakistan relations.

The comments which the two leaders made at the press conferences at the end of their talks reflected the differences in the two men, and in the policies and orientation of their governments. Nehru stressed the great similarity in "texture" between the cultures of India and Pakistan, and he

[3] *Pakistan's Foreign Policy: An Interpretation* (New York: Institute of Pacific Relations, 1957), p. 8.

quoted lines from Coleridge to explain the psychological depths of the bitterness:

> To be wroth with one we love
> Doth work like madness in the brain.

Ayub Khan took a less philosophical and less detached approach. He told the reporters that he had got Nehru to admit that Kashmir was a "problem," and he warned: "All the things achieved in other fields will be nullified if the Kashmir dispute is not solved."

Relations between India and Pakistan soon took a turn for the worse, and they have steadily deteriorated ever since. On October 6, 1960, hardly a week after his talks with Nehru, Ayub Khan made a speech in the capital of Azad Kashmir, in which he coupled a strong restatement of Pakistan's determination not to rest until the Kashmir question was resolved satisfactorily with bitter criticism of India. Indian spokesmen replied in kind, and soon the more cordial atmosphere of 1959–60 was clouded by a miasma of recrimination. In 1961 and 1962 the tone and contents of editorials and news stories in the press of both countries, the critical statements of leading figures, and the reactions in one country to the developments in the other raised the level of hostility to an alarming degree. The critical tone in the press was noticeably muted after Nehru and Ayub Khan, in early December 1962, announced their agreement to hold talks on the Kashmir question; but as talks on the ministerial level failed to produce significant areas of agreement, the journalistic feuding was resumed.

India's enlarged crisis with China did not, unfortunately, lead to an improvement in relations. India's plight received precious little sympathy in Pakistan, which was much more disturbed by the upsurge of Indian national spirit and the greater emphasis on military preparedness in India than by the Chinese threat to the entire subcontinent. Pakistanis seemed convinced that they were in greater danger than ever from an aroused and rearmed India, and that their Western allies had betrayed them by coming to India's aid.

Pakistan's post-October 1962 negotiations and agreements with China reveal a strange interpretation of current dangers and priorities. They suggest either that Pakistan does not regard the Chinese threat to the subcontinent as a major one, or that it is willing to risk its own security in order to play along with a Communist power which is endangering the security of India, or that it is still so obsessed with its hostility toward India and with its dissatisfaction over its alliances and allies that it is willing to continue to "play with fire" as far as China is concerned.

Some friendly outside observers feel that in the immediate aftermath of the Chinese attack both countries missed an historic opportunity to place their mutual relations on a new and more cooperative level. Among the great "might-have-beens" of modern history the following questions may be filed: What would have happened if Pakistan had shown sympathy and had given support to India after late October 1962, and had voluntarily agreed not to create additional complications for its harassed neighbor? Conversely, what would have been the result if India had made some generous gestures in Pakistan's direction, perhaps even including some real concessions regarding Kashmir? Both countries, for reasons which they must have regarded as compelling, followed a wholly different path, and as a result, in spite — or perhaps partly because — of the talks on Kashmir, Indo-Pakistan relations reached new lows of bitterness and vituperation and mistrust. Thus, the danger of which responsible leaders of both countries have often warned has become all the greater, as India and Pakistan "go on squabbling with each other," while the external threats to their security and very survival have visibly increased.

To the twisted images of each other, based on decades of intimate but not always happy contacts and on communal differences, are now added distorted views of the present situation and of the aims and policies of the other country. Many Pakistanis seem convinced that the nearly 50,000,000 Muslims of India are a terribly oppressed minority, and that their Muslim brethren in the India-held part of Kashmir are being governed ruthlessly against their will. Many Indians seem to believe that Pakistan cannot possibly survive, and that it is now little better than "a naked military dictatorship," in the words which Nehru himself used after the October 1958 "revolution."

Indians and Pakistanis now have relatively few contacts with, or sources of information about, each other. Restrictions on travel of nationals of one country to the other are extensive and humiliating. Newspapers and other publications of one country are not allowed to circulate freely in the other. In Pakistan, for example, only one Indian newspaper, *The Statesman*, which was British-owned until recently, may be distributed and sold, and in the spring of 1962 the sole Indian correspondent permitted in East Pakistan, representing *The Statesman*, was asked to leave on what appeared to be trumped-up charges. A special correspondent of the same paper, who was allowed to visit Pakistan for two weeks in March 1962, reported that he had to pay nine visits to various police stations during his brief visit. He was fair enough to add that "the condition about reporting arrival and departure at a police station is enforced almost as rigorously in India." While he encountered "a great deal of friendliness and hospitality," the answers he got to his inquiries were "depressing and disheartening"; "the same persons who overwhelmed me with courtesy usually displayed an astonishing measure of hostility when they spoke of India as a country or nation ... there was nothing for which they did not seem to blame India."[4]

In general, the news of developments in the one country which is printed

[4] Krishan Bhatia, "Vicissitudes in Relations with India," *The Statesman* (New Delhi), March 15, 1962.

in the press of the other is slanted, negative, and often vituperative. The Pakistani press, which presumably reflects the views of the Pakistan government, probably excels the Indian papers in the volume and level of vituperation and critical comment, but the difference is one of degree and not of kind. Indian journals seem to regard Pakistan as a "fouled-up" country which is trying to divert attention from its internal failures and divisions to external threats and pressures. "The cardinal aim of Pakistan's domestic and foreign policy," declared *The Indian Express*, one of the more sober Indian papers, "is how best to embarrass India."[5]

Statements by leading figures of India and Pakistan often add to the mutual bitterness and distortion. Undoubtedly the top leaders of both countries genuinely desire to reverse the present trends in Indo-Pakistan relations, and to lay the basis for "peaceful co-existence"; but sometimes one wonders to what extent the strained relations become useful to these leaders as a rallying cry for national unity and as a justification for policies which would otherwise be quite unpopular. Leaders of both countries are under strong internal pressures to take a strong stand, and they are constantly faced with a dilemma, namely to what extent should they bow to these pressures and to what extent should they try to check them? And if certain groups become more influential politically, such as the orthodox *ulama* or Muslim fanatics in Pakistan or Hindu communalists in India, relations would almost certainly change for the worse.

The problems of the two countries are emotional and psychological, as well as material. They are in a sense problems of communalism and of regionalism rather than of foreign policy.

Major Issues in Dispute

As already noted, the relations between India and Pakistan are perhaps as much aspects of their domestic politics as of their foreign relations. In addition to rooted antipathies and suspicions, innumerable issues have arisen to complicate the already strained relations and to divert attention from basic problems of unity and development. Some of these issues have been resolved, or have ceased to be of major significance. Notable among these have been most of the border disputes, many of the evacuee property claims (although there has been much dissatisfaction over the nature of the settlement of these claims), and the canal waters dispute. Other issues in dispute are still unresolved; among these the Kashmir question stands out as the greatest single divisive factor in Indo-Pakistan relations. A few issues have assumed radically different complexion over the years; these include a wide range of economic relations, which have changed what formerly were com-

[5] "Strange Alliance" (editorial), *The Indian Express*, May 28, 1962.

plementary economies into virtually autonomous ones, with little mutual dependence or contacts.

From the gamut of issues in dispute between India and Pakistan, brief attention will be given to seven: migration and refugee problems; communal disturbances; border problems; evacuee property; economic relations; and water disputes, with particular attention to the canal waters dispute which led to the Indus Waters Treaty of 1960. The Kashmir question must be given a somewhat fuller treatment, not only because it has bedeviled India and Pakistan since independence, but also because the United States, for better or for worse, has been deeply concerned and involved in it.

1. Migration and Refugee Problems

Speaking in the Indian Parliament on August 7, 1950, Nehru declared: "The main thing to remember is that we have been suffering in India . . . — and probably in Pakistan also — from a fever, from a sickness which did not begin with the partition but which the partition certainly aggravated."[6] The fever mounted rapidly just before and after partition. It led to widespread rioting, looting, and pillage, to the massacre of several hundreds of thousands of people, mostly in both parts of divided Punjab, and to the movement of perhaps twelve million people across the new borders, creating one of the greatest refugee problems in this "century of the homeless man." The fever has never wholly abated, but fortunately it has never risen again to its former heights. Within a few months after partition most of the Hindus in West Pakistan had migrated to India, and most of the Muslims from areas within the Indian Union who decided to cast their lot with Pakistan had moved to their newly adopted country. The great exception was in divided Bengal, where the movement of refugees from one side to the other has continued, with peaks of migration and disturbances. The movement was by no means a one-way traffic, but considerably larger numbers crossed from East Pakistan into West Bengal; if figures issued by the government of India are correct, their numbers were about 4,000,000 during the first three years of independence. Communal riots and disturbances usually produced spurts in migration. Naturally most of the refugees from East Pakistan were Hindus. Even today, however, East Pakistan, unlike West Pakistan, has a sizable Hindu minority, numbering at least 7,000,000, and perhaps even more. Almost all the persons moving into East Pakistan were Muslims, but West Bengal, Assam, and Tripura, the Indian areas adjoining East Pakistan, still have many millions of Muslims. A particularly troublesome problem has been the continued illegal migration of Muslims into Assam, one of the most underdeveloped states in India, where friction between Assamese and Bengalis has frequently led to violence. West Bengal still has special refugee

[6] Jawaharlal Nehru, *India's Foreign Policy* (New Delhi: The Publications Division, Ministry of Information and Broadcasting, Government of India, 1961), p. 462.

problems, because most of those who do cross the border resist any efforts to settle them outside of Bengal.

In West Pakistan and most of India the refugees have been largely absorbed. In Karachi and Lahore, New Delhi and Bombay the concentrations of the flimsiest kinds of temporary shelters, in which mud huts were almost a prestige symbol, have largely disappeared; where such settlements still exist, they are usually inhabited by itinerant laborers and others who have flocked to the overcrowded cities rather than by refugees, most of whom have found a place in the communities in which they have settled. If they still remain together, they are likely to be living in the settled and substantial communities which the governments of India and Pakistan have built for refugees, such as Faridabad, south of New Delhi, or Korangi, outside of Karachi.

Forced to abandon their homes and most of their possessions, and haunted by memories of the massacres and other tragedies accompanying partition, most of the refugees have created psychological and foreign policy problems for the countries to which they fled. The bitterness in their own hearts has inevitably increased the level of bitterness in the relations between India and Pakistan. Later migrations, generally disapproved by both countries, have added to the human tragedies and to the social costs of partition, and have been a continuing source of tension.

2. Communalism and Communal Disturbances

The very act of fleeing, plus the stories the refugees tell of persecution and hardships, have convinced people in one country that the minority groups in the other are being badly mistreated and are regarded as second-class citizens, despite the constitutional guarantees of equality and the assurances that these guarantees will be enforced. Unfortunately, there is considerable basis for the complaints. In spite of the genuine desires of the top leaders and the legal safeguards, Muslims in India and Hindus in East Pakistan are often regarded with suspicion, as if they were really disloyal citizens, and they are discriminated against through economic and social restrictions. This problem is primarily a domestic one for both countries, but it inevitably involves their mutual relations. It is complicated by the differences over the so-called "two-nation theory," which Jinnah propounded and which India has never accepted, and by the differences in approach between a state founded on Islamic principles and one which proclaims itself to be a secular state.

Whatever the nature of their approach, Pakistan is primarily a Muslim state, and in a different sense India is a Hindu state, since more than three-fourths of its population are Hindus. India naturally takes a special interest in the fate of the Hindus in East Pakistan, and Pakistan seems to feel some kind of special responsibility for the fortunes of the nearly 50,000,000 Muslims in India, whether these people wish to have such special solicitude or not. In fact, some Pakistanis go so far as to insist that Pakistan is really a state of some 150,000,000 people, rather than 100,000,000, which gives a strange religious twist to modern nationalism.

That majority and minority communities in South Asia have not yet learned how to live peacefully with each other, and will respond all too quickly to appeals to emotionalism or fanaticism, is revealed by the frequent clashes between communal groups. These disturbances are more common in India than in Pakistan, perhaps mainly because there are so many more Muslims in India than Hindus in Pakistan. They are reported in an exaggerated and distorted way in Pakistan. The government of Pakistan claims that there have been nearly 600 major communal disturbances in India since independence; it maintains a kind of check-list of these disturbances, and it is assiduous in distributing its versions of these affairs, not only in Pakistan but abroad as well. Unfortunately there is real substance to these claims, although the Pakistani versions are usually models of biased reporting and disregard for the actual facts, which are difficult enough to ascertain even by objective on-the-spot observers, who seldom are brought into the picture. India has a very serious communal problem, and it is deeply concerned about it; but it does not appreciate the way in which this grave internal problem is used for propaganda purposes by Pakistan. Communal disturbances seem to be increasing again; in 1964 both India and Pakistan witnessed the most serious wave of communal rioting and bloodshed, and the most extensive refugee movements, since partition.[7]

3. Border Problems

Just prior to partition a tribunal headed by Sir Cyril Radcliffe was appointed to determine the exact frontiers between the new states. The Radcliffe award, announced immediately after independence, was largely accepted, although quite naturally there was a good deal of dissatisfaction with some of the precise boundary demarcations. Pakistan, for example, com-

[7] Unlike the situation at the time of partition, the areas most seriously affected in 1964 were East Pakistan and West Bengal (and to a lesser extent Assam, Bihar, Orissa, and Madhya Pradesh). Official Indian estimates indicated that in the less than five months following serious communal riots in East Pakistan in January 1964, 312,000 refugees crossed over into India, chiefly into West Bengal. "Refugees in India Now Put at 312,000," dispatch from Calcutta, May 7, 1964; in *The New York Times*, May 8, 1964. The government and the press of India and Pakistan gave extensive publicity to and inflammatory accounts of the communal troubles and the treatment of minorities in the other country. President Ayub Khan addressed a message to President Radhakrishnan, stressing the gravity of the situation in Calcutta and elsewhere in West Bengal, and calling for "effective action immediately to restore order and peace in West Bengal such as would create a sense of security in the minds of the Muslim minority and enable these refugees to return to their homes." For the text of this message see *Pakistan Affairs* (issued by the Embassy of Pakistan, Washington), January 16, 1964. The government of India charged that in East Pakistan Christians as well as Hindus were being persecuted. See P. N. Sharma, *Pakistan Persecutes Christians* (Delhi: Tej Press, 1964), a profusely illustrated booklet distributed in the United States by the Information Service of India.

plained bitterly over the award of the Gurdaspur District in the Punjab to India, even though this district had a small Muslim majority. The Gurdaspur award was particularly important because it gave India access by land into Kashmir, an access which was utilized in a dramatic way in late 1947, following the tribal invasion of Kashmir and the accession of the Maharaja of Kashmir to India. Pakistanis objected to the award, not only because the district had a Muslim majority but because, they insisted, without it "India had no claim whatever to Kashmir."[8]

Because many questions arose regarding the interpretation of the Radcliffe award, another tribunal, chaired by Mr. Justice Bagge, was appointed to consider the disputes in the borders of East Pakistan and to make appropriate recommendations. The Bagge award, submitted in 1950, was also generally accepted, but it still left many border problems unresolved. Most of these involved relatively small pieces of territory, but they were of the kind that could stir up deep-seated emotions and hostilities. Intermittent negotiations produced few agreements, and the border problems continued to be a source of tension and trouble. When Pakistan's Prime Minister, Feroz Khan Noon, visited India in August 1958, many of the border questions were resolved in the resulting Nehru-Noon agreement. In accordance with procedures agreed upon by the two Prime Ministers, agreement on the borders of East Pakistan was reached in the fall of 1959, and on the borders between India and West Pakistan, as far as Jammu and Kashmir, in early 1960. The signing of these two border agreements was hailed as major landmarks in the efforts to deal with the issues in dispute by direct negotiations and in a peaceful way.

The Government of India strongly objected to the Pakistan-China border agreement, signed in Peking on March 3, 1963. Among its reasons was the claim that Pakistan had no right to enter into an agreement for the delimitation of the boundary between Sinkiang and a section of Kashmir which, according to India, Pakistan was occupying illegally. The one remaining border problem on which India and Pakistan are at complete loggerheads is, of course, in the Kashmir area, but this involves far more important considerations than the exact position of boundary lines.

4. Evacuee Property

The problem of evacuee property is one unresolved consequence of partition. "The refugees left behind their vast immovable property uncared for, their movable property was either lost or destroyed to a great extent, and not much of what remained could be carried by the early migrants to

---

[8] See Michael Brecher, *Nehru: A Political Biography* (London: Oxford University Press, 1959), pp. 359–361. Lord Birdwood, who knew the Punjab well and whose father was Commander-in-Chief of the British Indian Army, has maintained that if India had not had access to Kashmir through the Gurdaspur District, the issue in that disputed area might have been different. Few outside observers, however, would go as far as Lord Birdwood in supporting the extreme Pakistani claims regarding the Gurdaspur award and Kashmir. Lord Birdwood, *India and Pakistan: A Continent Decides* (New York: Praeger, 1954), pp. 36, 235–236.

their new homes."[9] No reliable figures are available, but it is clear that the value of non-Muslim evacuee property in Pakistan was far greater than that of Muslim evacuee property in India — according to the Indian claim, by as much as five to one. The issue was discussed immediately after partition, but it has not yet been completely resolved. It has of course been a source of vast discontent for the millions of people directly concerned. "The issue has embittered Indo-Pakistan relations to a great extent and it is no exaggeration to say that the Indians attach as much importance to it as the Pakistanis do to Kashmir."[10]

At first both governments acted on the assumption that most of the evacuees would return to their homes and would regain possession of their properties; but when this assumption proved to be unrealistic, India took the position that the entire question should be dealt with on a government-to-government basis. Accordingly, India decided to take over the claims of evacuee owners, and to use the proceeds from the sale of the property of Muslim evacuees who went to Pakistan in partial compensation for those who fled from Pakistan, leaving property behind. Both governments have enacted stringent laws by which evacuee property has been allotted to refugees or has been sold to compensate refugees for their losses in the other country. Aside from personal hardships and injustices which this procedure has involved, major complications have arisen because of the great disparity in the value of the properties left behind, the failure to agree on a fair value of the properties in question, and Pakistan's manifest unwillingness to meet the heavy claims which non-Muslim evacuees can make upon it. Although some compensation has been given, the problem of the disposition of and payment for immovable property has never been finally resolved. Agreements regarding movable property have been more definite and more generally implemented.

In addition, many other financial issues arising out of partition have been troublesome. The two new nations could not agree on an equitable division of the cash balances of undivided India. When an arbitral tribunal, in January 1948, fixed Pakistan's shares at Rs. 750 million (approximately $157,500,000), Sardar Patel tried to link implementation of the award with a settlement of the Kashmir dispute. At this stage Gandhi began a fast to stop the communal killings and disturbances, which was also considered to be a silent rebuke to the Government of India for its failure to honor the financial agreement. The next day the Government announced that the agreement would be implemented.

5. Economic Relations

Partition disrupted the normal economic patterns of the subcontinent, and strained relations added to the economic woes. The wheat lands of

[9] J. B. Das Gupta, *Indo-Pakistan Relations, 1947–1955* (Amsterdam: Djambatan, 1958), p. 188.
[10] *Ibid.*

West Punjab had produced the surplus made available to food-deficit areas elsewhere. Most of the raw jute was grown in East Pakistan, but all of the jute mills were in or near Calcutta. Most of the textile mills were in India, but most of the cotton was grown in West Pakistan.

Under a tentative "Standstill Agreement" concluded on August 5, 1947, the *status quo* regarding all trade and economic relations and movements between the two new states was to be maintained until February 29, 1948, and no trade or customs barriers would be imposed. Almost immediately, however, disagreements led to the imposition of retaliatory import and export duties, after Pakistan had rejected an Indian proposal for a customs and excise union and India had refused to share the jute duty with Pakistan. Some trade agreements were concluded in 1948 and 1949, but both countries complained of alleged violations.

When Pakistan, unlike other countries in the sterling area, failed to devalue its currency in September 1949, India, which already had an adverse trade balance, was compelled to pay much more for products from that country. As a result of friction over this issue and others India and Pakistan soon became involved in a costly trade war, which lasted for several months. Interim agreements in 1950 and 1951 brought the war of devaluation to an end. In general, trade between the two countries has declined markedly, with major declines in 1949–50 and in 1953–54. In 1958–59 the volume of trade was less than one-tenth of the amount in 1948–49. Except in 1952–53 and 1958–59, India has had an unfavorable balance of trade with Pakistan.

On March 21, 1960, a new agreement was signed. India agreed to supply Pakistan with larger quantities of iron and steel, coal, cement, and a variety of other products. Pakistan, in return, agreed to increase exports to India of raw jute, cotton, and other items.[11] There seems to be little prospect, however, that trade between India and Pakistan can be substantially increased, or that they will be willing to establish a customs union or even to reduce the existing barriers to their mutual trade. The former economic interdependence of the subcontinent has been largely replaced by relatively separate economies.

6. Water Disputes — the Indus Water Treaty

Partition also gave rise to a major dispute regarding the waters of the Indus River system, and of the elaborate canal irrigation system using these waters. Next to the Kashmir dispute, this was the most important of the many issues that arose in Indo-Pakistan relations; it was literally a matter of life or death for several million people living in Bahawalpur and other parts of West Pakistan, who were dependent on the waters of the rivers running through India for their very existence. The eventual resolution of this dispute, after difficult and protracted negotiations, was a major achieve-

[11] The text of the joint communiqué issued in New Delhi on March 21, 1960 is given in *Indiagram* (issued by the Embassy of India, Washington), No. 13, April 1, 1960.

ment and raised hopes that it would pave the way for the settlement of other issues.

The Indus River system, whose total flow is about twice that of the Nile, consists of the Indus River itself and various tributaries, notably the Jhelum, the Chenab, the Ravi, the Sutlej, and the Beas. The last three rivers rise in India and flow through Indian territory for some distance before they enter West Pakistan. In the nineteenth century British engineers constructed an elaborate irrigation system in the Punjab. With the division of the Punjab, this network of canals was cut by a political boundary. The Punjab Partition Committee held that "there is no question of varying the authorized shares of water to which the two zones and the various canals are entitled,"[12] and in December 1947 the Chief Engineers of East and West Punjab signed a Standstill Agreement for a continuance of the normal water supplies to canals in Pakistan from the headworks in India. When this agreement expired at the end of March 1948, however, India almost immediately stopped the supply of canal waters. The supply was restored in May, and in an agreement worked out in an inter-Dominion Conference in Delhi in the same month Pakistan agreed to accept a progressive reduction in the supply of water from the Indian rivers and India agreed to give Pakistan time to develop alternative sources of supply, through link canals and other works. Pakistan maintained that it had signed under duress, and in December 1950 it announced that it would no longer consider the agreement to be binding.

In 1951, on the basis of a first-hand investigation of the canal waters problem, David E. Lilienthal, former Chairman of the Tennessee Valley Authority, proposed in an article in a popular American magazine[13] that India and Pakistan work out a comprehensive joint plan for the development of the water resources of the Indus system, which he regarded as adequate for all the water needs of those sections of the two countries in the Indus basin. He also proposed that the International Bank for Reconstruction and Development be called in to assist in the development of the Indus basin plan and its financing. Seldom has an article in a popular journal had more fruitful results. Although his assumption that the water resources were adequate and that a comprehensive plan was possible proved to be wrong, Mr. Lilienthal did outline the kind of approach which eventually provided the solution to a most sensitive and complicated problem. Eugene Black, President of the World Bank, suggested to India and Pakistan that the good offices of the Bank might be useful in helping them to resolve their dispute, and in March 1952 both governments accepted Mr. Black's offer.

Eight years of technical study and diplomatic negotiations followed, with the World Bank serving in an advisory and intermediary role. Engineers

[12] Ministry of External Affairs, Government of India, *Correspondence which Has Taken Place between the Prime Ministers of India and Pakistan on the Subject of No War Declaration* (New Delhi: Author, 1950), Part II, p. 6.

[13] "Another Korea in the Making?" *Collier's Weekly,* August 4, 1951.

from India, Pakistan, and the World Bank, under the direction of General Raymond A. Wheeler, an American, composed the main technical group. They soon concluded that the development of the water resources of the Indus Basin on a joint basis was politically impossible, and recommended a new approach.[14] In brief, they proposed that the waters of the three eastern rivers — the Ravi, Beas, and Sutlej — should be for the use of India, that the waters of the three western rivers — the Indus, Jhelum, and Chenab — should be for the use of Pakistan, and that there should be a transition period, during which Pakistan would construct link canals and other works to replace the supply of water which it had been receiving from the three eastern rivers, the cost of these projects to be borne by India. This proposal, formally presented by the World Bank, was accepted by India with only a few minor reservations. Pakistan accepted it in principle, but felt dubious about it and asked for further technical studies. With the assistance of a firm of American engineers, Pakistan prepared a plan in accordance with the principles of the World Bank proposal, which envisioned an expenditure of some $1.25 billion, most of which should be provided by India.

For four years negotiations between India and Pakistan on the canal waters question were carried on, mostly in Washington, with Mr. W. A. B. Iliff, Vice President of the World Bank, available as needed. In June 1957 the Bank proposed that any difference over its proposal of 1954 be submitted to arbitration. Pakistan eventually accepted the proposal for arbitration, and it also offered to submit the entire dispute to the International Court of Justice. India showed no enthusiasm for any form of arbitration. In 1954 it began to withdraw water for the newly opened Bhakra Canal, a first stage of the vast Bhakra-Nangal project in the Punjab, which is now in operation. Although it entered into a series of interim agreements with Pakistan regarding the withdrawal of waters for its canals, it refused to pay the costs of link canals and other works in Pakistan to offset these withdrawals.

In spite of these differences, the negotiations finally resulted, in May 1959, in an agreement on the basic principles of a settlement. The actual text of the Indus Waters Treaty was agreed to in late August 1960, and on September 19 the treaty was signed in Karachi by Ayub Khan, Nehru, and W. A. B. Iliff. In general it followed the main outlines of the Bank's proposal of 1954, with the same division of the waters and with an elaborate program for canals, dams, and other works to be constructed over a period of some ten years. An Indus Commission, composed of a representative of each country, was to supervise implementation of the treaty.

The estimated cost of the program was more than one billion dollars. Recognizing that this sum was far beyond the capacity of India and Pakistan to meet, without external assistance, the World Bank had taken the initiative

[14] For an analysis of the World Bank proposal of February 1954 see Das Gupta, cited, pp. 171–183.

in working out an Indus Basin Development Fund Agreement, which was signed, simultaneously with the Indus Waters Treaty, by representatives of India, Pakistan, four other Commonwealth countries — Australia, Canada. New Zealand, and the United Kingdom — the United States, West Germany, and the World Bank. About 70 per cent of the funds pledged in this agreement were to be provided by the United States — a grant of $177 million, a foreign exchange loan of $70 million, loans and grants in local currency of $235 million, all to Pakistan, and a loan of $33 million to India. Pakistan and India would also contribute foreign exchange and local currency to the project.[15]

The implementation of the Indus Basin plan will be a difficult and lengthy venture that may well lead to many disagreements between India and Pakistan. Contracts for the building of the Mangla Dam, the first major project to be undertaken, have been awarded to an American construction firm, and work on this huge new dam is now in progress. It will be built across the Jhelum River, at a site practically on the borders of West Pakistan and Azad Kashmir. Before the Indus Waters Treaty was agreed upon, Pakistan had been making plans for a dam at Mangla, and India had protested, even to the extent of complaining to the United Nations. India objected because the site was in Azad Kashmir and because the waters contained by the dam would cover territory which India claimed. Furthermore, since the cost estimates for the Indus Basin project have risen substantially since the conclusion of the Development Fund Agreement, the necessary financial support for the project is by no means in sight. Pakistan has already been in touch with the signatories to discuss the increased financial needs.

Water troubles between India and Pakistan are by no means at an end. Pakistan has frequently protested the construction by India of the Farraka Barrage across the Ganges, which, it claims, will affect the supply of water in East Pakistan; and India has objected to the inauguration of the Karnaphuli Dam at Kaptai in the Chittagong Hill Tracts, on the ground that Pakistan has not lived up to its agreements which were reached some years ago, when the dam was first contemplated.

The Kashmir Question

United States involvement in the Kashmir dispute dates from the earliest stages of its reference to the United Nations Security Council and is an inescapable concomitant of the increasingly close relations with both India

---

[15] For a detailed summary of the provisions of the Indus Waters Treaty and the Indus Basin Development Fund Agreement, see *Pakistan News Digest*, October 1 and 27, 1960. For the broader implications of the Indus Waters agreement see Eugene Black, "The Indus: A Moral for Nations," *The New York Times Magazine*, December 11, 1960.

and Pakistan, between whom Kashmir stands as the great divide. This difficult question has become even more complicated since 1947. Ironically, both India and Pakistan seem to agree that the proper "solution" is a fairly simple one; the trouble is that they are poles apart regarding the proper solution.

Approaches to the Question

India and Pakistan approach the Kashmir question from very different premises. "The basic difference between the approach of India and Pakistan to the Kashmir problem," wrote Frank Moraes in *The Indian Express* in 1961, "is that while India fastens on aggression, Pakistan concentrates on a plebiscite." In each case the position is an entrenched one, and there seems to be little likelihood of any significant concessions. One important consideration is that the leaders of India and Pakistan are subject to powerful pressures on the Kashmir issue, and their room for concession and maneuver is probably quite narrow. Pakistan will feel insecure and incomplete until the present situation in Kashmir is changed to its advantage, and India will feel insecure if any significant change is made in this situation. On logical grounds the question should be capable of satisfactory resolution in any one of a number of ways; but Kashmir is more of an emotional than a logical issue.

Pakistan insists that there can be no peace in the subcontinent, and no prospect of concentrating on the basic internal problems and external challenges, until and unless the Kashmir question is "solved." In an article in January 1964 Ayub wrote: "For if the security and welfare of the Indian subcontinent are the objective, then what is needed is not the injection of massive doses of military aid into India but a rapprochement between India and Pakistan, such as would ensure a disengagement and could even open the way to a reduction of the Indian and Pakistani forces. Such a rapprochement can be brought about only through a just and honorable settlement of the Kashmir dispute. It can be achieved in no other way."[16]

Pakistan holds that the Kashmir question is an explosive one, a "time bomb in Asia," and that it is a grave world issue. Its spokesmen have declared that if this question can be "solved," there will be no major issues in dispute between them. This view is doubtless overly optimistic, but it is certainly a fact that the Kashmir question intrudes itself wherever any efforts are made to improve Indo-Pakistan relations. Like Banquo's ghost, it is present at every feast.

Pakistanis often insist that the "solution" of the Kashmir question is a matter of life and death for them. Whatever the reasons for such extreme claims, they are undoubtedly deep-seated, and lie in the realm of psychology and national prestige. Aside from these intangible factors, which are

[16] "The Pakistan-American Alliance: Stresses and Strains," *Foreign Affairs*, January 1964, p. 208.

perhaps more basic than any tangible considerations, the main Pakistani concern apparently revolves around questions of security and water.

Kashmir occupies an important geopolitical position at the meeting-point of India, Pakistan, Afghanistan, the Soviet Union, and China. If Chinese or Russian forces pushed over the Himalayas or the Hindu Kush and established themselves in Kashmir, both India and Pakistan would face a grave security threat. Pakistan is as well aware as India of the need to ward off any such threat (its recent flirtations with Communist China and the Soviet Union have had other motivations). But Pakistan also regards the presence of Indian armed forces in Kashmir as a special threat to its security, a much more real and immediate one than any emanating from across the mountains to the north. Even though Pakistan has long and more vulnerable frontiers with India, the Indian occupation of part of Kashmir still looms as a kind of sword thrust between Pakistan and its "rightful" northern boundaries.

The water problem is closely related to the question of security. The three western rivers of the Indus River system all flow through Kashmir, and two of them — the Jhelum and the Chenab — flow into Pakistan after passing through the India-held portion of Kashmir. Moreover, if Pakistan is to conserve substantial amounts of the waters of the western rivers, the most logical place for some of the dams or storage basins is in or adjoining parts of Kashmir.

In Pakistan, or at least in West Pakistan, feeling on the Kashmir question is an explosive mixture of frustration, irritation, and anger. This is expressed in statements by the leaders of the country, in broadcasts over Radio Pakistan, in editorials in Pakistani newspapers, in the almost hypochondriac preoccupation with any developments relating to Kashmir, and in the interjection of the Kashmir issue into almost every discussion which a representative of Pakistan has with people from other countries. Ayub Khan tried to bring his talks with Nehru in September 1960 around to this question, but he found the Indian Prime Minister quite uncommunicative whenever this approach was tried. In his talks with President Kennedy in Washington in July 1961, and in his speeches during his American visit, Ayub Khan went out of his way to call attention to the Kashmir question and the necessity of finding some satisfactory resolution to it. He has repeatedly promised his fellow-countrymen that he will never let the issue die until it is satisfactorily resolved. He has at times even given assurances, which it will be difficult for him to fulfill, that "justice" will be done in Kashmir. He has been compelled by public pressure to take a particularly strong stand on Kashmir; and his own strong statements have perhaps added to the popular feeling and resentment over this issue.

In an atmosphere of frustration, irritation, and anger, many illogical things can happen. There may, therefore, be some basis for Indian apprehensions that in such an atmosphere even the responsible leaders of Pakistan may be pressured into taking measures in Kashmir which might lead to military hostilities between India and Pakistan, or, as is more likely, that Pakistani fanatics may, even in defiance of their government, take some extreme steps which could lead to serious trouble between the two countries.

For wholly understandable reasons the Indian approach to the Kashmir question is relatively calm, particularly on official levels. When the question was again brought before the Security Council in late 1961 and early 1962, Prem Bhatia of *The Times of India* observed: "Years of familiarity with the Kashmir issue have given to senior officials in the External Affairs Ministry a certain immunity against panic. The question has been before them for fourteen years and its various aspects have by now acquired the distasteful intimacy of a rag which has been chewed by a long succession of specialists."[17] This "business-as-usual" attitude is particularly annoying to Pakistan. After all, India holds the choice parts of Kashmir, including the famous Valley — an extraordinarily small piece of real estate to be the focal point of so much controversy. It regards Kashmir as an integral part of India, and is not likely to agree to any proposals which might result in Kashmir's detachment or which would run counter to its concept of a secular state or which would inflame Hindu-Muslim relations elsewhere in India.

If India was faced with a real danger of losing its position in Kashmir, its present calm attitude would soon give way to intense excitement. Some Hindu communalist groups try to make political capital out of the Kashmir question. At the least they demand a much tougher policy toward Pakistan generally, and some favor armed action to oust Pakistan from those parts of Kashmir which it now holds. Obviously if such groups become really influential politically, and if they have more influence on Nehru's successors than they had on the anticommunalist Nehru, relations between India and Pakistan will take a grave turn for the worse, although this danger is not imminent.

The Kashmir Story

The "story of Kashmir" has often been told, but perhaps never in a way which interested outside observers would find both objective and intelligible.[18] Official documents, statements, publications without number, and extensive press coverage are available; but since the Indian and Pakistani versions of the story are so greatly at variance, and since so much of this material is of a frankly propagandistic nature, the materials must be used with caution and skepticism.[19]

[17] "Two Angles on Kashmir," *The Times of India*, January 16, 1962.

[18] For details of the "Kashmir story," especially since 1947, see Michael Brecher, *The Struggle for Kashmir* (New York: Oxford University Press, 1953); Josef Korbel, *Danger in Kashmir* (Princeton University Press, 1954); Lord Birdwood, *Two Nations and Kashmir* (London: Robert Hale, 1956); and J. B. Das Gupta, *Indo-Pakistan Relations, 1947–1955* (Amsterdam: Djambatan, 1958).

[19] Once one is familiar with the main outlines of the Kashmir story, perhaps his most reliable source of information would be the five lengthy reports submitted by the United

By August 1947, the rulers of nearly all of the more than 550 princely states that dotted the subcontinent had entered into some kind of association with either India or Pakistan. The major exceptions were the rulers of the two largest princely states, Hyderabad and Jammu and Kashmir. The Nizam of Hyderabad tried to maintain a separate status, and he refused to accede to India until Indian troops entered the state in 1948 and forced his accession. The Maharaja of Kashmir likewise was reluctant to cast his lot with either country, although he did enter into a Standstill Agreement with Pakistan. Only when he was convinced that he could not drive back the tribal invaders without help, in October 1947, did he appeal for Indian military assistance. India in effect forced or at least speeded up his accession by insisting, on Lord Mountbatten's advice, on accession as a price for military support.

In a letter to Lord Mountbatten dated October 26, 1947, the Maharaja of Kashmir stated: "With the condition obtaining at present in my State and the great emergency of the situation as it exists, I have no option but to ask for help from the Indian Dominion." On the following day Lord Mountbatten accepted the accession of Kashmir to the Dominion of India and made the following pledge: "In consistence with their policy that in the case of any State where the issue of accession has been the subject of dispute, the question of accession should be decided in accordance with the wishes of the people of the State. It is my Government's wish that, as soon as law and order have been restored in Kashmir and its soil cleared of the invader, the question of the State's accession should be settled by a reference to the people.[20]

This pledge was repeated many times in 1947 and 1948, and less frequently in subsequent years by Prime Minister Nehru and other Indian spokesmen. It was reaffirmed, with the specific mention of "a plebiscite or referendum," in the letter which the Government of India addressed to the President of the UN Security Council on January 1, 1948, asking the Council to "call upon Pakistan to put an end immediately to the giving of . . . assistance [to the invaders of Kashmir] which is an act of aggression against India." It was incorporated in the resolutions of the United Nations Commission for India and Pakistan of August 13, 1948 and January 5, 1949,

---

Nations Representative for India and Pakistan, Dr. Frank Graham, in 1951–1953. See UN Security Council, *Official Records; Special Supplement No. 2, Report of the United Nations Representative for India and Pakistan,* S/2375/Rev. 1 (New York: Author, 1951); *Special Supplement No. 2, Second Report of the United Nations Representative for India and Pakistan,* S/2448 (New York: Author, 1952); *Special Supplement No. 2, Third and Fourth Reports of the United Nations Representative for India and Pakistan,* S/2611 and Corr. 1, S/2783 and Corr. 1 (New York: Author, 1952); and *Special Supplement No. 1, Fifth Report of the United Nations Representative for India and Pakistan,* S/2967 (New York: Author, 1953).

[20] The texts of the letters exchanged between the Maharaja of Kashmir and Lord Mountbatten on October 26 and 27, 1947, are given in Korbel, cited, pp. 80–83.

which both countries accepted.[21]   The latter resolution declared that "The question of the accession of the State of Jammu and Kashmir to India or Pakistan will be decided through the democratic method of a free and impartial plebiscite." In an address to the Indian Parliament on March 28, 1951, Nehru declared: "From the very beginning it has been our declared wish that the people of Kashmir should themselves decide their future. *We will continue to adhere to our policy whatever happens.* In pursuance of our policy, we agreed to hold a plebiscite *provided the conditions necessary to its peaceful conduct were fulfilled.*"[22]

So many new factors have been introduced into the Kashmir scene in the intervening years that it is difficult to determine whether India still adheres to this announced policy. To judge from many statements by Indian spokesmen, particularly V. K. Krishna Menon, and even by Nehru himself, India no longer regards the pledge of a plebiscite in Kashmir as valid or binding. Nehru, however, usually justified his obvious dislike for a plebiscite on the ground that Pakistan has never fulfilled "the conditions necessary to its peaceful conduct." These conditions, laid down in the UN resolutions, include a withdrawal of Pakistan troops from Kashmir and other necessary steps before a fair verdict of the people through of a plebiscite can be obtained. Virtually all of the efforts of Dr. Frank Graham and other UN representatives were devoted to obtaining agreement between India and Pakistan on the demilitarization of Kashmir and other preconditions. At one stage, in 1952, India and Pakistan, under UN urging, agreed to appoint a plebisicite administrator before the following April, but this step was never taken.

In other words, despite the early pledges of India and Pakistan, the UN resolutions, and the efforts of UN representatives, the two countries have never come close to setting the stage for a plebiscite. As far as Pakistan is concerned, the Indian pledge is as binding now as it was when first voluntarily made in 1947. As far as India is concerned, the pledge is virtually a dead letter, although India has not finally repudiated it, and it cannot possibly be honored until many other conditions are disposed of to India's satisfaction.

The United Nations and Kashmir

India, not Pakistan, brought the Kashmir question before the Security Council. Its letter of January 1, 1948 to the President of the Security Council requested the Council: "(1) to prevent Pakistan Government personnel, military or civil, from participating or assisting in the invasion of the Jammu and Kashmir State; (2) to call upon other Pakistani nationals to desist from taking any part in the fighting in the Jammu and Kashmir State; (3) to deny to the invaders: (a) access to and use of its territory for operations

[21] For the texts of the two resolutions see *ibid.*, Appendices II and III, pp. 312–319.
[22] Nehru, cited, p. 466. Italics added.

against Kashmir, (b) military and other supplies; (c) all other kinds of aid that might tend to prolong the present struggle."[23] Since India chose to limit its reference to the Security Council to these three items, and since it invoked Articles 34 and 35 of the United Nations Charter, relating to "the pacific settlement of disputes," rather than Chapter VII of the Charter, dealing with "action with respect to threats to the peace, breach of the peace, or act of aggression," India did not base its charges against Pakistan on grounds of aggression. However, its letter of January 1 did state that Pakistan's assistance to the invaders of Kashmir "is an act of aggression against India," and the charge of aggression was frequently levied by Indian spokesmen in the months that followed.

From the very beginning of the long deliberations the Kashmir issue became bogged down and obfuscated by many Pakistani countercharges, by basic disagreements on facts and priorities, and by honest bewilderment on the part of the Security Council members. After weeks of discussion, the Security Council set up a Commission and instructed it "to proceed at once to the Indian subcontinent and there place its good offices and mediation at the disposal of the Governments of India and Pakistan." The Commission spent most of July and August in India and Pakistan, and in September it was able to conduct some first-hand investigations in Kashmir. When it arrived in Karachi, it learned for the first time that regular units of the Pakistan armed forces had been in Kashmir since May, as "an act of self-defense." This admission, to which Nehru pointed as proof positive of Pakistan's aggression in Kashmir, came as "a bombshell" to the members of the Commission, and introduced a "new and most important element in the picture." On August 13, 1948, it passed a resolution in three parts, calling for a cease-fire in Kashmir, for the withdrawal of Pakistan's troops from Kashmir, which should be followed by the withdrawal of "the bulk" of the Indian forces, and for a reaffirmation by both India and Pakistan of their agreement "that the future status of the State of Jammu and Kashmir shall be determined in accordance with the will of the people." On January 5, 1949, in a second major resolution, the Commission directed that "the question of the accession of the State of Jammu and Kashmir to India or Pakistan will be decided through the democratic method of a free and impartial plebiscite," to be arranged for and supervised by a plebiscite administrator, appointed by the UN Secretary-General.

Both resolutions were accepted by both India and Pakistan, although they objected to some of the provisions, and are the basic documents in the United Nations approach to the Kashmir question. This question has been continuously before the Security Council, although since 1952 it has been considered at length only in 1957, 1962, and 1964. Pakistan claims that India has consistently flaunted the United Nations by its refusal to agree

[23] UN Security Council, *Official Records*, January 2, 1948, S/628 (New York: Author, 1948).

to a plebiscite in Kashmir. India usually justifies its refusal either on the basis of the failure of Pakistan to withdraw its troops from Kashmir or on the basis of new elements that have entered into the issue since 1949.

In late December 1948, in accordance with the recommendation in the UNCIP resolution of August 13, India and Pakistan agreed to a cease-fire in Kashmir, effective January 1, 1949. Since that time a small group of UN military observers has been continuously on the spot in Kashmir, patrol-ling the cease-fire line, which was formally demarcated in mid-1949, and reporting to the two governments and to the UN Secretary-General on all incidents along the cease-fire line. This almost forgotten group, numbering usually between thirty and fifty men, has been performing useful work, under difficult conditions and with little recognition, for many years. Until 1954 it included an American contingent, but after the announcement of the decision to extend military aid to Pakistan the contingent was withdrawn, at India's insistence.

In February 1949 UNCIP returned to the Indian subcontinent to arrange for the implementation of the terms of the truce agreement and for the holding of a plebiscite. In March the Secretary-General nominated Fleet Admiral Chester W. Nimitz as plebiscite administrator. The Commission, however, could not resolve the differences between India and Pakistan on the conditions for the demilitarization of Kashmir, the necessary precondi-tion for the holding of a plebiscite. On this rock its efforts foundered.[24]

Feeling that its usefulness was at an end, the Commission recommended that it be replaced by a single United Nations Representative, and, early in 1950, Sir Owen Dixon of Australia was appointed to this new post. After less than three months in the subcontinent, Sir Owen concluded that there was no hope of bringing India and Pakistan into agreement regarding Kashmir, and he asked to be relieved of his assignment. Every proposal that he advanced, including partition and a plebiscite, was rejected by India or Pakistan. "In the end," he reported frankly to the Security Council, "I became convinced that India's agreement would never be obtained to demilitarization in any . . . form, or to provisions regarding the period of the plebiscite."[25]

---

[24] On its return to New York, the Commission submitted a report to the Security Council, which contained a mournful but accurate commentary on the real obstacles in the way: "The roots of the Kashmir dispute are deep; strong undercurrents — political, economic, religious — in both Dominions have acted, and do act, against an easy and prompt solution of this outstanding dispute between India and Pakistan. These currents, which at this early stage of national formation are often antagonistic, account to a con-siderable degree for the misgivings, reluctance, and hesitation which the Commission felt was often present in the negotiations and which restricted both governments in the concessions which they might otherwise have been prepared to make to facilitate agree-ment." UN Security Council, *Official Records: Special Supplement No. 7, Third In-terim Report of the United Nations Commission for India and Pakistan,* S/1430/Rev. 1 (New York: Author, 1949), p. 60.

[25] UN Security Council, *Official Records: Supplement for September-December 1950,* S/1791, September 15, 1950 (New York: Author, 1950), p. 16.

In 1951 the Security Council asked for the appointment of a new UN Representative, and Dr. Frank P. Graham of the United States was named for this thankless assignment. For the next two years Dr. Graham carried on negotiations, drew up twelve proposals, and submitted five reports to the Security Council.[26] In his first report he expressed some hope for agreement between India and Pakistan; in his fifth he concluded that there was no further basis at that stage for a continuance of his negotiations.

For nearly four years the Kashmir question was not brought before the Security Council. Then, in January 1957, Pakistan requested that it be taken up once again.[27] This was a particularly unpropitious time for India, which was on the eve of its second general elections. Krishna Menon expounded India's position at length, in the longest speech ever made to the Security Council. He returned to India to be welcomed as "the hero of Kashmir" and to be elected to the Indian Parliament from North Bombay.

On February 19 a resolution in the Security Council, re-emphasizing the necessity for a plebiscite in Kashmir and expressing the belief that a proposal advanced by Pakistan for "a temporary United Nations force in connection with demilitarization . . . would deserve consideration," was defeated by a Soviet veto, and was indignantly rejected by India. The Council thereupon requested its President, Gunnar V. Jarring of Sweden, to proceed to the Indian subcontinent "to examine . . . any proposals which, in his opinion, are likely to contribute towards the settlement of the dispute." To no one's surprise, Mr. Jarring's brief trip led to no progress in resolving the dispute. In his report he seemed to suggest some acceptance of India's contention that the Kashmir question had changed considerably since 1947–48, and that India's offer of a plebiscite could not remain open indefinitely.

In December 1957, at Pakistan's request, the Security Council agreed to ask Dr. Graham to take up his task again. After one month of negotiations Dr. Graham submitted a report, which asked India and Pakistan to refrain from statements and actions that would aggravate the situation, urged them to agree on the interpretation of the UNCIP resolutions of August 1948 and January 1949, suggested that pending a final "solution" of the Kashmir problem the two governments should consider the stationing of a United Nations force on the Pakistani side of the border after the withdrawal of Pakistani forces from Kashmir, and recommended that the Prime Ministers should meet "at the earliest practicable date," under Dr. Graham's auspices. Dr. Graham reported that Pakistan had accepted all of these proposals, but that India had rejected them *in toto*.

Because they were unacceptable to India, the proposals advanced by Dr. Graham in 1958 gathered dust in the files of the United Nations, although the Pakistani representative, Zafrulla Khan referred to them often in his state-

[26] See above, n. 20.
[27] In 1957 the Security Council devoted 28 meetings to the "India-Pakistan question."

ments before the Security Council in the spring of 1962, when, again at Pakistan's request, the Kashmir question was reopened.

Pakistan asked for a reopening on the ground that the matter had assumed a new urgency because of mounting tensions. The Council did not accede to India's objections to the reopening of the question, but it did agree to an Indian request to postpone further consideration until after the third general elections in India and the formation of the new government. In early May, and again in early June, the question was considered at some length. On June 22 a resolution, introduced by Ireland, calling for direct negotiations between India and Pakistan for the implementation of the UN resolutions of August 1948 and January 1949, was defeated by a Soviet veto.

India had let it be known that it was opposed to this resolution, and would regard a vote in its favor as an unfriendly act. The Soviet vote was hailed in India as another evidence of Russia's true friendship, and although the resolution seemed to be innocuous enough, the United States and Britain incurred India's ill will by reaffirming a position which India had itself apparently accepted many years before.

In 1964, when, at Pakistan's insistence, the Kashmir question was again considered by the Security Council, all attempts to obtain Council approval of a formal resolution were abandoned because of the certainty of another Soviet veto. India, backed by the Soviet Union and Czechoslovakia, opposed a direct mediation role by UN Secretary-General U Thant, as proposed by Pakistan. The Council ended debate on May 18, with appeals by some of its members to India and Pakistan to resume their talks and to exercise restraint in dealing with this controversial issue.

For nearly two decades the Kashmir question has been before the United Nations Security Council. Almost the only concrete results of much labor and concern have been the important UNCIP resolutions of August 1948 and January 1949; the cease-fire in Kashmir, which has been in effect since January 1, 1949; numerous proposals by Dr. Graham and other UN representatives, most of which have been accepted by Pakistan, sometimes with reservations, and rejected by India; extensive documentation; and growing frustration and disappointments. It would be difficult to say whether the extensive UN efforts, although obviously they have been well-intentioned, have been really helpful, except in preventing a military showdown between India and Pakistan. India has often expressed regrets that it ever brought the question before the Security Council, which from the beginning became entangled in innumerable complications and tended to bypass the issues in which India was interested, and which has generally been more critical of India than of Pakistan. Pakistan's case has usually been more convincing to the Security Council, and to world opinion, than has the position of India; but verbal sympathy and support in the form of resolutions have not gained for Pakistan the concessions to which it feels entitled, and have only strengthened Pakistan's feelings of frustration and disillusionment. The Soviet "veto" of the resolution introduced into the Security Council in June 1962, and the abandonment of efforts to introduce any resolution at all in the Council during the debate in 1964, seemed to signify that the Council had come to a dead end as far as Kashmir is concerned. Pakistan has toyed with the idea of referring the question to the General Assembly, but this would be nothing but a futile gesture, for the majority of the members of the United Nations will almost certainly not vote against India on such an issue. Pakistan may from time to time ask for a reopening of the Kashmir question in the Security Council, chiefly for the purpose of keeping the issue open.

Mounting tensions in Kashmir in August 1965 led to the outbreak of open warfare between India and Pakistan. The latter country insisted that a necessary condition for a cease-fire was "an honorable settlement" of the Kashmir question. This was not, however, a condition of the cease-fire to which Pakistan reluctantly agreed, under pressure from the UN Security Council, on September 22. Speaking before an early morning session of the Council on that date, Foreign Minister Z. A. Bhutto warned that Pakistan might withdraw from the United Nations unless the Kashmir question were settled "once and for all." Thus even after the blood-letting of August-September Kashmir continues to be the main focus of Indo-Pakistan bitterness and the main barrier to improved relations between the two South Asian neighbors.

The Failure of Direct Negotiations

Far from contributing to the resolution of the dispute, the Security Council's deliberation in 1962 and 1964 apparently increased tensions between India and Pakistan. This suggests that the only real hope for a resolution of the issue is for India and Pakistan to reach agreement by bilateral negotiations, with or without the help of the UN or other international agencies of representatives. Unfortunately, in spite of an expressed willingness to deal with each other, India and Pakistan have never been able to "get down to brass tacks" on Kashmir, let alone to agree on the necessary preliminaries.

In November 1962 the American Government, disturbed by the critical reactions in Pakistan to its military assistance to India to meet the Chinese threat, and realizing that in its forthcoming struggle to persuade the Congress to approve appropriations for additional military aid to India, the question of Kashmir was bound to be brought up again and again, in cooperation with the United Kingdom brought strong pressure on Nehru and Ayub Khan to agree to direct talks on Kashmir. Each government sent high-level delegations to South Asia. Duncan Sandys, Secretary for Commonwealth Relations, and Averell Harriman, then Assistant Secretary of State for Far Eastern Affairs, secured the agreement of Nehru and Ayub to hold direct negotiations, first on a ministerial level and later, if the signs were hopeful, by a face-to-face meeting. This was not a major concession for Pakistan, in spite of its new sensitivity over India's *bona fides*, for it had always been willing to discuss Kashmir. India, which has in the past been the reluctant negotiator, was making a more marked departure from previous policy.

This agreement paved the way for the first really extensive series of direct talks between India and Pakistan on the Kashmir question.[28] The first round of talks was held in Rawalpindi on December 27–29, 1962. On the eve of the talks Pakistan announced that it had reached a settlement with China regarding the Kashmir-Sinkiang border. The timing of this announcement was interpreted by India as an effort to prejudice the Rawalpindi talks, which opened in an atmosphere of suspicion and distrust, and which produced only a preliminary exchange of views. Pakistan still wanted to talk about a plebiscite, or some other equally "just" solution, and India wanted to explore the possibilities of agreement on the partition of Kashmir, if Pakistan would not promise to abandon its claims to the territory which it has held, directly or indirectly, since 1947.

After exploratory discussions the two parties agreed to resume their talks in mid-January in New Delhi. Four more rounds of talks were held between February and mid-May, but at the end the representatives announced that no agreement could be reached, and Indo-Pakistan relations seemed to be at a lower ebb than ever. India charged that Pakistan's border agreement with China showed that Pakistan was not seriously interested in securing an agreement, and Pakistan charged that India's refusal to make significant concessions indicated that it did not intend to permit a peaceful resolution of the problem. Each country apparently expected the United States and the United Kingdom to exert pressure on the other to make one-sided concessions.

The Situation Within Kashmir

Conditions within Jammu and Kashmir have changed considerably since 1947–48. India and Pakistan have kept rather close control over the parts of Jammu and Kashmir which they occupy, although Pakistan maintains the fiction of an "independent" Azad government in most of the section of Kashmir on its side of the cease-fire line, and India has treated Kashmir in a special way while steadfastly maintaining that it is an integral part of India. Very little real freedom has been permitted in either part, although the India-held part has been more open to outside contacts.

In the first six years after partition Sheikh Abdullah, "the Lion of Kashmir," was the unquestioned leader on the Indian side of the cease-fire line. Although a Muslim, "Sheikh Sahib" had cooperated with the Indian Na-

---

[28] Detailed reports on the talks were published in the newspapers of India and Pakistan. For summaries of the talks see the pertinent issues of *India News* and *Pakistan News Digest*.

tional Congress, and he had cast his lot with India. In the fall of 1952 the rule of the Maharaja was officially terminated, and his son, the Yuvraj Karen Singh, was appointed as the head of the state. By 1952 or early 1953, Sheikh Abdullah apparently began to think in terms of greater autonomy, or perhaps even of complete independence, for Kashmir. This led to disagreements within the top leadership of the National Conference, and in August 1953 to the arrest of Abdullah and the appointment of his Deputy Prime Minister, Bakshi Ghulam Mohammed, as Prime Minister. The extent of Indian involvement in these moves, which were taken in the name of the Yuvraj Karen Singh, has never been determined. Nehru denied that India's hand was back of the sensational events of August 1953, and he expressed his regret over the fate that had befallen his "old comrade in arms"; but in all probability he gave his approval of Abdullah's deposition and arrest.[29]

From August 1953 until April 1964, with the exception of two brief periods of freedom, Abdullah was in custody. Even in custody he was a burden on the conscience of Nehru and other Indian leaders. When he was temporarily released, he was outspoken in his criticisms of Indian policy toward Kashmir. Presumably he was being tried for his alleged offenses, but his trial dragged on for many months, with no end in sight. Neither the Bakshi Ghulam Mohammed regime nor the Government of India was eager to condemn Abdullah, for this would simply make him a martyr in the eyes of many Kashmiris. On the other hand, failure to proceed against him would raise further doubts regarding the legality as well as the wisdom of his arrest and long confinement.

While Sheikh Abdullah was in custody the governments of Bakshi Ghulam Mohammed and of India took several steps to associate Kashmir more closely with the Indian Union. In the States Reorganization Bill, passed by the Indian Parliament in August 1956, the state of Jammu and Kashmir was listed as one of the fourteen Indian states. In November, the Kashmir Constituent Assembly adopted a new constitution, which declared Kashmir to be an integral part of India. All these steps were bitterly criticized by Pakistan, which appealed to the Security Council to declare such steps to be contrary to India's commitments under the UN resolutions. In January 1957 the Council, with no opposing votes but with the Soviet Union abstaining, adopted a resolution declaring that the constitutional developments linking part of Kashmir more closely with India were contrary to the commitment to a plebiscite. India refused to accept this ruling, and instead, on January 26, 1957 (Republic Day), it confirmed Kashmir's accession. Nehru, Krishna Menon, and other Indian spokesmen frequently asserted that no change could henceforth be made in Kashmir's status without the concurrence of the Constituent Assembly of the state. Bakshi Ghulam Mohammed repeatedly declared that Kashmir is irrevocably linked to India.

[29] See Norman D. Palmer, "The Changing Scene in Kashmir," *Far Eastern Survey,* November 1953, pp. 157–163.

Several events after 1953 brought the Kashmir dispute more directly into the arena of the cold war. The signing of a mutual defense assistance agreement between the United States and Pakistan, and Pakistan's entry into SEATO and CENTO were regarded by Mr. Nehru as creating an entirely new situation and destroying "the roots and foundation of the plebiscite proposal in Kashmir." During a visit to Srinagar, in 1955, Nikita Khrushchev declared flatly that "the question of Kashmir as one of the States of the Republic of India has already been decided by the people of Kashmir." After this declaration, until India and Pakistan became involved in armed hostilities in the fall of 1965, the Soviet Union openly backed India's position on the Kashmir issue. Naturally the Soviet stand aroused extreme bitterness in Pakistan. Ironically, some of this bitterness was transferred to the United States, on the ground that Pakistan had not received the kind of support that India had received from the Soviet Union.

When several Indian Cabinet members and Chief Ministers resigned en masse in August 1963 in a move to revitalize the Congress party organization, Bakshi Ghulam Mohammed resigned as Prime Minister of Jammu and Kashmir. At the same time he resigned as head of the Kashmiri National Conference and joined the Congress party. One of his last official acts was to propose an amendment to the state's constitution to change the title of his successor from Prime Minister to Chief Minister, in accordance with the practice in other Indian states, and to authorize other measures to "integrate" Kashmir more fully into the Republic of India. Pakistan protested strongly against the proposed amendment, which it attributed to Indian initiative.

In April 1964 the legal proceedings were abandoned and Abdullah was released. His release was hailed in Srinagar and elsewhere in Indian-held Kashmir, but it was received with mixed reactions in most parts of India and in Parliament. Nehru was greatly embarrassed by Abdullah's refusal to accept the official Indian view that Kashmir was an integral part of India and by his open championing of a very different approach to the Kashmir question, based on referring the question of Kashmir's future to the people of the State.[30]

The release of Sheikh Abdullah was only one of several events in 1964 which put India more on the defensive than ever regarding Kashmir. Other complicating developments were the growing evidences that the people of the Valley of Kashmir did not support the tie with India, the obvious lack of popular support of the feeble successors of the unpopular Bakshi Ghulam Mohammed, the communal riots sparked by the theft of a "hair of the Prophet" from a mosque in Srinagar, and the adverse reactions in Pakistan, in other countries, and even within India to these gloomy signs of more

[30] See Thomas F. Brady, "New Moves to Settle Kashmir," *The New York Times,* May 24, 1964. In May, 1965, on his return from a trip abroad, Abdullah was again apprehended and placed in custody, this time in South India.

trouble ahead. And the most complicating development of all was the death of Jawaharlal Nehru on May 27.

In Pakistan and elsewhere — even at times in India — the sentiment was often expressed that India would be unyielding on the Kashmir issue as long as Nehru, a descendant of Kashmiri Brahmins, was at the helm in India. But in the last months of his life there were indications that Nehru was willing to moderate his previous position on Kashmir. He was largely responsible for the release of Sheikh Abdullah, and in spite of continuing criticisms he met with Abdullah and encouraged the Kashmiri leader to explore various possible "solutions" for the Kashmir question — most of which he did not approve himself — and to visit Pakistan as well as the Valley of Kashmir for a study of the existing situation and an exchange of views. There is some indication that if Nehru had lived, he and Ayub Khan would have met in mid-1964 to seek agreement on Kashmir. Thus Nehru's death may have diminished rather than enhanced the prospects of some Indo-Pakistan reconciliation regarding Kashmir. Both Ayub Khan and Prime Minister Lal Bahadur Shastri have publicly expressed a desire to work for such a reconciliation, and they have been discreet, and even complimentary, with reference to each other. Shastri is known to be eager to find some way out of the Kashmir impasse, and he seems to be less adamant on this question than most other Indian leaders. But it is doubtful that he will dare to make significant concessions, for these would be strongly opposed by extremist groups in India, and he does not have the prestige or the popular following which Nehru enjoyed. Sheikh Abdullah is in a strategic position to seek a settlement, but the mercurial Kashmiri leader is known to harbor views which are equally unacceptable to India and Pakistan, and his own hold on the Kashmiri people, after so many years of forced retirement from public life, as well as his capacity for real statesmanship, remain to be tested.

India or Pakistan — the Clash of Views

Both India and Pakistan will be satisfied with nothing less than complete support of their respective positions. This poses a dilemma for countries like the United States which seek to help bring them into agreement rather than pass judgment on their claims. Both sides in fact have a strong case, which is not always well presented and is encumbered with many irrelevancies.

India emphasizes the "fact" of accession by the Maharaja of Kashmir, which it claims gives it legal title to all of Jammu and Kashmir, the "fact" of "aggression" by Pakistan in 1947 and 1948, and the "fact" of the legal integration of Kashmir (or that part on the Indian side of the cease-fire line) into the indissoluble Indian Union. It maintains that Pakistan is illegally and forcefully occupying territory in Kashmir which rightfully belongs to India, and it insists that Pakistan "vacate its aggression."

"Our position," Krishna Menon declared in 1962, "is that we will not be treated like two peas in a pod in this matter. And there can be no question of any intervention, any good offices or anything. . . . We will never consider this question on the basis of equality of Pakistan and India . . . the accession is full, it is complete, it is final."[31] It is clear, however, that India is willing to negotiate a settlement on the basis of the *status quo* in Kashmir, subject to minor boundary and other adjustments. As early as 1955, and afterward, Nehru offered a settlement on the basis of the *status quo*, but Pakistan rejected this idea.

Regarding a plebiscite, India points out that this was conditioned on Pakistan's vacating the "aggression." It holds that the conditional promise is no longer valid or feasible, because Pakistan has not observed the preconditions, American military aid to its ally has created an entirely different situation, and conditions have changed radically in other ways since the plebiscite pledge was made.

India does not accept the contention that since Kashmir is a Muslim-majority state, it should be associated with Pakistan rather than with India. This would imply an acceptance of the "two-nation theory," which India has always rejected, and would be in violation of India's desire to build a secular state, in which people of many religions would coexist peacefully and on terms of equality, with the right to exercise their religion freely.[32]

India is genuinely apprehensive of the effects of "an upset of everything in Kashmir," to use Nehru's words, upon the communal situation throughout the country. It maintains that any radical change in the status of Kashmir would have dangerous effects on the relations between Hindus and Muslims in other parts of India. For this reason alone India would almost certainly refuse to permit a plebiscite in Kashmir, even under international auspices.

Pakistan insists that the Kashmir question can be readily "solved" if India will live to its pledge of 1947 to refer the question of the future status of Kashmir to the Kashmiri people, and abide by the United Nations resolutions. "The fundamental question involved here," declared Zafrulla Khan in 1962, "is the self-determination of the people of Kashmir, the right to decide their own future freely without interference from one side or the other."[33] Obviously Pakistan is confident that if the Kashmiri people are given such an opportunity, they will opt for Pakistan. Presumably the choice offered would be a simple one: India or Pakistan? If, contrary to Pakistan's expectations, the people of Kashmir opted for India, Pakistan has promised to accept this verdict in good faith. It is less certain what its attitude would be if a third choice, namely independence, were among the options, or if a

[31] UN Security Council, *Official Records*, May 3, 1962, S/PV.1009, pp. 22, 32.
[32] One prominent Indian journalist wrote in January 1962 that "the Kashmir problem is essentially no more than the final challenge or test to older generations of Indians and Pakistanis of Mr. Jinnah's two-nation theory." B. G. Verghese, in *The Times of India*, January 26, 1962.
[33] UN Security Council, *Official Records*, February 1, 1962, S/PV. 900, p. 46.

plebiscite were limited only to the Valley of Kashmir, as has sometimes been proposed, with Jammu and Ladakh assigned to India and the rest of the state to Pakistan, without reference to the Kashmiri people.

Pakistan points out that it has accepted every major UN proposal and offer of mediation, whereas India has either not abided by those it accepted, or has flatly rejected them. Kashmir, it insists, is a matter of great international concern, and the United Nations has a special responsibility to facilitate a settlement.

The Pakistan Constitution of 1962 contains the following interesting provision (Article 221); "When the people of the State of Jammu and Kashmir decide to accede to Pakistan, the relationship between Pakistan and that State shall be determined in accordance with the wishes of the people of that State." It reads "when" and not "if," which may be an expression of hope rather than of genuine expectation.

Once the premises of the two countries are understood, the reasons for their present position can be more sympathetically examined. India is the satisfied country in this instance. It clearly regards the Kashmir question as already settled in its fundamentals, and it is not inclined to significant concessions. In its view, Pakistan should accept the "fact" that it is not going to get the Valley and other parts of Kashmir which India now controls, and should turn its attention to other and more pressing matters; and other nations should exert pressure on Pakistan to this end. Pakistan is the aggrieved party. It feels that India has been in the wrong from the beginning and that India's adamant position stands in the way of peaceful relations between the two countries and is in fact a threat to world peace. It is critical of other countries, and especially of the United States and Britain, for their failure to bring real pressure on India to "do justice" in Kashmir.

Even a cursory examination of the records of the United Nations and of editorial comments in the newspapers of Western countries will reveal that on the whole the Pakistani case has been more convincing than the Indian position; at least, it has certainly received a more sympathetic response. As an astute English observer of the South Asian scene, Taya Zinkin, wrote in 1962: "Pakistan always scores and India always loses when it comes to the presentation of the Kashmir case to the ignorant unprejudiced outsider. This is because when a Pakistani presents the case he understates and omits whereas when an Indian presents it he overstates and cheats."[34] India feels that its case is not properly appreciated or understood; but in the meantime it holds the choice parts of Kashmir, and is obviously determined, as Nehru said in January 1962, to hold fast to what it has "always and ever."

At the least, Pakistan is determined to see to it that neither India nor the world is allowed to forget the Kashmir question. At one moment it warns

[34] "Kashmir Tangle," *Opinion* (Bombay), February 27, 1962, pp. 4–5.

that some acceptable "solution" is a matter of the gravest urgency, while on other occasions it obviously thinks in long-range terms.[35]

The United States and the Kashmir Dispute

The United States has been reluctantly involved in the Kashmir dispute ever since it was first brought before the United Nations. The dispute has been considered at more than 100 meetings of the Security Council, and the representatives of the United States have had to express views and cast votes on matters relating to it. Since late 1961, because of pressure from Pakistan and the repercussions of the Sino-Indian crisis, the Kashmir question has become "active" again, in ways which have further exacerbated Indo-Pakistan relations and affected United States relations with South Asia.

Having prompted a direct exchange of views between Indian and Pakistani representatives on the Kashmir issue in 1962 and 1963, the United States and the United Kingdom became deeply involved in the final outcome. It was a calculated gamble that did not pay off. When the negotiations led to the same dead end that all previous efforts had reached, tensions between India and Pakistan were accentuated, and the Kennedy Administration was placed in a difficult position in hearings on Capitol Hill on requested appropriations for military assistance to India.

From the point of view of the United States, especially of many members of the American Congress, an Indo-Pakistan agreement on Kashmir has become more imperative than ever because of the dangers of continued friction within the subcontinent at a time of growing pressures from the north. This point of view was specifically and strongly expressed in a report of the House Committee on Foreign Affairs, in 1963:

> The United States has given extensive economic aid to India and Pakistan to strengthen their economic base. It has also made substantial amounts available for the improvement of Pakistan's military forces and, as a result of recent Communist Chinese pressures against India, has inaugurated military assistance to that country. The continued dispute between India and Pakistan over Kashmir jeopardizes the security of both countries, and not until an amicable solution is achieved will it be possible for both nations to attain their economic objectives. The committee recognizes the complexities of the Kashmir question. It does not presume to pass judgment on the claims of either party, but it is mindful of the fact that, to the extent that the dispute embitters relations between India and Pakistan, it reduces and may even nullify our assistance to both. The committee carefully considered an amendment that would drastically reduce our aid to both countries until such time as the issue is resolved. It noted the small but encouraging measures that have been taken by both parties to remove this issue. It will keep the matter under continuous review.

[35] On the second anniversary of the October 1958 "revolution" Ayub Khan said that the Kashmir question was "a time-bomb never far removed from the flash point," which must be defused as quickly as possible. On February 1, 1962, Zafrulla Khan told the Security Council: "I do wish very solemnly to assure members of the Council that not fifteen years, but if 150 years were to pass this dispute will not be settled except through the freely expressed wishes of the people of Kashmir."

Should there be no evidence of an improvement in the situation, the committee is prepared to recommend curtailment of aid to both parties.[36]

However logical this position seems to be, it is based on a profound misunderstanding of the nature and causes of the differences between India and Pakistan and of the urgency of American economic assistance to both countries. It would be most unfortunate to condition this assistance on a resolution of the Kashmir question, although the United States should of course continue to urge the two countries to cooperate in every possible way. The Kashmir question is a most complex one, and the positions taken by India and Pakistan rest on different premises and involve basic consideration of national policy. It is not the kind of question that can be resolved quickly, under pressure from external threats or from outside powers, unless one side or the other abandons its basic position, or unless both sides drop their whole approach and agree on a compromise formula, such as a division of Kashmir along the present cease-fire line, a condominium in the Valley of Kashmir, a United Nations trusteeship, or an autonomous Kashmir state. Clearly if the Kashmir question could be resolved, a major stumbling block to improved Indo-Pakistan relations would be removed; but it does not necessarily follow that a solution would lead to such a basic improvement in relations that the two countries would henceforth drop their suspicions of each other and cooperate in dealing with their serious internal and external problems.

It would have been folly for the United States, in 1954, to condition its military assistance to Pakistan on a solution of the Kashmir question, and it would be just as unwise for the United States to condition its military assistance to India on any such agreement. There is a world of difference between friendly pressure and curt insistence. Members of the American Congress have every right and reason to express concern over the unhappy state of Indo-Pakistan relations at a time of increased danger, but they should not insist that the immediate resolution of an issue as complex as the Kashmir dispute is a prerequisite to either economic or military assistance in the present emergency.

Thus far the United States has not had much success in its efforts to bring pressure to bear on India and Pakistan to resolve the Kashmir question. By Pakistan its efforts have been regarded as half-hearted, and by both countries as often ill-advised, if well-intentioned. Both countries are rather resentful, Pakistan because it feels that it is being pressured to make concessions so that India can concentrate on the Chinese threat, India because it feels that its crisis with China is being used as a pretext for forcing it to abandon its essential position in Kashmir. The United States should make it clear that it is interested only in being of assistance in promoting an agreed-

---

[36] *Foreign Assistance Act of 1963*, Report of the House Committee on Foreign Affairs, 88th Cong., 1st Sess. (Washington: Government Printing Office, 1963), pp. 6–7.

upon settlement on Kashmir, acceptable to both parties, and that it is not trying to force one country to yield to the other.

The United States has generally taken an in-between position on the Kashmir question, which has been unsatisfactory to both India and Pakistan. Each country (Pakistan openly and emphatically, India in a more reserved way) hopes and expects that the United States will be helpful in the eventual resolution of the dispute. Each believes that its position is the correct one, and that therefore the United States should support it whole-heartedly and exert pressure on the other to accept it, too, in good faith. Each seems to be convinced that the United States can and should force the other to yield on Kashmir; each seems to have an exaggerated idea of the capacity of the United States to exert leverage on the other.

The fact that the United States position regarding Kashmir has been satisfactory to neither India nor Pakistan may suggest that it is a relatively sound one, for any in-between position is bound to be unsatisfactory to nations which hold diametrically opposite views and are convinced that their views are correct. There would seem to be no point in the United States championing any particular "solution" of the Kashmir question. Innumerable "solutions" have been proposed, but none has been acceptable to both India and Pakistan. In such a situation there is no one right or wrong "solution." Any one of several "solutions" is possible if India and Pakistan will agree to it. The United States, therefore, should favor any reasonable proposal which is acceptable to the two countries, and it should urge them at every opportunity to resolve the dispute by direct negotiations. It should also continue to express willingness to be of assistance in dealing with this question, if both countries so wish. For the most part its overtures should be made unobtrusively, with due regard to the sensitivities of both countries.

Since the United States has been involved in the Kashmir question in various ways almost since its inception, and since this question stands in the way of improved Indo-Pakistan relations, it would be idle to suggest that the United States should have as little as possible to do with the whole issue; but its role should be peripheral and not central, unless the two countries directly involved ask it to take a larger responsibility. The United States should not make public proposals regarding Kashmir unless asked to do so by both countries, and unless it has some reason to believe that such proposals would be given serious consideration. It should not give its unqualified support to either India or Pakistan on this issue; but it should be available for almost any role that they desire it to play.

The United States should continue to support the UN resolutions of 1948 and 1949. It should make it clear that it supports all parts of these resolutions, which called for the withdrawal of Pakistani troops from the state and for the restoration of peace and order there as well as for the implementation, under UN auspices, of measures for ascertaining the wishes of the people of Kashmir. Likewise, the United Nations should be available and should stand by, without prejudging the issue, ready to be helpful if an opportunity presents itself.

Before the Kashmir question can be resolved, however, India and Pakistan must, by direct contacts and negotiations, agree on some fundamental matters. The responsibility for the resolution of this troublesome question rests directly on them. Neither the United Nations nor the United States can do more than to exert pressure on India and Pakistan to accept this responsibility and to offer assistance and facilities if such services are desired by both of the contending parties.

CHAPTER TEN

India and Communist China: From Panchsheel to Protracted Conflict

THE EMERGENCE OF INDIA as an independent state in 1947 and the Communist victory in China in 1949 were obviously two of the major developments in the postwar era. Until 1959 the relations of the two Asian giants, with some exceptions, seemed to be friendly, if not really close. Since 1959, however, these relations have gone from bad to worse. India and China have engaged in a series of border engagements which have led to increasing tensions between the two countries, and, in the fall of 1962, to what amounted to an undeclared war.

The reasons for this abrupt reversal of Sino-Indian relations and its full implications cannot yet be adequately appraised.[1] From the Chinese point of view it is obviously part of a broader and deeper plan — a plan whose successful implementation would, in the minds of the Chinese leaders, offset

---

[1] See G. F. Hudson, "China's Southward Push," *The Radical Humanist,* December 6, 1959; P. C. Chakravarti, *India's China Policy* (Bloomington: Indiana University Press, 1962), pp. 139–152; Robert Trumbull, "Peking Explains Anger at Nehru," and A. M. Rosenthal, "Battle Between India and China Has Wide Impact," *The New York Times,* November 4, 1962; Norman D. Palmer, "Trans-Himalayan Confrontation," *Orbis,* Winter 1963; H. Arthur Steiner, "China Across the Himalayas: A Failure of the Hard Line," *China Quarterly,* No. 13, January-March 1963; A. Appadorai, "Chinese Aggression and India: An Introductory Essay," *International Studies* (quarterly journal of the Indian Institute of International Studies), New Delhi, July-October 1963, pp. 15–18 (this is a "Special Double Issue" on "Chinese Aggression and India"); C. N. Satyapalan, *India's China Policy: The First Decade, an Analytical Interpretation* (unpublished Ph.D. dissertation, University of Pennsylvania, 1964); George N. Patterson, *Peking Versus Delhi* (London: Faber and Faber, 1963), a book which has been banned in India. Mr. Trumbull's dispatch summarizes a lengthy article in the October 27, 1962 issue of *Jenmin Jih Pao,* the official organ of the Chinese Communist Party, analyzing Communist China's long-term policy toward India. Mr. Trumbull describes this article as "a political document of major importance," and he states that the wording "strongly indicates that no accommodation Mr. Nehru could make on the border issue would alter China's hostility to India's political course under Mr. Nehru's leadership."

the obvious costs, such as the loss of their friendship with India and of much of the large reservoir of goodwill which they had built up by several years of patient and generally friendly cultivation of the countries of non-Communist Asia. In characteristic Communist fashion, however, the Chinese have tended to play down the significance of their difficulties with India, including the border disputes and even the military hostilities, and have insisted that these difficulties are of little import when measured against the "long-standing friendship" between the two countries.[2]

Before 1959 Prime Minister Nehru obviously tried to convince himself that the distribution of Chinese maps showing large parts of the North East Frontier Agency and Ladakh as Chinese territory, and the infrequent Chinese incursions into parts of this territory, were not harbingers of trouble ahead. But after the Chinese suppression of the uprising in Tibet in March 1959, the flight of the Dalai Lama to India, the strong public reactions in India to these events, and above all, the Longju incident and many other border incursions by Chinese troops in the fall of 1959, he made no further efforts to conceal the facts from his people or to minimize the significance of the crisis. Speaking in the Lok Sabha on November 27, 1959, he said: "We are dealing . . . not with a small or casual matter but with a matter of the utmost significance to the present and future of India and Asia." As the crisis continued most observers became convinced that Nehru's latter-day insights and not the Chinese Communists' protestations of minor rifts in "long-standing friendship" were closer to the mark.

Now that American arms and military equipment are being sent to India, it is obvious that the United States is deeply involved in the Sino-Indian dispute. In a basic sense it has been thus engaged from the beginning, for it has a great and continuing stake in the survival and development of free India and in the containment of Chinese power.

Sino-Indian Relations: The Historical Record

During the "honeymoon period" in the modern relations between India and China, the two or three years following the conclusion of the Sino-Indian Treaty regarding Tibet in 1954, Indian as well as Chinese spokesmen often referred eloquently to "the long-standing friendship" and the intimate contacts between their countries, extending, so they claimed, over a period of

---

[2] The report of the Chinese officials on the border issues, in December 1960, which was highly critical of the Indian position on these issues, contained a bland observation: "The people of China and India have maintained a profound friendship for generations. . . . Compared with this long-standing friendship, the current boundary dispute between the two countries is only an issue of a temporary and limited nature." Ministry of External Affairs, Government of India, *Report of the Officials of the Governments of India and the People's Republic of China on the Boundary Question* (New Delhi: Author, 1961), p. CR-190. Hereafter cited as *Officials' Report*.

some two thousand years. In actual fact, relations between the two main centers of Asian civilization, separated by vast distances and different historical experiences and cultural characteristics, were never extensive and seldom, if ever, really intimate. The contacts during the first ten centuries of the Christian era were largely confined to those of Buddhist monks, scholars, and traders who journeyed back and forth by the long and arduous routes through Central Asia or by sea. Buddhism has of course had a profound impact on Chinese civilization. No comparable impact of China on India can be discerned. "It was . . . largely a one-way traffic. India gave: China received. Indian thought deeply tinged Chinese civilization; but India received hardly anything in return."[3]

After this long period of intermittent spiritual, cultural, and commercial contacts, intercourse of any kind between India and China virtually ceased. "With the conquest of India by Islamic invaders from the northwest, and the virtual disappearance of Buddhism from Indian soil, the old spiritual and cultural links between India and China were . . . snapped."[4] To most Indians through the centuries the world that mattered ended with the snowy fastnesses of the Himalayas, where the gods kept their vigil and where mortal men were not invited to intrude. "What lay beyond," in the words of K. M. Panikkar, "was the region of unexplored mystery. The great empire of China was cut off from India for all practical purposes."[5]

In the nineteenth century the two countries were linked in a distant way as a result of the consolidation of British control in India and the extension of British influence in China after the so-called "Opium War" of 1839–42. An extensive opium trade developed. Opium grown in India was carried, largely in British vessels, to the port of Canton. After the British gained spheres of influence following the "carving of the Chinese melon" among various Western powers in the 1890s and the early twentieth century, India and China were more closely linked as parts of Britain's Asian imperium.

Contacts of this sort were between India and China as areas of British imperial interests, but they were hardly between Indians and Chinese. The two peoples began to get acquainted, however, as a result of foreign domination and their own resistance to it. In his famous lectures on the "Three Principles of the People" in 1924, Dr. Sun Yat-sen referred to the methods of noncooperation and nonviolence inaugurated by Mahatma Gandhi, as a model for China. The Indian National Congress frequently expressed its sympathy with China in its struggle against British and, after 1931, Japanese "ruthless and inhuman imperialism" as well. In 1937 and 1938 the Congress sent financial assistance and an ambulance corps to China and organized a boycott of Japanese goods in India. Nehru made his first visit to China in 1939. Three years later Chiang Kai-shek came to India, chiefly to confer with the British authorities, but he did arrange to have long

---

[3] Chakravarti, cited, p. 2.
[4] *Ibid.*
[5] "The Himalayas and India's Defence." *India Quarterly,* April-June 1947, p. 132.

talks with Gandhi, Nehru, and other nationalist leaders. While he publicly expressed the hope that the British "without waiting for any demands on the part of the people of India, will as speedily as possible, give them their political powers," he also urged the Indian leaders to support the war effort. When Gandhi persuaded the Congress to take a different course, and to initiate the "Quit India" movement at a crucial stage of the war, he wrote to Chiang Kai-shek to explain the reasons for his position and to assure the hard-pressed Generalissimo that "my appeal to the British power to withdraw from India . . . is not meant in any shape or form to weaken India's defence against the Japanese or to embarrass you in your struggle."[6]

For a decade following the Communist take-over in China, India seemed to be on good terms with the new regime; but it did not get along well with the Chinese Nationalists in the last years of their ascendancy, which coincided with the first years of Indian independence, and it has not recognized the existence of the Nationalist regime on Formosa since it extended recognition to the People's Republic of China in the latter part of 1949, the second non-Communist state to take such action. At the unofficial Asian Relations Conference in March 1947 the Chinese delegates were manifestly unhappy to be playing a secondary role to their Indian hosts. They objected strenuously to a map of Asia in the conference hall which showed Tibet as a separate entity, they were displeased because Tibet had been invited to send delegates, and they differed openly with India regarding the character and location of a proposed permanent Asian organization. At the official Asian conference on Indonesia in January 1949, convened by India, delegates from eighteen countries participated, but China was represented only by observers.

The Chinese Nationalists share the same views regarding the legal status of Tibet as the Chinese Communists. In spite of their bitterness toward their successful rivals for supremacy on the Chinese mainland, they have not expressed the slightest support for the Indian position on Tibet, nor for that matter have they been noticeably critical of the pressures being exerted on India along the northern borders. Nationalists as well as Communists have shown what may be called a typically Chinese view toward those parts of Asia, including parts of Indo-China, all of Burma, Nepal, Bhutan, and large portions of Northern India and Pakistan, which were at one time or another, in one way or another, linked to the Chinese empire, especially after the vast expansion of Chinese suzerainty during the T'ang Dynasty (618–907 A.D.).

The New India and the New China

After the proclamation in October 1949 of the Central People's Government of the People's Republic of China, India became the most active

---

[6] Quoted in Chakravarti, cited, p. 6.

champion of the new regime of any non-Communist country. It advocated the recognition of the Communist Government as the rightful representative of China, and it refused to have any further dealings with the Nationalist Government. It was critical of the United States and other countries which refused to extend recognition to the Communist regime and opposed its entry into the United Nations. The general tone of public pronouncements and press comments in India was very friendly toward China.

To all of these gestures of friendship and goodwill the Chinese Communists made very little response. From the beginning the Sino-Indian courtship was "a one-sided love affair." In conformity with the international party line Peking in 1949 still labeled Nehru as "a running dog of imperialism."

In 1950 the Chinese Communists sent troops into Tibet and took other steps which evidenced a determination to establish a firm control over the "Tibetan region." Even at the time these steps aroused grave apprehensions in India.[7] They altered the balance of power in all of Inner Asia, and they created a major security problem for India, a problem whose full dimensions India seemed to comprehend only in 1959 — or perhaps only in October 1962.

So long as Chinese suzerainty over Tibet was nominal and so long as Chinese authorities respected the autonomy of Outer Tibet, India was faced with no real threat. This situation was changed by a dramatic announcement from Peking on October 25, 1950, that "Units of the Chinese People's Army have been ordered to cross over into Tibet in order to free three million Tibetans from Western Imperialist oppression and to consolidate national defenses on China's western borders." When the Government of India expressed its "surprise" and "regrets" at this move, the Chinese authorities replied caustically that "The problem of Tibet is entirely the domestic problem of China." Warning that "no foreign interference will be tolerated," Peking intimated that "the Indian viewpoint was affected by foreign influences hostile to China." In response to a further Indian note, expressing the hope that a settlement could "be effected by peaceful negotiations, adjusting the legitimate Tibetan claim to autonomy within the framework of Chinese Suzerainty," Peking rebuked India for having "attempted to influence and obstruct the exercise of its sovereign rights in Tibet"; but it also suggested

---

[7] Speaking in the Indian Parliament on November 27, 1959, Prime Minister Nehru said: "Ever since the Chinese revolution, we naturally had to think of this major fact . . . and what this new China was likely to be. We realized that this revolution, apart from the change over, was going to be a big factor in Asia and in the world too, and in regard to us. . . . We knew this much history that a strong China is normally an expansionist China. . . . And we saw or felt that the two factors taken together, the great push towards industrialization of that country, plus the amazing pace of its population increase, would create a most dangerous situation. . . . So if anybody thinks that we followed our policy in regard to China without realizing these obvious consequences, he is mistaken." *Lok Sabha Debates*, 2nd series, November 27, 1959, no. 10, Cols. 2203–2204.

that the problems relating to "Sino-Indian diplomatic, commercial and cultural relations with respect to Tibet may be solved properly and to our mutual benefit through normal diplomatic channels."

With the knowledge and acquiescence of India, the Dalai Lama's government appealed for help to the United Nations, and on November 15, 1950, El Salvador requested that the Tibetan appeal be placed on the agenda of the General Assembly. But the Assembly was preoccupied with the Korean question, which had reached a grave turn with the intervention of the Chinese Communist forces in North Korea, and India, contrary to its assurances to the Tibetan government, decided not to support a resolution of censure of China for its actions in Tibet. In explaining the decision the Indian representative stated: "The Indian Government was certain that the Tibetan question could still be settled by peaceful means, and that such a settlement could safeguard the autonomy which Tibet had enjoyed for several decades while maintaining its historical association with China." The General Committee of the Assembly thereupon voted unanimously not to consider the resolution. With no prospect of outside support the Dalai Lama was forced to submit to China's terms in the Sino-Tibetan agreement of 1951. Even in this agreement, however, as the Dalai Lama explained in 1959 after he had fled from Tibet, the Chinese government promised not to change the political system in Tibet or the powers, status, and functions of the Dalai Lama.

Whatever his apprehensions, Nehru was apparently restrained by a knowledge that he was not in a position to prevent the Chinese moves, by a belief, later shaken, that the Chinese would respect the autonomy of Tibet, and by a conviction that the problems in dispute, including India's rights in Tibet, could be resolved by peaceful negotiations. He was also restrained by an apparent conviction that Tibet was not an independent state and that basically it was associated in some way with China. Unfortunately, he further befogged the question by a reference in December 1960 to "suzerainty over Tibet or sovereignty over Tibet," as if these were interchangeable terms, and he failed to link a recognition of Chinese suzerainty with an insistence on Chinese observance of Tibetan autonomy, as had been done in the famous Simla Convention of 1914 and also by the British. "The conclusion thus seems to be irresistible that India wrote off Tibet in her defense calculations, and decided to lean on Sino-Indian friendship for the security of her northern frontier. Conversely, it may be stated that the Chinese policy of aggression against Tibet was based on the sure knowledge that India would not stand in their way."[8]

The beginnings of the crisis in Sino-Indian relations since 1959 can therefore be traced to the Chinese take-over in Tibet in 1950 and to the Indian reactions to this move. Only in 1959 and subsequently, however, did Indian

[8] Chakravarti, cited, p. 38.

public opinion become fully aware of the implications of the Chinese actions in Tibet, nearly a decade before.

In spite of its unhappiness over the Chinese behavior in Tibet, India continued to champion the cause of China in the United Nations. It warned the United States that crossing the 38th parallel in Korea would bring the Chinese Communists into the war, and it took a tolerant view toward the Chinese intervention when it did occur; it voted against the resolution introduced into the General Assembly by the United States condemning Chinese aggression in Korea, and it abstained on a resolution in the Assembly to impose an arms embargo against China. It refused to participate in the San Francisco conference in September 1951, convened to agree on a peace treaty with Japan, partially on the ground that Communist China was not being asked to sign the treaty. It exchanged a number of official and "cultural" delegations with Communist China.

The Chinese Communist leaders did not hesitate to trespass on Indian tolerance and faith by eliminating India's traditional contacts north of the Himalayas. After the protests and diplomatic exchanges of 1950 and 1951 the Indian Government did little to press its claims in Tibet, while the Chinese exerted steady pressure to eliminate all Indian influence there, and also in Sinkiang, which was declared a "closed area," with the result that India had to close its Consulate-General in Kashgar and was cut off from virtually all trade with Central Asia.

Relations with China reached another low in November and December 1952, when the Chinese authorities condemned in vitriolic language a draft resolution submitted by India and accepted by the General Assembly, containing provisions for the release and repatriation of prisoners of war in Korea. Again Peking accused India of allying itself with "the Anglo-American camp."

In late 1952 and thereafter there were some signs that China was veering around to the new international party line, which seemed to be changing from a hard policy toward developing non-Communist countries to a softer line emphasizing political action and "peaceful co-existence." Proclaimed at the Asian and Pacific Peace Conference in Peking in October 1952, this policy became more marked after the death of Stalin in the following March.

Panchsheel and the "Honeymoon Period"

The new order in Tibet, and the exclusionist policies of the Chinese Communists, led India to seek a clarification of its treaty rights there. On April 29, 1954, after four months of negotiations, an "Agreement on Trade and Intercourse between the Tibet Region of China and India," which was to remain in force for an original period of eight years, was signed.[9] India

[9] For the text of the agreement see Chanakya Sen, *Tibet Disappears* (Bombay: Asia Publishing House, 1960), pp. 82–85.

gave up all the extraterritorial rights and privileges which it had inherited from past British agreements. It was permitted to retain three trade agencies. There were specific regulations for markets, trade, pilgrimage, and travel. By agreeing to the rather unfortunate phrase "the Tibet region of China," India in effect recognized Chinese sovereignty, especially since the agreement contained no guarantees of Tibetan autonomy. Unfortunately India did not insist on this or other *quid pro quos,* such as a definite understanding that China accepted the borders between Tibet and India and Nepal which had been traditionally recognized and demarcated, at least in general terms, in various agreements in British days.

Although the 1954 agreement confirmed India's acceptance of its loss of rights in Tibet, it was widely proclaimed in India as a diplomatic triumph. One reason for this optimistic view was that the agreement embodied for the first time in a formal document the now-famous *Panchsheel (Panch Shila),* or Five Principles of Peaceful Coexistence — "mutual respect for each other's territorial integrity and sovereignty, mutual nonaggression, mutual noninterference in each other's internal affairs, equality and mutual benefit, and peaceful coexistence." Two months later Prime Minister Chou En-lai came to New Delhi, and joined with Nehru in reaffirming the Five Principles and in expressing "confidence in the friendship between India and China." In October of the same year Nehru was enthusiastically welcomed during a ten-day visit to China.

Most Indians seemed to see in the *Panchsheel* evidence of China's goodwill and peaceful intentions. For the next four and a half years they seemed to regard *Panchsheel* as an adequate substitute for careful attention to India's security interests along its northern borders.

These developments ushered in the "honeymoon" — the *"Hindi Chini bhai bhai"* ("Indians and Chinese are brothers"!) — period. Indians were apparently convinced that the Chinese Communists were sincere converts to the Five Principles. For very different reasons the Chinese leaders cultivated a posture of "sweet reasonableness" in their approach to India and to Asia generally.

At the Bandung Conference in April 1955 Chou En-lai made a great impression by his affability and moderation. The delegates to this conference endorsed the Five Principles and added a few more for good measure. Although Nehru was reported to have been rather irritated at the attention showered on the Chinese Prime Minister, Chou's performance convinced many Indians, who were more than ready to be convinced, that their favorable expectations regarding Chinese intentions were being realized.

Exchanges between India and China reached an all-time high. Chou En-lai visited India four times between June 1954 and January 1957, and was always given a warm welcome. India and China joined in various types of political and cultural collaboration. In October 1954 they concluded an important trade agreement, which led to a marked increase in trade between the two countries — but not in trade between India and Tibet.

"Cartographic Aggression" and Border Problems

Even during the "honeymoon period," however, and especially after the general hardening in China's international attitudes and policies, which became increasingly apparent after 1956 and 1957, some jarring notes marred the Sino-Indian symphony. The main differences which arose related to Chinese maps showing some 50,000 square miles of Indian territory, mostly in the North East Frontier Agency and Ladakh, as belonging to China, and to an increasing number of Chinese incursions into Indian territory, beginning as early as 1954.[10]

Year after year China continued to issue maps showing large portions of traditional Indian territory (some 42,000 square miles) as belonging to China. When Nehru raised the question of the maps during his talks in Peking in October 1954, he was told that the maps to which he objected "were really reproductions of old pre-liberation maps" which the People's Government "had had no time to revise." Chou En-lai gave Nehru the impression that he attached little importance to this matter, and that China had no intention of making an issue of the territory in Ladakh and south of the McMahon Line in NEFA. In 1958, when similar maps were published in both Chinese and Russian journals, the Government of India again protested. Again the Chinese Government replied that the maps were undoubtedly reproductions of old maps, but it also added that it had "not yet undertaken a survey of China's boundary, nor consulted with the countries concerned," and it promised that pending such steps it would "not make changes in the boundary on its own." The Indian authorities were understandably disturbed.

In the meantime developments more serious than "cartographic aggression" had aroused the apprehensions of India's leaders: actual physical intrusions of Chinese into Indian territory. Ironically, the first formal complaint came from China. Less than a month after the Nehru–Chou En-lai meeting of June 1954 the Chinese Government charged that "over thirty Indian troops armed with rifles crossed the Niti Pass on 29 June 1954, and intruded into Wu-Je of the Ali Area of the Tibet Region of China," which it identified as "one day's journey from the Niti Pass."[11] The Indian reply was a denial and a countercharge that some Tibetan officials "tried to cross into our territory in Hoti Plain," southeast of the Niti Pass. Charges and countercharges of incursions north and south of the Niti Pass were made over the next four years. The exchanges revealed that both govern-

[10] The difficulties with China in the period 1954–59 were dramatically revealed in a White Paper published by the Ministry of External Affairs, Government of India, in September 1959, entitled *Notes, Memoranda and Letters Exchanged and Agreements Signed Between the Governments of India and China, 1954–1959.* Hereafter referred to as *White Paper I.*

[11] *White Paper I,* p. 1.

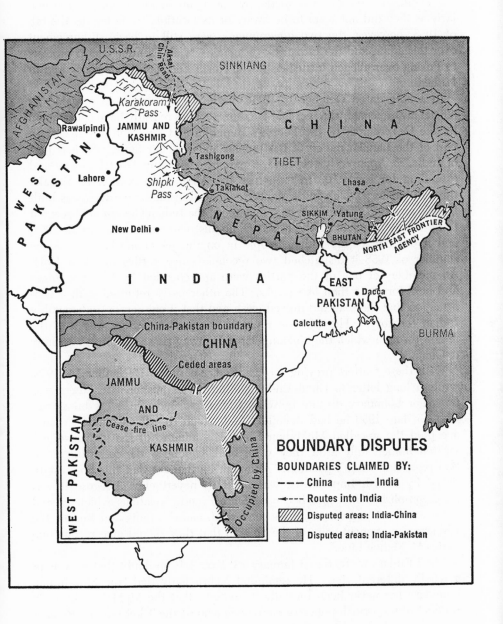

BOUNDARY DISPUTES

BOUNDARIES CLAIMED BY:
--- China ——— India
◄--- Routes into India
▨ Disputed areas: India-China
▨ Disputed areas: India-Pakistan

ments were hazy about the geography of the region in dispute. India did not take a very serious view of the dispute; apparently it "concluded that the claim to Barahoti was made by the Chinese in ignorance, particularly as they did not seem to be aware of its location."[12] As late as the fall of 1958, however, the two governments were still in basic disagreement over this affair, and the Indian Government was also sending sharp protests to Peking over alleged intrusions in the North East Frontier Agency and in Ladakh.

In a note dated October 18, 1958, India for the first time revealed its official awareness of "the fact that a motor road has recently been constructed by the Government of the People's Republic of China across the eastern part of the Ladakh region of the Jammu and Kashmir State, which is part of India."[13] Apparently this road, a part of a Sinkiang-Tibet highway and extending for some 100 miles across the Aksai Chin section of Ladakh through territory which India claimed was well inside its borders, was built in 1956 and 1957. Incredible as it may seem, the Indian Government seemed to be totally unaware of the existence of this road until sometime in 1958, and it did not let the Indian people in on the secret until 1959. In the summer of 1958 it dispatched two reconnaissance parties to Aksai Chin. All members of one of the parties were apprehended by Chinese forces and held for more than five weeks. The other party returned with a confirmation that the road did indeed exist, and that it cut across "indisputably Indian territory." The Chinese reply to the Indian protest was that the region through which the Sinkiang-Tibet highway passed belonged entirely to China.

With these matters preying on his mind, Nehru, on December 14, 1958, wrote a long letter to Chou En-lai, stating his impression that "there was no major boundary dispute between China and India." In his talks with Chou in late 1956 he had definitely understood that the Chinese Premier accepted the so-called McMahon Line. His minutes of the conversations, written immediately after they were held, contained the following notation regarding Chou's position: "Although he thought that this line, established by British Imperialists, was not fair, nevertheless, because it was an accomplished fact and because of the friendly relations which existed between China and the countries concerned, namely, India and Burma, the Chinese Government were of the opinion that they should give recognition to this McMahon Line."

Chou En-lai's reply, dated January 23, 1959, left no doubt that he was of a wholly different view. He reminded Nehru flatly that "the Sino-Indian boundary has never been formally delimited," that the McMahon Line, "a product of the British policy of aggression against the Tibet region of China

---

[12] "Sino-Indian Boundary: Leading Events During 1947–1962," *India News,* August 27, 1962, p. 6.
[13] *White Paper I,* p. 26.

. . . cannot be considered legal" and "had never been recognized," and that therefore "border disputes do exist between China and India."[14]

The Revolt in Tibet and India's Response

After this exchange of notes, the Indian leaders could no longer doubt that they had a problem of the greatest seriousness on their hands. Nevertheless, they kept the story of growing difficulties with China from their own people. But in 1959 the lid of secrecy was blown off by the revolt in Tibet, which brought the era of the *Panchsheel* to an abrupt end.

The Indian Government was not unaware that a serious situation was developing in Tibet. The Chinese did not hesitate to violate the terms of their 1951 agreement with the Dalai Lama. When he came to India in November 1956, the Dalai Lama decided not to return but was persuaded to reverse his decision by Nehru himself, who sought and obtained renewed assurances from Chou En-lai that the person of the Dalai Lama and the autonomy of Tibet would be respected. Less than two years later, when Nehru planned to visit Tibet, he was curtly informed by the Chinese Government that the invitation to him had been withdrawn.

In March 1959 the Tibetans, goaded beyond endurance by Chinese behavior and policies since 1950, rose in open revolt against the Chinese occupation of their country. The Chinese retaliated with ruthless vengeance, and crushed the revolt in a few days. Although the news of the tragic happenings in Tibet was rather scanty for some days, the sympathies of the Indian people with the Tibetans were powerfully expressed, in the Parliament and throughout the country.

A Chinese communiqué complained of a discussion of the developments in Tibet in the Indian Parliament and indicated that China "considers such discussion of the internal affairs of a friendly country to be impolite and improper."[15] This position was indignantly attacked in the Indian Parliament, and by Nehru himself in his statement in Parliament on March 30. On the following day the Dalai Lama and a party of about eighty persons, after a dramatic two-week flight, crossed the frontier into Indian territory and requested political asylum. This privilege was promptly granted, but the Dalai Lama was instructed not to carry on any political activities while he was enjoying Indian hospitality. Several thousand Tibetans followed their leader into voluntary exile, and were given assistance and asylum in India. India was bitterly attacked by all the organs of Chinese propaganda for its reactions to the Tibet uprising and for its reception of the Dalai Lama and other Tibetan refugees.

The events in Tibet in March 1959 gave the Indian people, almost for

[14] *White Paper I*, pp. 52–53.
[15] Quoted in Chakravarti, cited, p. 89.

the first time, an inkling of the real nature of Chinese behavior and intentions and of the new perils in store for them to the north. They also marked an abrupt reversal in Sino-Indian relations, and revealed the limitations of the *Panchsheel* in dealing with Chinese pressures and expansionism. The demand for "a realistic reassessment" of the bases of India's foreign policy, and also defense policy, mounted steadily. It led to considerable soul-searching and reappraisal; and while Nehru consistently insisted that the Chinese actions did not invalidate in any way the bases of India's policy of nonalignment or the fundamental wisdom of the *Panchsheel* approach, he was obviously affected by the behavior of the Chinese and by the strong reactions in India. The remarkable national consensus on foreign policy still continued, but, as an Indian observer noted, "for the first time since independence the foreign policy of India has become a matter of controversy."[16]

Border Clashes, Diplomatic Fencing, and Military Preparations

In late August the apprehensions of the Indian people were further aroused by the announcement, for the first time, by their own government of the frequent intrusions in Indian territory ever since 1954. The immediate occasion for these startling revelations was a series of three unusually serious intrusions, one in Ladakh and two in the NEFA area, including Chinese forcible occupation of the Indian post at Longju. In two important statements Nehru recounted the border difficulties with China and announced a "double policy" of strengthening the border defenses and repelling any further invasions, and at the same time of attempting to "settle matters by conference."

Not long after these events the Chinese gave further evidence that they were determined to give India real trouble over border questions. In a letter to Prime Minister Nehru, dated September 8, 1959, Chou En-lai charged that "The fact that India does not recognise the undelimited state of the Sino-Indian boundary and steps up bringing pressure to bear on China militarily, diplomatically and through public opinion cannot but make one suspect that it is the attempt of India to impose upon China its one-sided claims on the boundary question." He stated again that "the so-called McMahon Line" was "decidedly illegal."

In his lengthy reply, dated September 26th, Nehru reiterated India's firm position regarding the Sino-Indian border. He recognized, however, that since the border had not been demarcated on the ground, disputes might arise "at some places," and he agreed that these disputes "should be amica-

[16] Sisir Gupta, "The Problem," *Seminar*, No. 19, March 1961, p. 10.

bly and peacefully settled." In the meantime he insisted that "neither party should seek to alter the *status quo* in any manner."

For a time, in early October, the Chinese seemed to be adopting a more moderate position, and Nehru and other Indian spokesmen deliberately tried to allay anti-Chinese sentiment in India. But on October 20 an Indian police party on patrol in the Kongka Pass in the Chang Cherno Valley in Ladakh, some forty to fifty miles inside Indian territory as shown on Indian maps, was attacked by a larger and more heavily armed Chinese force. In the skirmish nine Indians were killed, and another seriously wounded. The Chinese took the Indians, dead and alive, to their patrol post, and kept them for five days in the bitter cold in torn tents, without bedding of any kind, and without medical attention. In the bitter diplomatic exchange that followed receipt of the news of the Kongka Pass incident, the Chinese insisted that the affair had occurred in "indisputably Chinese territory."

Having stirred up another hornet's nest, China changed its tactics and resorted again to diplomatic moves. Apparently to avoid a united front against it and doubtless also to prove its "reasonableness" on border and other disputes, the Chinese initiated negotiations to settle their border disputes with Burma and Nepal and their "nationality" dispute with Indonesia. On November 29 Chou En-lai proposed to Nehru that "the two Prime Ministers hold talks in the immediate future," and that in the meantime, to avert further border clashes, "the armed forces of India and China each withdraw twenty kilometers at once from the so-called McMahon Line in the East, and from the line up to which each side exercises actual control in the West." As a counterproposal Nehru suggested that in the NEFA area the McMahon Line should remain the frontier and that neither side should send out patrols across that Line; and that in Ladakh India should withdraw its personnel to the west of the line shown as the boundary in Chinese maps of 1956, while China should withdraw to the east of the boundary as shown on Indian maps. Chou En-lai rejected this proposal as "lacking in fairness," but repeated his suggestion that he and Nehru should meet in the near future. To this Nehru replied: "I do not see how we can reach agreement on principles when there is complete disagreement about the facts."[17]

On January 13, 1960, Nehru told a press conference that since he found no common ground between the Indian and Chinese points of view he saw no point in meeting in the near future. Three weeks later, however, he invited Chou En-lai to meet with him in New Delhi. The reasons for this *volte-face* remain a mystery, and it was criticized by many persons and newspapers in India.

[17] Ministry of External Affairs, Government of India, *Notes, Memoranda and Letters Exchanged Between the Governments of India and China, March, 1960–November, 1960* (New Delhi: Author, 1960), pp. 45–46, 56, 58. Hereafter referred to as *White Paper III*.

On his many previous visits to India the Chinese Premier had received a warm welcome. During the week that he spent in New Delhi in April 1960, however, he was treated with studied coolness and given no public welcome. He had only to read the Indian press to realize how deeply the Chinese actions of the past months had alienated the Indian people. On April 25, after six days of talks, the two Prime Ministers admitted in a joint communiqué that their face-to-face sessions had not succeeded in resolving their differences.[18] The reasons for this impasse were crystal clear.

At a press conference on the eve of his departure, and apparently in his talks with Nehru, Chou En-lai proposed a "solution." He stated again that "the so-called McMahon Line is absolutely unacceptable to China," but indicated that China would nevertheless be willing "to accommodate the Indian point of view in the eastern sector," if India would "accommodate China in the western sector."[19] Since this would have maintained the *status quo* in the North East Frontier Agency and left China in possession of some 12,000 square miles of territory which India claimed as its own in Ladakh, it is hardly surprising that this proposal fell on deaf ears in New Delhi. But it raises some intriguing speculations regarding the real aims of the Chinese pressures on India.

Almost the only concrete result of the Nehru–Chou En-lai talks, which was hardly more than a face-saving gesture, was the decision that "officials of the two Governments should meet and examine, check and study all historical documents, records, maps, and other material relevant to the boundary question . . . and draw up a report for submission to the two Governments." Accordingly, Indian and Chinese representatives held three lengthy meetings in 1960. The fruit of their labors was not one report, but two, representing the same differences of facts and interpretation. In February 1961 both reports were published in full by the Government of India.[20] The report of the Indian officials has never been published in China; even the Chinese report was withheld until May 1962, when a "garbled truncated version" was made public. Although these reports were hardly more than propaganda documents, or at best fuller restatements of familiar and divergent positions, they and the many White Papers issued by the Government of India provide the fullest documentation of the course of the Sino-Indian dispute.

The Sino-Indian Agreement on Tibet was to remain in force for eight years. In December 1961 China suggested that it be renewed, but the Government of India, holding that China had violated both the letter and the spirit of the agreement, refused to consider an extension of the agreement, and it therefore lapsed on June 2, 1962.

[18] For the text of this communiqué see *The New York Times*, April 26, 1960.
[19] The full text of Chou En-lai's press conference is given in *The Peking Review*, May 3, 1960.
[20] *Officials' Report*, cited.

Trans-Himalayan Confrontation: Implications for India[21]

To most Indians the Chinese actions since 1959 are as incomprehensible as they are alarming. Indians found it hard to understand why China would deliberately forfeit the friendship of India, which had been China's leading champion among the non-Communist states. As Nehru expressed his own feelings of bewilderment regarding the motives and aims of the Chinese: "We had very friendly attitude towards the Chinese but they attacked us. This was completely a meaningless thing which one could not understand."[22] While one can understand Mr. Nehru's feelings of bewilderment and even of helplessness, one can hardly agree that the Chinese actions toward India since 1959 are "completely a meaningless thing." We must assume that in their sudden change-over to a hard policy the Chinese leaders felt that their gains would outweigh their losses.

Until the fall of 1962, at least, it was still possible to make a fairly logical case for the Chinese behavior on the ground of limited objectives and the pursuit of traditional Chinese claims. In retrospect, the immediate source of the Sino-Indian controversy was Tibet. India acquiesced in the Chinese decision to establish direct control over the "Tibetan region," but later protested against, first, the consolidation of Chinese control at the expense of Tibetan "autonomy," and then against the ruthless suppression of the uprising in Tibet in March 1959.

Chinese pressures on India have been explained on grounds of historical Chinese expansionism, militant nationalism, and "the revolutionary zeal of communism"; but the relative influence of these factors cannot be determined with any accuracy. Certainly, for an explanation of China's recent actions neither history nor ideology should be overlooked.[23]

A glance at a map showing the stages of the expansion of the Chinese empire will reveal that during the T'ang Dynasty (618–907 A.D.) China laid claim to all of the Himalayan regions, including the territory now in dispute with India, plus Nepal, Bhutan and some parts of northern India south of the Himalayas. Chinese control of these regions was never more than a shadowy one, but the fact that they were once regarded as part of the Chinese empire has never been forgotten.

As Chinese nationalism became a fairly strong force in the twentieth cen-

---

[21] This section is a revised and condensed version of the author's article, "Trans-Himalayan Confrontation," cited, pp. 513–527.

[22] Address at a meeting organized by the Delhi Citizens Committee for Disarmament and against Nuclear Arms and for National Integration, New Delhi, October 2, 1962.

[23] A. M. Rosenthal showed an awareness of both considerations when he expressed the opinion that "Peking's decision to attack was based on a political basket of fears and ambitions growing out of Chinese history and Marxist ideology." "Battle Between India and China Has Wide Impact," *The New York Times*, November 4, 1962.

tury, whether under Sun Yat-sen or Chiang Kai-shek or Mao Tse-tung, ancient historical precedents and claims were occasionally revived; but until the rise to power of the Chinese Communists no Chinese regime had a strong base for operations and control in the Himalayan regions. "China's main motive," in the opinion of Guy Wint, "is to take back what she believes is her own. The Communist revolution has restored her sense of strength, and she is determined to right the wrongs which she considers were done against her in the past. She wants to regain her old frontiers to the utmost extent."[24]

The element of "revolutionary zeal," however, stems from the stage of Communist militancy in which China is now engrossed, and therefore adds a new dimension to the threat of Chinese expansionism. As the stronghold of Communist orthodoxy, China seems to regard itself as a true defender of the faith. It has taken an uncompromising stand in opposition to deviation from the more inflexible tenets of Marxism-Leninism, with a strong flavor of Stalinism as an added ingredient.

Foremost among other explanations for China's recent actions are the beliefs that Chinese pressures on India were prompted by internal problems and pressures, and that they are a by-product of differences between China and the Soviet Union.

If internal troubles help to account for the Chinese actions against India, they are interwoven with other considerations. G. F. Hudson, an experienced English student of Chinese policy, has emphasized the internal compulsions in the broader framework of other possible motivations:

> It remains to ask why the Chinese have been so recklessly antagonising Indian national sentiment by their claims and encroachments. The main reason is undoubtedly that the Chinese Communists base their power on national chauvinism as much as on their social doctrine, and it is especially necessary for them to beat the patriotic drum when the Chinese people are feeling the strain of the party's economic policies. The reconquest of Tibet was for the Chinese the recovery of a portion of "China" lost through imperialist intrigues; it involves also the revision of the frontiers to which China has never given its formal consent. In view of Tibetan turbulence, moreover, it is necessary to round off the reconquest of Tibet by incorporating as far as possible all ethnically Tibetan areas which can be foci of continuing national resistance. If all this means a quarrel with India, Peking does not greatly care, for in Chinese Communist eyes the Indians have already been guilty of impertinent behaviour by criticizing Chinese actions in Tibet, and it is doubtless considered that they are militarily incapable of an effective defence of their northern frontiers — at least as long as their main strategic dispositions are directed against Pakistan.[25]

Since these words were written in 1959, the Chinese have followed up their initial demands and intrusions with "further military action in the frontier area," and the crisis in Sino-Indian relations has entered a new and more alarming stage. So too has the crisis in Sino-Soviet relations. Despite

[24] "India and China," *The Radical Humanist,* January 17, 1960, p. 28.
[25] "China's Southward Push," *The Radical Humanist,* December 6, 1959, p. 578.

much analysis of the rift between the Communist giants no really definitive conclusions have emerged. It may spring from the fact that the two countries are at different stages of ideological as well as economic development, or from rivalries for leadership and influence in the Communist bloc, or from personal rivalries.

Soviet-Chinese rivalry seems to be especially focused on Asia. Chinese influence in Communist circles in Asia is increasing, and China seems to be deliberately engaged in undermining or curbing Soviet power and influence in Asia, as it is in humiliating and weakening India. One of China's aims in abandoning its pretense of friendship with India may have been to strengthen its position in the Himalayan regions and the Indian subcontinent *vis-à-vis* the Soviet Union. One of Russia's aims in maintaining its friendly ties and in continuing its military as well as economic assistance to India may be to resist further Chinese inroads and to maintain its influence in other parts of Asia. The Soviet Union may be almost as much interested as is India in the containment of China. Thus India may have been a factor in the power struggles within the Communist bloc.

India and China have often been described as inevitable rivals in Asia, and much depends on their relative progress, or lack of it. Each country is trying to deal with quite similar problems in fundamentally different ways. India is an open and China is a closed society. India has deliberately chosen the democratic way, whereas China has come under the control of some of the most fanatically devoted Communists in the world. If China makes much more rapid progress than India, this will have a profound influence on other developing countries, regardless of the cost of this progress. If, on the other hand, it becomes apparent that communism has brought to the Chinese people not only totalitarianism but economic misery and greater human suffering, while India manages to move slowly toward a better deal for its growing millions, the power of example may be compelling. In any event, if China wants to promote the spread of communism in Asia or even to extend its own physical presence and power, India stands squarely athwart its path.

China's basic aim, therefore, may be to weaken and humiliate India, to gain strategic superiority over its Asian rival, to lessen Indian power and influence generally, especially in Southeast Asia, and to hamper India's economic progress. If it could slow up the already painfully slow rate of Indian economic development, it would score several gains at one and the same time: it would weaken India greatly, and therefore would give China an even greater edge in the test of strength. In any event, the Chinese assault on India, as A. M. Rosenthal of *The New York Times* wrote a few days after it occurred, "has brought about a great confrontation that Asia had not expected for years and perhaps decades to come."[26]

---

[26] Rosenthal, cited.

The full implications of the Sino-Indian dispute cannot be properly assessed at this stage. It is far more than a border dispute, and far more than a challenge to India. It is already having profound effects on the balance of forces in Asia, and it will probably have greater effects on India than on China.

The United States and the Sino-Indian Dispute

For reasons which many Americans as well as Indians could not understand, the United States did not officially express its "full sympathy" with India in the dispute with China until August 1962, and it did not officially state that it regarded the McMahon Line as the legitimate boundary between India and Tibet in the NEFA area until October 27, 1962, shortly after Chinese forces had launched a major offensive in NEFA and only two days before Nehru formally requested arms aid from the United States. Why did the United States remain silent so long in this developing dispute?

Until 1959 the Government of India played down the Chinese occupation of Tibet, the consolidation of Chinese control there, and the growing number of border incidents. It deliberately kept the news of the growing friction with China from the Indian people and even from members of the Parliament. It is hardly surprising, then, that prior to 1959 the United States had little to say about the Sino-Indian disputes and made no effort either to express public support for India or to intervene in the dispute. In August 1962, according to *The Indian Express*, Ambassador J. K. Galbraith "revealed that two of his predecessors, Chester Bowles and Sherman Cooper, both well known for their friendliness toward India, had urged upon the United States administration a policy of reticence on the ground that closer American interest and espousal of India's cause would be misconstrued by the Chinese, as also by the world as a whole, as intrusion of the cold war into the India-China dispute, which would have made the problem all the more intractable and combustible."[27] Presumably this "policy of reticence" was understood and approved by the Indian Government.

The feeling of bewilderment in India over the standoffish policy of the United States in the Sino-Indian dispute turned for a time into active indignation when, in the fall of 1959, the American Secretary of State, Christian Herter, indicated that the United States was rather uncertain about the relative merits of the border claims of India and China. His statement is quite understandable in view of the fact that, as the Indian Government freely admitted, the borders between India and Tibet and Sinkiang had never been demarcated on the ground, and that no Chinese government had ever recognized the legality of the so-called McMahon Line. But, like the

---

[27] "Welcome Move" (editorial), *The Indian Express*, August 16, 1962. Ambassador Galbraith's revelations were made in an address in New Delhi, August 8, 1962.

even more hotly resented statement by Secretary Dulles about Goa nearly four years before, it was made at an unfortunate time and left an unfortunate impression, contrary to Mr. Herter's real intentions.

At long last, in August 1962, the United States indicated its open support of the Indian position on the border dispute. Ambassador Galbraith assured the Indian people that the United States had "full sympathy for the sombre tasks" India faced on its northern frontiers. He also affirmed America's "hope for a settlement and our desire to do nothing that might prejudice it."[28] On October 27 he gave the first official American endorsement of the McMahon Line: "The McMahon Line is an accepted international border and is sanctioned by modern usage. Accordingly, we regard it as the northern border of the NEFA area."[29]

After the Chinese attack, when Nehru made preliminary inquiries regarding the willingness of the Western powers to supply arms and other military needs to India, he was assured that such aid would be promptly forthcoming, upon request, and that the terms of payment could be worked out later. Therefore, on October 29, 1962, in a sharp departure from previous policy, Nehru formally requested military aid from the United States, the United Kingdom, and other Western powers. Within three days the first American C-135 jet transports took off from American bases in Frankfurt, Germany, loaded with light infantry weapons, artillery, and communications and transportation equipment. Very shortly C-135s were flying arms to India on a round-the-clock airlift from Germany.

Under these emergency circumstances the United States became directly engaged in the Sino-Indian dispute. Indians were profoundly impressed by the response of the United States in their hour of crisis, acceding to Nehru's request without delay, any haggling over terms, or preachments about India's past sins. At a critical time India's leaders showed that they could discard old illusions and face new realities, and the American leaders showed that they recognized the great stake of the United States in India's future.

The prompt decision of the President to give military assistance to India was almost universally supported by the American people. The decision was made while the United States was engaged in a serious test of will with the Soviet Union, over the Russian missile bases in Cuba, and while the American people were in the closing stages of an unusually intense off-year election campaign. Almost all American newspapers, whatever their feelings about the President or about India, backed the President's decision. Unfortunately, most of the American press and much of articulate American public opinion were not able to resist the temptation to link support of American military assistance to India with "snide" comments about India's

[28] Address in New Delhi, August 8, 1962.
[29] Quoted in *India News,* Special Supplement, October 30, 1962.

past failings, and about the anti-Western proclivities of V. K. Krishna Menon and even Nehru.[30]

One of the most common popular American reactions to the abrupt shift in India's policies as a result of the Chinese "invasion" was an insistence that Nehru now must prove that he was really ready to face realities by allying India with the West and by dropping his opposition to military alliances. The Sino-Indian crisis provoked a spate of cartoons in American newspapers; and many of these rang the changes on the collapse of "neutralism" or "neutrality" in India.

The Philadelphia *Inquirer*, on November 6, 1962, expressed the popular American view bluntly and forcefully:

> Nehru cannot shun and oppose indefinitely the Western system of collective security without forfeiting its protection. A free ride for Nehru, on the back of neutralism, would be grossly unfair to SEATO countries and others that have staked their future and their treasure in the collective security system. The Prime Minister of India could alter the course of history — and give the freedom of mankind an enduring impetus — by acknowledging that his theory of neutralism has been proved by time and events to be impractical and dangerous, by renouncing neutralism, by joining the collective security system of the Free World and urging other neutrals to do likewise before it is too late.

In demanding that India renounce its policy of nonalignment — erroneously called "neutralism" — presumably by joining SEATO or some other military alliance, many Americans were asking for a reorientation of India's basic approach to foreign affairs which is probably both impossible and undesirable. The American Government did not make the same mistake.

---

[30] For a good summary of American reactions see Sisir Gupta, "The United States' Reactions," *International Studies*, July-October 1963, pp. 57–67. Mr. Gupta, a research scholar with the Indian Council of World Affairs, was in the United States before, during, and after the Chinese invasion.

Even the more responsible American newspapers coupled expressions of sympathy with India and support of American arms with comments on past Indian policies and attitudes which, in their opinion, contributed to the present predicament. *The New York Times* (October 23, 1962) declared: "The free world will surely lend its sympathy and moral support to India, regardless of India's unrealistic policies in the past that ignored the real nature of the Chinese Communist regime and its tendency toward subversion and aggression." "If Mr. Nehru had been a realist," observed the *Christian Science Monitor*, "if he had accepted the offer of Pakistan's President Ayub two years ago to form a common defense of the area against Peking, if some adjustments of the mutual conflict over Kashmir had been found and the troops of both sides released from their common frontier, the present Chinese attack might not have occurred."

On the day following Mr. Nehru's request for American military assistance, and the day prior to Mr. Menon's dismissal as Defense Minister, India voted in favor of the admission of Communist China to the General Assembly of the United Nations. The American press denounced this vote as "amazing," as "shocking beyond reasonable explanation." It seemed incredible to the Philadelphia *Inquirer* (October 31, 1962) that India would continue to support the Chinese aggressor, "while the Himalayan snows are stained red" with Indian blood. Actually, India was adhering to its oft-expressed belief in the principle of universality of membership in the United Nations and in the sobering effect of UN membership upon Communist China.

It did not condition its military aid to India on any such demand. India should not be asked to enter any formal military alliance as a price for Western support. Nonalignment is a deeply rooted Indian policy — or approach — to world affairs, and it cannot be abandoned immediately or *in toto*. Even as he announced to his people, on October 22, 1962, that "everything else has to be sacrificed in this great crisis," Prime Minister Nehru reaffirmed his faith in nonalignment: "I believe in that policy fully and we shall continue to follow it. We are not going to give up our basic principles because of the present difficulty."

There is no reason under present circumstances for the United States to make an issue of the abandonment of India's nonalignment. In its recent soul-searching and reappraisal the Indian approach to nonalignment has assumed a very different character, and it no longer stands in the way of meaningful association with aligned states.

The United States and other aligned states, in turn, are taking a new look at the nature and value of military alliances. Formal military alliances may be of little value in the underdeveloped world, but meaningful ties can still be formed between developing countries and the West. The Indian experience suggests a possible pattern for association, short of formal military alliance but far superior to previous relationships. India is now linked with the West in ways that would have been inconceivable a short time ago; yet it is possible to argue that the bases of this relationship have existed all along, but have been obscured by superficial differences in policies and approaches. India may now be ready to accept the conclusion which a distinguished Indian critic of India's China policy expressed in 1961: "The main task of Indian statesmanship, today and in the immediate future, is to adopt positive measures to fight against Chinese pressure and infiltration across the Himalayan frontier and to promote, indirectly and adroitly, a common policy of defense against Communist China without an open alliance with the West."[31]

[31] Chakravarti, cited, p. 161.

CHAPTER ELEVEN

South Asia and the Other Communist Countries

SINCE THE BOLSHEVIK REVOLUTION IN RUSSIA, and particularly since the end of the World War II, communism has scored massive gains in Asia. Occupying nearly three-fourths of the land mass of the largest of continents, the Soviet Union and China hang like a menacing shadow over all the states to the south. Whatever the differences between them, the two head-centers of world communism are united on long-range goals of the promotion of communism throughout the world.

Asia has been a particularly fertile field for Communist activity, and the results in some instances have been spectacular. With Lenin's theories of imperialism and of social revolution the Communists have been skillful and successful in exploiting the strong feelings of anticolonialism and nationalism. "Belief in dialectical materialism never blinded the Soviet leaders to the strength of nationalism in Asia. On the contrary, from the time of their coming to power they have had a carefully thought-out policy on nationalities and the colonial question."[1] With all of the shifts in the party line during the past forty-five years and more and all the differences over strategy, tactics, and leadership, the relentless and unceasing pressures of international communism have been felt throughout Asia, as elsewhere.

From the early days until the present the international Communist movement, whether directed by the Comintern or by its successor agencies and channels, has been trying to promote conditions in South Asia which would be most conducive to further penetration. The Communist Party of India (CPI) has generally followed the twists and turns of the international party line, with some temporary lags and deviations, in spite of poor organization and rivalries among the top leaders and occasional ideological splits.[2] For

[1] John C. Campbell, *The United States in World Affairs, 1948–1949* (New York: Harper, for the Council on Foreign Relations, 1949), p. 264.

[2] See John H. Kautsky, *Moscow and the Communist Party of India* (New York: The Technology Press and John Wiley, 1956).

many years the Communist Party of Great Britain was the immediately directing agency.

On the whole, the Soviet Union and the leaders of international communism have tended to follow the Leninist policy of working with the national liberation movements (i.e., the Indian National Congress) and the national bourgeoisie (a category which would include Nehru and most other Congress leaders), even at the expense of support of the CPI. Khrushchev's policy of peaceful co-existence and of the peaceful transition to socialism has especially appealed to India's leaders. This policy has, however, been publicly criticized by the Chinese Communists, who, ironically, seem to be champions of an approach toward former colonial countries which is reminiscent of M. N. Roy's contentions in a famous debate with Lenin in the early 1920s. Roy, India's most famous Communist (who later abjured communism), held that the national bourgeoisie were agents of the imperialist order, and that only the Communist parties in colonial areas, however weak and persecuted, were to be entrusted with the revolutionary tasks.

At the "summit" conference of leaders of eighty-one Communist parties in November 1960, the Chinese delegates attacked Khrushchev for " 'curbing the anti-imperialist struggle in Asia, Africa, and Latin America,' especially in Iraq, India, and Algeria. They attacked his 'friendship' with Nasser, Kassem, Nehru, and Sukarno, and demanded that the Communist parties in those leaders' countries should behave more aggressively toward them and the 'national bourgeoisie' at large."[3] The final declaration of the conference was a compromise between the Russian and Chinese views. The national bourgeoisie were declared to be unstable and inclined to compromise with "internal reaction and imperialism"; nevertheless, they could play a useful role in the "revolutionary struggle," and, furthermore, Communist parties would "support the actions of national governments which undermine the positions of imperialism." The main object, however, would be to turn each former colonial country into an "independent State of national democracy." "This is a new category of States in communist parlance.... It is not as advanced, in the Communist sense, as an East European People's Democracy, but it is at a stage where the advent of communism is brought appreciably nearer."[4]

From the Communist point of view all of the countries of South Asia could become "national democratic States," but all now fall far short of

[3] Isaac Deutscher, "The New Communist Manifesto," *The Reporter*, January 5, 1961, p. 28.

[4] "The Cold War Manifesto," *NATO Letter* (Paris), February 1961, p. 16. According to the Moscow declaration, to qualify for the title of "national democratic state" a country must, among other things, "defend its political and economic independence, fight against imperialism and its military blocs and against military bases on its territory; fight against the new forms of colonialism and the penetration of imperialist capital . . . give its people the chance to struggle for the implementation of agrarian reform and the implementation of other demands in the sphere of democratic and social reforms."

qualifying for this designation. Communist parties are active in all of these countries but are not in a strong position anywhere, except in two or three states of India. In Pakistan and Nepal the Communist Party is banned, and has to operate clandestinely. In Ceylon the main Communist groups are Trotskyite in ideology, and have therefore deviated from the mainstream of international communism. The CPI is active in most parts of India, and is the largest opposition party in the central Parliament and in several State Assemblies; but it is weak and divided.[5] It has been further weakened by a split between pro-Russian and pro-Chinese leaders and factions, and, in spite of its own critical views of the Chinese pressures on India, it is inevitably under a cloud of disapproval and suspicion as a result of the actions of the Chinese Communists. Thus far, in fact, the South Asian states have been a disappointment to the leaders of world communism; but obviously Communists will continue to exploit every possible opportunity to transform them into "national democratic States" and finally to full-fledged "people's Democracies."

India and the Soviet Union

Since the Bolshevik revolution of 1917 most of the leaders of modern India have been attracted and repelled by Communist policies and actions in the Soviet Union, regarding it as at once an example and a warning. They have been impressed by the economic theories and the great physical accomplishments of the Soviets, by the claims of success in creating a multiracial society, and by the support given to the national and anticolonial movements, the while they have been disturbed and sometimes alarmed by the methods which the Soviets have employed in their harsher moments at home and abroad. But all in all, the Indian image of the Soviet Union has been a rather favorable one.

Nehru was flattered and wooed by the Soviet leaders and other spokesmen of international communism; he was also criticized and attacked. He frequently expressed his admiration for the Soviet Union, and he also at times used such terms as "communist aggression." On the whole, he was obviously reluctant to criticize the Soviets, and he was occasionally described in Western circles as being "neutral on the side of the Soviet Union." In these mixed reactions and statements he reflected the feelings of most of his fellow-countrymen who have any views at all on such matters.[6]

[5] See Harry Gilman, "The Communist Party of India: Sino-Soviet Battleground," in A. Doak Barnett, ed., *Communist Strategies in Asia: A Comparative Analysis of Governments and Parties* (New York: Praeger, 1963), Chapter 4, pp. 101–147.

[6] Writing in Ahmadnagar Fort prison in 1944, Jawaharlal Nehru reflected on the probable role which the Soviet Union would play in the postwar era, and on the strong and weak points of the Soviet system: "The Soviet Union actually is probably poorer than it was prior to the war, owing to enormous destruction, but its potential is tre-

Until 1954 or 1955 contacts between India and the U.S.S.R. were limited to trade, the exchange of cultural delegations, official visits, and regular diplomatic relations. In 1951, during the height of a food crisis, India entered into a barter deal with Russia to exchange a variety of Indian products for Russian wheat, although in a much smaller amount than the $190,000,000 wheat loan extended to India by the United States at the same time. Yet, despite a five-year bilateral agreement of 1953, India's trade with the U.S.S.R., or for that matter with the entire Communist bloc, has never been more than a very small percentage of its total foreign trade.

A high point in Indo-Soviet relations came in 1955. In June Nehru visited the Soviet Union and was given a warm welcome; in November and December Nikolai Bulganin and Nikita Khrushchev made a highly publicized official visit to India, Burma, and Afghanistan.

Since 1955 the Soviets have directed a many-pronged "offensive" toward India, featuring encouragement of a policy of "neutralism" and opposition to military bases and alliances, extensive economic aid, and a great variety of cultural exchanges. In a little more than a decade India has received over one billion dollars of economic assistance, mostly in the form of low-interest loans payable in rupees or in products, from the countries of the Communist bloc, chiefly from the Soviet Union. This kind of assistance has been especially welcome to India, for it removes the stigma of charity or of "gifts," imposes no drain on foreign exchange, and has easy repayment terms. The Soviets have made some outright grants to India, mainly in the educational and cultural fields. Of all non-Communist countries India has been by far the largest recipient of Communist bloc economic assistance.[7] Since it has also been by far the largest recipient of American economic aid to developing nations, India offers the best case study of the relative nature and impact

mendous and it will rapidly make good and go further ahead. In physical and economic power there will be none to challenge it on the Eurasian continent. Already it is showing an expansionist tendency and is expanding its territories more or less on the basis of the tsar's empire. How far this process will go it is difficult to say. The socialist economy does not necessarily lead to expansion, for it can be made self-sufficient. But other forces and old suspicions are at play, and again we notice the fear of so-called encirclement. In any event the U.S.S.R. will be busy for many years in repairing the ravages of war. Yet the tendency to expand if not in territory then in other ways, is evident. No other country presents such a politically solid and economically well-balanced picture as the Soviet Union, though some of the developments there in recent years have come as a shock to many of its old admirers. Its present leaders have an unchallengeable position, and everything depends on their outlook for the future." *The Discovery of India* (New York: John Day, 1946), pp. 553–554.

[7] See Joseph S. Berliner, *Soviet Economic Aid* (New York: Praeger, for the Council on Foreign Relations, 1958), Hans Heyman, Jr., "Soviet Foreign Aid as a Problem for U.S. Policy," *World Politics*, July 1960, pp. 525–540; Barbara Ward, "The Other Foreign Aid Program," *The New York Times Magazine*, June 17, 1962; George S. Carnett and Morris H. Crawford, "The Scope and Distribution of Soviet Economic Aid," and Leon H. Herman, "The Political Goals of Soviet Foreign Aid," in *Dimensions of Soviet Economic Power*, studies prepared for the Joint Economic Committee, U.S. Congress, 87th Cong., 2d Sess. (Washington: Government Printing Office, 1962), pp. 457–485.

of American and Communist economic assistance. Most Americans seem to regard India as the center of competition of economic policies and programs with the Communist countries, rather than as an area of possible cooperation and "commingling."

The largest single Soviet-supported project in India, or indeed in any other non-Communist country (with the possible exception of the Aswan Dam in the U.A.R.), is the huge public-sector steel plant at Bhilai in Madhya Pradesh. In February 1955 India signed an agreement with the Soviet Union for Soviet technical and financial assistance in the construction and operation of the plant at Bhilai. The Soviet Union agreed to supply equipment, materials, and technical assistance to the value of about $132,000,000, payment to be made in twelve equal installments, at the low interest rate of 2½ per cent. The payments, moreover, would be made in rupees, which the Russians would use for the purchase of commodities in India. Some 700 Indian engineers, technicians, and skilled workers were trained in the Soviet Union, and many more, plus perhaps 4,500 unskilled workers, were given special training in India by Soviet experts. The first main units of the Bhilai plant were officially inaugurated early in 1959, and by the end of the Second Five Year Plan in 1961 the plant was operating close to its planned capacity of 1,000,000 ingot tons of steel each year. The capacity of the Bhilai plant will be expanded to 2.5 million tons, with continued Soviet supervision and assistance.

For the Soviet economic offensive Bhilai was a show-window project, and since it seemed to proceed with greater speed and efficiency than the comparable British and German supported projects at Durgapur and Rourkela, Bhilai was an impressive Soviet political and propaganda feat, as well as an economic achievement of unquestioned magnitude.[8] The same comment could be made about the Soviet agreement, announced in May 1964, to help to finance and build a new steel plant at Bokaro, with an initial capacity of 1.5 million tons, and an eventual capacity of at least 4 million tons. In this case, the Soviet's political and propaganda gains were all the greater because it stepped into the breach created by the collapse of the protracted negotiations with the United States for assistance in financing and building the Bokaro plant.[9]

There are many other Soviet-assisted projects in India, mostly in heavy industry, almost all provided under the same generous financial arrangements as were agreed upon for the Bhilai plant. In November 1957, for example, the Soviet Union agreed to provide the equivalent of about $126,000,000 in

---

[8] See Douglas Cater, "India: A Tale of Two Steel Mills," *The Reporter*, October 2, 1958, pp. 29–33. The two steel mills referred to in the article are the Bhilai plant, and the privately-owned concern at Jamshedpur of the Tata Iron & Steel Company, where the capacity is being doubled with the assistance of an American construction company, the Kaiser Engineering Overseas Corporation, with funds supplied by the World Bank and private New York bank loans.

[9] See above, "The Bokaro Story," pp. 146–151.

credits, chiefly for the construction of a heavy machine-building plant, a coal-mining machinery plant, an optical glass factory, a thermal power station, and a number of projects connected with mining and the treatment of coal.

On the political as well as the economic and cultural fronts the Soviets have scored obvious successes in India since 1955. Indians have particularly appreciated the Soviet position on Kashmir. When the discussion of the Kashmir question was revived in the Security Council of the United Nations in 1957, and again in 1962, resolutions unacceptable to India were blocked by Soviet vetoes. The Suez crisis of 1956, in which India and the Soviet Union expressed the same views, although doubtless for different reasons, would have redounded even more to the Soviet advantage had it not been for the far more ruthless Soviet action in Hungary at almost the same time. Indians were apparently honestly bewildered and confused by the events in Hungary, and they were slow in condemning the Soviet actions in that country.

As India's relations with Communist China went from bad to worse after 1959, its relations with the Soviet Union seemed to become increasingly close and cordial. Instead of supporting its fellow-Communist state, the Soviet Union let it be known that it did not approve of China's behavior in precipitating the border dispute with India — a dispute which Khrushchev in 1959 called "a sad and stupid affair" — and it professed to be eager to be of assistance in mediating the dispute. "This was the first time in Bloc history that the U.S.S.R. has taken a neutral position in a dispute between a Communist and a non-Communist state, a position which Peking undoubtedly regarded as a betrayal of 'proletarian internationalism.' "[10] Many Indians came to believe that in the event of real trouble with China India could depend on the Soviet Union to remain neutral or even to come to the assistance of India rather than China.

When the Sino-Indian dispute flared up into an undeclared war in the fall of 1962, the Soviet Union, which was just then involved in a direct confrontation with the United States over Cuba, still tried to avoid giving any impression that it sided with either China or India. Not until October 24 did any of the organs of Soviet propaganda mention the fighting in NEFA and Ladakh.

The first Soviet reactions to India's enlarged crisis with China convinced many Indians that the Soviet Union could not be counted on in any showdown with China and that the requirements of the Sino-Soviet alliance would always be given precedence over any Soviet desires to build up India as a makeweight against China or even to remain on good terms with India. The Soviet Union, as some of its propaganda releases stated, regarded China as a "brother" and India as a "friend."

[10] Donald S. Zagoria, *The Sino-Soviet Conflict, 1956–1961* (Princeton University Press, 1962), p. 283.

In late 1962 the U.S.S.R. was virtually forced to abandon its previous position of "neutrality" in the Sino-Indian dispute, and it had to come down, to the extent that it could not avoid a decision, on the side of China. But its actions in late 1962 were not wholly satisfactory to either China or India. Both the Cuban crisis and the Sino-Indian dispute, in fact, widened the gulf between the Soviet Union and China.

While the fast-moving events along the Sino-Indian border apparently forced him to take a more definite position regarding the Sino-Indian dispute than he had previously revealed, Khrushchev still tried to preserve Soviet influence in and links with India. He gave the impression that the Soviet Union would continue to supply India with all of the military equipment which it had promised to send. The Soviet Ministry of Foreign Trade expressed the belief that trade between India and the U.S.S.R. would continue to increase. The announcement in May 1964 of the Soviet agreement to provide financial and technical assistance in building a steel plant at Bokaro seemed to give support to the widely held belief in India that the Soviet Union could be relied upon for continued economic assistance through long-term credits, in spite of China's open hostility toward India and the new military ties between India and the major non-Communist powers of the West. Some Indians seemed to look on the Soviet Union as the main bulwark against China. In a sense, therefore, India seemed to have become a focal point of the relations between the Soviet Union and the Western powers. The kind of nonalignment which prevailed in India after October 1962 seemed compatible with closer ties with both the Soviet Union and the Western powers. Only toward Communist China could India henceforth not be "neutral," and the change in Sino-Indian relations was precipitated by the actions of China, and not of India.

Pakistan and the Soviet Union

Pakistan's relations with the Soviet Union, especially from 1953–54 until recently, have been distant and cool. There is suspicion on both sides. Pakistan fears the huge size and immense power of the Soviet Union, its revolutionary ideology, and its keen desire to find access to an ice-free port. The Soviet Union finds Pakistan too close to its soft belly and fears that Pakistan may be used as a base against it.[11] These and other factors, such as the Soviet stand on Kashmir, have created the "state of mutual distrust" which has generally characterized Soviet-Pakistan relations.

Quite naturally, the U.S.S.R. strongly disapproved of the basic orientation of Pakistan's foreign policy after 1953–54, and of Pakistan's affiliations with

[11] Aslam Siddiqi, *Pakistan Seeks Security* (Lahore: Longmans, Green, 1960), p. 38.

SEATO and CENTO, its military alliance with the United States, and its acceptance of American military aid. For years the two countries engaged in a series of vitriolic diplomatic exchanges. In April 1958, for example, the Soviet Union warned of the "grave consequences which will inevitably await Pakistan if its territory will be allowed for the establishment of military bases with the purpose of using them against the Soviet Union and other peace-loving countries." The note added: "In case of aggressive actions against the U.S.S.R. the latter will be forced to use all the means at its disposal to launch a counterblow upon the aggressor as well as upon the aggressor's bases in foreign territories." When it was learned that the American U-2 plane shot down over the Soviet Union in May 1960 had taken off from the airfield at Peshawar, the Soviet Union accused Pakistan of lending its territory for the carrying out of aggressive acts against it, and Khrushchev threatened to wipe out the Peshawar airfield. To all of these protests and warnings Pakistan replied by firm denials and countercharges; but the Soviet threats, particularly after the U-2 incident, seem to have raised some apprehensions among many Pakistanis.

Pakistan has viewed with particular apprehensions the growing Soviet influence in Afghanistan, with which diplomatic relations were severed in September 1961. Since 1955 Afghanistan has been a major target of the Soviet economic, political, and cultural offensive, for when Bulganin and Khrushchev stopped in Kabul, they made all kinds of promises to Afghanistan, including the extension of a Soviet loan, on the usual easy terms, of about $100,000,000. Total Soviet economic aid to Afghanistan has been more than double this original loan, and has been slightly greater than total United States aid to Afghanistan since 1946.

As a result of several barter and other agreements since 1955, more than half of Afghanistan's total foreign trade is now with the Soviet Union. Furthermore, the closing of the main route for non-Communist trade and supplies, and for American assistance as well, through Karachi and Peshawar, as a result of the severance of diplomatic relations between Pakistan and Afghanistan, turned Afghanistan even more strongly toward the U.S.S.R. The Soviets have trained and equipped the Afghan army and seem to have considerable influence in that army. They have also built roads of great strategic importance from the Soviet border to key centers in Afghanistan, even by-passing the Hindu Kush.[12]

To add to Pakistan's apprehensions and alarms, the Soviet Union has encouraged Afghanistan to revive and press the Pakhtunistan issue, which Pakistan regards as palpably an effort to keep the Pathans and other tribesmen of the frontier areas stirred up and to create unnecessary security and tribal problems for Pakistan over a "phony" issue. On March 4, 1960, in

[12] *Ibid.*, pp. 31–32.

Kabul, Khrushchev joined with the Prime Minister of Afghanistan in a communiqué which proposed that the Pathans on the Pakistan side of the Durand Line should be given the right of self-determination in accordance with the principles of the United Nations Charter.

As a result of these and other signs of Soviet intervention, the leaders of Pakistan are convinced that Afghanistan is to all intents and purposes a Soviet satellite, a fact that raises grave security problems, not only for them and for India, but also for their Western allies. Since the United States does not officially share this view of the extent of Soviet penetration in Afghanistan, they regard America's Afghan policy as at best naive and at worse hazardous.

Until 1961 Pakistan had shown little interest in trade with the Soviet Union, or in receiving Soviet economic assistance. A few trade missions were exchanged between the two countries, and some trade agreements were concluded. On several occasions — as during Mikoyan's visit in March 1956 — the Soviet Union offered substantial economic assistance to Pakistan, but these offers were always turned down.[13] In 1961, however, the government of Ayub Khan reversed this long-standing policy, and on March 4th concluded a $30,000,000 loan agreement with the Soviet Union for the provision of equipment and technical assistance in carrying out oil exploration in Pakistan. This first formal aid agreement with the U.S.S.R. was also the first concrete evidence of a desire on the part of Pakistan's leaders to improve their relations with the Soviet Union.

In 1963 Pakistan concluded several important agreements with Communist countries, including the much discussed border agreement with China, air agreements for landing and onflying rights with both the Soviet Union and China, and a barter agreement with the U.S.S.R. for the exchange of cement for jute, valued at about $2,000,000. Additional aid and cultural agreements were signed during Ayub Khan's official goodwill visit to the Soviet Union in early April 1965, the first visit ever made to the Soviet Union by a Pakistani chief of state.

Although Pakistan has shown a greater interest than formerly in establishing some limited contacts with the Soviet Union, in all probability no marked pro-Soviet shift in Pakistan's policies is in the offing. Apparently this new orientation is a part of the "new realism" that has characterized Pakistan's foreign policy since 1960 or 1961.

---

[13] In 1956 the Soviet Union offered to help Pakistan in the peaceful uses of atomic energy and in the construction of a steel mill. In 1958 the leader of a Soviet Parliamentary delegation to Pakistan repeated the Soviet offers of economic and technical assistance, either on the basis of bilateral agreements or through the United Nations, in the fields of irrigation, agriculture, flood control, and the eradication of salinity and waterlogging of the soil. *Pakistan Times*, February 4, 1958. In March and again in November 1958 the Soviet Ambassador to Pakistan offered agricultural and other machinery on a credit basis, repayable in rupees.

Pakistan and Communist China

Pakistan extended recognition to the Communist regime in China in early 1950, but relations were quite limited until 1961, apart from the exchange of several official visits and cultural delegations.[14] In orientation and in attitudes the two countries were far apart. China, like the Soviet Union, denounced Pakistan for its various military associations. Yet Pakistan has for some years maintained closer contacts with China than with the Soviet Union. Besides the usual desire for economic relations (an important trade agreement between Pakistan and China was signed as early as May 1956), the obvious political reason was the hope of obtaining Chinese support on Kashmir.

Although consistently taking the view that the Communist regime should represent China in the United Nations, simply on the ground that it has effective control over the Chinese mainland, Pakistan has not been a vigorous champion of China, as was India. In 1950 it supported an Indian-sponsored resolution for the seating of the Peking regime in the General Assembly and in 1961, a Soviet-sponsored one. Each year in the interval, however, it voted for United States-sponsored resolutions for the postponement of the question of the representation of China.

In April 1959, shortly after the Chinese had ruthlessly suppressed the uprising in Tibet, the Foreign Minister of Pakistan, Manzur Qadir, repeatedly expressed his misgivings and fears about Communist expansionism and urged other Asian countries to join collective security arrangements. At about the same time President Ayub Khan renewed his offer to enter into a joint defense arrangement with India, subject to certain conditions — an offer which Nehru spurned. China asked Pakistan to indicate against whom the joint defense was intended to be organized. The answer was obvious, but Pakistan did not press the point. It did, however, support a resolution on Tibet which condemned the violation of human rights by China, while India opposed the inclusion of the question of Tibet on the agenda of the General Assembly.

Pakistan obviously has been keeping an alert eye on the developments in Tibet and Sinkiang, and especially in Ladakh and in the areas which it controls in northern Kashmir and Hunza, along the Sinkiang border. In September 1959, for example, it protested to China against repeated violations of its air space. It was also well aware that Chinese maps indicated that China claimed some five or six thousand square miles of territory which Pakistan controlled, including the area around Mount Godwin Austen (K²), the second highest mountain in the world, and some 15,000 square miles in Ladakh, in which Pakistan also claimed to have a special interest.

[14] See S. M. Burke, "Sino-Pakistan Relations," *Orbis*, Summer 1964, pp. 391–395.

While India's difficulties with China were increasing, Pakistan began to "chum up" with China, to use Nehru's words. The first concrete evidence of this rather puzzling policy shift came in 1961, when Pakistan and China announced an agreement to enter into negotiations regarding the demarcation of the border between Sinkiang and the Pakistan-occupied portion of Kashmir and Hunza, from the Karakoram Pass to the borders of Afghanistan (a distance of approximately 250 miles). The talks have continued intermittently ever since, and apparently have covered a wide range of subjects. In late December 1962, on the eve of the first round of high-level Indo-Pakistan talks on Kashmir, Pakistan and China announced that they had reached agreement on the demarcation of the border between Sinkiang and Hunza and the Pakistan-held portions of Kashmir, and on March 3, 1963, between the third and fourth rounds of discussions of the Kashmir issue, Foreign Minister Z. A. Bhutto signed the border agreement in Peking. In 1963 Pakistan and China concluded several other agreements, including a trade agreement in January, an air agreement in August, and a barter agreement to exchange jute for cement in September.[15] Early in 1964 Premier Chou En-lai stopped in Karachi on his way to Africa, and in March he was warmly welcomed during an eight-day official visit. A year later President Ayub Khan was given the "red carpet" treatment during an official state visit to China.

In "chumming up" with China, Pakistan seemed to be primarily interested in getting a specific agreement on its northern borders with Sinkiang, whereas China seemed to be more interested in entering into some kind of nebulous nonaggression agreement along the lines of the *Panchsheel.* Apparently China believed that such an agreement would help to convince the naive and unwary that China is a great devotee of peaceful co-existence, while at the same time it would tend to wean a now rather disgruntled Pakistan away from its military alliances. Pakistan's objectives were less clear, although the professed objective of its border negotiations was a simple one, namely, as Ayub Khan stated at a CENTO meeting in Teheran in 1959, "to prevent a dispute similar to that which led to a border clash between China and India."

When Chou En-lai visited Karachi in the spring of 1964, he publicly endorsed Pakistan's position on the Kashmir question; and the Chinese Communist Government unequivocally sided with Pakistan when India and Pakistan became involved in military conflict in the fall of 1965. This support, which contrasted with the "neutral" position of the United States, the United Kingdom, and the Soviet Union, was greatly appreciated by Pakistanis. Undoubtedly it strengthened Pakistan's pro-Chinese orientation.

It is no secret that the United States is troubled by the recent Pakistani overtures to China, especially at a time when the Chinese have been taking

[15] See Norman D. Palmer, "New Directions for Pakistan," *Current History,* February 1964, pp. 74–75

an intransigent line on most international issues. That its wooing of China embarrasses the United States as well as India may not disturb Pakistan at all, and may indeed have been one of the reasons for opening negotiations with China. Pakistan does not intend to be taken for granted by its great Western ally. If the United States insists on paying close attention to India, Pakistan apparently asks why it should accept this orientation without taking compensatory moves on its own part. It also insists that an agreement with China on the precise delimitation of the common border will remove the danger that the United States and Pakistan's SEATO and CENTO allies generally might become involved in a South Asian war over disputed boundary claims.

If Pakistan continues to maintain a "neutral" position in the Sino-Indian dispute, as in the past, this will be evidence that disillusionment and the "new realism" are exerting a greater influence on its politics and attitudes than any other considerations. As long as it is dominated by such a frame of mind, it will be a difficult ally for the United States.

In this critical situation the United States, while giving firm support to India, should encourage Pakistan to take a more realistic view of the Chinese threat and to refrain from actions which will create added problems for India. The United States should make it clear, however, that in coming to India's aid in a time of crisis, it is not neglecting its South Asian ally.

India, Pakistan, and the Lesser Communist Countries

India and Pakistan have established diplomatic relations with the Communist states of Eastern Europe, but these contacts have been limited. Representatives of the East European regimes have visited India, and some cultural delegations have been exchanged. India has received some economic aid from East European countries, involving small loans and the provision of a few score of technicians for specific projects and purposes, and it has carried on a limited volume of trade with Eastern Europe.

With some significant exceptions, India and Pakistan have showed little interest in developments in Eastern Europe, and they have not been well posted on the complicated pattern of events in a distant portion of the Communist world. The main exceptions have been a special interest in Hungary during the crisis of 1956, and, for India but not for Pakistan, a special interest in Yugoslavia.

Since the Hungarian crisis exploded while the Suez crisis was occupying the focus of world attention, India and Pakistan were so absorbed in condemning the invasion of Egypt by British, French, and Israeli forces and so puzzled by the bewildering events which occurred in Hungary in rapid succession, that they did not speak out on Hungary as vigorously as they did on Suez. Pakistan, however, was fairly prompt in denouncing the Soviet brutalities in Hungary, and it played an active role in efforts in the United Nations to put pressure on the Soviet Union to withdraw its troops from Hungary and to permit the Hungarian people to decide their own future. It supported and co-sponsored several draft resolutions condemning the Soviet action.[16]

India took a softer attitude toward the Soviet actions in Hungary. It co-sponsored an amendment to the American draft resolution on Hungary in the General Assembly which sought to remove all words of condemnation of the U.S.S.R., and when this amendment was defeated, it abstained when the vote on the resolution was taken. It voted against the paragraph in the draft resolution co-sponsored by Pakistan which called for free elections in Hungary under UN auspices; and in the end it voted against the resolution as a whole.

The hesitation shown by Krishna Menon in the consideration of the Hungarian question in the United Nations, and by Nehru himself, was widely criticized in Western countries, and even in India. Gradually, however, as the details of the Hungarian tragedy became clearer and as public opinion in India demanded a stronger stand against the Soviet Union, Nehru spoke out more bluntly and more critically.[17]

Indian interest in Yugoslavia is quite pronounced, and is indeed an interesting phenomenon of contemporary international relations. In November 1956 Nehru remarked in the Lok Sabha that "Yugoslavia is a country with which we exchange our appraisals of the world situation more frequently than with any other country." Nehru visited Yugoslavia on several occasions, and Tito has visited India, where he was given a warm reception. Nehru, Nasser, and Tito held "neutralist summit meetings," and were frequently described as spokesmen of different forms of neutralism in today's world. From Nehru's point of view Yugoslavia occupies an important in-between position in world affairs; as a Communist state — though a maverick one — it is in touch with the Soviet Union and other bloc countries, and it has special ties and contacts with non-Communist countries. According to Nehru, "good relations between Yugoslavia and India will prove . . . that countries with different set-ups can co-exist."[18]

Neither India nor Pakistan has shown much interest in North Korea, apart from India's role in the repatriation of the prisoners of war in 1953–54. India has been somewhat involved in the affairs of North Vietnam by virtue of its chairmanship of the Truce Supervisory Commission, which has responsibility for overseeing the observance of the terms of the Geneva Agreement of 1954. For a time its representatives were regarded as being more sympathetic

---

[16] K. Sarwar Hasan, *Pakistan and the United Nations* (New York: Manhattan Publishing Company, 1960), pp. 267–271.

[17] For Nehru's major statements on "the tragedy in Hungary" see Jawaharlal Nehru, *India's Foreign Policy* (New Delhi: The Publications Division, Ministry of Information and Broadcasting, Government of India, 1961), pp. 555–564.

[18] *Ibid.*, p. 581.

with North Vietnam than with the non-Communist regimes in Southeast Asia, but these criticisms have not been heard so often in recent months. Nehru and Ho Chi Minh have exchanged official visits. India seems to be somewhat more in sympathy with the regime in Hanoi than with that in Saigon, whereas Pakistan, without professing any love for Ngo Dinh Diem, or his successors, is a member of SEATO, which has thrown the mantle of its protection over the non-Communist states of former Indo-China.

It is quite obvious, in short, that India and Pakistan are not particularly familiar with the happenings and trends in the lesser Communist states and have relatively limited direct contacts with them. On the whole, the relations between the Communist states and South Asian countries have been primarily relations with the Soviet Union, and to a lesser extent with Communist China.

Ceylon, Nepal, Bhutan, and Communist Countries

At present the smaller countries of South Asia are being "wooed" by China and the Soviet Union, and they seem to be impressed by the Communist blandishments. Ceylon established relations with the Soviet Union immediately after its independence in 1948, and with the Communist regime in China in early 1950; Nepal has had increasingly close ties with both Russia and China since about 1958; and China is now attempting, thus far without much apparent success, to make inroads in Bhutan.

Ceylon

During the ministry of Sir John Kotelawala, a staunch anti-Communist, Ceylon made a much-discussed agreement with Communist China, according to which China supplied substantial quantities of rice in return for rubber. Strongly criticized in the United States, the Government of Ceylon defended this agreement on the grounds that it was necessary for Ceylon's survival and that it was quite consistent with Ceylon's policy of nonalignment. At the Bandung Conference in April 1955, Kotelawala surprised almost everyone by speaking out vigorously about new and more dangerous forms of colonialism, with obvious reference to Communist policies. In this stand he sided with Pakistan, the Philippines, and other aligned countries represented at Bandung, and differed openly with Nehru and most of the other leaders, including Chou En-lai, who seemed to make a greater impression on other "neutralists" than he did on Sir John. Following Kotelawala's defeat at the polls a year after the Bandung Conference, the governments headed by Mr. and Mrs. Bandaranaike retreated from Sir John's position and followed a policy of nonalignment which seems to have been "softer" toward the Communist countries.

Occasionally, to be sure, a representative of Ceylon, in United Nations organs or agencies or at some international conference, has been critical of Communist or Soviet policies. Perhaps the best known example of this occasional deviation came in 1957, when the Ceylon member of a UN commission investigating the facts of the Hungarian crisis joined with his fellow-members in endorsing a report which is still regarded as one of the most damning indictments of Soviet policies that has been submitted to the UN or any other body. For this endorsement Ceylon's representative was criticized in many nonaligned countries and at home, but he defended his action effectively by maintaining that no man of honor could have taken any other position.

Ceylon has been a recipient of Soviet economic aid since 1955. The amount has not been large — about $30 million, roughly equal to American development assistance to Ceylon since 1955[19] — and it has been directed largely to impact projects and has been extended on favorable terms, in accordance with standard Soviet practice. A marked swing toward a more pro-Soviet orientation set in during the ministry of S. W. R. D. Bandaranaike, and it continued during the ministry of his wife. The controversy between the government of Ceylon and British and American oil companies, which led to the suspension of American economic assistance to Ceylon in February 1963, redounded to the benefit of the U.S.S.R.[20]

Since the Korean War China has been supplying huge quantities of rice to Ceylon, presently amounting to about one-fourth of Ceylon's rice needs, and has been receiving rubber in return. Ceylon is the only country outside of the Communist bloc which has received about as much aid from Communist China as from the Soviet Union.[21]

When China and India became involved in an undeclared war, Mrs. Bandaranaike took the initiative in convening a meeting of five neutralist countries to make proposals for a pacific settlement of the dispute. The Colombo proposals were at first welcomed by China, but after India accepted the proposals as a basis for negotiations, China reneged. This has been one of several events which have produced a slight cooling in relations between Ceylon and China. When Chou En-lai visited Ceylon in February 1964, his visit was "marked by a decided absence of popular enthusiasm," and the final communiqué revealed that he and Mrs. Bandaranaike had been unable to agree on two basic issues, namely the Colombo proposals for the resolution of the Sino-Indian dispute, and the Chinese proposal for another Bandung-type conference rather than a conference of nonaligned nations, advocated by India and supported by Ceylon.[22]

---

[19] U.S. development assistance to Ceylon up to 1964 amounted to about $29 million. In addition, surplus foods valued at approximately $65 million were made available.

[20] See above, pp. 151–152.

[21] See Paul Hurmuses, "Lessons for Chou En-lai: Ceylon Proves Money Doesn't Buy Friends," *The Philadelphia Inquirer*, March 1, 1964.

[22] See Thomas T. Brady, "Chou and Mrs. Bandaranaike Are Unable to Agree," dispatch from Colombo, February 29, 1964; in *The New York Times*, March 1, 1964.

As a result of general elections in March 1965 the government headed by Mrs. Bandaranaike was replaced by one formed by the United National Party, with Dudley Senanayake as Prime Minister. The new government has been following a more truly nonaligned policy, without the pro-Communist orientation which characterized the governments of Mr. and Mrs. Bandaranaike.

Nepal

Since December 1960, when he dismissed the Koirala government and the Parliament, imprisoned Koirala and other former Cabinet officers, and assumed direct control of Nepali affairs, King Mahendra has been playing a kind of Himalayan balance-of-power game, featured by various shifts in personnel and policies inside Nepal, by strains in Indo-Nepali relations, and by the conclusion of various agreements with the Soviet Union and China.[23]

Both the Soviet Union and China now have diplomatic missions in Kathmandu, as have India, the United Kingdom, the United States, and Israel. The two Communist states have provided some assistance to Nepal, on a scale roughly comparable to United States aid to that country as far as commitments are concerned (nearly $70 million in each case to the end of 1963) but far less in terms of actual expenditures (about $7 million for China and the U.S.S.R. combined, compared with $53 million for the United States, to the end of 1963).

In recent years the relations between Nepal and the Soviet Union have been carried on in a "low key." The Soviets have won friends in Nepal by their policy of apparent moderation and limited demands. Chinese pressures on Nepal have been more obvious. China would clearly like to wean Nepal away from its heavy dependence on India and the United States as well. China has cultivated King Mahendra and the Nepalis in every possible way. China and Nepal have reached agreement on the demarcation of their common borders. The Sino-Nepali agreement of 1961 for the building of a road north into Tibet was particularly disturbing to India, for its construction, already well under way, will provide a motorable link from Tibet into India and open up Nepal to further Chinese penetration. King Mahendra and his ministers have rejected Indian protests about this agreement, which they have insisted blandly is prompted wholly by economic considerations. Apparently they are trying to gain a small degree of freedom of maneuver and to lessen their heavy dependence on India.[24]

Another rather disturbing development is "the Nepal government's increasing interest in using Nepali communities abroad as an instrument of

[23] Leo E. Rose, "Sino-Indian Rivalry and the Himalayan Border States," *Orbis*, Summer 1961, pp. 198–215; and "Nepal: Under Same Management, Business as Usual," *Asian Survey*, February 1965, pp. 77–78.

[24] See Shen-Yu Dai, "Peking, Kathmandu and New Delhi," *The China Quarterly*, November-December 1963, pp. 86–98; and Satish Kumar, "Nepal and China," *The Indian Journal of Political Science*, January-March 1963, pp. 79–93.

Nepal's foreign policy. Certain factions in Kathmandu, with close ties to the present regime, are urging the government to adopt a more positive position on this question aimed at weaning Nepalis in Sikkim, Bhutan and the hill areas of West Bengal away from their orientation toward Delhi."[25] In the past these people of Nepali origin have shown little interest in or support for the more adventurist programs of the Nepali government, and they have been generally pro-Indian in their sympathies.

The efforts of "certain factions in Kathmandu" to woo Nepalis living outside of the country may also play into the hands of the Chinese, whether or not this is the intent of those who are promoting such a program. This danger is pointed out clearly by Leo E. Rose, a leading American specialist on the Himalayan border areas:

> The most vocal elements on this subject are those generally adhering to a "pro-China" (though . . . not necessarily, "pro-communist") line. . . . If the oft-exaggerated reports from the border area can be relied upon in this instance, Peking has already commenced an unofficial but widespread propaganda campaign on its own supporting the establishment of a "Greater Himalayan" state that would, apparently, include all the sub-Himalayan hill area from Bhutan to Kashmir (though not the hill areas to the east of Bhutan which China claims for itself).[26]

Sometimes the Chinese proposals for Himalayan "confederation" are more limited, as for example for a "federation of Sikkim and Bhutan," and sometimes they seem to include the North East Frontier Area, Nagaland, and even parts of Assam and North Bengal. Some Nepalis seem to be greatly interested in the idea of a kind of Greater Nepal, or Gurkhastan. Indeed, according to George N. Patterson, "the most significant development in Nepal today is the interest in the Chinese proposal for a 'Confederation of Himalayan States'."[27]

Disturbed by the unhappy state of its relations with King Mahendra, India has been making special efforts, with some success, to improve them. It has also been disturbed by King Mahendra's apparent willingness to open up his country to Communist influence and to make agreements with the Soviet Union and China. This is a situation which calls for special caution on the part of both India and the United States. If the Chinese resume their military offensive against India, or even if they simply continue their stepped-up campaign of propaganda and subversion in the Himalayan areas generally, Nepal may yet prove to be a vulnerable part of India's defensive frontiers.

[25] Leo E. Rose, "Sino-Indian Rivalry and the Himalayan Border States," *Orbis*, Summer 1961, p. 214.

[26] *Ibid.*

[27] "Recent Chinese Policies in Tibet and Towards the Himalayan Border States," *China Quarterly*, No 12, October-December 1962, p. 197.

Bhutan

The even more isolated Himalayan border kingdom of Bhutan — a "state" whose precise legal status is rather uncertain — is gradually showing some signs of a desire to emerge from its self-imposed isolation, and is being subjected to both pressures and diplomatic flattery from the Chinese. India provides an annual subsidy to Bhutan, and under a treaty of 1949 the Maharaja of Bhutan agreed to accept India's guidance in foreign affairs and in certain other subjects. China refuses to acknowledge or to accept this arrangement. In 1959 it suggested direct discussion with Bhutan about the border between Bhutan and Tibet — a suggestion which the Maharaja rejected. In 1960, when representatives of China and India held several lengthy meetings to make a detailed study of conflicting border claims, the Chinese refused to discuss the border between Bhutan and Tibet with the Indian representatives.

India is naturally concerned about Chinese pressures on Bhutan, especially since Bhutan occupies another vulnerable part of India's northern frontiers, and since many of the people of Bhutan are of either Nepali or Tibetan stock and are therefore racially and religiously related to the people of Tibet and adjoining regions under Chinese control.

Indian engineers have built a motorable road into Bhutan, and at least one more road linking India and Bhutan is under construction. There are even reports that an airfield capable of accommodating jet planes will be built in that remote country. Communications generally are still primitive, but the opportunities for Chinese influence and infiltration, chiefly through agents of Tibetan or Nepali or Bhutanese stock, are extensive.

A team of experts from India's Planning Commission helped to draft Bhutan's First Five Year Plan, launched in 1961. "This Plan, now being implemented with Indian aid, is modernising Bhutan's agriculture, building new industries in Bhutan, and breaking the country's physical isolation by developing the means of communication."[28] The assassination of Premier Jigme Dorji in April 1964 was a great blow, for the Premier was an effective leader in his country and a good friend of India. Quite naturally, India suspected Chinese Communist implication in the plot. "It is obvious that Peking, in its pursuit of territorial aggrandisement in the Himalayas, would have found a weak and friendless Bhutan much to its advantage."[29] Bhutan, however, seems to have survived its great loss, and to be carrying on along the lines charted by its late Premier.

[28] "Outlook in Bhutan," *Indian and Foreign Review* (New Delhi), June 1, 1964, p. 5.
[29] *Ibid.*

The United States and South Asian-Communist Ties

The United States is concerned about the nature of the relations between Communist states and the nations of South Asia, and about the extent of internal and external Communist pressures. The crisis with China has taught India a hard lesson in the unreliability of Communist promises and professions. A prolonged "national emergency," however, may sap the economic strength of the country, the energies of its leaders, and the morale of its people; and continuing Chinese pressures short of further armed conflict will keep all of South and Southeast Asia in a state of uneasy tension. The states of this area will be particularly sensitive to any evidences of American determination and capacity to assist them in any eventuality, or alternatively of any lessening of interest and support or any failure of will. America's capacity for enlightened statesmanship will be subjected to some stern tests indeed in a vital and vulnerable part of the "free world."

CHAPTER TWELVE

South Asia and the United States: A Look Ahead

A SURVEY OF THE SOUTH ASIAN SCENE — the heritage, the experience since independence, and the present situation — provides ample grounds for either optimism or despair. It is indeed impossible to say precisely what the "facts" of South Asia mean. Political independence has been won, but economic and social independence are still unattained goals. National integration, economic development, indeed national and human survival, are still pressing problems. As Albert Mayer once remarked, "any estimate of India's future must be an ambivalent one"[1] — a remark that applies with equal or greater validity to the other countries of the area.

Official and unofficial contacts between the United States and the South Asian countries, though increasing, are still rather limited and superficial; they do not yet rest on solid foundations of mutual understanding. In a sense, the real United States-South Asian encounter has just begun.

This concluding chapter stresses the need for extending and stengthening the ties between the United States and South Asia. It recommends a reappraisal of the whole gamut of relations, and of basic American policies, specifically those concerning economic aid, trade, military assistance, cultural relations, and intraregional disputes. It gives little attention, except by indirection, to desirable changes either in the general foreign policies of the South Asian countries, or their policies toward the United States. A great deal can — and perhaps should — be said about them by way of explanation, criticism, or commendation, but relatively little will be said here, for the focus of the study is on United States policy. Obviously, however, these subjects are interrelated, and most of the recommended changes in United States policy are dependent, at least in part, upon concomitant changes in the policies of the South Asian countries.

The alternatives which American policy-makers weigh in their decisions

---

[1] "Social Analysis and National Economic Development in India," *Pacific Affairs*, XXXV (Summer, 1962), p. 140.

on South Asia sometimes carry greater implications than are immediately recognized, and often the freedom of choice is more limited than outsiders imagine. Nevertheless, certain rather obvious background considerations that are not always observed in practice can facilitate, even if they cannot resolve, the difficult decisions facing policy-makers. Among these considerations are six very patent guidelines. Briefly stated, United States policies toward South Asia should:

1. always be considered in the light of American national interests in their worldwide extent;
2. recognize the present heavy American involvement and great stake in the future of the countries and peoples of the area;
3. develop an integrated approach that gives due attention to the impact of specific actions and of long-term policies on the balance of forces there;
4. pay special attention to the internal dynamics of the political and social systems;
5. be based on independent appraisal to avoid any impression of simply endorsing the positions of other countries in the area or outside; and
6. avoid any pressure to "choose" between India and Pakistan.

It is also helpful to distinguish levels on which United States policies toward South Asia can be considered, namely, the level of regular diplomatic relations or the "normal intercourse with governments," the level of foreign assistance, providing "help in fortifying economic and social structures against the tensions of modernization," and the level of policies relating to intraregional disputes, which, unhappily, are numerous and intractable.[2] To these may be added a fourth level, that of unofficial contacts in the United States-South Asian encounter.

Political Development

First of all, United States policy should pay closer attention to the internal situation in each of the South Asian countries. At present the political situation in each country seems to be relatively stable, but beneath the surface many signs of impending changes may be detected. The United States should follow these trends with particular care and interest. At the hazard of being accused of intervention in the internal affairs of these countries, it must take as much interest in their political as in their economic development, for economic and social progress in freedom is not possible without adequate political and administrative institutions and leadership. The object should not be political stability *per se*, but political change by

[2] *Foreign Assistance Act of 1962*, Hearings before House Foreign Affairs Committee, 87th Cong., 2d Sess., March 29, 1962 (Washington: Government Printing Office, 1962), pp. 570–571. Testimony of Phillips Talbot, Assistant Secretary of State for Near Eastern and South Asian Affairs.

orderly rather than disruptive means, which may in time lay the basis for genuine political stability.[3]

Political development cannot occur without effective leadership, something generally lacking in most developing countries. In South Asia political leadership has in the past been confined largely to certain privileged groups, but new patterns are emerging as leaders are being drawn from wider strata of society. The United States must establish contacts with younger leaders at all levels, including those persons with whose views it is not sympathetic and those who are presently out of favor with the people who wield effective power. At present, the United States is not doing well in this respect. It is out of touch with many persons who are already stepping to the fore as leaders, and it seems unaware of the importance of also cultivating those who come from unfamiliar backgrounds and hold unfamiliar views.

Many of the new leaders of South Asia will be far less Westernized and far less at home in international or even national circles than the leaders who have thus far dominated the political scene. Difficult though they may be to deal with, they will probably be more genuinely representative of the interests and the prejudices of the people.

India

As Congress dominance will probably continue at the Center, and in most if not all of the states, for the indefinite future, particular attention should continue to be paid to the leaders of this party. But all is not well with the Congress. It is weakened by internal divisions and rivalries, and opposition to it is growing. It has lost its great charismatic leader, its main unifying force. But it has survived the crisis of leadership after Nehru's death in May 1964; indeed, the transition from charismatic to collective leadership has been remarkably smooth and peaceful. There is no dearth of leaders in the ranks of the Congress, whether those who were in the second echelon of command in the later stages of the Nehru era, or those who are emerging at state and local levels.

For some time now the Chief Ministers in the states have been exercising an increasing influence in Congress affairs. It is probable that most future Prime Ministers of India will have served as Chief Ministers. At district and local levels new leaders can already be identified, and more will emerge as the politicization of caste brings more representatives of the lower castes into the political arena, and as election to the various tiers of Panchayati Raj becomes a means of obtaining real political power.

[3] Dankwart A. Rustow has suggested that "we should elevate what may be termed 'political development assistance' to a level of equal or greater dignity with the more traditional forms of economic and technical assistance." This, in his judgment, requires that "we should resolutely abandon the illusory quest for political stability and instead encourage political development as rapid and as orderly as circumstances in individual countries permit." "The Vanishing Dream of Stability," *AID Digest*, August 1962, p. 16.

Another possibility is a split of the Congress. In this event two democratic parties may emerge, one grouped around the leftist members of the Congress and the Socialist parties, the other around the more conservative Congress members and non-communal conservatives, drawn perhaps from the present membership of the Swatantra Party. As politics in India would still remain within an essentially democratic framework, this change would involve no major policy dilemmas for the United States.

There seems to be little likelihood that a more violent shift to the extreme right or the extreme left will occur by political means. If violent means are used to achieve power, it would probably be either a Communist take-over or a military coup. In either eventuality the United States would be forced to evolve new policies.

Fissiparous tendencies are so strong in India that the danger of political fragmentation on regional, linguistic, communal, or north-south lines cannot be wholly discounted, although it seems even less likely than a swing from the experiment in parliamentary democracy to some kind of extreme left- or right-wing authoritarianism. The danger of fragmentation seemed to be growing in recent years, aggravated by political appeals to the divisive forces of caste or communalism, and to regional or linguistic loyalties. But that danger seems to have receded somewhat in the wake of the Chinese invasion in the fall of 1962, which produced an unprecedented upsurge of national unity and determination. More recently the linguistic riots and other demonstrations in South India revived the fears of Hindi–non-Hindi, or north-south fragmentation.

Obviously the United States should be alert to all signs of impending changes, whether of a violent or of an orderly nature. It should do what it can to strengthen the forces of unity and of democracy against the pressures tending either toward an authoritarianism of the right or the left or toward political fragmentation. Clearly this involves a deep concern for India's political development, no less than for its economic and social progress.

Pakistan

Pakistan's second effort to make the institutions of democracy work, this time under a presidential rather than a parliamentary system, has got off to a rather shaky start. From Ayub Khan's point of view, the National Assembly has been behaving badly, and some of the old and discredited political parties seem to be reappearing in new guises. East Pakistan continues to be a dissatisfied wing of the country.

Early in 1965 Ayub Khan was re-elected as President of Pakistan by a sizable majority, and thereby received a clear mandate for another five years. In all probability he will continue for some time to dominate the political life of Pakistan. But it is not at all certain whether he will be willing to endure the trials of operating under the new Constitution and will permit the gradual relaxation of controls and the revival of political activities, or whether he will put an end to the new experiments in representative government, as he and General Mirza did to the previous experiment in October 1958. If martial law comes again to Pakistan, it will probably last longer and will be more difficult to "phase out" in favor of a subsequent effort to give Pakistan a democratic system.

The United States should continue to be interested in and sympathetic with the efforts of the Pakistan authorities to deal with their very grave problems. It should not be too critical of the present regime, but should make clear that it regards some of the methods which have been and still are being employed to a considerable degree as justified only under emergency conditions and for limited periods. If responsible American officials and friends can persuade the powers-that-be in Pakistan to pay more attention to the popular desire for more representative institutions and the restoration of more normal political activity, with all of the attendant risks, they will have made a real contribution to mutual long-range interests, as well as to the immediate problems of political reawakening. Without taking a utopian or theoretical view of the prospects for democracy in Pakistan, the United States can and should encourage the present leaders to be bolder in moving in a generally democratic direction. If these leaders show that their hearts are not in this kind of effort, the United States should not neglect to express its reservations about any "backsliding" or even to show an interest in other leaders and groups more democratically inclined. Surely the American interest in political development includes progress in democratic procedures as well as the consolidation of national unity and the establishment of a stable government.

The United States should also establish contacts with Pakistani leaders who are not associated with the present regime, including those who are very much out of favor. It should pay special attention to the problems of East Pakistan, whose people and leaders feel that they have been badly neglected, not only by the West Pakistanis but by Americans also. (It is interesting to note that Americans in East Pakistan, almost to a man, seem to share this feeling.) East Pakistan is bound to be increasingly dissatisfied unless it truly becomes an equal partner in the nation's development. This will involve a greater share in development and other expenditures of the central government; the appointment of much larger numbers of East Pakistanis to the civil services, the armed forces, and political positions (including the Cabinet); and greater attention to the needs and interests of East Pakistan generally. By establishing more extensive contacts in East Pakistan and becoming more familiar with the conditions of the area and with the complaints and aspirations of the people, the United States will perhaps be able to take a more balanced view of Pakistan's affairs.

The situation in East Pakistan is potentially an explosive one, which could even lead to the disruption of Pakistan itself, either by secession or by pressures in West Pakistan to cut the ties. This would create further problems and divisions in South Asia. The United States should express a continued interest in all efforts to solidify the bonds of unity between the two "wings" and to achieve a more balanced development of the country as a whole.

Nepal and Ceylon

In Nepal King Mahendra has imposed his personal rule on the country, with the assistance of weak ministers and against the opposition of almost all the former political leaders, most of whom are now in prison, or carefully watched, or in exile. He seems determined to maintain his firm control, although he has been experimenting with his own version of "Basic Democracies" (which he calls "Panchayat democracy") and with other concessions. Since he believes — probably correctly — that former Prime Minister B. P. Koirala and other leaders would try to abolish the monarchy if they were restored to power, he wants none of them and their forms of "democracy."

In this unstable situation the United States is establishing limited contacts of an official nature, and is giving a substantial amount of economic assistance. While maintaining formally correct relations, the United States should attempt in discreet ways to discourage trends toward greater authoritarianism or toward a more pronounced pro-Soviet or pro-Chinese orientation. It should also keep in touch, to the limited degree that is possible under present circumstances, with Nepali leaders who are in opposition to the present regime as well as with those who support it. Contacts on unofficial levels are still quite limited, although channels are being opened at various levels, and should be extended and broadened. The United States is not yet taking full advantage of this opportunity to get acquainted with Nepal.

Ceylon is the only country in South Asia where an opposition party has come into power through the electoral process. Like India, it has retained its parliamentary system, which has been working in a rather strange and spasmodic way. The economic and foreign policies of the governments headed by Mr. and Mrs. Bandaranaike (1956–1965) gave no comfort to the United States. The oil controversy of 1962–1965 is but one of several recent indications that the present state of United States-Ceylonese relations is far from satisfactory. Fortunately these relations have improved considerably since the return of the United National Party to power in 1965. Since there is every reason why the United States and Ceylon should be on good terms, a special effort to resolve misunderstandings and to lay the basis for improved relations is in order. In this effort the United States should take the initiative.

Foreign Policy

Although relatively weak states, both India and Pakistan have been playing a role in world affairs that is out of keeping with their actual power.
Despite different internal and external policies and strained mutual relations, they have tended to agree far more than they have disagreed on most
international issues. Their voting records in the General Assembly of the
United Nations show that they have usually voted in the same way, and
that more often than not their positions have been at variance with those
taken by the United States and the Soviet Union.

Among the nations of the underdeveloped world India and Pakistan
occupy a very special place that is not merely a reflection of their large
populations. Both are among the more underdeveloped in terms of per
capita income and other crucial indices, but both have had more experience,
and greater success, in economic planning and development than almost
any others. Because they are of such significance, the United States must
perforce give special attention to them, particularly since what has been
called the North-South problem is becoming about as serious as the East-
West problem.

Both India and Pakistan have to tread delicately in international affairs,
for, in addition to their internal weakness and mutual difficulties, they have
to deal rather directly and on many levels with the three giants of the
contemporary world — the United States, the Soviet Union, and Communist
China. Until the Chinese taught them a lesson in *realpolitik,* Indians
fancied that their relations with China were cordial, based on the *Panchsheel.*
They learned the hard way that China had other motivations, and now
Indians regard it as a dangerous rival and threat. Until 1963 Pakistan had
very limited contacts with Communist China; but the two countries have
entered into a number of agreements and Pakistan seems to be interested
in even closer relations, dictated chiefly, no doubt, by dissatisfaction with
its alliances and by mounting fear of an India becoming militarily stronger
week by week, with the assistance of Pakistan's own allies. The United
States should constantly bear in mind the reasons for the change in attitude
of both South Asian states toward China, and the limited nature of the
apparent shift that has occurred.

India has been encouraged by the refusal of the Soviet Union to support
the Chinese actions in the Himalayas, and by the continuance, and indeed
the stepping up, of Soviet military as well as financial assistance. It obviously wishes to cultivate the Soviet Union as a counterweight to China. It
hopes to continue to be a major beneficiary of both Soviet and Western
economic and military assistance. Thus in a peculiar way India has become
a factor of some significance in both Sino-Soviet and United States-Soviet

relations.[4] Nehru and other Indian spokesmen have often suggested that India might be an area of 'commingling" as well as of coexistence of Soviet and American programs, and that some forms of cooperation in South Asia, however limited, might be useful by way of experimentation regarding ways and means of lessening Soviet-American tensions.[5] This is an idea which is worth exploring, and perhaps even trying on a tentative basis, although clearly it opens up special difficulties as well as opportunities.

Since 1959 Pakistan, in evincing a desire to develop closer relations, has entered into a few limited agreements with the Soviet Union. Quite evidently it does not intend to permit its growing contacts with Communist China to lead to a commitment in the Sino-Soviet dispute, or to interfere with its efforts to establish more, though still limited, contacts with the U.S.S.R. This does not mean that Ayub Khan has forgotten the facts of geopolitics; but it does indicate that he and his associates seem to be so concerned with the military strengthening of India that they are willing to gamble a bit on the intentions and capabilities of both Communist giants in return for possible benefits which they seem unable to achieve by themselves or with the assistance of their "incredible allies." Pakistan is willing to risk the displeasure of the United States, assuming no doubt that its American ally, whose commitment seems to be firm in regard to economic and military assistance and unreliable in regard to support against India, will do no more than criticize and protest. The United States should not be overly concerned with Pakistan's present flirtations with China and Russia, so long as they do not open that country, or South Asia generally, to Communist invasion or further penetration, and so long as Pakistan continues to take a strong anti-Communist position internally and to adhere to its alliances and other commitments.

As has been pointed out, the policies of India since late 1962 and Pakistan since 1960 have been characterized by a "new realism," which has both good and bad features. Before the "new realism" set in, the United States was generally more satisfied with the foreign policy of Pakistan than of India. Now the situation seems to be reversed. But the apparent pro-American swing of the pendulum in India and the anti-American swing in Pakistan may simply be the latest phases of the ups and downs that have characterized United States relations with both countries since their independence. In any event, the United States should seek to take advantage of the opportunity provided by the improved relations with India to establish them on a sounder basis of understanding. It should also try to "mend fences" with Pakistan. Nor should it identify itself too strongly with the

---

[4] See Sisir Gupta, *India and Regional Integration in Asia* (Bombay: Asia Publishing House, 1964), pp. 18–26.

[5] *Ibid*, p. 24. See also R. K. Karanjia, *The Mind of Mr. Nehru* (London: George Allen and Unwin, 1960), pp. 44, 88, 100–101; and Wilfred Malenbaum, *East and West in India's Economic Development* (Washington: National Planning Association, 1959), p. 3.

position of either country on issues in dispute between them; rather it should seek bases of general agreement. In this effort it should be diverted neither by the continued Indian insistence on describing India's foreign policy as one of nonalignment, nor by Pakistan's apparent movement away from a policy of alignment, while still adhering to it, at least formally. After all, thanks to China's actions rather than to America's preachments, Indians are now more willing to take strong measures, even in cooperation with aligned countries, to strengthen their country and to resist external threats.

Because of the change in India's views, all this is now possible and within the framework of continued adherence to a policy of nonalignment, which has inevitably taken on a different complexion in recent years. It is the kind of nonalignment which makes cooperation with the United States possible on a wider front, in areas that were "out of bounds" prior to October 1962. It has produced a more realistic understanding of the true meaning of Jawaharlal Nehru's oft-quoted statement, first made in his address to the American Congress in October 1949: "Where freedom is menaced or justice threatened or where aggression takes place, we cannot be and shall not be neutral." This is the kind of assurance which Pakistan has freely given, at least since 1953–54; and there is no reason to doubt that its shift toward a more "independent" policy, still within the framework of formal alignment, has made it less dedicated to such a commitment.

Since the United States will be increasingly involved in the affairs of South Asia, it should adjust its approach and its policies accordingly. This calls for sustained interest in and support of developments and trends regarded as constructive. Yet there is little hope of spectacular results by short-term nostrums or novel techniques. Quiet diplomacy is likely to produce better results over the long pull. The United States can probably advance its true interests more effectively by working quietly and persistently behind the scenes, rather than by siding with any state or states in matters of intra-South Asian disagreement, or by openly and loudly criticizing the policies of existing governments and leaders.

Overstrenuous diplomacy may defeat its own purposes, for it can boomerang and leave matters worse than they were before. Some rather dramatic and highly publicized efforts may be cited as examples of the perils of overstrenuous diplomacy. Such examples include the Livingston Merchant mission to attempt to help in resolving the differences between Pakistan and Afghanistan in 1962; the joint United States-United Kingdom effort to persuade India and Pakistan to hold talks on the Kashmir issue shortly after the Chinese attack; the failure of the United States, after lengthy negotiations and publicly expressed interest, to provide assistance for the construction at Bokaro of a steel mill in the public sector; and the suspension of American economic assistance to Ceylon in early 1963. Possibly even United States arms aid to Pakistan in 1954 and subsequently, and American military assistance to India, if it is continued on a fairly large scale for an indefinite period, might also be included in this list of spectacular and well-intentioned efforts whose negative effects may outweigh the positive results. The United States, in short, should recognize the desirable limits as well as the growing scope of its involvement in South Asian affairs and the peripheral, though important, role which it can and should play in that part of the world. On most issues on which strong divisions exist in the area, either within or between the different countries, it should recognize the desirability of in-between positions and the dangers of commitment. Americans, we are told, prefer clear-cut "solutions" to in-between positions, but in the conditions of South Asia few clear solutions are possible, and even fewer are conceivable as a product of external pressures, however well-intentioned. Reflecting on these matters, Selig S. Harrison has written: "This is inescapably the continent of partial, maybe-can-do involvements in situations where the U. S. can have at best halfway roles." It would therefore be better for the United States to accept this situation and to seek no larger roles, even though "the thought that the U. S. should make significant but qualified commitments and hedge its bets from the beginning runs against the grain." According to this line of reasoning,

India at the present moment illustrates the limits and opportunities of the American role in Asia . . . . the contract made today with a representative national leadership could turn out in five or ten years to be non-negotiable if the Congress should move too far to the right or drift into fragmented impotence. This does not mean that the U.S. should steer clear of significant involvement. But it does suggest that the intimacy of the involvement should be about what it is now, and that the responsibility for Indian success — or failure — in defense and development should remain clearly Indian.[6]

These comments of a long-term student and a pessimistic but friendly observer of South Asian affairs suggest both the limits and the possibilities of the American commitment in South Asia. Obviously, too, they have implications for United States policy which extend far beyond the subcontinent.

India and Pakistan — The Perennial Dilemma

For all friends of India and Pakistan the real object of concern with respect to foreign policy is the unhappy state of their mutual relations. For reasons which lie deep in the history and psychology of the peoples of the subcontinent and which should be more fully appreciated by those who, impatient with the failure to resolve the problem, demand such a resolution as a price for continued support, India and Pakistan have been unable to lay the basis for cooperative relations. Instead they have diverted energies

[6] Selig S. Harrison, "How Far Can U.S. Intervene in Asia?," *The Washington Post*, October 5, 1963.

and resources from more basic needs and have jeopardized their prospects for unity and survival in unproductive "squabbling." This is not an East-West issue; but it is one of the most intractable problems in contemporary international relations, with implications which extend far beyond the bounds of South Asia.

Indo-Pakistan relations have been even worse than usual since late 1962 or early 1963; but while there seems to be little prospect of a fundamental improvement in the immediate future, some developments in 1964 indicated that responsible people in both countries were seeking to reverse the deterioration. Among these developments were numerous evidences, including the release of Sheikh Abdullah and the toleration of the Sheikh's outspoken utterances on the Kashmir question, that in the last months of his life Nehru was giving special attention to relations with Pakistan and was taking an unusually flexible attitude toward Kashmir and other issues in dispute; the conciliatory statements of Ayub Khan and the new Prime Minister of India, Lal Bahadur Shastri, immediately after Nehru's death; and fresh efforts and proposals on the part of Jayaprakash Narayan and other Indian leaders who are particularly interested in finding a way out of the Kashmir impasse. Unhappily, more recent developments, including various steps by the Government of India to integrate the portion of Kashmir which it controls more closely into the Indian Union, armed hostilities in the Rann of Kutch, and the open warfare in August-September 1965, have added fresh tensions to Indo-Pakistan relations.

The particular dilemma for the United States is frankly stated by an Indian scholar: "As long as India and Pakistan fail to settle their differences, United States policy in South Asia is bound to remain comparatively ineffective."[7] Obviously the United States would like to develop friendly relations with both countries by being helpful in persuading them to resolve their differences and to cooperate in the interests of mutual survival. But its efforts often boomerang, and its programs often seem to conflict or even to negate themselves and to create imbalances and special problems for one country while they favor the other. Pakistan, for example, insists that there is no real difference between economic and military aid, and that the substantial economic assistance to India has made it possible for that country to allocate other resources to a military build-up against Pakistan. India, in turn, has alleged that the United States complicates India's development efforts by giving arms aid to Pakistan, because of which India is forced to divert needed resources to unproductive military purposes. India is becoming dissatisfied with the limited amount of military aid from the United States since the Chinese attack; and Pakistan is vociferously dissatisfied with any American military assistance, for whatever reason, to its already stronger neighbor.

[7] M. V. Pylee, "Challenge for Indian Leadership," *Current History*, February 1964, p. 81.

One of the clearest statements of the United States dilemma was made by President Kennedy at a press conference on September 12, 1963. He was asked the following question: "Mr. President, the prime minister of Pakistan said yesterday in his interview [with Selig Harrison] that he may have to make an alliance with China because of his fear of our arming India further. Is there any way this government can or has it been able to give assurances either to Indians or to the Pakistani which would quiet the mutual fear which seems to plague both of them?" The President's reply is well worth quoting at some length:

> I can tell you that there is nothing that has occupied our attention more over the last nine months. The fact, of course, is we want to sustain India, which may be attacked this fall by China. So we don't want India to be helpless as a half billion people. Of course, if that country becomes fragmented and defeated . . . that would be a most disastrous blow to the balance of power. On the other hand, everything we give to India adversely affects the balance of power with Pakistan which is a much smaller country. So we are dealing with a very, very complicated problem, because the hostility between them is so deep . . . .
>
> I think we are going to deal with a very unsatisfactory situation in that area. My judgment is that finally Pakistan will not make an alliance with China. I think she will continue to make it very clear to us, her concern about the re-armament of India and her strong conviction that she must not be put at a military disadvantage in relationship to India . . . .
>
> So we are trying to balance off what is one of our most difficult problems. . . . I think we are just going to have to continue to work with this one.[8]

The United States is under strong pressure, both at home and in Karachi and New Delhi, to choose between India and Pakistan. This would probably be the worst possible policy, which would lead to endless and unnecessary complications. Moreover, the grounds for a real choice do not exist. As President Kennedy pointed out, it is a continuing, complex problem.

If Indians and Pakistanis operate on the principle that "my enemy's friend is my enemy," as many of them seem to do, then the efforts of the United States to be the friend of both countries are bound to be unacceptable to both. If Indians and Pakistanis insist on judging countries according to their attitudes on specific issues — such as Kashmir or Goa — as they often do, then again the United States cannot be regarded as a true friend. Both countries seem to feel that the proper course for the United States is to give them all-out support on the issues in dispute between them — an impossible feat of diplomatic juggling — and each seems to have an exaggerated notion of the influence that the United States can exert upon the other.

The pressure to choose between the two countries is also strong in the

[8] The full text of the President's press conference is printed in *The Washington Post*, September 13, 1963.

United States, as reflected in newspaper editorials, in the general reactions of the "man in the street," in business circles, and above all in the American Congress. Almost every year, when the foreign aid appropriations are being considered, some influential members of key Congressional committees will ask representatives of the State Department or other government officials why the United States should not choose between India and Pakistan and frame its foreign aid policies and programs accordingly. A variant query is to ask why aid should be given when the two countries cannot get along with each other and dissipate much of the aid by military expenditures aimed at each other and by a failure to develop cooperative policies.[9] Still another variant is to ask why aid should not be conditioned on the "solution" of Indo-Pakistan differences, especially over Kashmir.

There can be no doubt that India and Pakistan are dissipating their limited energies and resources in their mutual rivalries and antagonisms, and that this situation lessens the effectiveness of outside assistance, weakens them internally, and makes it more difficult for them to deal with outside pressures. Their differences, however, are deep-seated, and can be mitigated, but probably not removed, only in time, and only by the most

[9] During the hearings before the House Committee on Foreign Affairs on the Foreign Assistance Act of 1964, the following interesting exchange occurred between the Chairman, Representative Thomas E. Morgan, and the Assistant Secretary of State for Near Eastern and South Asian Affairs, Phillips Talbot:

Chairman MORGAN. Mr. Secretary, when the President of Pakistan was here and addressed a joint session of Congress I was quite impressed with some of the flag waving on behalf of the free world. From what I read in the press he is willing to gamble the great friendship he professes for this country in his quarrel with India. I think our position ought to be pointed out to both of these countries. If they don't get down to business and settle their quarrels we should lessen the rate or stop aid altogether. We don't seem to be making any progress. They may be making progress economically in these countries but I don't think it is doing the position of the free world any good to have squabbling going on all the time between these two nations.

Mr. TALBOT. You are right. It is not doing the position of the free world or doing either of these countries good to continue these deep differences. The differences do distort their energies and divert their resources that are badly needed for development. So far as our aid programs go, our concern, of course, is to balance the various aspects of our relationship, and our interests with that area. If Kashmir were the most important thing in the world to us, then I think that it would be our duty to say no more aid to either country until Kashmir is settled. If, on the other hand, in the subcontinent it is more important to us to limit the opportunities of Communist powers to move in, to limit the potential of disintegration and chaos in these two countries so that they can develop viability, and they can be relatively effective nations of the world, then it seems to me, Mr. Chairman, that we should take what measures we can to help them constructively, and in our diplomatic efforts try very hard to help them to soften these bone-deep cultural, religious, social, economic, and political disputes.

Chairman MORGAN. It seems to me when 80 per cent of the money you have requested here today — approximately that — is for these two countries, I think our position ought to be firm that they are able to live with each other or we shouldn't make the investment.

Foreign Assistance Act of 1964, Hearings before House Foreign Affairs Committee, 88th Cong., 2d Sess., April 8, 1964 (Washington: Government Printing Office, 1964), pp. 238–239.

delicate diplomacy on the part of friendly nations and the two countries themselves.

Under no circumstances should the United States "choose" between India and Pakistan. It should adhere to its announced desire to develop close and friendly relations with both countries, and to be as helpful as possible in encouraging both to resolve their differences and to lay a new basis of cooperative co-existence.

The United States has every reason for being particularly concerned about the evolution of India, the largest of the world's democracies, the giant among the developing nations of the non-Communist world. There are dangers, however, in a policy that is too much India-oriented. This will be viewed with suspicion by Pakistan, by Nepal, which seems to fear that India is seeking to dominate it, and by Ceylon, which has some unresolved disputes with India and lives uneasily in India's vast shadow. It will also be viewed with suspicion by the countries of Southeast Asia and the Middle East, many of which, for various reasons, would like to see India's influence and power diminished rather than enhanced. Too much American absorption with India will convince other Asians that there is no point in incurring the risks of alignment and that, in spite of the vagaries of India's domestic and foreign policies, the United States is concentrating on India just because it is big and not because it is particularly worthy of special attention.

Obviously, as the United States is neither a free-wheeling nor an omnipotent force in world affairs, it has to shape its policies in the light not only of its commitments and responsibilities but also of its limitations and its capabilities. In considering the policies and interests of other countries in its dealings with South Asia, it has to weigh the extent to which its own interests will best be served by following along lines similar to those of other countries, or by working closely with certain of them. But in all cases it should attempt to develop "independent" policies, and not simply accept those of other countries.

A common charge in the region is that the United States has no real interest in South Asians, other than simply using them for the prosecution of the cold war against the Soviet Union and international communism. Another charge is that America's South Asia policies are largely influenced by its NATO allies. Add to these the suspicions of the several South Asian countries regarding American policies toward their neighbors. These feelings reduce America's effectiveness as a possible mediator in South Asia's intraregional disputes, and create further special problems.

Since the United States can hardly avoid such suspicions, it should be particularly conscious of them and make special efforts to counteract them. As a general principle, while it may side with a particular country on a particular issue, it should not give blanket endorsement to the internal or external policies of any country, whether it be Pakistan because of the military alliance or India because of its obvious importance. Where, as in the case of military assistance to either India or Pakistan, its actions tend to heighten intraregional tensions, it should make special efforts to mitigate these adverse effects by attending specially to the objections of the neighboring countries and by providing such guarantees or compensations for the adverse impact of its actions as would seem feasible under the circumstances. But no South Asian country should have in effect a veto on actions which the United States feels are desirable, even if these measures lead to temporary strains in relations. Whenever possible, the United States should try to encourage the resolution of intraregional disputes and tensions, and the expansion of intraregional cooperation — ends toward which it can work through the United Nations, through multilateral lending and developing agencies, and through bilateral relations. By developing a more integrated approach to South Asia as a whole, it may be able to bring its policies and actions more clearly in line with its objectives in its dealing with individual states, large and small.

The United States and South Asian Defense

Military alliance and assistance to Pakistan represented a considerable United States involvement in South Asia. It definitely affected the balance of power within the subcontinent to the detriment of India, and had an adverse effect on Indo-American relations. But it is doubtful that the military association with Pakistan was sufficiently beneficial to offset the adverse consequences. It involved the United States in South Asian affairs in ways that proved embarrassing and that interfered with its desire to remain "neutral" in Indo-Pakistan disputes. On balance the alliance may have been a mistake, but it was a logical consequence of policies which the United States has been following, with rather general approval of the American people, ever since the beginning of the cold war, and it may have contributed to overall objectives during a critical decade. In any event, even before 1962 both the United States and Pakistan were entertaining increasing doubts of the benefits of the alliance, and they were entering a stage of critical evaluation of the basic policies which led to it.

In the aftermath of the Chinese attack on India both the United States and Pakistan embarked on new directions in foreign policy which tended to widen the gulf that was opening between them and to place the alliance and the military assistance program in a new light. With military assistance the situation has changed considerably because of the new program of arms aid to India; and there is perhaps no way out of the dilemma facing the United States in this respect. It wants to help the South Asian countries develop a better defense posture against any possible threats from the Communist countries to the north, and it recognizes the determination of the existing regimes to build defense forces to maintain law and order and to provide some protection against internal and intraregional foes. But in the long run the United States may have to consider whether a military build-up in South Asia is not so self-defeating and dangerous because of its effects that it vitiates whatever advantages it may have by way of strengthening the area against possible Communist aggression.

Had the decision to extend arms aid to India not been taken, the United States might have been well advised to consider ways and means of terminating its military assistance program to Pakistan. But it would make no sense at all to talk about ending military aid to Pakistan while similar aid is being extended to India. This step has already changed the balance of power in South Asia in India's favor, and the termination of arms aid to Pakistan and its continuance to India would be intolerable to Pakistan and would place the United States in a virtually untenable position. The United States must now consider its dual military assistance efforts in terms not only of their possible self-defeating effects but also of the South Asian balance and the beneficial results of a militarily stronger India and Pakistan in the context of external threat.

If further external threats to South Asia do not arise, the United States should then consider the possibility of reducing and eventually ending its direct military assistance programs to both India and Pakistan. This does not mean that the United States should refuse to support the efforts of both countries to develop an adequate defense posture, but it does imply that the United States should not contribute directly to Indo-Pakistan tensions by military aid to both sides, with all the unfortunate consequences of such self-defeating actions. It should recognize that in the present state of their national development neither country has the resources to provide for adequate defense without outside help, but this help should be extended in the form of economic rather than direct military assistance.

In all probability the economic assistance programs should be increased to compensate for the phasing out of military assistance, so that the two countries can press on with their economic development programs and at the same time maintain a defense establishment adequate to ward off external dangers and to ensure internal stability. In reply to the inevitable argument that there is really little difference between economic and military assistance, the point can be made that the difference is in fact very great, in both tangible and intangible ways. Specifically, the ending of military assistance will free the United States from its present position of embarrassment and involvement in the military programs of both countries. It will give India and Pakistan greater scope and responsibility for procuring the arms and military equipment they need from such places as they choose and for determining their own military policies and programs, free of the commitments which arms aid inescapably carries with it.

Such a change in policy, impossible for the immediate future, is desirable in the long run. It will not lessen American interest in or concern for the defense of South Asia. In the last analysis, the defense of South Asia must devolve on the countries of the area, and not on the United States. Of course, the United States will continue to stand ready to give advice and assistance under conditions of greater mutuality, and its aid will be available if the South Asian countries are involved in attack from outside its borders on a scale and of a kind with which they cannot cope without assistance from the major nuclear power.

Economic Development and Foreign Economic Relations

India and Pakistan have now reached a "crisis of development" in which their needs for domestic and external resources are particularly great. They must mobilize greater resources to achieve the targets of the Five Year Plans. In order to fulfill even minimal needs they must step up the pace of development considerably. This will require far more than economic measures.

Non-Economic Requisites for Development

The United States can do, and in fact is doing, a great deal to assist these countries in developing a more effective administrative structure, in training administrative personnel and orienting them to the tasks of welfare and development as well as to the traditional duties. It can do, and is doing, much to help improve the educational system at all levels and in all parts of India, Pakistan, and other countries. The official American efforts are being ably supplemented by assistance from private American foundations, notably the Ford, Rockefeller and Asia Foundations; by land-grant and private American universities through such arrangements as inter-university contracts; by other private American agencies, and by countless individual Americans who serve in South Asia under individual arrangements. Nor should the work of thousands of American missionaries in welfare and education be overlooked.

In the crucial area of family planning official Washington is virtually hamstrung by certain inhibitions to which it is subjected, notably the pressure of the Catholic Church. Some private American foundations can be of limited assistance in birth control measures, especially by providing technical experts and funds for research and experimentation. Moreover, the United States contributes to several international agencies, notably the World Health Organization, which are giving substantial support to the effort of India and Pakistan to achieve real population control by various family planning techniques. But the efforts of the two governments, with some outside assistance, are still pitifully limited, and they have made no appreciable impact on the population growth rate, which is well over 2 per cent a year and means an annual increase of over 13,000,000 people.

In the difficult task of persuading the masses to identify themselves with and to participate in the development effort no outside country can do much except to encourage and applaud the work of those in India and Pakistan who are laboring in this field. The comprehensive programs of Basic Democracies and Panchayati Raj have as a major objective precisely the mobilization of popular participation and support. For this and many other reasons the United States should take a greater interest in these programs, which have been described as among the most exciting programs of their kind in any developing country. These programs need to be appreciated and understood not only in their specific economic and technical objectives, but also in their large implications, for they may provide models for democratic decentralization and popular mobilization which other developing countries might emulate.

Approaches to Planning

Although the United States is not enamored of national planning, it recognizes the imperative necessity of such planning in the South Asian countries, and it is giving major assistance to the programs there. This assistance should be continued at present or even expanded levels. The object is to assist in what may be termed "Operation Survival," and to support the national development plans, but it is not to endorse the objective of a "socialist pattern of society" or to increase economic and political centralization. For all the talk about socialism in India, the approach of the Indian planners, as well as of their counterparts in Pakistan, is a pragmatic one. Both countries are really mixed economies, in which the private sector accounts for by far the greater part of the gross national product, even though the public sector is expanding rapidly.

The United States should continue to encourage the two countries to follow a pragmatic approach in economic as well as political and social policies, and to maintain a true mixed economy, with ample scope for the private as well as the public sector. Wherever possible and desirable, it should give special assistance and encouragement to the private sector, and should encourage the governments of the South Asia countries to do the same. But it should recognize that private enterprise is operating under severe limitations in that part of the world; that it is rather suspect, and to some extent rightly, because of its heavy concentration in the past on exploitative rather than productive undertakings; that it cannot be expected to operate in certain essential areas of development where the prospects of monetary returns are not good, at least for some years to come; and that some things that must be done to further the national plans are beyond the capacity of indigenous private enterprise. Thus, the United States should not be disturbed because much of its assistance is going to the public sector, and it should not hesitate to give even direct aid to public enterprises whenever it is convinced that there is no real alternative. So long as India follows pragmatic and not rigid or dogmatic economic policies, the public dedication of the government to the "socialist pattern of society" should probably be no more of a barrier to Indo-American economic cooperation than nonalignment is to political cooperation on many fronts.

Trade, Not Aid

Although foreign aid bulks larger in the relations between the United States and India and Pakistan, trade could and should be a more important dimension of these relations. The United States ranks next to the United Kingdom as the best market of the South Asian countries, and it is the major source of their imports. By unnecessarily illiberal and restrictive trade policies it can more than undo all the good effects of the substantial amounts of foreign aid that it is making available to the two countries; and conversely, relatively small concessions in the trade field can be more effective than larger amounts of foreign aid.

For these reasons the South Asian states look to the United States for assistance in export promotion, for favorable opportunities for selling their products, including raw materials and semi-manufactured and manufactured products, for the provision of imports needed for development and other purposes at favorable prices and terms of payment. They also look to the United States to take the leadership in the liberalization of world trade; they welcomed the Trade Expansion Act of 1962, and the general trade policies of the Kennedy Administration. They hope for American leadership in the conclusion of various international commodity agreements, in pressing for the reduction of tariffs and other barriers to trade, and in granting special concessions to developing nations because of their weak competitive position. They would like the United States to continue to work for trade liberalization in the General Agreement on Tariffs and Trade, and to make GATT an agency more responsive to the particular needs of the developing countries. In particular, they hope that the United States will give special attention to the needs of the developing countries as advanced in the eight-point memorandum prepared by Raul Prebitsch for the United Nations Conference on Trade and Development in the late spring of 1964, and in the resolutions supported by the developing countries at this conference. They were rather disappointed at the limited concessions which the United States was willing to make, and at the failure of the United States to exert pressure on other economically advanced countries to make concessions.

Naturally the United States has its own problems in international trade, such as balance of payments difficulties and the demands for assistance to domestic interests engaged in international trade; and it can hardly support all the desires and demands of the developing states. But it should give special attention to these desires and demands, and it should do all it can to give meaning to the "trade, not aid" objective. For unless India and Pakistan are able to earn more foreign exchange and compete through more substantial participation in international trade, they will never be able to achieve their growth objective without continued infusions of foreign aid. They must do all they can to improve their competitive position through increased production and improvements in quality and price of export products; but they must also receive greater assistance in the foreign trade arena from the more developed countries, and most of all from the United States.

American Private Investment in South Asia

For obvious reasons the bulk of foreign private investment in South Asia has been and still is British. Only limited amounts of private American capital have been invested in South Asia, and although more companies are now investing there, especially through joint venture arrangements, the total amount is still quite small. Although there seems to be little prospect for the kind of stepped-up American private investment that would make much of a difference to the Indian economy, efforts to achieve higher levels should be pursued more vigorously by private American concerns, and more strongly encouraged by the American and South Asian governments.

On the whole the investment climate in India and Pakistan is favorable. Both countries grant special concessions to private investment, foreign or domestic. These concessions could perhaps be further liberalized. A great stimulus to American investors would come from steps to simplify governmental requirements, to relax controls, to eliminate some of the "red tape" and the bureaucratic delays and frustrations, and in general to simplify the procedures and expedite the necessary clearances for foreign investors. The establishment of the Indian Investment Centre, with headquarters in New Delhi and a branch office in New York, has been a welcome development. The Centre has been able to act as an intermediary and to provide answers to many of the questions of American concerns which might be interested in investment in India if the opportunities seem attractive.

Private American companies have been unduly cautious and slow in embarking on business ventures in South Asia. For most of them this is an unfamiliar part of the world. Moreover, they can find opportunities for profitable investment elsewhere, either at home or in areas such as Western Europe or Latin America with which they are more familiar. They have been reluctant to invest in countries where the private sector seems to be under such tight controls, to battle all the frustrating delays and the "red tape," and to accept less than a majority equity in joint ventures. Yet such ventures are currently favored by the governments of the South Asian countries, and they offer attractive investment opportunities in virtually monopoly market areas.

The American Government has been trying to encourage American concerns to invest in South Asian countries. It has provided a variety of investment guarantees and incentives; it has furnished valuable information and advice about investment opportunities and governmental requirements and incentives in South Asia; it has tried to influence the governments of South Asian states to provide incentives and favorable opportunities for foreign private investment; and it has made limited funds available, chiefly through "Cooley loans," to certain American companies for operations in South Asia or to local concerns which wish to enter into joint ventures with American counterparts. All of these activities are commendable, and should be continued and expanded. Other measures looking to the same objectives should also be considered. One real stimulus would be the conclusion of tax treaties with India and Pakistan, but apparently these would not be approved by the United States Senate.

Foreign Aid: Special Considerations and Problems

If India and Pakistan are to achieve even their minimal objectives of development, they must continue to receive substantial amounts of foreign aid for some time to come. For this they are and will continue to be particularly dependent on the United States, the major supplier of such aid. Indeed, India is now the largest recipient of American economic assistance, and Pakistan the second largest. Foreign aid tends to overshadow all other aspects of United States-South Asian relations. It creates an unnatural and unhealthy relationship, and it is a constant embarrassment to both giver and recipients. Yet in present circumstances there seems to be no alternative to its continuance at existing or higher levels. It is a marginal, but nevertheless important, kind of assistance to the South Asian countries, and it constitutes a relatively insignificant drain on the American economy. In fact, American economic aid to India now amounts to hardly one-tenth of one per cent of the gross national product, and aid to Pakistan is an even more insignificant percentage. Seldom have such relatively small sums been the object of so much criticism and so much scrutiny.

The reasons for the extension of American aid to developing countries are clear and compelling. Relatively small amounts of economic assistance may make the difference between collapse and survival, or between closed patterns and relatively open societies, and they may therefore represent as much an investment in America's future as in the future of the developing world. As President Kennedy said in his foreign aid message in March 1962:

> Our efforts to help them help themselves, to demonstrate and to strengthen the vitality of free institutions, are small in cost compared to our military outlays for the defense of freedom. Yet all of our armies and atoms combined

will be of little avail if these nations fall, unable to meet the needs of their own people and unable to stave off within their borders the rise of forces that threaten our security.

Looked at from this point of view South Asia looms as an area of special need and special opportunity. One of the more underdeveloped portions of the world, it is also an area in which substantial economic progress has been made. India, in particular, seems to deserve special attention because of the magnitude of its needs, the extent of its development efforts, and the dedication of its leaders to "progress through democracy."

In a previous chapter a number of special problems and considerations with regard to American economic assistance to the South Asian countries were discussed. Some broad conclusions relating to a few of these problems may be summarized here:

1. In general, the conditions or "strings" which the United States imposes upon its foreign aid should be economic and technical and not political. Nonpolitical conditions are undoubtedly necessary. The United States must take certain precautions to assure itself as best it can that the aid extended will be used constructively and employed effectively. Some supposedly economic conditions to which developing countries particularly object, notably project tying and country-of-origin tying, may be prompted more by political than economic reasons, and by domestic rather than external circumstances. Greater flexibility should be sought in defining such conditions.

2. The whole problem of the political conditions and motivations of foreign aid is a delicate one, which has been evaded rather than faced squarely by both the United States and the recipients. As the United States does not use economic aid as a means of securing satellites, or of dictating the national policies of other states, political conditions of a more specific nature should, in general, likewise be avoided. Thus, aid to India and Pakistan should not be conditioned on the settlement of the Kashmir question or other matters in dispute between them. It was probably unwise to write the Hickenlooper Amendment into the Foreign Assistance Act, and to use foreign aid as a threat to prevent recipient nations from expropriating the property or investments of private American concerns without adequate compensation. Other ways should be sought to promote the worthy objective of the Amendment.

Obviously, however, political considerations enter into the foreign aid program, at least to the extent that it is inescapably related with American foreign policy generally. Such considerations often lead to a limitation or an expansion of foreign aid to particular countries, as the cases of Indonesia and Pakistan illustrate. And though economic aid may be extended without political strings, its political impact is great. Foreign aid constitutes a massive intrusion into the affairs of recipient countries, with considerable impact on their domestic and often their foreign policies. A stimulus to change, it penetrates into some of the innermost recesses of the economy and the political and social structure.

These points were clearly stated in a report of the Senate Foreign Relations Committee on the Foreign Assistance Act of 1962.[10] The Committee's report also asked whether tests such as progress toward self-government, stability, and anti-communism should be employed to determine the recipients of foreign aid and the magnitude of the assistance, and it concluded that "This question can only be answered on a country-by-country basis, against the background of conditions in a given country," an observation of special relevance to the countries of South Asia. None of them would be able to satisfy all three criteria cited, though not necessarily endorsed, by the Senate Foreign Relations Committee. "Progress toward self-government" seems to characterize India, but is a doubtful description of any other South Asia country, although there are grounds for hope for such progress in all. None of the countries could pass the test of anti-communism, except in terms of some aspects of domestic policy. None could pass the test of stability, except in a superficial way, and one may properly question whether stability should be the objective in South Asia. In any event, in South Asia as elsewhere the United States is necessarily interested in the political as well as the social and economic development of the countries receiving its economic assistance, and it can hardly be impervious to the political consequences and impact of its aid programs.

3. A collateral problem is the extent to which the United States should be involved in the planning process. It has been rather directly involved, through the provision of American advisers, through encouragement of certain projects and of certain approaches to planning, and through the project-tying of much of its aid. The Ford Foundation has also been rather directly involved in the planning process, especially through the activities of the so-called Harvard Group which it made possible, whose members have been closely associated for some years with Pakistan's top planners.[11] This kind of direct involvement can lead to serious complications; but if it is in response to the avowed request of the governments concerned, and if it does not also lead to too intimate involvement in sensitive areas of domestic politics, it should probably be continued. Certainly it offers an unusual opportunity for effective assistance in national planning.

4. Aid should be funneled to South Asia through both bilateral and multilateral channels, assuming many forms. The current emphasis on loans rather than grants is satisfactory, although not necessarily preferable, so long as the bulk of the loans are "soft" and not "hard" ones. The choice is more

[10] *Foreign Assistance Act of 1962,* Report of the Senate Foreign Relations Committee, 87th Cong., 2d Sess., May 28, 1962 (Washington: Government Printing Office, 1962), p. 10.

[11] See *Design for Pakistan,* a Report on Assistance to the Pakistan Planning Commission by the Ford Foundation and Harvard University (New York: Ford Foundation, February 1965).

of a political than an economic nature, arising from American rather than South Asian preferences. Economically speaking, soft loans, carrying low rates of interest and repayable over a fairly long period of time, may be indistinguishable from grants. This is especially true if repayment may be made in nonredeemable local currencies, most of which will be made available to the debtor country for purposes of economic development. If they are repayable eventually in dollars, as most American development loans now are, this may create foreign exchange problems in the future, but long before the due dates of repayment other arrangements may be worked out.

The United States should continue to make assistance available through the various channels and agencies which it now employs, both bilateral and multilateral, in the form of both hard and soft loans, as well as technical assistance. This aid should be on approximately the present scale and with approximately the present balance between bilateral and multilateral channels, except that larger contributions and more positive support should be given to the International Development Association and to the UN programs of technical assistance. Assistance at present levels or higher will probably be necessary for at least another five years, and perhaps much longer.

5. The problem of blocked rupee funds, arising largely out of the accumulation of counterpart funds, in both India and Pakistan seems to be getting out of hand, and may well become a source of friction, if only of a psychological nature, between them and the United States, unless some acceptable way is found to check the pyramiding of these funds, and to use them more extensively and more effectively. Certainly they should not be allowed to be, or even to appear to be, a threat to the monetary and fiscal systems of India and Pakistan. Surely some ways can be found by mutual agreement for the more rapid use of these blocked rupees for basic development purposes, and for such valuable collateral and supporting programs as education, cultural and educational exchange, and perhaps even for family planning, without creating an inflationary threat or upsetting the fiscal structures of the two countries. Perhaps the long-run solution is for the United States to agree to write off that portion of the blocked funds which cannot be effectively channeled into the development programs. In the meantime, it should give positive assurances to both countries that these mounting credits in blocked rupees will be used only in ways that are approved by the governments of the countries in which they have accumulated.

6. The United States should give careful consideration to some projects so large in scope and so costly that they cannot possibly be undertaken by India or Pakistan unless most of the financing is made available from outside sources, and whose support would call for additional American appropriations and commitments, above existing levels. The United States has already made a commitment to the Indus Basin Development Project in West Pakistan, although it has not yet agreed to increase its promised contribution in the light of new and far higher cost estimates. If these estimates seem

realistic, as determined by responsible experts, the United States probably should and will agree to increase its pledged contributions to this important project.

Another large undertaking, which will involve vast sums of money and many years of effort and in which the United States has taken a special interest, is the program to deal with the serious problem of waterlogging and salinity of the soil, especially in West Pakistan. The United States has already given some technical and scientific assistance in studying this problem, in experimenting with various ways to check waterlogging and salinity, and in drawing up a twenty-five-year plan. It has made some limited commitments of funds, and in all probability will, and should, make larger commitments as the plan develops.

American support for the proposed fourth steel mill in the public sector in India, to be located at Bokaro, would have been another such commitment. The refusal of the United States, because of Congressional opposition, to agree to support this project, after the Administration had indicated great interest in it and after lengthy and costly feasibility studies, was probably an unwise decision, both politically and economically.

Other large projects of special importance to which the United States might give substantial support have been noted, including programs for the economic development of East Pakistan, for urban development and renewal, especially in India, and for rural development. Some of the assistance which the United States is now providing to India and Pakistan is being used for all of these purposes, along with substantial domestic resources, but apparently much larger programs costing far more must be launched before really substantial progress can be made. The Ford Foundation has been especially interested in the problems of urban and rural development, and it has allocated several millions of dollars, largely for technical assistance. Particular praise may be given to the Foundation's support for the Delhi and Calcutta "Master Plans," and for the so-called "package program" in rural India, involving an intensive effort in rural development in one district of each state of the Indian Republic.[12]

7. The United States is currently giving even more economic assistance to Nepal than is India. This assistance goes mainly for health, education, and other basic needs, not for impact projects. The King and his ministers have been rather critical of the American approach to aid to their country, and of American policies generally. It is doubtful that American aid is achieving either the political or the economic objectives which the United States would like to achieve in Nepal, and it should be continually reappraised with a critical eye, bearing in mind the difficult conditions prevailing in Nepal and the consequences of the discontinuance of American assistance.

8. Recent United States-Ceylonese relations were complicated by the im-

[12] See *Roots of Change: The Ford Foundation in India* (New York: Ford Foundation, November 1961).

passe between the Government of Ceylon and American and British oil companies, some of whose properties have been expropriated, and by the arrangements for the imports of oil and other petroleum products from the Soviet Union and other bloc countries, as well as the U.A.R. For more than two years after the aid program was suspended in February 1963, little if any progress was made in resolving the oil controversy and United States-Ceylonese relations were adversely affected in many tangible and intangible ways. Without completely endorsing the position of the American oil companies — Esso Standard Eastern and Caltex — the representatives of the American government should do what they can to effect a settlement and should point out to the Ceylonese officials some of the complications created by the deals with the Communist countries.

Monetarily the stakes were not high, for the investments of the American oil companies in Ceylon and the amounts of American aid to that country amount to only a few million dollars; but the principle was important to all parties concerned. The oil companies felt that if Ceylon could expropriate their properties and, while promising to make adequate compensation, could drag out negotiations indefinitely and could make offers which are little better than expropriation without compensation, a dangerous precedent would be set which might be followed in other countries, such as India, where the oil companies have a far larger investment. The American government felt that it had to try to protect American companies from the risks of expropriation without compensation, and the Congressmen who supported the Hickenlooper Amendment felt so strongly about this matter that they supported the move to cut off foreign aid as a means of putting pressure on a recalcitrant government.

This was a test case not only for the application of the Hickenlooper Amendment to the Foreign Assistance Act but also of the effects of the suspension of American aid to a country with which the United States is on friendly terms. It is a highly dubious procedure at best, and raises questions about the basic purposes of foreign aid and about the desirability of bringing this kind of pressure, amounting almost to sanctions, to bear upon a friendly government, at the almost certain cost of resentment and retaliation. Surely a more suitable means may be found to resolve problems arising between a foreign government and private American concerns.

The Growing United States-South Asian Encounter

It is perhaps unfortunate that economic relations have been so important in the total context of United States-South Asian relations; but in view of the urgency of development efforts and the desperate need for substantial outside assistance, this situation could hardly have been avoided. The antidote, to the extent that there is one, must be to give greater emphasis to other kinds of contacts between Americans and South Asians, on both official and un-official levels, without neglecting or minimizing the economic relationship.

It is hardly surprising that United States-South Asian contacts are still rather limited and superficial, and that Americans and South Asians really know very little about the history, culture, institutions, and ways of life that exist in these very different societies "half a world away." This lack of basic contacts and understanding, however, limits severely the scope of United States-South Asian relations, and gives an air of unreality, or at least a false glow, to any claims or apparent evidences that an era of understanding has really opened.

The United States is faced with a tremendous task of education and mental reorientation that must be carried on at various levels, and by official and unofficial agencies and individuals. In the United States it involves a massive effort to encourage greater interest, knowledge, and understanding on the part of the American people generally; a more concentrated effort to promote the same objectives with respect to opinion leaders and elite groups; and greater encouragement and support for official and unofficial programs for the training of specialists in South Asian affairs. Americans should also concentrate far more than they have in the past on the many hundreds of South Asians who are in this country every year as students and teachers. These people include many future leaders; and if they have a worthwhile experience in the United States, including opportunities to get some real understanding of the "American way of life" and to establish personal contacts with different kinds of Americans (not just those in academic posi-tions), this will undoubtedly pay rich dividends in the future.

In South Asian countries the educational task faced by the United States includes giving assistance to educational development, as well as making efforts to promote a better and more widespread understanding of "the American way of life." It embraces educational, cultural, scientific, and general information programs. These are expanding in scope and effective-ness, but have not yet made much of an impression on most South Asians. Programs of educational and cultural exchange should also be broadened. Fortunately, the Fulbright and Smith-Mundt programs are being expanded, but these have their own built-in limitations and represent only a small part of the effort that is needed.

In an address in New York in May 1963, shortly before his departure to assume the post of American Ambassador to India, Chester Bowles declared: "The Chinese attack on India and the Sino-Soviet dispute mark a sea-change in history that may well offer the United States a new possibility to use our power and influence on behalf of free societies in Asia." A less optimistic observer might have added that these epochal developments have also generated new tensions in Asia and placed new burdens on already over-burdened nations and societies, and that they have made it more difficult for "free societies" to defend themselves and have created new dilemmas and difficulties for the United States in its efforts to find ways to assist and to shore up these "free societies" and thereby to further American national interests. Today, it is clearly in America's national interests to base these broadening commitments on sounder foundations of understanding and on more extensive contacts on official and unofficial levels, and thereby to give depth and meaning to the United States-South Asian encounter.

Bibliographical Note

United States-South Asian Relations

No COMPREHENSIVE TREATMENT of the relations of the United States with South Asia, or with any of the countries of that important area, has yet been published. The story of pre-independence contacts has been traced in several unpublished doctoral dissertations, based largely on consular dispatches and missionary records. Harold Isaacs, in *Scratches on Our Minds* (John Day, 1958), has isolated various American images of India, formed mainly from impressions and stereotypes rather than from first-hand contacts or special knowledge. In several articles in *The New Republic* — notably three on "India, Pakistan and the United States" in the issues of August 10 and 24 and September 7, 1959, and one on South Asia and U.S. Policy" in the issue of December 11, 1961 — and in many dispatches to *The Washington Post*, Selig S. Harrison has commented on various aspects of United States-South Asian relations, particularly the implications of American military aid to Pakistan. The story of these relations, and of developments in South Asia since independence, has been told most fully for Americans in the dispatches of correspondents of the few American newspapers, notably *The New York Times*, which have maintained reporters in the Indian subcontinent, usually based in New Delhi.

Shortly after India's independence, Lawrence Rosinger published a useful study of *India and the United States: Political and Economic Relations* (Macmillan, 1950). Phillips Talbot and S. L. Poplai, *India and America: A Study of Their Relations* (Harper, 1958), which appeared eight years later, is a joint analysis of the main areas of agreement and disagreement between India and the United States, prepared by an American and an Indian scholar and sponsored by the Council on Foreign Relations and the Indian Council of World Affairs. No studies of comparable scope have been made of United States-Pakistan relations.

Innumerable articles on various aspects of United States-South Asian relations have appeared in magazines published in the United States, India, Pakistan, and elsewhere — for example, various articles by M. S. Venkataramani and others in *India Quarterly* (the organ of the Indian Council of World Affairs), by N. D. Palmer in *Current History* and other journals, and an authoritative article by President Ayub Khan, entitled "The Pakistan-American Alliance: Stresses and Strains," in *Foreign Affairs*, XLII (January 1964). For the detailed story of these relations in the post-independence era a few newspapers in the United States (notably *The New York Times, The Washington Post,* and *The Christian Science Monitor*), India (*The Hindu, The Times of India, The Statesman, The Hindustan Times, The Indian Express,* and others), and Pakistan (*Dawn, The Morning*

News of Karachi and Dacca, and *The Pakistan Observer*) should be consulted.

On the official level special attention should be given to the speeches and statements of the President of the United States, the Prime Minister of India, and the President of Pakistan (Prime Minister before October 1958), the Foreign Ministers of these countries, as well as other responsible spokesmen. Statements of key members of the national parliaments may be found in the *Congressional Record*, the Lok Sabha and Rajya Sabha debates, and the records of the National Assembly of Pakistan. Public addresses by top leaders of all three countries are reported extensively in leading newspapers.

Details regarding American foreign assistance to the countries of South Asia are available in various reports and other publications of the Agency for International Development and its predecessor agencies. Another valuable source is the annual hearings on the Foreign Assistance Act before the Senate Committee on Foreign Relations and the House Committee on Foreign Affairs, and on the annual Foreign Assistance Appropriations Act before the two Appropriations Committees. Chapters 10, 11, and 12 in John P. Lewis, *Quiet Crisis in India: Economic Development and American Policy* (The Brookings Institution, 1962), contain a clear and intelligible discussion of specific aspects of the economic aid program in India. More general and often theoretical considerations are presented in Charles Wolf, *Foreign Aid: Theory and Practice in Southern Asia* (Princeton University Press, 1960), and John D. Montgomery, *The Politics of Foreign Aid* (Praeger, 1962).

Various examples of American-South Asian joint ventures, the main vehicle for American private investment in the South Asian countries, are described in Wolfgang C. Friedmann and George Kalmanoff, eds., *Joint International Business Ventures* (Columbia University Press, 1961). The Indian Investment Centre, which has headquarters in New Delhi and a branch office in New York City, is another good source of information about Indo-American joint ventures, and investment opportunities in India. The Department of Commerce and the Agency for International Development provide extensive information and assistance to American businessmen interested in exploring such opportunities in South Asia, or elsewhere.

P. T. Bauer, *United States Aid and Indian Economic Development* (American Enterprise Association, 1959), is a conservative approach to the subject. Indian analyses of the role and impact of foreign aid on India's development efforts are given in V. K. R. V. Rao and Dharm Narain, *Foreign Aid and India's Economic Development* (Bombay, 1963), and in the *Report of the Committee on Utilisation of External Assistance* (V. K. R. V. Rao, Chairman), issued by the Ministry of Finance, Department of Economic Affairs, Government of India, in 1964. Similar analyses have been issued by the Planning Commission of Pakistan.

Government and Politics

Since this study deals primarily with South Asia since World War II, and particularly since the independence of India and Pakistan in 1947, no attempt will be made to suggest readings on the political heritage of the independent states of the area. The interested reader is referred to two excellent bibliographies:

Patrick Wilson, *The Government and Politics of India and Pakistan, 1885–1955: a Bibliography of Works in Western Languages* (Institute of East Asiatic Studies, University of California, 1956), and J. Michael Mahar, *India: A Critical Bibliography* (University of Arizona Press, 1964). W. Norman Brown, *The United States and India and Pakistan* (revised edition, Harvard University Press, 1963) is an authoritative presentation of the whole South Asian panorama, from the earliest times to the present. It also contains excellent bibliographical suggestions. A more popular account is Beatrice Pitney Lamb, *India: A World in Transition* (Praeger, 1963). Amaury de Riencourt, *The Soul of India* (Harper & Brothers, 1960), is a stimulating, if controversial, interpretation, full of challenging statements and penetrating insights.

A sophisticated interpretative essay on the politics of India and Pakistan since independence is Hugh Tinker, *India and Pakistan: A Political Analysis* (Praeger, 1962). Briefer but equally stimulating interpretations are contained in Saul Rose, ed., *Politics in Southern Asia* (London, 1963), and C. H. Phillips, ed., *Politics and Society in India* (Praeger, 1962). A forthcoming volume, *Religion and Politics in South Asia* (Princeton University Press, 1966), edited by Donald E. Smith, will contain two introductory chapters on this important subject, twelve on India, six on Pakistan, and five on Ceylon.

An invaluable and reasonably priced reference work, which gives extensive information and bibliographical references pertaining to the contemporary political, economic, social, and military scene in India, with some attention to historical background, is the *U. S. Army Area Handbook for India,* prepared for the Department of the Army by the Foreign Areas Studies Division of the Special Operations Research Office, the American University (Department of the Army Pamphlet No. 550-21, Government Printing Office, July, 1964).

For contemporary Indian politics, particularly since independence, the following fairly comprehensive treatments are recommended: Michael Brecher, *Nehru: A Political Biography* (London, 1959), a "life and times" biography which is in essence a political history of contemporary India; W. H. Morris-Jones, *The Government and Politics of India* (London, 1964); N. D. Palmer, *The Indian Political System* (Houghton Mifflin, 1961); M. V. Pylee, *Constitutional Government in India* (Bombay, 1960); K. V. Rao, *Parliamentary Democracy in India* (Calcutta, 1961); and the chapters on India by N. D. Palmer in George McT. Kahin, ed., *Major Governments of Asia* (second edition, Cornell University Press, 1963), and by Myron Weiner in Gabriel Almond and James Coleman, eds., *The Politics of the Developing Areas* (Princeton University Press, 1960). Richard L. Park and Irene Tinker, eds., *Leadership and Political Institutions in India* (Princeton University Press, 1959), contains many excellent chapters on various aspects of Indian political and social life. A widely-discussed and rather pessimistic approach to the Indian political scene is Selig S. Harrison, *India: The Most Dangerous Decades* (Princeton University Press, 1960). Another general work containing useful material is B. N. Varma, *Contemporary India* (Asia Publishing House, 1964). An important characteristic of the Indian political system is discussed at length in Donald E. Smith, *India as a Secular State* (Princeton University Press, 1963).

Two books dealing with significant aspects of the central government of India are K. M. Munshi, *The President under the Indian Constitution* (Bombay, 1963), and W. H. Morris-Jones, *Parliament in India* (University of Pennsylvania Press, 1957). K. I. Santhanam, *Union-State Relations in India* (Asia Publishing House, 1960), deals with aspects of Indian federalism. The civil service, public administration, and the politics of planning are some of the topics considered in various chapters in Ralph Braibanti and Joseph J. Spengler, eds., *Administration and Economic Development in India* (Duke University Press, 1963). Among the many reports on public administration in India, the most famous are those by A. D. Gorwala (1951) and Paul H. Appleby (1953).

The lack of an adequate general work on state politics in India will soon be remedied with the appearance of a volume on this subject, edited by Myron Weiner. The organization of city government is outlined in a chapter by R. Bhaskaran in William Robson, ed., *Great Cities of the World* (London, 1955), and the problems of growing urbanization are considered in Roy Turner, ed., *India's Urban Future* (University of California Press, 1962). David C. Potter gives a good brief description of district administration in *Government in Rural India: An Introduction to Contemporary Administration* (London, 1964). This small volume includes chapters on community development and Panchayati Raj. The latter program was introduced largely as a result of the report of the Balvantray Mehta Study Team in 1957 — *Report of the Team for the Study of Community Projects and National Extension Service*, prepared at the request of the Committee on Plan Projects of the Planning Commission. The literature on Panchayati Raj is already formidable. Good general studies are: B. Maheshwari, *Studies in Panchayati Raj* (Delhi, 1963); *Agenda Papers: Seminar on Public Administration in Panchayati Raj* (Mussoorie, 1962), prepared for the Central Institute for Community Development; and R. V. Jathar, *Evolution of Panchayati Raj in India* (Dhawar, 1964).

Articles on political parties in India abound, but, surprisingly, there is no good book-length study of the Congress Party in its post-independence phase, or indeed of any other party except the Communist Party. In *Political Parties in India* (Princeton University Press, 1957) Myron Weiner dealt with some of the main opposition parties. In *The Politics of Scarcity* (University of Chicago Press, 1962) the same author explored the still-neglected subject of interest and pressure groups in India. Gene D. Overstreet and Marshall Windmiller, *Communism in India* (University of California Press, 1959), is the most comprehensive treatment of the CPI, but it should be supplemented by more recent studies.

Detailed statistics on the three general elections and other elections have been issued (usually long after the elections have been held) by the Election Commission. S. V. Kogekar and Richard L. Park edited a series of state-by-state *Reports on the Indian General Elections, 1951–52* (Bombay, 1956). No similar study has been prepared for the second and third general elections, although many books and articles on aspects of these elections have been published. A series of nine articles under the general title, "The Third General Elections: Studies in Voting Behaviour," planned and organized by Myron Weiner and Rajni Kothari, appeared in the *Economic Weekly*, July-September, 1962. V. M. Sirsikar, using modern techniques of field work and analysis, presents an unusually interesting electoral case study in the city of Poona — *Political Behaviour in India: A Case Study of the 1962 General Elections* (Bombay, 1965).

Studies of equal quality on Pakistan are more limited. Two good general books on Pakistan during the early stages of the Ayub Khan regime are Ian Stephens, *Pakistan* (Praeger, 1963), and Wayne A. Wilcox, *Pakistan: The Consolidation of a Nation* (Columbia University Press, 1963). Two excellent studies of the politics of Pakistan in approximately the first decade of its existence are Keith Callard, *Pakistan: A Political Study* (London, 1957), and Khalid Bin Sayeed, *Pakistan: The Formative Phase* (Karachi, 1960). G. W. Choudhury, *Democracy in Pakistan* (Dacca, 1963), is a good text on the government and politics of Pakistan since October, 1958, by a competent Pakistani political scientist. It should be supplemented by reference to the *Report of the Constitution Commission, Pakistan, 1961*, a report that was not made public by the Government of Pakistan until March, 1962, and to Karl von Vorys, *Political Development in Pakistan* (Princeton University Press, 1965), a sophisticated analysis of Pakistan's political system during the same period.

Henry G. Goodnow, *The Civil Service of Pakistan: Bureaucracy in a New Nation* (Yale University Press, 1964), is an excellent case study of the higher governmental bureaucracy. Two reports by American specialists on public administration in Pakistan, by Rowland Egger in 1953 and by Bernard L. Gladieux in 1955, attracted widespread attention and comment, even though neither has been published in its entirety. Valuable materials on administration and development are contained in a volume on *Bureaucracy and Development in Pakistan*, edited by Inyatullah (Peshawar, 1963). A great deal of information regarding Basic Democracies is provided in government publications, as well as in reports and studies of the Pakistan Academies for Rural Development in Peshawar and Comilla (especially the latter) and the Social Science Research Centre in Lahore.

Planning and Economic Development

Among the innumerable works on the Indian economy, including economic development and foreign economic relations, the following are particularly recommended: P. T. Bauer, *Indian Economic Policy and Development* (London, 1961); D. R. Gadgil, *Economic Policy and Development* (Poona, 1955), and *Planning and Economic Policy in India* (Poona, 1961); John P. Lewis, *Quiet Crisis in India* (The Brookings Institution, 1962); Wilfred Malenbaum, *Prospects for Indian Development* (London, 1962); W. B. Reddaway, *The Development of the Indian Economy* (Richard D. Irwin, 1962); B. R. Shenoy, *Indian Planning and Economic Development* (Bombay, 1963); and H. Venkatasubbiah, *Indian Economy since Independence* (Bombay, 1958). A more popular analysis is presented in Barbara Ward, *India and the West* (W. W. Norton, 1961). The "human factor" in India's economic development is stressed in a fascinating book by Kusum Nair, *Blossoms in the Dust* (London, 1961).

The Planning Commission is a mine of information on India's development efforts. It has published the texts of the Five Year Plans and many commentaries on the Plans. The reports of its Programme Evaluation Organisation, its Committee on Plan Projects, and other affiliated agencies, are particularly useful. The Commission has also sponsored a popular exposition of the development program, geared largely for Western readers: *The New India: Progress Through Democracy* (Macmillan, 1958). Valuable studies and reports have also been

322 *Bibliographical Note*

issued by many research organizations and institutes in India, notably the National Council of Applied Economic Research (New Delhi), the Gokhale Institute of Politics and Economics (Poona), the Indian Statistical Institute (Calcutta), and the Institute of Economic Growth (Delhi).

In Pakistan the Planning Commission (formerly the Planning Board) has assumed major responsibility for preparing the Five Year Plans, and it has issued many reports and studies on the progress of the planning efforts. The texts of the three Five Year Plans provide the most complete information on the nature and dimensions of these efforts. The planning process and organization are clearly outlined in Albert Waterston, *Planning in Pakistan* (The Johns Hopkins Press, 1963), a publication of the Economic Development Institute of the International Bank for Reconstruction and Development. The most substantial study of Pakistan's economy is J. Russell Andrus and Azizali F. Mohammed, *The Economy of Pakistan* (Stanford University Press, 1958). Agha M. Ghouse, *The Economy of Pakistan: A Review* (Lahore, 1961) is a briefer treatment, which gives special attention to import controls and export promotion.

Defense and Security

Prior to the Chinese attack in late 1962 materials relating to problems of defense and security were scarce in India. The most prolific writer on such subjects was the scholar-diplomat, K. M. Panikkar. Among his many books were *India and the Indian Ocean* (London, 1945), *Geographical Factors in Indian History* (Bombay, 1951), and *Problems of Indian Defence* (Bombay, 1960). Three other particularly useful studies are *Defence and Security in the Indian Ocean Area,* based on the discussions of a study group of the Indian Council of World Affairs and included in papers presented to the 13th Conference of the Institute of Pacific Relations (Vol. 2, No. 4, 1958); *Seminar,* No. 35 (July, 1962), an issue devoted to the question of "India's Defence"; and H. M. Patel, *The Defence of India* (Bombay, 1963). Detailed information regarding the organization of the armed forces is contained in Jaswant Singh, ed., *Indian Armed Forces Year Book* (Bombay, issued annually). Since the Chinese attack, Indian newspapers and magazines have devoted a great deal of attention to problems of defense and security, but no satisfactory book-length study of these important subjects has yet appeared.

From the beginning of its existence as an independent state Pakistan has been absorbed in problems of defense against India and in developing an adequate defense posture, since 1954 with substantial assistance from the United States. Few serious studies of these matters have been published, however. Almost the only remotely satisfactory work is Aslam Siddiqi, *Pakistan Seeks Security* (Lahore, 1960). Briefer and more politically-oriented analyses are K. Sarwar Hasan, *The Strategic Interests of Pakistan* (Karachi, 1954), and M. A. Choudhry, *Pakistan and the Regional Pacts* (Karachi, 1958). As would be expected from a professional soldier who has assumed the top political post in the country, President Ayub Khan has shown a broad grasp of problems of defense and security and of geopolitical realities, as illustrated in his well-known article entitled "Pakistan Perspective" in *Foreign Affairs,* XXXVIII (July, 1960).

Foreign Policy

For a generation Jawaharlal Nehru was the chief architect and spokesman of India's foreign policy, and his statements and speeches form the main source for a study of this subject. They have been reprinted in several volumes. A convenient one-volume collection, covering the period from September 1946 to April 1961, is Jawaharlal Nehru, *India's Foreign Policy* (Delhi, 1961), issued by the Publications Division of the Ministry of Information and Broadcasting. Chapter XIX of Brecher's *Nehru*, previously cited, is a good overall account of the nature of Indian foreign policy in the Nehru era, and also of Nehru's views on "India and the World."

For the roots of India's foreign policy Bimla Prasad, *The Origins of Indian Foreign Policy* (Calcutta, 1960) and N. V. Rajkumar, ed., *The Background of India's Foreign Policy* (New Delhi, 1952) are useful references. A satisfactory one-volume study of the foreign policy of independent India has yet to be written. J. C. Kundra, *Indian Foreign Policy, 1947–1954: A Study of Relations with the Western Bloc* (Groningen, 1955), is a competent work on a major aspect of the subject in the early years of independence. Unfortunately the series on *India in World Affairs* being issued under the auspices of the Indian Council of World Affairs is sadly behind schedule. The volumes that have appeared, however — two by K. P. Karunakaran covering the periods 1947–1950 (Bombay, 1952) and 1950–1953 (Bombay, 1958), and a formidable tome by M. S. Rajan dealing with the years 1954–1956 (Bombay, 1964) — provide the most comprehensive coverage of India's foreign policy in the first decade of its independence. Two issues of *Seminar* — No. 19 (March 1961), "Our Foreign Policy," and No. 37 (September 1962), "Our Neighbors" — are particularly pertinent. Sisir Gupta, one of the most perceptive Indian students of foreign affairs, explored India's attitudes toward regionalism in *India and Regional Integration in Asia* (Bombay, 1964). J. S. Bains, *India's International Disputes: A Legal Study* (Bombay, 1962) is a series of case studies of such interesting questions as the Indo-Pakistan water dispute, the Kashmir question, the status of persons of Indian origin in Ceylon, Tibet, the Sino-Indian border dispute, and Goa, from the point of view of an Indian student of international law. India's role in the United Nations is the subject of two useful volumes: *India and the United Nations* (Manhattan Publishing Company, 1957), based on the work of a study group organized by the Indian Council of World Affairs; and Ross N. Berkes and Mohinder S. Bedi, *The Diplomacy of India: Indian Foreign Policy in the United Nations* (Stanford University Press, 1958).

The pros and cons of the Sino-Indian dispute, which broke out into the open in 1959, and the conflicting claims of the two countries, are exhaustively documented in the eleven White Papers — *Notes, Memoranda and Letters Exchanged Between the Governments of India and China* — issued by the Ministry of External Affairs, Government of India, since September 1959 (White Paper No. I covered the period from July 1954 to August 1959, and later White Papers have carried the story into 1964), and in the *Report of the Officials of the Governments of India and the People's Republic of China on the Boundary Question*, issued by the Ministry of External Affairs in February 1961. A few of the many studies of Sino-Indian relations, and especially of the post-*Panchsheel* era, are:

P. C. Chakravarti, *India's China Policy* (Indiana University Press, 1962); Girilal Jain, *Panchsheela and After* (Bombay, 1960); Chanakya Sen, *Tibet Disappears* (Bombay, 1960); George N. Patterson, *Peking versus Delhi* (London, 1963), a book which has been banned in India; Margaret Fisher, Leo E. Rose, and Robert A. Huttenback, *Himalayan Battleground: Sino-Indian Rivalry in Ladakh* (Praeger, 1963); S. P. Varma, *The Struggle for the Himalayas* (Jullundur, 1965); V. P. Dutt, *China's Foreign Policy* (Bombay, 1964); *Seminar*, No. 19 (March 1961); and the July-October issue of *International Studies*, the organ of the Indian School of International Studies (a "Special Double Issue" on "Chinese Aggression and India").

Relations between India and Pakistan have been the object of continuing interest and concern, and have been discussed *ad nauseam* by the responsible spokesmen of both countries — in the national Parliamentary bodies, in the newspapers, on innumerable public platforms, and in the Security Council of the United Nations. One of the best overall treatments covering the first decade of the independence of the two countries is J. B. Das Gupta, *Indo-Pakistan Relations (1947-1955)* (Amsterdam, 1958). In both countries publications and statements on the Kashmir question, the main issue in dispute, are incredibly voluminous and often incredibly biased. The differing viewpoints of India and Pakistan have been fully presented in the debates on the Kashmir question in the UN Security Council, which has devoted more than 100 sessions to this question. Five lengthy reports to the Council by Dr. Frank Graham, the United Nations Mediator for India and Pakistan, provide a valuable source of information. These reports may be found in the official records of the Security Council. At the time of their release, digests appeared in Indian and Pakistani newspapers. Among the more objective studies of the Kashmir question by non-South Asians who are familiar with the Kashmir area through first-hand observation and research are: Michael Brecher, *The Struggle for Kashmir* (Oxford University Press, 1953); Josef Korbel, *Danger in Kashmir* (Princeton University Press, 1954); and Lord Birdwood, *Two Nations and Kashmir* (London, 1956).

Papers on various aspects of Pakistan's foreign policy, originally prepared for a symposium conducted by the Department of International Relations of the University of Karachi in March 1962, are included in *Foreign Policy of Pakistan: An Analysis* (Karachi, 1964). For Pakistan's foreign policy prior to 1958 useful references are Keith Callard, *Pakistan's Foreign Policy: An Interpretation* (Institute of Pacific Relations, 1957), and K. Sarwar Hasan, *Pakistan and the United Nations* (Manhattan Publishing Company, 1960). Since 1958 the main source has been the statements and speeches of President Ayub Khan himself, as well as those of his Foreign Minister, Manzur Qadir, Mohammed Ali, and Z. A. Bhutto. Several volumes of Ayub Khan's speeches have been published. Of special value are three of his articles: "Essentials of Pakistan's Foreign Policy," *Pakistan Horizon*, XIV (Fourth Quarter, 1961); "Pakistan Perspective," *Foreign Affairs*, XXXVIII (July, 1963); and "The Pakistan-American Alliance: Stresses and Strains," *Foreign Affairs*, XLII (January, 1964).

Newspapers and Journals

For the continuing story of the developments in South Asia and of the foreign policies of the area, including United States-South Asian relations, the best source is the newspapers. Reference has already been made to the leading English-language newspapers of India and Pakistan and to the few American papers which give reasonably good coverage to news from and relating to South Asia. The International Edition of *The New York Times* is available in the major cities of India and Pakistan shortly after publication. *The Hindu,* the *Hindustan Times,* the *Statesman,* and *The Times of India* publish overseas weekly editions. Several American libraries receive daily editions of leading Indian and Pakistani newspapers by airmail. Many interested Americans receive the weekly *India News* and the biweekly *Indian and Foreign Review* (published in New Delhi from the Information Service of India, and the weekly *Pakistan Affairs* and an airmail edition of the biweekly *Pakistan News Digest* (published in Karachi) from the Embassy of Pakistan. Similar publications are distributed in India and Pakistan by the United States Information Service.

Among the scores of journals published in India and Pakistan the following are especially recommended: *Economic Weekly* (Bombay); the *Eastern Economist* (New Delhi); *Seminar* (New Delhi); *Asian Recorder* (Delhi); *Indian Recorder and Digest* (Delhi); the *Indian Journal of Political Science;* the *Indian Journal of Public Administration; Indian Quarterly; International Studies; Pakistan Horizon;* and the *Journal of the Pakistan Academy for Rural Development, Comilla.* Many journals published in the United States carry articles on South Asia or on United States-South Asian relations, including the *Department of State Bulletin, Current History, Foreign Affairs, Asian Survey,* and the *Journal of Asian Studies.* Useful journals published in other countries are *Pacific Affairs* (Vancouver), *International Affairs* (Toronto), the *Journal of Commonwealth Political Studies* (London), *Political Studies* (London), *Round Table* (London), *Parliamentary Affairs* (London), *Political Quarterly* (London), and the *Far Eastern Economic Review* (Hong Kong).

Nepal and Ceylon

Since the focus of this study has been on the major countries of South Asia and the relations of the United States with these countries, only peripheral attention has been given to Nepal and Ceylon. A basic reference book for Nepal is the *U. S. Army Area Handbook for Nepal (with Sikkim and Bhutan)* (U. S. Government Printing Office, May, 1964). Three other important works on Nepal are: Girilal Jain, *India Meets China in Nepal* (Bombay, 1959); Anirudha Gupta, *Politics in Nepal: A Study of Post-Rana Political Developments and Party Politics* (Bombay, 1964); and Eugene B. Mihaly, *Foreign Aid and Politics in Nepal* (Oxford University Press, 1965). A convenient summary of the Nepali press, the *Nepali Press Digest,* compiled in Kathmandu, is available in an airmail edition. The need for a comprehensive treatment of Nepali politics since the overthrow of the Ranas in 1951–52 will soon be met with the publication of Bhuwan

Lal Joshi and Leo E. Rose, *Democratic Innovations in Nepal* (University of California Press, 1966).

For the Western reader, at least, the most useful volume on contemporary Ceylon is W. Howard Wriggins, *Ceylon: Dilemmas of a New Nation* (Princeton University Press, 1960). Some attention to Ceylon since independence, against the background of the long historical past, is given in B. H. Farmer, *Ceylon: A Divided Nation* (London, 1963), S. Arasaratnam, *Ceylon* (Prentice-Hall, 1964), and S. A. Pakeman, *Ceylon* (London, 1964). More specialized studies are Bruce Ryan, *Caste in Modern Ceylon* (Rutgers University Press, 1953) and Marshall R. Singer, *The Emerging Elite: A Study of Political Leadership in Ceylon* (The M.I.T. Press, 1964). "The Politics of Buddhist Resurgence" in Ceylon will be explored in five chapters in the forthcoming volume, *Religion and Politics in South Asia* (Princeton University Press, 1966), edited by Donald E. Smith. For day-by-day news of developments in Ceylon, the *Ceylon Daily News* (Colombo) should be consulted regularly.

Index

228–247; and Korean crisis, 172, 254; lack of military tradition, 188; land reforms, 93; and League of Nations, 169–170; and North Vietnam, 282–283; and Pakistan, 26, 36, 167, 177–178, 186–188, 190, 213–247, 298–303; political development, 291–292; political leadership, 60, 63, 291; political parties, 55, 57; political system, 67–68; private investment in, 108, 117–127, 308–309; public enterprises in, 101–103; regionalism, 84–85; reorganization of states, 49; role of military, 65–66; and Tibet, 191, 251–260; and UN, 170–173, 215; urban planning in, 83–84; and U.S., 7, 9–10, 13–14, 16–20, 23–27, 60, 181–183, 295–298; U.S. economic aid to, 5, 21, 136–142, 144–151; U.S. military aid to, 5, 211, 304; and U.S.S.R., 15, 157–158, 187–188, 198–200, 272–276, 295–296

Indian Investment Centre, 119, 308
Indian National Congress: consequences of split in, 60; effects of Nehru's death on, 58; and foreign policy, 163–164, 166; "groupism" in, 58, 61–62; and Muslim League, 46, 165; opposition in states, 58; political dominance, 57; representation in Lok Sabha, 56
Indian Ocean, defense of, 192
Indian Oil Company, 123–124
Indus Basin Development Fund, 91, 227
Indus Waters Treaty, 226–227
Industrial Credit and Investment Corporation of India (ICICI), 103
Industrial estates, 101
Industrial policy resolution, 73, 122
Industrial production, in India and Pakistan, 98
International Bank for Reconstruction and Development, 96, 130, 154, 225–227
International commodity agreements, 130
International consortia, 131, 154; Aid-to-India Club, 22, 88, 138–139; Aid-to-Pakistan Club, 139–140
International Development Association, 131, 154
International Monetary Fund, 131

Jammu and Kashmir, *see* Kashmir
Jan Sangh, 58–59
Japanese Peace Treaty, 16
Jarring, Gunnar V., 235

Jinnah, Mohammed Ali: and creation of Pakistan, 46; death of, 63; Governor-General of Pakistan, 50; and partition, 165; "two-nation" theory, 46–47, 165
Joint ventures, in India and Pakistan, 125–127

Kamaraj, K., 58, 61–62
Karnaphuli project, 100, 145–146, 227
Kashmir, 229; events of 1947–1948, 231–232; political status of, 239–240
Kashmir, Maharaja of, 231
Kashmir National Conference, 59
Kashmir question, 25, 187, 190, 207, 216, 218–219, 227–247
Kennedy, John F., 12–13, 22, 35, 130, 300, 309–310
Kerala, 59, 63
Khan, Liaquat Ali, 63, 65
Khan, Sir Syed Ahmad, 46
Khan, Zafrulla, 170, 235, 242
Khrushchev, Nikita, 19, 276
Knoppers, Dr. Antonie, 76
Korean crisis, 14, 172, 254
Kotelawala, Sir John, 283
Kripalani, Acharya, 65–66
Krishnamarchari, T. T., 88

Ladakh, 256, 258, 261
Land reforms, in South Asia, 93–94
League of Nations, India's role in, 169–170
Lewis, John P., 117, 154, 156
Lilienthal, David E., 225
Lokanathan, P. S., 131

McMahon Line, 256, 258, 261, 266–267
Mahendra, King, 285–286, 294
Malaviya, K. D., 122–124
Mangla Dam, 227
Meany, George, 20
Mehta, Asoka, 88
Mehta, Balvantray, 96
Mehta, G. L., 121
Menon, V. K. Krishna: Defense Minister, 24, 65–66, 196, 199; and Kashmir question, 235, 242
Merchant, Livingston, 297
Military aid programs, U.S.: to India, 5, 211, 304; to Pakistan, 3, 5, 17–18, 35–36, 195, 202, 208–212, 303–305
Mirza, Iskandar, 50, 63
Mohammed, Bakshi Ghulam, 239–240
Mohammed, Ghulam, 63

Warsak Dam, 145
Waterlogging and salinity, in Pakistan, 95, 313
West Pakistan, 85

Wheat loans to India, 10, 15, 141
Works Program, in Pakistan, 91

Yugoslavia, 282